The Children's Encyclopedia

VOLUME NINE

Chief Contributors to
The Children's Encyclopedia

Literary	Art
T. THORNE BAKER	FREDERICK ANGER
HAROLD BEGBIE	HILDA M. COLEY
ERNEST A. BRYANT	A. FORESTIER
JOHN DERRY	F. R. HINKINS
ARTHUR D. INNES	J. R. MONSELL
MARGARET LILLIE	GEORGE F. MORRELL
CHARLES RAY	WAL PAGET
C. W. SALEEBY	S. B. PEARSE
J. A. SPENDER	T. H. ROBINSON
J. ARTHUR THOMSON	W. B. ROBINSON
R. F. TOWLER	CHARLES M. SHELDON
H. N. TYERMAN	E. F. SKINNER
SYDNEY WARNER	S. E. TRANTER
H. C. WHAITE	S. J. TURNER
PERCY M. YOUNG	

Printed in Great Britain by
The Amalgamated Press, Ltd., London

HANDEL THINKING OUT THE HALLELUJAH CHORUS

THE CHILDREN'S ENCYCLOPEDIA

FOUNDED
by
ARTHUR MEE

VOLUME NINE

THE EDUCATIONAL BOOK COMPANY LIMITED
LONDON

CONTENTS OF THIS VOLUME

iv

BRITISH MOTHS AND THEIR CATERPILLARS

1. Broad-bordered Yellow Underwing 2. Spurge Hawk 3. Large Emerald 4. Goat 5. Elephant Hawk 6. Brimstone 7. Pale Tussock 8. Six-spotted Burnet 9. Scarlet Tiger 10. Leopard 11. Copper Underwing 12. Emperor 13. Privet Hawk 14. Clifden Nonpareil 15. Lime Hawk 16. December 17. Peach Blossom 18. Black Arches 19. Lappet 20. Buff-Tip 21. Cinnabar 22. Pebble Prominent 23. Oleander Hawk 24. Lackey 25. Small Eggar 26. Humming-Bird Hawk

See page 6197

The Story of the Boundless Universe and All Its Wondrous Worlds

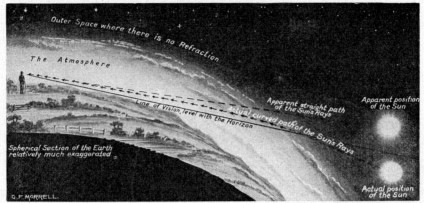

Why we see the Sun after it has actually set

WHERE COLOUR COMES FROM

WE may now consider one of the most marvellous and mysterious things in Nature, the wonderful colours that we may see in light.

Light, as we know, consists of electro-magnetic waves which originate in atoms, but there is a certain range only of these waves which cause the sensation of sight ; waves shorter than these are the invisible ultra-violet rays, the X-rays, and the still shorter radiations from radium, while waves longer than the visible ones cause heat and extend into the wireless region of the spectrum.

As all waves of light travel with the same speed (186,000 miles a second), it will be clear that the shorter waves run more frequently past a given point, the longer waves less frequently. If peas and potatoes were travelling at the same rate on an endless band there would be more peas to the foot than potatoes. Similarly the short violet waves are more frequent than the longer red waves, or have a higher *frequency*, though they both travel with the same speed.

The shortest " violet " waves, which are really vibrations that cause the sensation of violet, are only about half the wave-length of the deepest red rays. Their wave-length ranges from 15 to 30

millionths of an inch, but is usually measured in millionths of a millimetre, or milli-microns, and while the extreme violet rays have a wave-length of about 400 milli-microns, the deepest red rays have a wave-length of nearly 800. That is just equivalent to an octave on the piano, where one note will be due to twice as many vibrations in every second as the same note an octave lower.

We can thus think of the colour of light as its *pitch*, and as we follow the colours of the spectrum from red to violet, it is as if we were listening to someone playing an octave on the piano.

The colours that we see when light passes through a prism or when a rainbow is formed in the sky are *pure* colours. An infinite number of shades of violet, gradually becoming more bluish, merge imperceptibly into the blue, the blue rays becoming greenish as they run into the green, and so on, until through a multiplicity of subtle oranges, each one redder than the previous one, the light becomes red, then ruby.

But in the things around us the colours are not really pure ; the yellow of a lemon really consists of a mixture of green, yellow, orange, and red rays. Most greens we see are actually mixtures

ASTRONOMY · GEOLOGY · GEOGRAPHY · CHEMISTRY · PHYSICS · LIFE

of blue and yellow or of blue, green, and yellow. Violet and mauve and purple colours are mixtures of different amounts of violet, blue, and red. If all the colours in the spectrum or rainbow are mixed, we know that they make white again, as Newton showed. But if we took away part of the spectrum, say the red rays, by passing a beam of light through a piece of coloured glass, the remainder of the spectrum colours only would get through the glass, and our eye would see *green*. Thus, when we see a colour it means that the coloured object has the power to destroy or filter out or absorb some of the spectrum colours so that our eye only sees the remainder, which are reflected back as a mixture.

A piece of green fabric appears green because the dye or pigment used in its manufacture kills or destroys all the other colours in the white light which falls upon it. An object thus appears coloured only when it contains a pigment or dye which destroys the other colours. If the coloured rays which it destroys could be mixed again and seen as a separate thing, we should see what is called the complementary colour. Thus violet is complementary to yellow, green to magenta, and red to bluish-green, and so on. Many of the most beautiful colour schemes in Nature are due to the delicate contrast of complementary colours in flowers.

WHY A PIECE OF BLUE CLOTH LOOKS BLACK IN A RED LIGHT

Again, if a piece of blue serge is put into red or orange or yellow light, it appears black. In blue light it looks blue, in violet light it appears violet, in green light it would seem to be green. All this is because its surface cannot reflect red or orange or yellow, but can reflect green or blue or violet. When white light, a mixture of all these colours, falls on it, it absorbs some of the waves and practically destroys their effect, but it reflects on to our eyes others of the waves, blending them so as to produce to our vision a blue effect.

Some colours used together are not at all harmonious, and are crude and displeasing. Different colours vary very much in the variety of waves of different pitch or frequency that they are made up of, and the eye usually takes these forms into consideration when, as we may say, it likes or dislikes certain colours or designs.

Just as in the case of sound it is possible to hear a chord, or the composite sound of several notes played together, so many different pure colours (or colours of a single pitch) can be—and almost always are—seen together. How necessary this must be can be understood when we know by how very little one pure colour differs from another. The violet waves are the shortest, and their wave-length is about fifteen millionths of an inch only from crest to crest.

THE GREEN OF THE GRASS CAUSED BY HUNDREDS OF DIFFERENT RAYS

In the wonderful spectroscope, with which it is possible to measure the wave-length, it is also possible to see a single pure colour, or spectrum line. Thus if we look through a spectroscope at the flame of a spirit lamp in which some salt is being burnt, we shall see a bright yellow line due to the metal sodium which has a wave-length of nearly 589 milli-microns. But if we use a still more powerful instrument, we shall see this yellow line split into two exceedingly fine lines, caused by rays having wave-lengths differing by only a few billionths of a millimetre. The simplest colours we see around us, the green of the grass, the peel of an orange, comprise hundreds of rays of different wave-length, and yet, as we have already seen, all the colours which the eye can appreciate occupy no more than a single octave of the vast keyboard of light visible and invisible.

We must next explain why we see colours at all. Why do rays of light of one wave-length give us the impression of blue, while if their wave-length is twice as great we see red, or if half as long again as the blue rays, we see green?

THE THREE SETS OF OPTIC NERVES WHICH GIVE US OUR COLOUR SENSE

Colours are only sensations, and all our enjoyment of the beautiful and varied colours in the world is due to the fact that Nature has given us three sets of optic nerves which connect the retina of the eye with the brain, and that one set of these nerves gives us the sensation of blue-violet, another of green, and the third of orange-red. A mixed bundle of rays from a natural object, consisting of a mixture of many *pure* colours, will stimulate these nerves in different proportions, and so by mixing so much blue-violet sensation with so much green and so much orange-red sensation the brain obtains the impression of that particular colour, and any colour we see is the sensation derived from these three primary ones.

One of the simplest ways to realise that colour is not a thing, but merely a sensation caused by the wave-length of a particular ray or a bundle of rays of light, is to consider the beautiful colours we see in the tail of a peacock, or on a film of oil on water. There are no paints or pigments in such things. The light falling upon them is merely broken up by a phenomenon known as diffraction into rays of different wave-length, which cause us to see the colours. The colour itself is merely a sensation, and the reason that grass looks green is because its natural pigment destroys the red rays from the white sunlight which falls upon it and only reflects the shorter wave-lengths which give us the sensation of green. If there were no absorption or destruction of some wave-lengths by substances, there would be no colours other than those caused by diffraction or the splitting up by a prism or other refracting medium. And if there were no such thing as reflection of light, then too we should live in a world of no colour.

THE LAWS THAT HOLD GOOD FOR LIGHT AND SOUND AND RADIANT HEAT

As in the case of invisible or radiant heat some substances admit light, and others soak it up or absorb it, and others will reflect it from their surface. There is still much we do not understand about the way different substances reflect or fail to reflect light ; we can, however, learn the laws of reflection.

We know that if a ball on a billiard-table is rolled gently against the cushion at an angle it will come off again at the same angle. The angle at which the ball approaches the cushion is called *the angle of incidence*, and the law for the billiard-ball, and for light, is that the angle of incidence and the angle of reflection are equal.

Another thing happens to light, radiant heat, and sound, and is called *refraction*. We must always distinguish this word from reflection, which means bending back. Refraction means breaking. When a ray of light passes from one thing to another its course is always changed, or

refracted, and this refraction also has laws. It is important, for we are able to see things only by means of refraction.

Behind the pupil of the eye there is a transparent lens which bends or refracts the rays of light that come in so that they shall all be made to fall on the retina, or curtain, at the back of the eye in such a way as to produce a clear image of the thing we are looking at.

HOW GLASSES, LIKE THE EYE, ALTER THE COURSE OF LIGHT

Eyeglasses of every kind are used for the same purpose. The use of them all, and of every kind of microscope and telescope, the glasses in front of a magic lantern, and so forth, is due to their power of refracting the rays of light.

Different things have different powers of refracting light. The diamond, for instance, alters the course of the rays of light passing through it much more than water does, this being the reason why the diamond is such a brilliant gem.

But the rays of light themselves differ in their power of being refracted ; some of the rays are more strongly bent or refracted than others. Newton's prism was a means for refracting the rays of light passing through it, and the success of his experiment depended on the fact that the different kinds of light are refracted each to a different degree in a regular way. The existence of the spectrum depends entirely on the possibility of refraction.

THE TWO MAIN SOURCES FROM WHICH COME COLOURS IN EVERYDAY LIFE

Colours as we meet them in everyday life come from two main sources. One of these is the natural pigments, such as the various mineral substances that are used in making paints. The other is the aniline dyes which are used in dress materials and textiles. Certain groups of atoms known as chromophores are necessary in an organic chemical substance if it is to give colour, and if a chromophore be combined with an auxochrome it will confer dyeing properties upon the combination and a fabric can be dyed with the colour.

If, then, we ask where colour comes from, the answer is that it may come from the mere diffraction of white light, or from the mineral and vegetable pigments in Nature, or from man-made dyes.

(Next chapter in this group, page 6059).

A GOOD WORKMAN BLAMES HIS TOOLS

SCOLDED BY HIS MOTHER FOR THE SMALLNESS OF HIS OUTPUT, YOUNG SAMUEL CROMPTON BLAMES THEIR
SPINNING JENNY, WHICH CONTINUALLY CAUSED HIS YARN TO BREAK

It was this trouble which eventually fired him with the determination to improve cotton-spinning machinery

MEN AND WOMEN

The Story of Immortal Folk Whose Work Will Never Die

Henry Ford   Lord Kelvin   Sir William Siemens   Joseph Jacquard   Edmund Cartwright

Elias Howe   Samuel Crompton   Eli Whitney   Henry Greathead   James Brindley

GREAT INVENTORS

THE world owes little of its happiness to kings, but to its inventors it owes more than it can pay. They have been the founders of our civilisation, the creators of the social world we live in, the preparers of future benefits for mankind.

We have only to look round to see that this is so. We see it in the story of the rise of our great industries. One of the greatest of them, one of the most important industries in the whole world, is our textile industry, and we can trace its rise to a few men who, while they lived and worked, were treated with cruelty and dishonesty and contempt. Sorrow has been the lot of the inventor from the beginning: it is rarely that his reward has come in his own time.

One of the first men behind our textile industry was a Lancashire genius who could neither read nor write—James Hargreaves. Born at Blackburn in 1745, he entered a mill owned by Sir Robert Peel's grandfather, where, as a shrewd and able man, he was set to work to improve a machine for carding cotton in order to abolish the old system of clearing and straightening the fibres by hand.

But he worked at home too. The cotton trade at that time depended largely on work done in cottages and little farms.

Part of the cotton had to be spun into thread to make the warp, and part into the weft (or woof) which crosses the texture. It happened that one day Hargreaves knocked over the simple little machine his wife was using for spinning weft, and to that action we may trace the work he did for himself, for his country, and for the world at large.

The machine was fitted with a wheel and spindle which spun only one thread at a time. When dislodged the wheel and the spindle, thrown from a horizontal into a vertical position, continued to revolve, tangling the thread.

Hargreaves saw that by widening the wheel and employing several upright spindles, he might spin a number of threads at the same time, instead of one as heretofore. He did so in secret, never dreaming that he was to found a new industry, but simply that he might have more material with which to work, and so earn more money to provide food and clothing for his family.

He made his first machine, the original spinning-jenny, and stealthily began to manufacture yarn in such quantities as no weaver had ever thought of producing. The result was that the Hargreaves household was soon making eight times as much

EXPLORERS · INVENTORS · WRITERS · ARTISTS · SCIENTISTS

material, and so helping the prosperity of everybody concerned in the mill, for yarn was the one thing they all needed.

But the narrow jealousy of the people of the neighbourhood was aroused at the suggestion, whispered abroad, that Jim Hargreaves was using machinery. Machinery—why, it would rob honest hand-workers of their living; it would drive all folk away from Blackburn and the surrounding towns. The tidings ran like fire, and the weavers of Darwen, Mellor, Tockholes, and Oswaldtwistle, assembled at Blackburn, and, with the local men, marched, an army of execution, to the poor cottage where Hargreaves lived.

They forced a way into the house, they smashed the machine, they demolished the furniture, and then they marched down to Peel's mill, where Hargreaves was at work, and wrecked that. That is how they taught a man to know better than to invent machines which were to bring millions and millions of pounds to Lancashire, though not for himself.

Hargreaves went to Nottingham and joined hands with a man named Thomas James, who had a little capital and a great faith. Together they began the manufacture of the spinning-jennies, but, having hounded him out of home and occupation, Lancashire was now using his jennies wholesale without paying him a farthing royalty.

THE POOR REWARD OF A MAN WHO MADE FORTUNES FOR OTHERS

The desperate inventor began an action to recover damages, but when his lawyer found how many dishonest cotton manufacturers in Blackburn alone had stolen the device, he threw up his brief in dismay, saying he could not fight an army. Hargreaves did not die in poverty, but when we know that at his death his share of the partnership was sold for £400, we realise that wealth had not come to this man who had placed at the disposal of his native county a device for building up unparalleled prosperity. He died in 1778.

Sir Richard Arkwright's story comes into this same time, with a greater hardship still, for here was a man with much more to offer, who had to triumph over still more extended injury. Born at Preston in 1732, the youngest of 13 poor, ill-educated children, he did not master spelling and grammar till he was rich and over fifty. He suffered great poverty in his youth, working as a penny barber, then as a travelling wigmaker; yet he found time to think out a better machine than that of Hargreaves.

He devised a spinning-frame which provided a stouter material strong enough to be used as warp. But he could not make it, and no one would help him, poor, ragged, and unkempt genius that he was. The instrument-maker to whom he applied for help would have nothing to do with him personally, but somehow was persuaded to lend him the services of a man named Kay to make the clockwork part of the apparatus.

THE BUSYBODIES WHO CREPT UP THROUGH THE GOOSEBERRY BUSHES

The trials were made in a little room in Preston, and the whirring of the machine in the guarded hovel at night drew the attention of two old crones who crept up through the gooseberry bushes to the window and listened, then forthwith went about reporting that there was witchcraft in the cottage, that they heard Satan tuning his pipes, and Arkwright dancing to the strains.

As soon as Arkwright reported his invention, the manufacturers cried out against machinery, and drove him to stocking making and calico manufacture. Then they turned against him an old Act of Parliament which decreed that no such fabric should be exported save under heavy tax, nor made at home at all unless it included a linen warp.

Still the gifted starveling struggled on, and patented an astonishing machine, which embraced the entire manufacture of cotton, carding, drawing, roving, spinning, and put the staple trade of Lancashire ahead of all competitors, where it has ever since remained. His reward was to see his patent infringed everywhere by rascally rivals, who denounced his machinery, used it themselves, and refused to pay royalty.

THE TRIUMPH OF ARKWRIGHT IN THE FACE OF FOLLY AND INJUSTICE

Nevertheless he set up his own factory at Chorley, near Preston, and it was wrecked by mobs. But fanatics among the workers, with robbers and pirates among rival manufacturers, could not defeat his iron resolve. He persevered in spite of all injustice and cruelty, made a fortune, educated himself, was knighted, created our factory system, enormously enriched the country, and died, in 1792, both rich and honoured at last.

Even today it is difficult to write without indignation of these pioneers of our national wealth, and especially when we come to Samuel Crompton, one of the most lovable of them all. Born near Bolton in 1753, he received as good an education as the local day school afforded, but the family was desperately poor. There was musical genius in Samuel, but no money for furnishing him with instruments; so he made himself a fiddle, and learned to play so well that he was able to earn eighteenpence a night by working in a Bolton orchestra.

He accounted himself passing rich on that sum, and bought books and materials for the making of his famous spinning-mule. This was a contrivance of great ingenuity which gave a better yarn than either Arkwright or Hargreaves could produce. He worked at cotton-spinning by day with the rest of the family, he played his fiddle at the theatre in the evening; then, when all the rest had gone to bed, he sat working far into the night on his mule.

The machine-smashing frenzy was running through the land, and poor

YOUNG NASMYTH SKETCHES GEORGE STEPHENSON'S ROCKET

THE WORK OF A WORM INSPIRES BRUNEL WITH THE IDEA OF TUNNELLING UNDER THE THAMES

Samuel used to take his machine to pieces and hide it, part by part, in a little secret chamber which he had made in the roof by cutting a hole through a ceiling.

It was perfected at last, and he turned out wonderful yarn with it, secretly made, of course, so that workmen should not rush in and smash his machine. The fame of his yarn soon spread, and from far and near men were sent to spy on him. He saw that he was in danger, that he could not preserve his secret, yet he was too poor to obtain a patent. " I was reduced to the cruel necessity of either destroying my machine," he said, " or of giving it to the public. To destroy it I could not think of; to give up that for which I had laboured so long was almost unbearable."

A Bolton manufacturer persuaded him that if he would make his secret public, eighty manufacturers in the town would each give him a guinea. All took the invention; sixty paid. Everybody made fortunes from its use. It extended all over Lancashire and right through the cotton manufacturing districts of Scotland. No one outside Bolton gave a penny to the creator of the splendid labour-saving device.

At last he appealed to the Government, showing that, whereas there were in use 156,000 spindles on the Hargreaves jenny, and 311,000 on the Arkwright machine, there were over four million in use on the Crompton mule. The man who had made huge fortunes for the cotton industry was at last awarded £5000, not by the men who had profited from his invention, but by the Government; and at last, in his poverty-stricken old age, the manufacturers of Bolton subscribed a sum which brought him in a beggarly £63 a year.

THE CLEVER COUNTRY PARSON WHO GAVE US THE POWER LOOM

Then there was Edmund Cartwright, the parson who first applied steam to textile manufacture and gave us the power loom. Born in 1743 at Marnham, Nottinghamshire, he was a man of rare gifts, a classical scholar, a poet, and instinct with inventive faculty. Hearing of the success of Arkwright's spinning machine, the good parson said, " Why not a machine to weave? " And when they answered him that such a thing was impossible, he cudgelled his brains till he had made the " impossible " apparatus.

It was a very rough, great thing, which took the strength of two men to handle, and was not a triumph; so the good parson, who really knew nothing of the practical side of weaving, went forth to see how men actually did weave. Then he returned and built a second machine which could do the work better, faster, and more surely than men. Not only so, but he had the audacity to build a little steam engine to drive his machine, and at once received an order for 400 machines.

The machine-wreckers were still abroad, and the factory for which the machines were furnished was burned to the ground; so the indomitable cleric invented a wool-combing machine which substituted mechanical action for men's labour and gave greatly improved results. Thereupon Parliament was petitioned to stop the use of this machine.

THE MAN WHO LOST A FORTUNE ON THINGS WHICH MADE MEN RICH

From one cause and another the wonderful parson lost £30,000 on these inventions which were to make the nation richer, and in the end Parliament could not but grant him £10,000 reward for his labours and losses. He died in 1823, happy, busy to the last, with inventions

and poetry, a singular blend of romance and practical realism. We forget his poetry today, but remember the far-reaching results which have flowed from those first power looms of his.

The pattern-making loom for lace is known as the Jacquard loom, and has a moving story behind it. Joseph Marie Jacquard was born in 1752 at Lyons, one of a family of lacemakers whose work was so hard, laborious, and ill-paid that he himself would not follow it, as he said, till the toil should be less wretched and the payment better. So he became bookbinder, type-founder, hat-maker, anything but a member of the family calling.

When Jacquard was fifty our Society of Arts offered a prize for a lace machine, and Jacquard, musing over the old problem, made a model for his own interest, and put it aside as a toy. But a workman with expert knowledge secretly carried off the model to the Mayor of Lyons. The mayor reported it to Napoleon, who was so delighted with the ingenuity of the scheme that he appointed the astonished inventor to the Conservatoire, there to complete his machine and to take charge of all the weaving.

HOW JACQUARD RESPONDED TO THE CALL OF HIS COUNTRY

Jacquard finished his machine and exhibited it at Lyons, where the mob carried it to the market-place and well and truly smashed it to fragments. Curiously enough the invention passed to England, and gave us a lace trade which has never died. Then, in self-defence, as it were, the French had to take up the machine, and begged Jacquard to resume control of his wonderful invention.

With that simple humility which marks all fine men, he did so, and was content to see a great trade spring from his machines, and to refuse princely offers to go elsewhere, and give to international rivals the benefit of his skill. He died in 1834, happy in the knowledge that lacemakers would never again toil miserably for wages so inadequate as had been the case with his own family in the craft.

So far we see inventions evolving for the rapid consumption of raw cotton, and the result was that demand for the raw material was outrunning supply. The need brings the man, and this man appeared in the person of Eli Whitney, born at Westborough, Massachusetts, in 1765. In

Georgia he was brought into contact with cotton growers who were in despair because the cotton had to be cleaned by hand after picking, and the slaves could manage only five to six pounds a day.

Whitney set to work as if the matter were a simple sum, and with amazing facility invented his famous cotton-gin, which enabled anyone to clean 1000 pounds of cotton a day. The invention left him as poor as he had been before, for rascally cotton growers broke into his little workshop, stole his plans, made machines of their own, and gave him nothing.

He therefore set up in business as a maker of firearms, and produced the first machine-guns; secured heavy Government contracts, introduced the system of sub-division of labour—later carried to perfection by Henry Ford—and died, in 1825, a wealthy man.

His first invention was for the profit of mankind, his second was for the destruction of men, and the first invention did more harm, indirectly, than the second did directly.

THE INVENTION WHICH PROLONGED THE CURSE OF SLAVERY IN AMERICA

For the cotton-gin fixed for another seventy years the shackles which had been about to drop from the slaves in the United States. They had become bad assets, with only five pounds of cotton cleaned a day; but, with a thousand pounds of cotton cleaned each day, every bond servant throughout the cotton area was converted into a wealth producing machine for his owner. We have only to look at the English figures to realise what happened.

Before Whitney invented his machine we could get only 138,000 pounds of cotton a year from America. Eight years later America was sending us 20 million pounds of cotton in the twelvemonth. So all thought of emancipating the slaves died suddenly in the Southern States of America, and it was this question that led to the great Civil War.

Invention never marches solitarily, it creates new needs and invents new ways of meeting them. The growing traffic arising from the trades to which these new gifts gave impetus, called for fresh avenues for transport. With all the facilities of our own age, traffic still keeps ahead of routes; we are hopelessly overcrowded in London and many other great areas of population.

Imagine what were the conditions in the eighteenth century and immediately beyond, when good roads barely existed.

The steam railway was not born; Macadam and Telford had not seamed the land with noble highways. Canals seemed a solution for traffic which existed, for traffic which might be created if new coalfields could be tapped and building sites for factories and mills placed in communication with the rest of the country. The man for the task was James Brindley; the man to summon him to it was the Duke of Bridgewater, who proved a notable patron.

THE APPRENTICE WHO PROVED HIMSELF A BETTER MAN THAN HIS MASTER

Brindley was a very rare genius, born at Thornsett, Derbyshire, in 1716, the son of an incompetent, negligent father, who mismanaged a tiny farm of his own, and let the brains of his children lie fallow. Jim had no more than a smattering of the three R's, never could more than sign his name and roughly scrawl down the figures of a simple sum.

Toil in the fields till he was 17 left the lad longing for a trade in which he could make things, and he apprenticed himself to a millwright, who, first thinking him a worthless dullard whom it was necessary to kick out of the dirty old foundry, lived to learn that the rough, unkempt lad was a better man than himself, who could right machinery which beat the old man, and who with noble honesty could run the business, support himself and the whole family of his master when that master fell ill and palsied of mind.

HOW JAMES BRINDLEY CARRIED BARGES AND CANALS THROUGH THE AIR

Jim Brindley could do anything. He could mend a broken machine, invent a new one, pump a mine by methods crazily original but marvellously effective. Whenever anything went wrong with a mine or a machine, they called on Jim. This boy never failed them. At last the Duke of Bridgewater was seized with his ideas for canals, so he, too, called on Brindley, whose first task under the new control was to link Manchester and Worsley by means of a canal, the first serious venture of the kind in England.

The work meant that this unschooled genius must tunnel here, raise great embankments there, and carry his canal across the River Irwell by means of a

23 A 9*

600 feet aqueduct. Professional critics laughed at the suggestion that barges and the water that bore them should thus be carried through the air; but in July 1761 barges were actually crossing the river by canal, and passing on their way from the tunnelled water at one end of Manchester to the tunnelled water at Worsley.

Next Brindley linked Manchester and Liverpool, by continuing his canal to the Mersey tideway at Runcorn, the course including two rivers and two deep valleys, the watercourses being crossed by aqueducts, the valleys by broad and lofty embankments. His resources were few and primitive. In the first 600 yards from the Mersey there is a rise of 82 feet, yet Brindley's locks mastered the difficulty.

Altogether Brindley gave England 365 miles of canals. He made the carriage of minerals so simple that it was worth while to open coalfields vital to Lancashire's growing trade; and he called new towns into being or greatly extended old and smaller ones by the facilities he furnished for their trade.

THE GREAT PROBLEMS JAMES BRINDLEY THOUGHT OUT IN BED

He had no ambition beyond canals and commerce. He believed, he said, that Nature meant rivers simply to feed navigable canals. That he was predestined to build the canals of his age he had as little doubt. Yet how slender was his equipment. He trusted entirely to his own strong, steady brain for his plans and conceptions. He drew no detailed plans: indeed he could not. He worked out no elaborate calculations on paper—it was all done in his head. At the end of profound thought he would jot down a few figures as reminders, then work on again, just as we do short sums in our heads as exercises in mental arithmetic.

If his problem were unusually stubborn he would go to bed and remain there for a day or two at a time. When he got up the sum was done. Quiet contemplation solved all his perplexities, and as the mists vanished from his brain, locks, embankments, tunnels, aqueducts, whole canals emerged, perfect, complete. When Brindley died in 1772 he had given us a system of inland waterways which should have put us ahead of nearly all other countries in the world, and would have done, had not selfish interests been allowed to render his work very largely useless.

Transport tales run naturally from canals to railways and steamships, which have no part in our present chapter, but we must note one of the great might-have-beens of the subject. This was Sir Marc Isambard Brunel. Born near Gisors, Normandy, in 1769, he served six years in the French Navy, where he invented an admirable quadrant. While he was home on leave he met an English girl named Sophia Kingdom, fell in love, and became engaged to her. The French Revolution drove Brunel to America, where he did notable work as chief engineer to New York; but charming Sophia was an irresistible magnet drawing him to England.

THE GREAT REWARD WHICH BROUGHT BRUNEL TO DISASTER

He came here with a new method of cutting blocks for ships' rigging, a scheme which had dawned on him while carving the initials of his beloved Sophia on a tree in the American wilds.

The Admiralty accepted his invention, paid him £17,000 for it, and made a saving of £24,000 a year for a generation by its aid. But it brought Brunel to disaster, for the sawmills which he erected were burned down and thus ruined him. He was working at the time on what must have been one of the first ideas for a steamship, and the Government, having encouraged him up to a certain point, revoked his authority, and left him to bear the expenses, so that in the midst of inventions giving us possible sewing machines, bootmaking machines, new type-making processes, bridge-building, and what not, he was seized and imprisoned for debt.

One of the finest spirits of the age was flung into prison for £5000 till the Government, shamed into action, paid the sum and released him. He went from the gaol to the building of the first Thames Tunnel, a grand conception, in which he introduced an indispensable new invention, product of a rare piece of observation.

HOW BRUNEL LEARNED A LESSON IN TUNNELLING FROM A MARINE WORM

We have a marine worm which tunnels timber and other substances, and, to effect its purpose, builds as it penetrates a limy cell of its own secretion so that the hollowed material cannot collapse on it. Brunel adapted the plan to human art. As he tunnelled the soft earth beneath the river he copied the worm by building up the walls and roof with masonry.

THE BOY WHO NEVER FAILED

YOUNG JAMES BRINDLEY MENDS THE BROKEN PLOUGH WHICH HAD BAFFLED HIS MASTER

It was an epoch-making plan, for all tunnelling inventions in yielding soil have been modelled on it ever since. In spite of this essential contrivance, the work was overwhelmingly difficult. Again and again the river broke into the workings, drowned men, crushed the machinery, wrecked the undertaking.

Married to his beloved Sophia, Brunel was now blessed with a splendid son, Isambard Kingdom Brunel (1806-1859), who toiled like a giant in the tunnel, sometimes working there day and night for 90 hours at a time. In spite of the efforts of father and son, the scheme was suspended, owing to lack of sufficient funds, for seven years.

THE WONDERFUL TUNNEL THAT ISAMBARD BRUNEL MADE

There the work stood crumbling into waste, waiting for a little money. Finally the public was goaded into action. A subscription was raised and the tunnel was completed, 18 years after its beginning. The work did not in the end serve the purpose for which it was intended, but was used as a railway tunnel. However, it was Brunel's greatest achievement and his monument, a pattern for the world to copy, and its author had the joy of seeing it perfect before he died in 1849.

Steamships came from other brains, but no ocean giants could yet arise, simply because there was no machinery large enough to forge the huge propeller shafts necessary to drive such ships. The hour called for new men and new methods, and James Nasmyth appeared. He was a native of Edinburgh, where he was born in 1808, son of the artist Alexander. James had his father's artistic faculty, but allied to a pronounced gift for mechanics. At 18 he was man enough to make a little steam engine to grind the colours for his father, and he had that inventive vision which enabled him to design machinery in his mind and then to draw it on paper.

THE WONDERFUL HAMMER WHICH A MAN INVENTED IN HALF AN HOUR

He could see what he wanted, he could imagine its operation, and he was able to sketch down all as if it existed in steel and iron. He served an apprenticeship under one of our grand old early tool-makers, Henry Maudslay, and then risking every farthing he had, £60, he set up for himself at Manchester, to build engines, machines, implements for other men's use.

So, when at last he was asked to provide something which would furnish great forgings for ships, he sat down and in half an hour had a wonderful new project on paper. Prior to this only the old anvil and hammers had been available, and the bigger the forging the less the power of the hammer, for the metal to be worked occupied the space on the anvil through which the hammer could have been travelling to gain momentum.

Nasmyth at once designed the hammer which bears his name. It is an invention which raises a great hammer-head high and clear of the object to be beaten, and lets it fall through space from such a distance as to make the blow like a force in nature. It can be regulated with such nicety as to crack an egg or a watch glass, or to beat with titanic force the biggest forging man can make. With that available, engineering was armed with entirely new powers, and before Nasmyth died in 1890 the whole character of the industry had been changed by his device.

As complete a change has been effected in the home and in a thousand industries by the invention of the sewing machine. But here the honour is due to more than one man. The first practical sewing machine was made by Barthélemy Thimmonier, a poor working tailor of Arbresle in the Department of the Rhône.

THE CLEVER TAILOR WHO NEGLECTED HIS BUSINESS FOR A MACHINE

His neighbours thought him mad, for he neglected his business to make his machine, which was patented in 1830. An inspector of mines who visited the Rhône recognised the worth of Thimmonier and took him to Paris. By 1841 eighty of Thimmonier's machines were in use there. They were made of wood.

As in the case of others, however, his invention was misunderstood by those whom it was to benefit. His machine never became the success it deserved to be, and he died in 1857, a poor man without friends.

The needle of Thimmonier's machine had a crochet hook, and a chain stitch was formed on the upper side of the material. Today sewing machines have needles with an eye near the point, and they work with a double thread and form what is called a lock-stitch. The first man to think of these ideas was an American, Walter Hunt, between the years 1832 and 1834, but for some reason he did not try to patent his machine.

Meanwhile, working quite in ignorance of Hunt's machine, Elias Howe (1819–67), born at Spencer, Massachusetts, had invented a practical sewing machine embodying these very ideas, besides many others. This machine was patented in 1846, after Howe and his wife and family had suffered many hardships.

It was the old story repeated. No American would buy or help the invention. Howe sold the English rights for £250, and came over to help the buyer to erect the machine. When he returned to America he found his young wife dead of consumption and starvation, while pirates were making his machines and gaining fortunes. He beat them, and died a wealthy man, but to the end there brooded over his success the vision of that young invalid wife who perished for lack of food.

An almost equal injustice drove Sir Henry Bessemer (1813–98) to great success. Of Huguenot extraction, he was a native of Hertfordshire.

From his youth up he poured out inventions, the first of which saved the

BRUNEL, IN A DIVING BELL, EXAMINES THE BED OF THE THAMES ABOVE HIS TUNNEL

YOUNG EDISON THROWN OUT OF A TRAIN

country £100,000 a year. It was a machine for perforating and dating the stamps embossed on legal documents.

He was promised a profitable position under the Government as a reward, but the promise was broken and he had to toil on to earn a livelihood.

Bessemer made a fortune from a secret preparation of bronze powder and gold paint, for which printers and painters had paid £5 10s. per pound. He gave them their material at a sixteenth of that cost, in unlimited quantities. Armed with funds, he began his researches on steel, and, nimbly profiting by accidental discovery, evolved a furnace through which steam, or a blast of air, was forced to cleanse molten pig iron of impurities and convert it into high grade steel. The plan was given out at first in an imperfect formula, and failed.

In its perfect form the Bessemer process was scoffed at by the trade. Henry Bessemer therefore built mills of his own, and very soon was supplying the world with admirable steel £20 a ton cheaper than any other that could be made. That won the day, and rivals flocked to him from all parts to make his product by licence. He gained a fortune, but his generation profited still more, for it had abundant and excellent metal for bridges, railways, and buildings, such as had never before been even dreamed of.

THE THREE BROTHERS AND WHAT THEY DID FOR THE WORLD

Next came Sir William Siemens, ten years the junior of Bessemer, and a native of Hanover. One of three inventive brothers, he was distinguished, with them, in electro-plating, and, not least, in the steel industry. By long and laborious experiment he perfected a furnace in which the open hearth principle was ingeniously exploited for the common good.

Gas was generated from coal consumed in closed chambers, and the gas formed the fuel for the steel process. The idea was novel and admirable, and at length proved an even greater boon than the Bessemer process. Systematically following up the subject, Siemens applied the principle of the recovery of waste heat to the superheating of steam and so enormously improved the whole scheme of steam raising. He died wealthy and honoured in 1883.

The story of Sidney Gilchrist Thomas and of his invention enabling inferior ores to be used in both these processes is on page 4103.

More and more Science advanced her frontiers, and the time came when a new generation thought mainly in terms of electricity. The outstanding figure of this new electric age was Thomas Alva Edison, who lived to 84, passing away in 1931.

He was a poor boy, born in 1847 at Milan, Ohio, and began his career as a hawker of newspapers on a railway train. But the papers were his own. He gathered news as the train travelled, set it up from his own type, printed it on a little machine of his own in the luggage van of the train, and sold it to the passengers and to people at stations where the train stopped.

HOW EDISON TURNED THE DREAMS OF OTHER MEN INTO REALITIES

He had also a little electric battery of his own making in that van, but, this setting fire to the compartment, he was kicked out of the train and left at a wayside station, where he was in time to save the stationmaster's daughter from being run over. The grateful father took the boy under his wing and taught him as much as he himself knew of telegraphy. Edison's first venture was to run a wire along fences from the station to the town and to transmit telegrams at a shilling apiece.

Without culture he had the old-time scholar's passion for travel and observation. He would wander like a tramp about the country, working here and there for a little while to earn money which, at the end of six months' hard saving, he would spend on a festival of strenuous experiment and invention.

In this way Edison developed a system of sending, by means of currents of varying strength, several messages over one wire at the same time. He made the first of the electric printing telegraphs for Stock Exchange and other news; he created new ideas of his own, he improved on those of other men.

Thus he ranks as one of the pioneers of the telephone. Pottering about with tin-foil on a revolving cylinder, to which were attached a diaphragm and a trumpet, he made the first phonograph, parent of all gramophones. Next came a still more astonishing invention, the kinetoscope, a primitive cinematograph patented in 1893, less than four years after William Friese-Greene, of whom we can read on page 6704, had made the first moving-picture camera.

LORD KELVIN, ONE OF THE GREATEST PHYSICISTS OF ALL TIME

Edison spent much money and time in perfecting a carbon filament lamp for electric lighting. An Englishman, Sir Joseph Swan, had actually made such a lamp in 1860, and was associated with Edison in this task. Few inventors have benefited their fellow-men to a greater measure than Thomas Alva Edison.

From this untaught genius of the poverty-stricken hovel we turn to William Thomson, known later as Lord Kelvin, the brilliant scholar of Glasgow and Cambridge Universities, the most famous professor of natural philosophy of his age, and one of the greatest physicists of all time. He lived from 1824 to 1907.

He was cradled at Belfast and became a professor at Glasgow University.

There he remained for 53 years, lecturing four days a week, twice a morning, to unique gatherings of students. They were unique, not for brilliance, but for boisterous lack of appreciation. He was too profoundly immersed in his great subjects to be understood by any but exceptional students. A few grand young minds comprehended and worked loyally with him; the others jested and went their way. With these few he worked marvels, not in a fine laboratory such as now exists, but in a class-room and in a tumble-down cellar.

The greatest mathematician of his era, Kelvin excelled in minute and complicated measurements, and only by this supreme power was he able to devise the important electrical inventions which immortalise his name.

The first Atlantic cables were useless because far too great a current was sent through them, a current which destroyed the cables meant to carry them. Kelvin saw that the plan must be weak current and intense power of magnifying the faint signals received.

To this end, he invented his mirror galvanometer, a dainty marvel weighing a few grains. For the advantage of mariners he gave us a new compass and a deep-sea sounding machine for use in any waters by ships travelling at any speeds. These are outstanding revolutions in science known to all the world, but other strokes of his commanding genius are too many and too technical for any attempted discussion in these pages.

TWO OLD WOMEN CREEP THROUGH THE BUSHES TO LISTEN AT ARKWRIGHT'S WINDOW

His inventions were numberless, his contributions to the literature of science almost a library to themselves—the text-books to which learning turns for data and guidance. Yet toward the end of his fruitful life he humbly told an international gathering this: "I know no more of electric and magnetic force, or of the relation between ether, electricity, and ponderable matter, or of chemical affinity, than I knew and tried to teach my class students in my first session as professor."

We turn to a very different type of genius in adding the name of Henry Ford to this roll of honour, yet this American manufacturer was, in his way, as considerable a wonder as Kelvin in his. He was born in 1863, as poor as Edison; he toiled on a little farm, hoeing and cultivating and pondering deeply. "I hoed ten thousand miles," he said, and he hated the monotony and toil.

His own experiences made him yearn to bring into existence machinery which would relieve human beings of this dreary labour. His escape was gained by way of one of the Edison factories, where he became a good mechanic, dreaming of a cheap motor tractor for the farm.

When he had saved up a little money and determined to start in business for himself, he realised that, farmers being conservative and opposed to new ideas, he must first teach them to be familiar with cars which they could drive before they would regard with favour a motor implement for the land.

So began the building of Ford motor-cars, cheap, ugly, but efficient. He had an enormous untapped market in America, and half the world beyond. To supply it he saw that he must standardise his productions, do everything by machinery. He brought to perfection the task of departmentalising industry, which his countryman, Whitney, had long previously begun.

Various partners were taken to help the almost friendless man, but they had different ideas from his. They wanted a new model every year; he aimed at one for all time, so that his machines could go on day and night turning out the same thing, in a continuous stream. He was right, they were wrong. They left, he went on, and became the greatest manufacturer history has known.

In order to secure efficiency from his workpeople, he cut down their hours from twelve to eight per day, and gave them all a pound a day as a minimum. That was in itself an industrial revolution, and benefits in unending succession followed.

THE WONDERFUL ORGANISATION BUILT UP BY HENRY FORD

The work grew to such an extent that he ceased to be merely a manufacturer. He used, for example, half a million tons of iron a year, and as he could not get regular supplies, owing to strikes, he bought his own iron mines. He bought his own coal mines, he bought a railway for the carriage of supplies and finished cars, he bought forests, he bought rubber plantations for his tyres, cotton plantations for the fabric of the hood; he even bought stretches of riverway which gave him immense horse-power in flowing water for driving machinery.

As the result of these far-reaching schemes Henry Ford became one of the richest men in the world. In his person a simple, kindly man, he proved a model employer, a model tradesman, fair to his workpeople, fair to his customers, always striving to raise his men's wages, while at the same time lowering the price of his cars to the public. He was indeed the pioneer of cheap motoring. He died in 1947, leaving a great fortune to be used for the benefit of his fellow men.

So far all the inventions we have looked at have been for commerce; let us conclude with one designed to profit the heart and not the pocket, the invention of the lifeboat. We are an island people, seagoers from the beginning, yet till a century ago our coasts were sea graveyards to all whose ships went down amid storms. People on shore would watch ships destroyed and men, women, and children drowned during tempests, when not a boat could leave the shore and live.

THE DISASTER WHICH INFLUENCED THE INVENTION OF THE LIFEBOAT

Pity for poor seafarers stirred a London coachbuilder named Lionel Lukin to make an attempt at a lifeboat in 1785. His idea was good, for the boat had airtight compartments, but the craft was so frail that it could not sail the seas whose violence alone called it into action. And there was a worthy old North Country beadle, in William Wouldhave, who contributed his quota to the fund of inven-

tion. But the hero of the achievement was Henry Greathead.

He was a native of Richmond, Yorkshire, where he was born in 1757, became a boatbuilder by trade, and tested boats and ships in many a tempestuous tide. In 1789 there was a particularly terrible wreck, with total loss of life of crew and passengers, at the mouth of the River Tyne, and so great was the sensation created that South Shields offered a premium for a lifeboat.

Greathead, to his lasting glory, gained the premium, as his own experiences of angry seas qualified him to do. His vessel was but a primitive version of the lifeboats we know now, but it could go out to sea in storms and rescue the perishing. It was the first to do so.

Greathead was honoured and rewarded in his lifetime; he is the patron saint of every station in the world from which a lifeboat is launched. He died in 1816.

THE MAN WHO FIRST THOUGHT OF JET-PROPULSION FOR AIRCRAFT

The inventors of our day, though their work is of equal importance, do not stand out like the pioneers whose achievements brought in the mechanical age. Industrial nations like Britain possess today thousands of different kinds of machinery for thousands of different purposes; yet all the time ingenious men and women are thinking out new processes or improvements of existing methods. Completely new inventions like radar and atomic energy are often the work of groups of scientists co-operating in research work.

Perhaps the greatest individual inventor of our time is Sir Frank Whittle, who by himself invented the turbo-jet engine. He first thought of jet-propulsion for aircraft when he was a young man, and he took out his first patent for his jet engine in 1930. He began the task of constructing one in 1933, and in 1937 his first jet-propulsion engine ran successfully.

Frank Whittle never asked for a penny as a reward for his great contribution to Britain's—and the world's—aviation, for he thought that as a serving officer in the R A F it would not be proper to do so. But the British Government awarded him £100,000 for this pioneer work.

The name of Sir Frank Whittle will be placed by history beside those of the world's other great inventors of means of propulsion.

The Great Stories of the World That Will Be Told for Ever

THE MAN WHO REFUSED A BRIBE

IN the days when the Commonwealth had come to an end and a king once more reigned in England, the fortunes of some of the bravest and wisest of the followers of Cromwell were at a low ebb. Milton, who had worked so hard for the Protector, was thrown into prison; and many other people were harshly treated by the Royalists.

There was one faithful follower of Cromwell, however, who had a great influence under the new Government. He was Andrew Marvell, a poet, and Member of Parliament for Hull. Though he seldom spoke, he was a most influential man. He bravely defended Milton.

It was Andrew Marvell's writings, however, that had most effect. They were called satires—that is, writings which bitterly ridicule the words, actions, or writings of another man. For instance, he was very indignant because Charles the Second was always getting money from Parliament and wasting it. The king and his ministers felt that this clever writer must be silenced, and the following story is told of him.

The vulgar monarch Charles the Second was often delighted to meet and entertain Andrew Marvell, taking pleasure in his ready wit and quick repartee. One morn-

ing his Majesty sent the Lord Treasurer, Danby, to seek Marvell, who was a very poor man, and earned but little more than the small salary which the town of Hull paid him as its Member. The crafty king knew this, and told Lord Danby to use every means to win Marvell to his side.

The Lord Treasurer had some difficulty in finding Marvell's lodging, but at last he discovered the house and entered abruptly.

" To what do I owe the honour of this visit? " asked Marvell, looking up from his writing.

" I come with a message from his Majesty, who wishes to know what he can do to serve you," replied Danby.

" It is not in his Majesty's power to serve me," said Marvell.

" But his Majesty wishes you to accept a post of honour at Court."

Andrew Marvell promptly refused to accept the honour, saying:

" I cannot accept any post with honour, for I must be either ungrateful to the king in voting against him, or false to my country in giving in to the measures of the Court. The only favour I beg of his Majesty is that he will esteem me as dutiful a subject as any he has, and realise that it is more in his interest for me to refuse than to accept his honours."

IMAGINATION · CHIVALRY · LEGENDS · GOLDEN DEEDS · FAIRY TALES

Danby then produced a bag containing a thousand pounds and placed it on the table, saying:

"The king has ordered me to give you a thousand pounds, which he hopes you will accept until you can think of some further boon to ask of his Majesty."

Andrew Marvell began to laugh.

"Surely, my lord, you do not intend to mock me by these offers? I do not need the king's gold. I have shelter, and as for my food, you shall hear of that from my landlady. Pray," said he, turning to her, "what had I for dinner yesterday?"

"A shoulder of mutton."

"And what shall I have today?"

"The remainder hashed."

"And tomorrow, my Lord Danby, I shall have the sweet blade bone broiled."

Danby was quite overcome by the stern simplicity of the poet, and picked up his bag of gold and returned to the king.

HOW ARSHAD SERVED HIS MASTER

HERE is the tale of a valiant man who met his death in a quarrel which was not his own.

There had been fighting for the throne in Persia. The ruler of that land was a boy of thirteen, and in his name ten million people were governed. This boy's father was Shah—the title of the Persian king—from 1907 until 1909, when, because he was so wicked, the people deposed him and made his little son Shah instead.

Mohammed Ali, the father, fled to Russia and plotted for the recovery of his throne, and with him was brave Arshad-ed-Dowleh, his commander-in-chief.

Early in September Arshad led an army into Persia to fight for Mohammed Ali. The general was unwell; his ill-ordered little army was quickly beaten, and he was wounded and taken prisoner.

Arshad was taken into camp late at night. He knew that as he had returned a rebel he could not hope for mercy.

For two hours he and his captors played a game. He was to have no inkling of his fate till morning came, and pride and caution alike prevented him from asking it. So they treated him as one of themselves, and the conversation was carried on in the complimentary language that in Persia even the most intimate friends employ to one another.

There he lay, reclining at his ease, while behind him, in the shadow, a crowd of silent soldiers leaned on their rifles, straining their ears to catch the talk.

Arshad told of the way in which he and the deposed Shah had striven to get together a force to recover the lost throne, and how Arshad himself had gone to Austria to learn military science to equip himself better for the task. And, with death staring him in the face, Arshad was proud of the fact that he had gained a diploma for his skill in military matters. Twice he mentioned his diploma. He told how he and the Shah had tried to borrow money from Russian officials and had failed, how they had pawned the queen's jewels and bought cannon. Arshad himself took the guns and ammunition across the Russian frontier labelled "mineral waters," and the Russian Customs officers believed the label.

It was late when the talk ended, and early in the morning he was seated on a chair in the place where they talked the night before. He was told, very gently, that he must die, for the State could not afford to let him live.

He looked as if he had slept well and had no fear. They gave him paper, and with a steady hand he wrote a letter to his wife, a royal princess, the daughter of Nasr-ed-Din, a former Shah.

Then he rose and made a speech, declaring that in all he had done he had ever been a man who worshipped his country. While he spoke the steady tramp of the firing-party was heard. It came up level with his left shoulder, marked time, and halted. He ceased, and turned to them. Between the files he went with them forty yards away. He stood erect, unfettered, without fear. When he heard the command "Ready!" he cried, "Long live my country! Fire!"

The volley rang out and he fell, but rose again to his knees with no sign of injury and cried, "Long live Mohammed Ali Shah!" The second section fired, and all was over.

The first section was Mussulman, and some say that each man fired wide, trusting to his neighbour's aim. The second section was Armenian.

Arshad-ed-Dowleh deserved a better master and a nobler cause.

L'HOMME QUI SE RAPPELA

This is a French translation of the story told in English on page 657

SEUL dans une petite pièce de son Palais de Bagdad le grand calife Haroun-al-Raschid reposait sur un divan, les mains immobiles sur ses genoux, les yeux fixés sur le mur vis-à-vis, la tête courbée comme sous le poids d'un fardeau. Il était si impassible, sa pose était si ajustée et si fixe, que l'on aurait pu le croire mort n'était-ce l'éclair extraordinaire de ses yeux.

Le plafond de cette petite chambre, ornée de pierres précieuses, était sculpté à l'imitation d'une fleur; les murs hexagonaux, en marbre, à part l'entrée et l'endroit où le balcon donnait à travers les cimes des arbres sur les toits de la cité, étaient divisés en panneaux d'ivoire ciselé, si magnifiquement travaillés que, tandis que le calife pouvait voir au travers, personne ne pouvait regarder dans la chambre parfumée, dont le plancher était parsemé de tapis doux et épais.

Une fine tapisserie recouvrait la voûte donnant accès de cette pièce secrète dans le reste du palais.

La lumière était pâle, l'air frais et parfumé on entendait un doux murmure de fontaine de la cour intérieure. Une branche de plante grimpante, avec toutes ses petites feuilles rayonnantes de lumière, pendait devant la croisée légèrement balancée par la bise.

Le grand calife était assis dans cette pièce, silencieux et immobile, l'âme profondément troublée. Sur son ordre, dans un accès de rage jalouse, le vizir avait été tué, le grand vizir Jaffar, adoré de la cité et tenu en grand honneur dans tout le califat, un homme bon et pur, bienveillant et juste, sincère et miséricordieux.

Haroun l'avait tué. Et, à présent, troublé de l'assassinat, amèrement repentant au souvenir de l'inconscient et abominable crime, il avait peur de son peuple. Car le peuple, contrarié de l'assassinat, avait laissé échapper un cri général d'affliction et de tristesse, une plainte qui était parvenue des rues populeuses de Bagdad jusqu'aux appartements mêmes du calife.

Jaffar était mort—Jaffar, l'ami des pauvres et des faibles, le juge équitable, le gouverneur bienveillant, le bon et saint homme d'abord facile et de vrai courage. Il était mort, ce protecteur des pauvres, ce juge miséricordieux et humain. Qui les aiderait à present ?

Ce cri de la cité arrivait terrible aux oreilles d'Haroun. Ce cri l'accusait et le menaçait. Le calife avait le droit de tuer qui il voulait; personne n'avait jamais osé lui contester ce droit. Tandis que maintenant—maintenant—

Dans sa colère il avait envoyé un ordre à travers l'Arabie entière disant que tout homme qui oserait dorénavant prononcer le nom de Jaffar serait condamné. L'homme était mort; il fallait que le nom mourût aussi. Haroun exigeait que sa mémoire fût à jamais effacée.

Et maintenant il était là, seul, sachant qu'on le défiait ; car des messagers étaient venus lui rapporter qu'un homme, nommé Mondeer, venait tous les jours crier le nom de Jaffar sur la place centrale, disant au peuple de le pleurer, de chérir sa mémoire, et d'entretenir les enfants de sa bonté, de sa justice, et de sa miséricorde, même au prix de la mort.

Haroun avait tremblé dans son fort intérieur à cette nouvelle. Mais son front s'était rembruni, ses yeux avaient étincelé, et, d'une voix de tonnerre, il avait ordonné que ce désobéissant coquin fût amené en sa présence.

Subitement il se leva du divan, grand, magnifique, rempli de grâce, c'était vraiment un bel homme; puis il enjamba rapidement, en silence, les tapis jusqu'au balcon, se tenant là un instant et contemplant tous les toits de la ville d'un regard troublé. Alors il se détourna et parcourut à nouveau la pièce, avec la même rapidité et dans le même silence, jusqu'à la voûte d'entrée, souleva la tapisserie et descendit l'escalier de marbre jusqu'à la cour où se jouait la fontaine.

Des esclaves se levèrent dans l'ombre de cette vaste et sombre cour, et se prosternèrent au passage du calife tandis que celui-ci poursuivait son chemin.

Il descendit de nouvelles marches, et arriva à la salle de l'audience dont des soldats gardaient l'entrée et où un grand nombre de ministres étaient réunis devant le trône. Il traversa la foule, qui s'effaça à son approche saluant jusqu'à terre, et atteignit enfin le trône, où il demeura debout, tournant le dos à l'assemblée silencieuse pendant un long moment, comme pour se recueillir et méditer sur la décision à prendre.

Alors, se retournant tout à coup et

s'asseyant, il fit un signe. Mondeer fut introduit tandis que des esclaves resserraient ses liens.

" Attachez bien, amis ! " cria le prisonnier. " Serrez fort et ne craignez pas de me blesser ! " Puis il leva les yeux, regarda le calife, et reprit, " Que les liens qui m'enchaînent soient les bienvenus, qu'ils soient bénis, car j'étais plus impuissant encore et mon sort était plus pénible quand Jaffar me rencontra et me délia pour me rendre la liberté. Ces cordes me rappellent sa belle action, elles réveillent en mon cœur une recrudescence d'affection pour lui, un élan d'amour, une vénération nouvelle, une plus profonde reconnaissance, aussi je les accueille avec joie. Que ton nom soit honoré, O Jaffar, toujours et toujours ! "

Tandis qu'il parlait l'âme du grand calife s'enflamma. Faire tuer un tel homme était au-dessous de la dignité d'un grand roi; l'honorer et le protéger serait reconquérir la faveur de l'opinion si éloignée du palais.

Une soif irrésistible de mériter un tel amour et une telle gratitude de son peuple s'empara du cœur d'Haroun. Il envia Jaffar dans sa tombe. Il envia la loyauté du prisonnier heureux de ses chaînes.

" Ami," lui dit-il, penchant son regard sur Mondeer, " tu portes la reconnaissance dans ton cœur, et la reconnaissance excuse tous les excès. Je te pardonne. De plus, puisque tu es sensible aux présents, avec mon pardon, je t'accorde la liberté et je t'offre ce gros diamant unique au monde, c'est la plus belle pierre qui brilla jamais sur la couronne tartare. Prends le et donne moi la place que tu voudras dans ton cœur."

Le prisonnier fut détaché. Il tendit les mains, ses yeux brillèrent avec plus d'éclat que le diamant, et, tournant ce cadeau sans prix vers le ciel, il leva la tête et s'écria avec amour :

"Ceci aussi je te le dois, O Jaffar ! Que ton nom soit honoré à jamais ! "

A WOMAN AGAINST A KING

THE wife of the Earl of Nithsdale, Jacobite leader condemned to death, came up to London to set her husband free.

But the Governor of the Tower would only allow her to enter on condition that she remained a prisoner. However, she could not then have helped her husband; so she bribed the guards, got admission daily, and quite won their confidence.

After fruitless attempts to obtain a pardon Lady Nithsdale made up her mind to help her husband to escape.

The evening before the date fixed for the execution of the earl and other prisoners Lady Nithsdale took two women with her into the Tower, and in turn brought them into and out of her husband's room, to take farewell of him. The first, a Mrs. Mills, had worn concealed garments, which the second, Mrs. Morgan, put on when quitting the Tower. Mrs. Morgan had taken off her outer garments and Lady Nithsdale had put them on her husband. Every little detail was thought out beforehand, and the cleverness, skill, and presence of mind shown by this resolute woman were very remarkable. Mrs. Morgan had been directed to come in crying and afflicted with grief, so that when Lord Nithsdale, who personated her, went out, he did so wearing a hood and with his face buried in a handkerchief to cover up his beard. Lady Nithsdale walked close behind him for a little distance to conceal his manly gait, and then returned to his room. The sham Mrs. Mills had been hurried off to fetch Lady Nithdale's maid.

In the deserted room Lady Nithsdale carried on a pretended conversation with her husband, asking questions and imitating his voice in answer, as well as striding up and down to make the people in the outer room think her husband was still there. Thus she allowed time for him to get clear of the Tower; then she opened the door, and, standing half in the room with her hands on the door, took a pretended farewell for the night, pulled the string through the latch of the door so that it could only open on the inside, and drove off in a coach.

The whole story, related by Lady Nithsdale some time after, shows wonderful self-control, skilful acting, and self-sacrifice, for she was hazarding her own life. The king was furious when he found what she had done, and issued orders for her arrest; but she escaped by her own clever wits, fetched her little boy from Scotland, and joined her husband in France.

THE FINEST THING IN THE WORLD

WHEN the King of Benares died the captain of his armies seized the crown and drove out of the country the three young sons of the king.

The three brothers crossed the mountains, and came to the edge of a great desert, where the track branched. Seeing an inn by the wayside, the brothers lodged there for the night; but instead of going to bed they sat up till daybreak, planning how to recover their father's kingdom.

"What is the finest thing in the world?" said Prince Deva, the eldest of the three brothers, suddenly, after a short silence.

When the meal was over the three princes paid for their lodging and food, and rode out into the desert.

"I will take the road to China, and come back armed with the power of money," said Prince Deva.

"I will go westward, and see if I can raise an army in Turkestan," said Prince Sanka; "and Amanda can do what he likes in Siam."

"But when shall we meet again?" asked the youngest brother.

"Let us meet here," said Sanka, "at this inn, on the first day of Spring ten

THE THREE BROTHERS SAT UP TILL DAYBREAK MAKING PLANS

"I do not know," said Prince Amanda, the youngest brother, looking at the innkeeper's pretty daughter, who came in to prepare the morning meal.

"It is power," said Prince Sanka, the second brother. "It was because he had command of all the power of the kingdom that our father's captain was able to rob us of our rights."

"No!" exclaimed Prince Deva. "The finest thing in the world is money. The wicked usurper of our kingdom acquired his power by bribing the soldiers."

The two elder brothers continued to argue the matter with great passion, but Prince Amanda was silent and thoughtful.

years hence. Then we will decide which of us three has obtained the finest thing in the world. Even if we only partly succeed, we ought to be able to recover our father's kingdom."

The three brothers agreed to all this, and, after saying good-bye, they separated. Prince Deva gaily mounted his horse, and joined a long caravan of Chinese merchants.

Prince Sanka set out on a lonely desert path, running into the wilds of Turkestan.

He was the first to disappear over the sky-line of the wide, bare, yellow desert. Then the caravan in which Prince Deva rode grew smaller and smaller in the distance.

Poor little Prince Amanda stood by the door of the inn, watching it with tears in his eyes until it disappeared. Very slowly and sorrowfully he at last rode down the southward track.

The ten years passed away. It was the first day of Spring. The little inn at the end of the mountain pass had grown lovelier in the lapse of time. Red roses climbed to the top of the walls, and all the roof was hidden with the beautiful flowers. In the doorway of the inn, framed in the roses, stood Saki. She had grown from a pretty girl into a beautiful woman. She held a little baby girl in her arms, and two red-cheeked little boys clutched her dress and stood on tiptoe, staring at the stretch of tawny sand.

Two great armies were approaching the inn, one from the east and one from the west. Along the track from China there slowly unrolled a broad, unending line of camels and ponies and men in blue robes. At the head of this vast and mighty caravan was a great elephant in golden harness; on its back with a howdah, which is a kind of little house. It was made of jewels, which shone with a dazzling light in the sunshine. In the howdah sat a pale-faced man, wrinkled and careworn.

The army that came out of Turkestan was terrible and enormous. A hundred thousand lean, fierce, savage horsemen, armed with long iron lances and great curious bows, galloped up on little wiry steeds. They shouted to each other with harsh, strange cries. Their faces were yellow, and beneath their low foreheads their dark, narrow, cruel eyes glittered with fierce joy. Then out from the centre of the host galloped a tall, strong man in bright chain-armour, an iron helmet on his head and naked sword in his hand.

"Deva!" he shouted to the man riding in from the west on the elephant.

"Sanka!" shouted the other.

They both alighted at the door of the inn, and embraced each other.

"How old and careworn you have grown, Deva!" said his brother.

"I have worked night and day for ten years," said Deva proudly, "but I do not regret it. I am now the richest man in the world. Look at this huge caravan. There isn't a camel or a pony or a porter carrying anything but gold and jewels."

"Yes, you are very rich indeed," said Sanka. "But are you still certain that wealth is the finest thing in the world? Look at the host I have collected. It took me ten years to get it together, and a hundred or more battles."

"But how can you pay a hundred thousand men?" asked Deva. "I tell you again, wealth is the finest thing in the world. I have only to offer your soldiers more money than you give them, and they would desert you and follow me.

"You are wrong!" said Sanka, in a furious voice. "Look at this trumpet. I have only to put it to my lips and give the order, and my men would slay all your porters, and this wonderful wealth of yours would be mine in less than five minutes."

Prince Deva's face was white. He looked at his brother in a strange way, and his eyes were narrow and cunning.

"I must admit you have the best of the argument, Sanka," he said at last; but his eyes grew more cunning in expression as he said it. "But where is little Amanda? I wonder what he thinks is the finest thing in the world."

"I am afraid the poor, simple little creature will be no use to us," said Sanka. "I have power and you have wealth. What else is there worth struggling for?"

A tall, handsome young man, with bright, gay eyes, came out of the inn. He was clad in a workaday dress. In the doorway of the inn Saki and the little girl and two boys stood watching him.

"It is poor Amanda," said Deva. "Well," he added, as his brother ran up and embraced Sanka and turned to him, "you do not look as though you have found the finest thing in the world."

"But I have," said Amanda, with a happy smile. "Instead of going to Siam I turned back, and I have never since left this inn. There is my wife at the door, and our three little children.

"Just like a silly boy," said Prince Deva, "to think that love is everything in life."

"It was not love that made me turn back to this little inn," said Amanda very softly. "Love came afterwards, with other blessings. I found here something without which love and wealth and power and everything are but dust and ashes."

"What was that?" said the two elder brothers. "Tell us, what was it?"

"The finest thing in the world—contentment!" said Amanda.

The two elder brothers were silent. They looked at each other, they gazed at their armies, and then they walked slowly up to the inn where Amanda's wife and children stood. Suddenly Prince Deva fiercely gripped Prince Sanka's arm.

"The boy is right!" he cried—"the boy is right! Do you know, Sanka, I was not even content with all my wealth, and I was scheming to bribe your army to betray you and get your power."

"And I had resolved to rob you tonight of all your wealth," said Sanka.

"I don't see why you wanted to scheme against each other," said Amanda.

"I must get an army to win back our father's kingdom," said Prince Deva.

"And I must get money to pay my soldiers, as I mean to lead them against the usurper," said Sanka.

"The usurper?" said Amanda. "He died nine years ago. Since then hundreds of messengers have come from Benarcs asking me to return and be king. But I am too contented to think of going."

Oh, how Deva and Sanka laughed! All their labours had been unnecessary.

In the end they had to give a great part of Deva's wealth to Sanka's army of fierce savages in order to induce the tribes to go back to Turkestan. The eldest brother would not accept the crown. He became a happy and contented inmate of Amanda's house; and though Sanka went back to India and became king, and had a long and happy reign, he often admitted that it was Amanda who had found the finest thing in the world.

THE GOOD SAMARITANS OF THE DESERT

THEY have no Victoria Cross in the United States or they would have awarded it to Louis Westcott Beck, and a special one to his big dog Rufus.

And yet, perhaps, they would not give medals at all. We do not give medals to the monks of St. Bernard or to their dogs; and Beck and Rufus have done in the blazing desert the work that the monks and their dogs do in the snowy Alps. It came about in a strange way.

Louis Beck was a miner seeking a lode of gold or silver which would make him rich. He had many adventures in search of wealth, but never reached the object of his dreams. In the course of his wanderings he found himself in Nevada, the most barren and desolate area on the American continent. For hundreds of miles stretches the almost sterile desert, with practically no vegetation and with only a few springs, miles apart.

Louis Beck, with some friends, wandered miserably on and on, in search of the gold and silver that were not there, down into the worst part of all the desert, a part which, from its horrible character, men have named Death Valley. They found nothing to reward them. Their food stores were dwindling; their water supply was exhausted before they could find fresh. They had a terrible march of two days and nights without a drop to drink. Their tongues were parched and swollen, so that they could not speak, and they were almost at the last gasp when they found a tiny stream trickling out of a cleft at the foot of the Panamint Mountains. They drank and lived.

Beck returned to civilisation a changed man, with a fixed purpose. Not for nothing had he seen those horrible desert sands strewn with dead men's bones. He remained among his friends during the winter, and in the spring he called up his big Newfoundland dog, Rufus, and set out again for Death Valley.

This time Beck took with him a load of thin metal strips, on which he could write directions. These strips he set up as signboards to guide dying miners to water and shelter.

Beck and Rufus continued their work until Death Valley is no longer a valley of death. With Rufus to help in carrying his luggage, Beck stalked through the valley finding new streams and marking them, piling up rocks and setting upon them his little metal strips, to tell the weary wayfarers where they may find the life-giving stream for which they are seeking. While still keeping an eye open for the gold-mine he yet hoped to find, Beck made himself more precious than gold to travellers in this dreaded valley.

Together he and Rufus continued to control the purple waste, Rufus, with his marvellous instinct, leading his master to where exhausted miners had fallen.

There is no medal for Beck, no medal for Rufus. The dog has earned a set of leather gaiters to protect his legs from snake-bite, and Beck has merely earned the gratitude of all mankind.

THE SPRING OF SAINT BONIFACE

HIDDEN away in the heart of the Black Forest there is a spring of water to which a beautiful legend is attached.

As early as the eighth century there came to this country, then a wild and savage place, a man who had grown up among the hills of Devon, Winfrid by name. This name was changed in after years to Boniface, and by that he is now known.

When he was quite a little boy, only five years old, his heart was stirred with a longing to devote his life to God; and, as he held to this purpose without changing, when he was thirteen he was allowed by his father to carry out his heart's desire, and from that time lived only to love God and serve his fellow-men.

When he grew to manhood he joined a band of missionaries who were going to the heathen tribes living in Germany.

One day when on a journey through the Black Forest he was fainting from thirst and fatigue, and begged a drop of milk from a woman whom he saw milking a cow. This woman, wild as she was, felt pity at the sight of his distress, and was about to give him milk when her husband suddenly appeared and brutally prevented her.

Boniface dragged himself on, and finally fell on the ground beneath a high granite rock, when suddenly, to his great surprise, there gushed out of it a stream of clear spring water, from which he gratefully drank. The woman, who had followed him and watched him, hastened up with a vessel in which to catch the welcome stream. The saint said to her, smiling: "Yes, to you it is granted, but remember, this fount will always be found dry when it is approached by the envious, the hating, and the unforgiving."

This story became so deeply rooted in the mind of the people of that country that right down to the nineteenth century the peasants living in the neighbourhood of the spring would warn people of ill-will not to approach it.

All those who came to seek the spring through the deep aisles of the trees must be in love with all mankind, or for them no waters would gush out.

It became known as the stream of St. Boniface, and it is pleasant to think that the good and holy man who gave it this name learned the love of God as a little child among the moors and hills of Devon.

THE WOLF THAT CAME IN THE NIGHT

IN the middle of last century a French lawyer, the Baron de Monthyon, left a large sum of money to provide an annual prize for "the poor French person who in the course of the year shall have performed the most virtuous actions."

The records of this annual award are a wonderful roll of golden deeds; but it is doubtful whether they contain a more heroic story than that of Madeleine Saunier, a young woman whose whole soul was fixed on doing deeds of charity, and who contrived to help others in a marvellous way.

A poor blind widow with a feeble daughter lived a mile and a half from her cottage, and for fifteen years Madeleine never failed to walk daily to them, to feed them, set their house in order, and cheer them up; and they waited eagerly for her coming the next day.

About as far off in another direction there lay in an outhouse a poor girl smitten with leprosy, and deserted by her friends. For eighteen months Madeleine visited her twice a day, to give her the little food she could take and to dress her frightful wounds, until at last the poor leper died.

In 1840 Madeleine was nearly drowned in trying to cross a swollen stream that lay between her and one of her daily pensioners, and when she was blamed for her rashness she only said:

"I could not help it; I could not go yesterday, so I had to go today."

One cold winter she had a terrible experience. She was nursing a dying woman named Mancel, who lived on the hillside in a hovel more like a wild beast's den than the home of a human creature. Toward the end of a long night Madeleine had lighted a few green sticks to try to lessen the intense cold when the wretched door was pushed aside, and she saw a wolf about to leap into the room.

She sprang to the door and held it fast, piling up everything she could to keep it shut, as the beast sprang against it; while she shouted as loudly as she could in the hope that the wolf might be frightened away. But all the rest of that terrible night she had to hold the door against the wolf.

A French translation of this story appears on page 6081.

Nature's Wonderful Living Family in Earth and Air and Sea

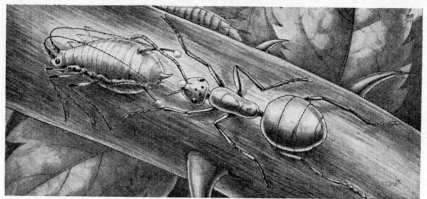

An ant milking an aphis

THE WONDERFUL ANT

WITH a certificate from Solomon for diligence and wisdom, the ants are perhaps the most impressive little creatures in the entire animal kingdom. Their social system is higher even that that of the beehive, and in many ways startlingly resembles that of mankind.

Aspects of ant life present themselves which outdistance the skill and instinctive habits of tribes of men known to science. These insects have a knowledge of hygiene, of the art of taming other creatures and employing them for service, which is a state immeasurably ahead of that of untaught savages.

The savage has no civic life, no home, no animals, no crops. The ant is a citizen of a considerable city marvellously planned, with ordered streets and highways, with nurseries for its young ones, with storehouses for its food, with quarters for its army and workers, with cattle abounding in stables which are in reality strong places of durance.

So proficient are ants in the technique of communal life that with a little care and patience an informed author might write a story of their routine in peace and war which might pass for a description of life in a human community.

They have many virtues comparable with human attributes, but they have vices as pronounced as ours, and of the same kind. The attitude of the ant towards nearly all animal life but their own and that of the creatures which they take as slaves and supplies into their nests, is one of intense hostility—if hostility is the correct term. Perhaps we had better say that they have an appetite for anything that lives, and that in gratification of that appetite they are merciless, and eat while the victim is alive and in agony from their thousand envenomed bites.

Courage is the badge of all the race. That they swarm to the attack of huge pythons which crush cattle is at first incredible; but then the snake can have no terrors for enemies whose numbers are overwhelming even after thousands may have been crushed by the writhing giant. The ants win in the end, and devour the great reptile. A snake is so huge and incomprehensibly formidable that they may slaughter it in ignorance of the wonder they perform.

A timid man in ambush may slay an elephant or a tiger, yet flee from the uplifted fist of a puny member of his own race and sex. How, then, does the ant fare against an antagonist whose powers it may reasonably be expected to appreciate ? There is no better answer than personal experience furnishes.

PREHISTORIC LIFE · MAMMALS · BIRDS · REPTILES · FISHES · INSECTS

First, then, picture a swarming of brown garden ants. It was the day on which the young queens and drones were due to take their wedding flight, the most important day of the ant year. A series of ant cities were kept under observation by the writer, nests lying at intervals of from six feet to sixty yards and more apart, all separate, distinct, and without any communication with each other.

THE WORKER ANTS THAT RISE EARLY IN THE MORNING

Yet all swarmed on the same date, late in the autumn, a hot day, after a cold summer. The wingless workers were out and about in streams early in the day, but the winged queens and drones did not begin to appear till noon had passed. The workers assisted them out of the holes in a stuccoed wall which formed the exits from the city.

Timorous and unwilling, the winged queens needed repeated support and encouragement to induce them to climb up the wooden posts of the garden from which they were to take flight. They were just like nervous girl brides leaving home, and demanding the sympathy and aid of their wingless relatives. They were petted and stroked; their wings were smoothed by the jaws of their attendants, and, towards the close of the exodus, it seemed as if the workers grew a little fretful and gave more than one shrinking queen a nip with their mouths to make them mount into the air.

Now, at the summit of one of the posts which was serving as a sort of springboard for the queens, there lurked a large wolf spider, which seemed to avoid the crowded area where workers and queens were congregated. But presently one queen, reluctant to launch herself, wandered away from the general assembly, as if to try another point of vantage from which to fly.

THE REVENGE OF THE ANTS ON A RAIDING SPIDER

With one spring the spider was on her. But before he could fasten his fangs in her, a worker ant, one-sixth his size, dashed at him. The spider retreated in alarm, followed by his little assailant. Other ants at once joined in the attack, and, like a man springing from a precipice to avoid foes on land, the spider leapt into the air, and dropped five feet to the ground, paying out a life-line of silk as it fell.

It alighted among an army of ants on the pavement. Strange stories are told of ants dropping food and larvae from a height to waiting allies below, and the suggestion is that there exists a sort of wireless communication between them. In the present instance there might have been such communication between the ants on high and those on the ground, for, quicker than one can tell it, the grim creature which fell among them was swarmed on by the ants on the pavement.

The spider seemed to recognise the hopelessness of the fight. After one attempt to run away, it crouched down as if dead. That served no useful purpose, but hastened its end. The ants rushed on it like furies. They bit it, they turned it over on its back, and in a trice they were hauling it to their hole.

It was too big to be dragged into so small an opening; its sprawling legs lay like hurdles across the portal. The ants bit off its legs, and carried the fat body in!

Picture the home of the ant—a labyrinth of highways, with halls and chambers, supported by pillars. There are nurseries for the babies, but as these are constantly hatching they are of various ages, and are grouped according to the stage of development they have reached.

THE LOVING CARE WITH WHICH THE ANTS TEND THEIR YOUNG

How old this wondrous city is, how old the citizens, cannot be guessed. Queen ants live, it is known, for fifteen years at least. The worker ants, too, attain seven or more years, in which they have a great advantage over worker wasps and bees.

Complex and unending is the activity in the city. The adult ants do for their little ones what the ideal State will do for human children: watch over them from birth, assist them through youth to maturity, and bury them when they are dead. The one respect in which the ant fails is that it does not tend its fellows when they fall sick.

Probably that consideration is not denied the young, for the solicitude of the workers for the offspring of their queen is unexcelled in any grade of life. It is perhaps unnecessary to emphasise the fact that the queen is the mother of almost the entire population of the colony. She appears to have the power to regulate the sex of her progeny; that is to say, she produces at the fitting season those which will develop into workers, which we call sexless, and later she produces future queens and drones.

A FEW OF NATURE'S LITTLE WORKERS

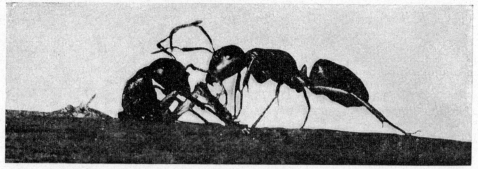

CARPENTER ANTS AT WORK

TAILOR OR SPINNING
ANT WORKER

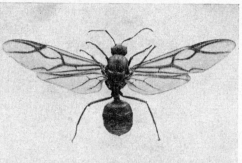

A WINGED FEMALE
SPINNING ANT

QUEEN WOOD
ANT

DRIVER ANT WORKER

RED WOOD ANT WORKER

HOUSE ANT QUEEN

ANTS REMOVING THE BODY OF A DEAD QUEEN

A SWARM OF BUSY ANTS

Practically all the citizens are her children, yet not quite all. The so-called sexless workers have the power, in time of need, to lay eggs, but, so far as has been discovered, these eggs always turn into male ants, the drones. When food supplies flag, the queen ant, like the queen bee in similar circumstances, is apt to produce a preponderance of male eggs, but otherwise she determines their advent, first laying the worker eggs, then the queen eggs, and finally the drone eggs.

This order is necessary, for the more the workers the greater is the supply of food brought in, and the larger the staff of little workpeople to carry on the labours of the ant community.

Let us imagine the summer hatching season in progress. The egg becomes a grub, legless, wingless, helpless. It is affectionately fed by the workers, who pre-digest the food for it in the same way as the bees do for bee larvae.

Not only are the grubs fed and cleansed, they are carried about the city daily for airing and exercise. The period occupied by the grub stage is variable, but probably in no case more than two or three weeks.

THE SILKEN JACKET THE ANT GRUB MAKES FOR ITSELF

At the end of that time the ant grub accomplishes a sort of natural miracle; it spins itself a vestment of silk, a cocoon in which it lies foodless and inert, while undergoing the change from a writhing maggot into a perfect ant. Three weeks is about the average term for this transformation. Throughout that time the workers tend the sleeping creature with all the loving assiduity which they displayed to the ravenous grub.

Daily it is visited by its careful attendants; it is even carried up to an outlet of the city and screened by some sheltering stone where it may derive the advantage of sunlight without the danger of observation. It is strange that these little people of the dark underworld realise the importance of sunlight to waxing life.

At last the slow wonder is achieved, and a little ant is ready to issue from the silken shirt which the grub wove. But it cannot do so unassisted. The workers have to aid in the removal of the imprisoning robe. It is a full-sized ant that creeps from the cradle bondage, for all development as to size takes place in the hungry grub period. But the new ant is not yet

fit to exchange buffets with its enemies in the outside world.

It must still be fed and nurtured by its elders; it must be taught its duties in the nest, like a new boy learning the regulations at school. For a fortnight or three weeks this probation may last, in which time the new ant is housemaid, scavenger, builder, nurse, all things by turn. Finally it joins the hunters and goes out into the world to battle and capture food.

THE FEEBLE DRONES WHICH LEAVE THE NEST NEVER TO RETURN

With the drones and queens the process is different. The queens enjoy a regal exemption from all toil but egg-laying. The drones do a little work, but are rather feeble folk, and cannot entirely feed themselves. On swarming day out they go to meet queens from other colonies. They never return. They are destroyed by birds, by other insects; winds and rains sweep them in multitudes to destruction, or they fall wearied at night to perish.

The queens, however, return to earth, and either enter an old city, to live in amity with the reigning queen, or start a colony of their own. Whichever the course, they have that one flight and that alone, for the first thing they do, on regaining the nest, is to bite off their wings. Should a returning queen be remiss in this respect, the workers bite her wings off for her; there is no second sallying forth for a queen, unless it be on foot, to change her nest with all her children about her.

Such an occasion is deeply interesting to watch, for we are able then to realise what a value the ants set on child life. Next to the queen herself, if indeed second at all, they rank the eggs and babies foremost in significance. No nomadic tribe ever showed more devotion to their children than these puny insects show for their eggs and infants. They are carried with a jealous affection which it is ill to challenge.

THE GREAT ARMY OF FOLLOWERS IN THE TRACK OF THE MIGRATING ANTS

Such a migration is marked by an unexpected revelation. The colony has a host of camp followers, various insects which are the living treasures of the owners of the city. There are many beetles, there are lesser breeds of ants, there are multitudes of green-fly.

These camp followers go where the ants go, some not voluntarily. The willing ones are either parasites or pets. Over

500 species of insects are known to inhabit ant nests. Some of them are kept because they diffuse odours pleasant to the senses of the ants. Some yield sugary secretions, some are unmistakably pets, things the ants rejoice to keep, feed, and guard, just as boys love to keep rabbits, birds, and caterpillars.

But the greatest wonder investigated up to now is in relation to the aphides. What do green-fly, creatures of the foliage and the open air, down in the gloomy recesses of an ant city ? They are the cattle of the ants, the milch cows. As we all know to our cost, the green-fly emits a sticky solution, which we call honey-dew. This is so plentiful when the green-fly are well fed that not only does it impart a glutinous sheen to the leaves of our trees, but actually drips to the ground.

That honey-dew is the dearest food treasure of the ants, and to get it they practise arts which we could not believe, had observation not been a hundred times confirmed. The ants take the aphides prisoners, carry them down into their cities, and build them into pens which have approaches large enough to permit the passage of an ant's body, but too small to permit a green-fly to get out.

HOW THE ANT CITY MAKES SURE OF ITS CATTLE SUPPLY

The aphis has to be kept alive, far from its natural food supplies. The food is brought to it by the worker ants, and the green-fly becomes as dependent on its captors as the caged birds in the Zoo on their human keepers.

The green-fly makes its return in the form of honey-dew, which it surrenders to the ant at a touch of the latter's antennae. We may see this done in the open, where an ant approaches a green-fly on a rose-leaf and there gently milks it, as it were.

But the green-fly, though prolific, are short-lived; how is the supply to be maintained ? In the autumn these amazing insects collect the eggs of aphides laid on plants in the open, carry them down into their subterranean nurseries, keep them there all the winter, and when they hatch out in the following spring, transfer the baby green-fly to the air and restore them to the food plant on which they will grow to strength and sufficiency of honey-dew.

If we consider that fact for a moment we see that it eclipses anything else in the way of prudent provision accomplished in the whole animal world, beneath the status of Man himself. That is not merely thinking of tomorrow, it is careful budgeting for next year's needs.

That happens in abundant instances in England, so we are prepared to find ants in warmer lands extending the same type of prevision to the products of the field. The agricultural ants of southern Europe, and of various places in the New World and elsewhere, garner grain for future use with superb skill.

THE LITTLE UNDERGROUND BARNS WHERE FOOD IS STORED FOR THE WINTER

They have been credited with too much talent. They have been said to set the seed and reap the harvest. What they actually do is to bite down, in the vicinity of their cities, all vegetable growth save the grasses, called ant rice, which form a large part of their food. This gives unchecked opportunity to the ants' cereal. When it ripens, they carry the seed down into their barns and store it against the coming of winter.

Buried grain germinates with heat and moisture, but not where an agricultural ant buries it. With supreme wisdom the little husbandmen bite off the radicle, the life germ of the grain, so that it cannot grow. But it is found that when they desire sugar they allow a certain proportion of their booty to begin growing, and eat the transformed product, while still maintaining an ample reserve of the dry sterilised grain.

A new vista of perplexity opens here, the relations of ants to the plant world. Eager as they are for flesh food, the majority of ants dote on honey in all its forms, and this craving makes them robbers in harvest scenes where they contribute no valuable return. Smooth-bodied and hairless, they are not pollen carriers as are the bees, so plants arm against them. The subject belongs more to botany than to the animal world, but the student of the ant must devote attention to it in the proper quarter.

THE FIERCE ARMIES THAT PROTECT AN ACACIA TREE OF AMERICA

We must, however, include here one amazing instance of mutual accommodation between trees and ants. The tree is a certain South American acacia, notably thorny and forbidding of aspect, yet generous of leaf, irresistibly alluring to hungering herb-eaters.

Now each of those threatening thorns on the acacia is simply the outward defence of what is a fortress within, garrisoned by ants ! The thorns are hollow, and inhabited exclusively by a specially virulent species of ants, which, when the tree is menaced by man or animal, dash out, swarm on him or it, and bite and inject poison as if they loved their task and their tree.

How does the tree lure the ants to itself ? The homes it affords are well enough, but if the ants had to roam in search of food the defence would be intermittent, and disaster might befall while the guardians sought their daily bread abroad. So the food is grown at home.

Each leaf of the acacia exudes honey in a generous stream, so that the garrison is furnished with meat, drink, and abode all on the same tree, and on the same terms as those on which the old man-made cities of Europe, and the feudal castles and estates of medieval England had their constant armed defences. Flowers spread their charms for the delight of bees, but this extraordinary tree is modified entirely for the reception, housing, victualling, of nothing but ants, and entertains its armed retainers in myriads.

THE RETURN OF THE RAIDERS UNDER THEIR PARASOLS

One of the functions of these acacia-haunting ants seems to be to keep off marauding ants of another species, the famous sauba or parasol ants, as they are called. Their second name is derived from their habit of cutting out sections of leaves and carrying them upright, like umbrellas, over their heads back to their own nests. In the wilds their practice is harmless, for though they strip a tree, recovery is easy in that generous climate. The danger arises when men advance into the ants' territory and there seek to grow coffee, oranges, and other products of civilised life. Here these leaf-cutters are a destructive terror to growers. Little wonder that they denounce the parasol ants and leave admiration to the naturalists. There is reason enough. The saubas have an invincible organisation. Included in their ranks are not merely ordinary military workers, but huge-headed soldier ants with terrific biting jaws.

When a leaf-cutting foray is coming, the soldiers marshal the workers into ranks, and themselves take guard on the flanks, where they attack and devour any enemy they may meet. In the same order the procession moves home with the booty. Enormous nests are made and stored with the leaves brought in—cities nearly 40 feet in diameter and ramifying below ground in ordered mazes of intricate town-planning.

THE DIVISION OF LABOUR AS PRACTISED BY THE SAUBA ANTS

Here are stored the stolen leaves, where after treatment by the ants, the vegetation throws up a mass of fungus, which forms the food of the ants. Some naturalists believe that the ants cultivate the fungus. We do not know. It is certain that the fungus grows after the ants have gnawed it; we have no proof that it grows without such treatment.

There is a scientific division of labour among the saubas, in the open as in the depths of the city. Multitudes scale the trees and drop the severed leaves to the ground, where waiting workers pick them up. But classification of tasks seems general throughout the hundreds upon hundreds of species of ants whose ways have been studied. Some of them have a perfect method of co-ordinating effort for the common good.

We see them transporting grains of corn, three or four ants to a grain, carrying prodigious burdens in proportion to the size of the bearers, half a mile and more. Others carry worms in the same way.

It takes three ants to support and move the particular worm they favour. To do the work, the three line up one behind another. Each straddles the worm and grips it with its jaws. Then they march, and, under a good magnifying glass, the bearers and their burden seem the living counterpart of those great vehicles which we employ for the carriage of tree trunks.

THE LIVING STOREHOUSE IN WHICH THE ANT KEEPS ITS FOOD

Nature has played her part in enlarging the ability of the ants to departmentalise life. Nothing stranger in the world is to be found in this direction than the honey-pot ants. This is a Mexican species in which certain of the workers remain ever in the city to act as animate honey-combs. The workers bring in their nectar and calmly pump it down the throats of the honey-pot receivers. The sweet fluid passes down the gullet of the receiver and into the strangest of all stomachs, a tough

AT HOME WITH THE ANTS

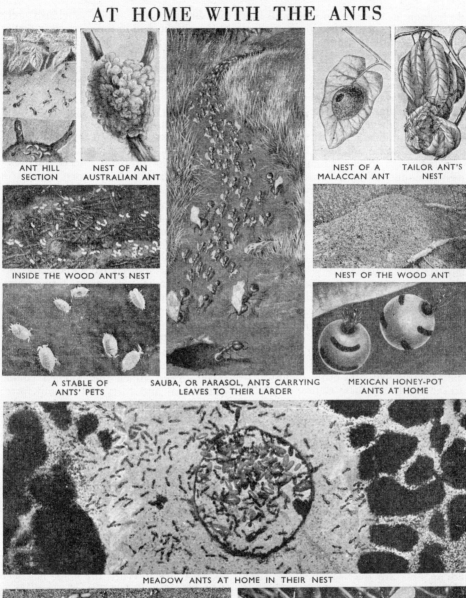

ANT HILL SECTION

NEST OF AN AUSTRALIAN ANT

NEST OF A MALACCAN ANT

TAILOR ANT'S NEST

INSIDE THE WOOD ANT'S NEST

NEST OF THE WOOD ANT

A STABLE OF ANTS' PETS

SAUBA, OR PARASOL, ANTS CARRYING LEAVES TO THEIR LARDER

MEXICAN HONEY-POT ANTS AT HOME

MEADOW ANTS AT HOME IN THEIR NEST

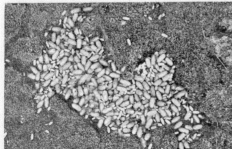

PUPAE OF THE BLACK ANT

ANTS CARRYING COCOONS

The pictures on these pages are by Messrs. Collins, Paul Griswold Howes, and others

little balloon, as it seems, in which all the natural digestive organs are present, but ridiculously reduced, simply to permit of an enormous extension of the crop for the storage of the honey.

The ancients imagined a Tantalus, whose fate it was ever to have luscious food and pleasant drink brought almost to his lips but never quite within reach. The ant Tantalus is filled to bursting with the spoil of innumerable flowers, but is not permitted to enjoy more than the barest amount of sweetness; it must receive at command and give back at a summons. The ants give, the ants take away, when they need honey.

That is the most curious adaptation we shall find; but there are others in the line we have considered. Some species have engineers which, when the workers move out, construct tunnels for them so that they make great marches in search of prey, well protected from observation.

THE FIERCE ATTACK OF A HOST OF BLIND RAIDERS

Others, of the aphis-loving kind, run tunnels up the trees in which the honey-yielding cattle live, and bring them down into the citadel by these routes, or coolly wall in the aphides where they are, and keep the tunnels for their own lines of communication.

Terrible to all other life in the vicinity are the operations of the larger and fiercer ants. The Eciton ants are notorious for the extreme severity of their attacks on all other living creatures within their range of action. They clear their line of march of every living thing, as if a flame had swept it. Birds and beasts, every type of insect, are attacked and eaten piecemeal. Even creatures which feed on ants are overwhelmed by sheer weight of numbers.

Human habitations are not proof against them. The ants swarm through them, clearing every particle of food, every rat and mouse, every spider and fly, all the vermin which negligent natives tolerate in their homes.

The curious thing is that these ants are blind. They were sighted once upon a time, but their habits of dependence on touch and smell have led, after millions of years, to complete loss of the sense of vision yet with no perceptible diminution of efficiency in the species. Perhaps

our British ants, which obviously rely little on sight, will in time lose their power of eye, too; already their ocelli, the three little eyes which they carry in addition to the two great many-faceted eyes, have practically lost their original function through lack of use.

THE TERRIBLE ARMAMENT OF THE SLAVE-RAIDING ANTS

That is not the most salutary loss that ants sustain. As we have already said the social life of these insects resembles human civilisation in its worst vices as in the highest of its virtues.

It is obviously but a short step from the domestication and imprisonment of green-fly and other insects to a regular system of enslavement. Many species of ants are confirmed slave raiders, the redoubtable Amazon ants especially. They are formidably armed with great biting jaws, and their habit is periodically to send out scouts to adjoining colonies of ants of lesser force, then, at a signal, to sally forth, thousands strong, to raid and enslave.

Added to their fighting qualities are military abilities of an impressive character. They attack the doomed citadel with a run and carry it by main force; or they surround it, place guards at every exit, then throw in what we must believe to be parties of picked fighters. Out come the rightful owners and battle is joined. The defence is hopeless. Soon the ground is littered with a horrible wreckage of ants bitten in two or torn to pieces. But while the fighters are thus wrestling in a death grapple, the raiders within are at the nurseries.

THE LAZY LIFE WHICH FOLLOWS A SUCCESSFUL RAID

Out they come, each one bearing an egg or a larva. When the home has been denuded of its infant life, the column is reformed and the living booty is carried back to the Amazon city. To what end? Simply that the larvae, waking to adult life in a hostile land, may know no other condition, but meekly accept bondage. They become the slaves of their captors.

Now there never was a condition in life which slavery did not undermine. Greece and Rome became helplessly weak through their dependence on slave labour and slave soldiers. The ancient Empires of the East rose and fell in tides, as slaves were many and faithful or few and unstable. Most of the dynastic tragedies in modern Oriental lands have sprung from the plots of slaves in the seclusion of the royal palaces.

And the greater the success of the raids of the slave-making ants, the more certain is the utter demoralisation of the conquerors. They cease to forage for themselves, leaving the task to their captives. They abandon habits of cleanliness, they neglect even to feed themselves, everything being done for them by their tireless slaves.

striking for the fact that the descent from pre-eminent fitness for existence comes about in the life, not of an almost everlasting species, but in that of an individual colony, an individual ant. Every ant born into the world appears a very darling of Nature, so amply equipped with gifts and cunning does it seem. We are always learning new things about these creatures, increasing our astonishment and sense of reverence.

For example, astonishment was caused in the autumn of 1922, when a great

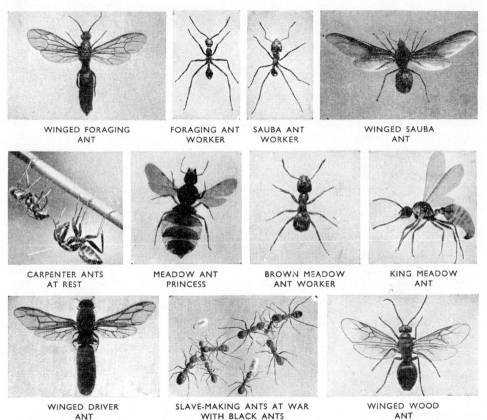

WINGED FORAGING ANT   FORAGING ANT WORKER   SAUBA ANT WORKER   WINGED SAUBA ANT

CARPENTER ANTS AT REST   MEADOW ANT PRINCESS   BROWN MEADOW ANT WORKER   KING MEADOW ANT

WINGED DRIVER ANT   SLAVE-MAKING ANTS AT WAR WITH BLACK ANTS   WINGED WOOD ANT

When the home has to be changed the slaves have to carry their masters, helpless as larvae. Left to themselves these conquerors, who slew citizens in thousands and wrecked strong places of defence, now starve and die, helpless if denied the daily service of the little slave ants to keep life in them by their ministrations. Self-help for ants as for humans has still its abounding merits.

Such a decline in skill, ardour, and independence as we see here, is the more

French naturalist returned to Europe from Indo-China to reveal a supposedly new species of ants to the French Academy of Sciences, in which the soldiers, enormous creatures, bear on their heads great hollow horns through which, when attacked, they eject poison gas, a vapour of formic acid.

A little later there was as great a surprise at home. Keeper Brow of the London Zoo's insect department was cleaning out a nest of our common wood ants when lo, the ants began to bombard him with what he thought to be the tear gas which was used in the First World War. With streaming eyes he made tests and found that his charges were deliberately fumigating him with vapourised formic acid, after the fashion of the Indo-Chinese ants. And it proves that our species can discharge their irritating gas to a distance of over eight inches.

THE PROFOUND WISDOM WHICH RESIDES IN A TINY HEAD

If the old writers of fables which formerly served for natural history had known but a little of the ways of ants, what a literature of the impossible they would have added to the common stock of travellers' tales.

But indeed they could not much have exceeded the wonder of the reality. There is their sense of values, their method of communication, their memory, their delightful deeds of art, cunning, reasoned initiative, and skill, all mysteries to us still, because we cannot imagine how such profound wisdom can reside in so tiny a horny head. Let us finally group one or two disconnected feats in order to enhance our respect for these little people.

There were the ants which for several days had to climb down a string to a jar which contained sugar, but presently ceased their journeys, yet got the sugar. Only three or four ants made the whole trip. They brought grains of sugar up the string and dropped it to a ledge below, where the bulk of the ants waited to carry it off to their nest.

Then there was a tiny company of wood ants which sought to get a great horny beetle home to their larder. It was alive and resisting vigorously, but it moved in the direction the ants desired. Two were in front, hauling, and two were behind, pushing, but as the ground was rough and the beetle's great legs waved and clutched, one could not understand how the tiny quartette were managing their huge burden. The mystery lay beneath, unseen. Underneath was a fifth ant, supporting the weight of the enormous body on its own.

THE WONDERFUL CLIMB OF A COMPANY OF ANTS

Best of all, perhaps, there is Mr William Beebe's picture of a great company of fighting ants struggling out of a five-feet pit which they had cleared of life: beetles, other ants, spiders, grasshoppers, frogs.

Their way up with their burden, he computed, was as if we had set men, each carrying a 200 pound weight, to scale a perpendicular cliff 1200 feet high.

It is a fascinating story, the way they did it, five columns strong, the majority heavily laden but with disciplined contingents thrown out to pick away loose grains of sand in the path that threatened destruction, to grip with feet and jaws and form living anchorages to which the toiling climbers could hold and climb over where places were smooth and treacherous.

But at the top of the ascent, the cliff, absolutely bare and slippery, overhung. Only a solitary ant could get up; the rest stayed, apparently defeated. But were they? No. The one successful ant was met at the top by numbers of other ants of the same tribe. There was a hurried consultation between the newcomer and the rest. Then there followed a rush of ants to the edge of the cliff. They formed themselves into a living mat, holding together one to another, each succeeding line of ants going lower and lower, as bees hang down in a skep hive, when about to form wax for their close-packed cells.

THE LIVING TUNNEL WHICH LED THE ANTS TO SAFETY

The living curtain hung several inches deep, when the lowermost ant with great excitement reached down its tentacles and touched the foremost ant of the column halted below. At once the ascent was resumed, aided by the ants hanging from above. The process was a sheer marvel of skill. The lower ants could come up only over the bodies of those hanging down, and that, seeing how they were burdened, was hazardous. So the hanging ants grouped themselves into a tube. And through the centre of this tube, this tunnel of living ants, the burden-bearers from below, including one which hugged a morsel of frog, climbed up to the tableland above. Such marvellous things these insects do.

There is still much to ponder and perceive in the way of an ant. With its great achievements, its high efficiency; its affection for its own, its love of play, its lordly entertainment of dependents of other genera; with its limitations and native vices, it ranks foremost in its claims on the interest of everyone who has the gift of imagination.

PICTURE-STORY OF A RAILWAY ENGINE

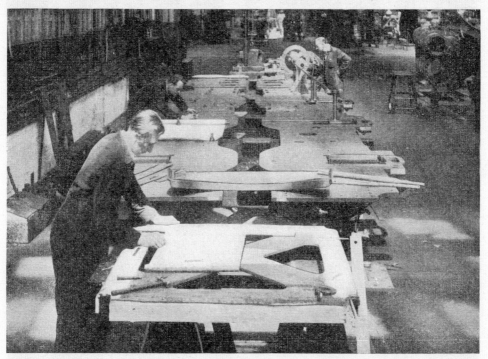

The first stage in the construction of a locomotive is to measure off from the designer's drawings the position of the cylinders, brackets, and so on, on the main frame, and to mark the holes for drilling.

When the main frame has been assembled on its supporting jacks, the two members are riveted together. The man in the foreground is using a riveting hammer operated by compressed air.

MAKING THE BOILER AND FIREBOX

Thick steel plate is first cut to size and shape, then passed through big rollers which bend the plate to the desired shape. The top roller is raised or lowered to suit the amount of curvature required.

The firebox is made of an outer steel casing (shown above) and an inner box of copper. Both boxes are joined together by numerous stays to form a water-jacket around the fire grate.

ELECTRIC & HYDRAULIC TOOLS FOR THE BOILER

The boiler barrel is lifted by an electric crane and connected to the firebox. The barrel will be drilled and the two parts securely riveted together. The rivets where the plates are joined together are clearly shown.

The engine boiler is lifted by a crane and lowered over a hydraulic machine which rivets the joints. While suspended in this way the boiler can be easily turned round and raised or lowered at the convenience of the riveter.

The boiler tubes are fitted into the end plate and made steamtight by expanding the tube ends by means of a tapering shaft fitted with rollers. This is placed in the ends of the tubes and rotated by an electric motor.

PREPARING THE ENGINE WHEELS

When the cast steel wheels and the steel axle have been machined, they are pushed onto the axles by means of a powerful hydraulic press. The press shown here can exert a pressure up to 120 tons.

The wheel tyres are turned to shape and size in powerful wheel lathes such as the one shown here. These great lathes are driven by 100-horse-power electric motors.

MACHINING THE ENGINE PARTS

This picture shows an engine cylinder casting being bored to size. The smaller hole is for the piston-type valve which controls the flow of steam into the cylinder.

Coupling and connecting rods are forged in the smiths' shop and then machined all over. Some rods are grooved or fluted and this is performed on a milling machine with rotating cutters, as seen here.

PUTTING THE BOILER ON THE WHEELS

The engine frame is lifted by an overhead crane and the wheels run into position on the rails underneath. The frame is then lowered onto the wheels until it rests upon the axleboxes.

The boiler is raised by the crane, and the ashpan, seen in the foreground, is fitted to the underside of the boiler firebox; the boiler is then lowered into the engine frame.

THE ENGINE IS READY FOR ITS TRIALS

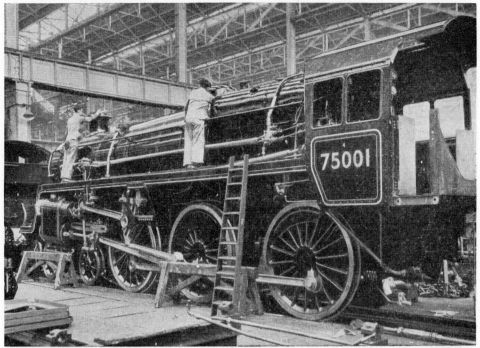

The engine is now nearing completion. The cab has been fixed and buffers, handrails, and other fittings have been added. It now receives its final paint and polish before its trial run.

Some engines are given a trial run on the rail track ; others are given a special test on the Test Plant as shown here. There the wheels can run on rollers at full speed while the engine remains stationary. Instruments are used to measure power, fuel consumption, and so on.

The pictures in these pages are by courtesy of British Railways

HOW A PETROL PUMP WORKS

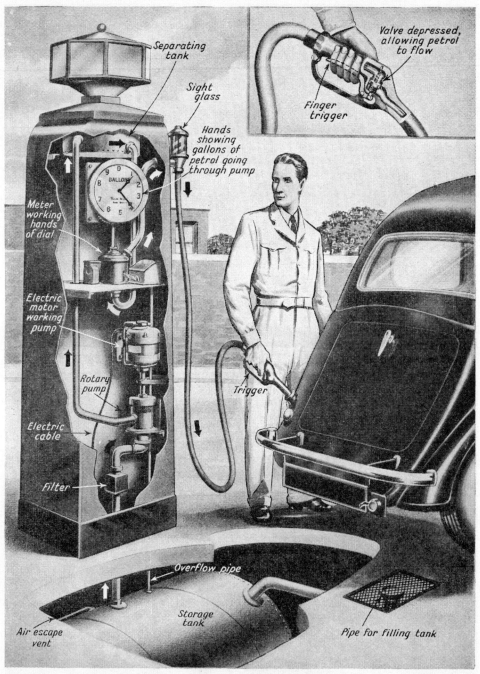

This sectional view of a petrol pump shows how the fuel is delivered to the tank of a car. First, the operator turns a knob which sets both hands of the dial to zero, or "twelve o'clock." He then switches on the electric motor which operates a rotary pump and draws the petrol from the main storage tank below ground. The petrol comes up through a filter and is passed up to a separating tank in which air and gases are eliminated. It next flows through a meter where pistons and valves measure the amount and actuate the hands of the dial. As the petrol leaves the pump and passes into the hosepipe it rotates a cylinder in a sight glass. The long hand of the dial makes one revolution for each gallon delivered, and the short hand registers each gallon. The inset diagram shows how the operator, by gripping a trigger on the handle of the nozzle, can control the flow of petrol into the tank in the car

Plain Answers to the Questions of the Children of the World

An artist's impression of London in Roman Days

HOW DID LONDON BEGIN ?

THE full story of the making of London can never be told. Its beginnings lie deeper than the fabric of the city. The London of today stands fully fifteen feet higher than the London Caesar knew. Waste and decay throw down matter, but do not destroy it. Rubbish collects and mounts, and buries a city beneath a city. Many successive Londons lie beneath the tide of modern traffic.

The makers of a city's unwritten history die, and with their voices records perish. As the old Londoners did not write, their narratives vanished with them; yet from the stuff of ruin we win here and there a little guide to strike light out of chaos. River mud and buried fragments yield from time to time a gleaming fragment into which modern learning is able to fit a tongue which sounds like a trumpet-call, a thrilling message from the dead past.

There was a London long before the Romans, and her sons were artists of high attainment. Two centuries before Caesar crossed our narrow sea there were men here working in metals with a skill and genius never excelled on the Continent of Europe. England had her copper coinage a century before Christianity dawned, and from the Thames has been rescued a shield from the Bronze Age as chastely wrought as anything produced by these wonderful craftsmen of olden times before the dawn of learning in Europe.

Relics of those early days show us that London and the surrounding counties stood high in the cultivation of beauty before the Roman invasion of Britain. They show, also, that our beauty-loving Britons were in regular communication with southern Europe before Rome was a great Power.

Here, then, is proof that the Britons of old London were travellers, men whose lives were sufficiently safe, peaceful, and leisured to allow of journeys, of indulgence in fine art, and of that luxurious labour in which the artistic soul finds its delight. An age which produced intrepid travellers, fearless warriors, and highly-skilled craftsmen, must have furnished more than wattle huts and rude stockades for so great a city as the London which received the Roman legions. Yet we know practically nothing of it at all. The name itself is Celtic, like the wonderfully worked metal the city entombs; and the name tells us that the site was fortified. We know that London was a rich city with a large population when Boadicea sacked and burned it about nineteen centuries ago. We know that the first Roman wall built to defend the city enclosed 380 acres, and that under the Romans London became the most important trading and financial centre of Britain.

FIRE · WIND · WATER · LIFE · MIND · SLEEP · HOW · WHY · WHERE

If we credit the old Celtic Britons with ability to raise a London of some dignity, what must have been the nobility and splendour of London as the capital of Roman Britain during the four centuries of wonderful Latin rule here? Even of that stately period we have no record.

The Romans returned to Rome—probably in the year 418—to prop a falling Empire, and London was submerged by waves of barbarism. The great city disappears for two centuries, like a sun eclipsed. From time to time it appears like island peaks above a flooded country, from out the waste of savagery, but not until the time of Alfred does the historian set his feet on sure continuous ground. Then London rises from the thirty years of ashes to which the Vikings had reduced it, and from that time to our own it has never lain at the feet of a Conqueror—for William the Conqueror did not take London; London took him. He was accepted by a vote of the citizens, on his promising to observe conditions which they laid down; and those conditions have never been modified in any reign.

We have peopled America and Australia on the terms that London demanded from the Conqueror. When Americans or Australians build a new city today, they know that every man in it will have the rights of a freeman, that every man will have the right to inherit his father's estate, and that the State will suffer no class to do them wrong. Those are the main clauses they unconsciously inherit as part of their birthright, because old London got them into the charter it demanded from Norman William nine centuries ago. No other nation has enjoyed such a schedule of foundation liberties as these which London taught all free men to demand.

Are There Flowers in the Antarctic?

While the Antarctic does not possess the abounding plant life of the Arctic, where at least four hundred species of flowering plants flourish, in addition to hundreds of lower forms, there are in the Antarctic many lowly mosses and seaweeds, and also two flowering plants. One of these flowers is related to our British wild campion and the other is a grass which was first discovered in the South Shetlands over a century ago, and has been found on the west of Graham Land, which faces Tierra del Fuego, and on one or two nearby islands. The campion-like plant has been found growing with the grass.

Owing to the extremely short Antarctic summer, and the low temperatures there, these plants are unable to mature their fruits, and so they do not reproduce their kind by seeds, but by vegetative processes, that is, by the development of cells which are actually a part of the general plant. In the Antarctic there are only four or five weeks in which plants can get the benefit of sunlight, and the ground is practically always frozen, so that there is not time for a flowering plant to complete its full cycle of life. Yet there are in the Antarctic fifty kinds of mosses, and over a hundred lichens. These, like the two flowering plants, mostly reproduce by vegetative processes. There are also about half a dozen liverworts, and about seventy species of seaweed. We know altogether about two hundred plants that contrive to live in Antarctica.

What is the Difference Between a Fruit and a Vegetable?

In ordinary talk we usually make a distinction between fruit and vegetables, but most people could scarcely say what the difference is. Everyone should know that all fruits are vegetable, even if we do not call them vegetables. All living creatures are divided into two classes, animal and vegetable, and every kind of fruit therefore belongs to the class of vegetables.

Still, though an apple or a strawberry is as much a vegetable as a cabbage or a potato, we can find a distinction between them. Many kinds of plants do not produce a fruit at all, but all the higher plants do, even the greatest trees. The fruit of a plant is that part of it which contains the seed. The fruit and the plant exist to produce the seed ; when we study the history of the fruit we find that it always comes from the flower. The purpose of the flower is to form the seed, and to allow it to be prepared for its future purpose ; and then the flower disappears and we have, instead, the fruit, holding the seed for its destiny—which is to be sown in the ground and produce a new plant.

Therefore, some of the things we call vegetables, such as tomatoes and cucumbers, are fruits in the proper sense of the word, because they bear the seed.

Why Cannot We Fly in the Air as We Swim in the Water?

The problems of swimming and flying are exactly the same in principle. In both cases the body is heavier than the thing around it, and the problem is, somehow or other, to prevent it from sinking. But in the water the thing around the body is much nearer the heaviness of the body itself than in the air, and so the task is much less difficult. It is still less difficult in sea-water than in fresh, because sea-water is heavier. It is possible, however, for a bat to fly, and the bat is an animal built on much the same principles as ourselves. Every airman knows what the bat appears to know—that if we want to fly we must expose a large surface to the air, so as to get all we can out of the supporting power of the air. So the bat, which has fingers of the same pattern as our own, has made them enormously long, and has stretched a web between them; and it can fly. We really see the same thing, as regards swimming, in the case of many web-footed birds, web-footed frogs and newts, and other similar creatures.

What Does the Barber's Pole Mean?

The barber's pole, which seems a comic thing to us today, is a memory of a very grim thing of olden days. Barbers used to act as surgeons in the days when bleeding was a common remedy. The pole represents the splint to which the patient's arm was bound, and formerly a basin was suspended from it. The red and white stripes round the pole represent the bandages employed.

How Many Words Are There in the Bible?

The Bible contains 66 books, of which 39 are in the Old Testament and 27 in the New. The Old Testament has 929 chapters, 23,214 verses, 592,439 words, and 2,728,100 letters. The New Testament has 260 chapters, 7959 verses, 181,253 words, and 838,380 letters. For the whole Bible the total is 1189 chapters, 31,173 verses, 773,692 words, and 3,566,480 letters. The Apocrypha contains 14 books, 183 chapters, 6081 verses, 152,185 words, and 1,063,876 letters.

The middle chapter of the Bible is Psalm 117, and the middle verse is verse 8 of Psalm 118. In the Old Testament the middle book is Proverbs, and the middle chapter is Job 29; but there is no middle verse as the number of verses is even; the middle comes between verses 17 and 18 of II Chronicles 20. In the New Testament the middle book is II Thessalonians and the middle verse is Acts 17, 17; but there is no middle chapter, owing to the even number. The middle comes between Romans 13 and 14.

How Many Words Has the English Language?

A dozen scholars might give as many answers to this question. One of them gave the number as 38,000, but a still greater scholar, Professor Max Müller, who was, perhaps, the greatest authority of his time on words, put the number of words in English at 100,000. He compared the growth and development of our language with the putting of grain in a sieve. Most of the chaff has been winnowed off, and with it have gone many good grains. Good old English words, which we now consider only dialect words or Americanisms, have gone out of the language. If we include all the words which have fixed places in the dialects of the country, and many which we know were spoken in earlier times, we shall have to put the total at over 500,000.

The number is constantly growing. Words have to be invented for new industries. When a new dictionary was made some years ago it was found that the new words made necessary by electricity numbered over 4000. A similar increase had taken place with regard to other arts and sciences. Most of them are purely technical words, but they become common words; and so the language grows.

In ordinary reading and writing, of course, we do not use a tenth of the words in the dictionary. The average educated man uses from three to five thousand words, but vast numbers of people manage with only a few hundred. Even some famous authors use a comparatively small number of words. Milton used only about seven thousand words for Paradise Lost, but Shakespeare used about 21,000.

What is a Baker's Dozen?

A baker's dozen means thirteen. Bakers used to be heavily fined for giving short weight, and so, to be quite sure that they were on the safe side, they gave an extra loaf to every dozen.

Why is there a Hollow in the Face of a Brick?

If we watch a bricklayer at work we shall notice that he places a lump of mortar on the last brick he has laid, smoothes it, and then places the next brick on the mortar, hollow downwards, so that it readily sinks into position. When it has dried, the mortar in the hollow becomes practically part of the brick, while it also helps to cement the brick more firmly to the whole, so that the completed wall is much stronger and more compact.

Why Does a Tooth Ache?

Headache and earache and toothache are caused by a great number of different things, most of which act on some special nerves, or on some part of the brain, causing a change in these structures which gives rise to a feeling of more or less intense pain. Sometimes the nerve swells up, and if it is in a tight place, the pain is very severe.

Why Does Bark Grow on a Tree?

If the bark did not grow on the tree, the tree would not grow. In the first place, the bark does one or two things which are useful but not very important. The outside of it is usually pretty tough, and has become more or less dead (like the outside of our skin), so that things do not hurt it, and it protects the living part of the tree inside. The inside of the bark is the most living part of the tree, we may say; it actually makes the tree. All the growth of the tree in thickness is due to the making of the wood, and it is the soft living part of the inside of the bark that has made all the hardest wood of the biggest and hardest tree-trunk. Also, there are channels in the bark through which the sap of the tree runs, in much the same way as the blood runs in our own blood-vessels.

Is it True that Nightingales Flourish Where there are Cowslips?

There is no direct connection between the cowslip and the nightingale, as this bird feeds on insects. The popular fallacy implied in the question probably arose because neither the nightingale nor the cowslip is to be found in Devon or Cornwall.

The nightingale comes to England across the narrowest part of the Channel and takes up its summer quarters in the counties on its direct route.

Why has a Tailor's Thimble no Top?

The reason why thimbles usually have tops is because in ordinary sewing the tip of the finger is used to push the needle through the material. But tailors sew through such thick material that they have to use the side of the thimble to drive the needle; so their thimbles need no tops.

What are the Little White Cups on the Telegraph Poles?

These little cups are made of earthenware, and known as insulators, and their object is to prevent the electric current escaping down the poles into the earth. Metal is a good conductor of electricity; wood is not, but when wet will conduct sufficiently to cause trouble, perhaps allowing current to escape through the poles into the ground. But certain materials, such as earthenware, are bad conductors of electricity, and are therefore used extensively as insulators.

What Were the Minute Men of America?

At the beginning of the American War of Independence the United States had no regular army, but many of the colonists belonged to the militia. When war broke out with England, most of these militia-men remained on their farms, but they pledged themselves to take the field when called upon at a moment's notice, thus earning the name of Minute Men. There is a monument to them at Concord, in Massachusetts, of which a photograph appears on page 3689.

What Makes the Fields White with Mist at Night in the Hot Weather?

The mist is water. It is exactly the same as a cloud, and if we pass through a cloud it looks like this mist. The hotter the air is, the more water-vapour it can hold. If the air is made very hot by the sun in the daytime, and if there is much water near, with little wind, then the air, as the day goes on, comes to hold a large quantity of water-vapour. This is a transparent gas, mixed with the other transparent gases that make the air, and so, of course, we cannot see it. But, as the sun sets, the air quickly gets cooler. Then it cannot hold as much water-vapour as it did before, and so a good deal of the water turns into liquid drops and makes a mist.

Is it Harmful to Smoke Tobacco ?

There has been a great deal of controversy on this subject in recent years. The tobacco plant contains nicotine (from the name of the Frenchman Nicot who discovered it). Nicotine is a poisonous alkaloid (one drop of pure nicotine will kill a dog) which acts as a drug, so even in its mildest form tobacco-smoking is a form of drug taking. Yet of course tobacco is not a drug in the sense in which that word is commonly used. Medical men seem to be agreed that, as with other things besides smoking, there is a danger in over-indulgence ; otherwise opinion on the subject appears to be about evenly divided.

Against the practice we read how doctors attached to the department of surgery at the Washington University School of Medicine drew up a report which stated that smoking increased the risk of getting lung cancer, and that more people die every year from nicotine poisoning than is generally realised.

On the other hand, physiologists of New York's Columbia University have reported that they can find no evidence that smoking is harmful, while not long ago some British doctors in Africa reported that tobacco-smoking natives had been known to escape malaria and sleeping-sickness in districts where these complaints usually took a heavy toll among non-smokers, which might support the argument sometimes made—that tobacco smoke is in some way a disinfectant.

It can certainly be said that, unlike alcohol, tobacco has not the power to change a man, affect his judgment, or make him foolish or quarrelsome. Thus the smoker cannot be said to be a menace to society, but the drunkard can bring about the ruin of others as well as of himself. This does not mean that there is any virtue in smoking. It may soothe the nerves, but innumerable healthy people whose nerves don't need soothing still enjoy smoking because they have acquired a liking for the smell and taste of tobacco. But if a person has never smoked, his body will never tell him that he *must* smoke in order to be well, in the way that it will tell him, through the feeling of hunger, that its energies need replenishing by food.

There is thus no reason why a person who has never smoked should ever want to do so, except to experience a new sensation, and that is where the danger lies. The new experience may give rise to a liking which may become a craving, resulting in a habit which is often difficult to break, and apart from any other considerations it is wrong and silly for us to become slaves to any habit. The smoking of tobacco, particularly, whether in the form of cigarettes, pipes, or cigars, can be an expensive habit, and you can probably think of lots of other things on which you would prefer to spend your money. Young people who are still growing should definitely not smoke, as it may impair their development, and even when they are fully grown, smoking is something which they should very well be able to do without.

Why Does Coal Burn and Not Stone ?

What really happens when a thing burns is that it combines with the oxygen of the air. When it has taken up all the oxygen it can, and has combined with it, it is completely burned and can burn no more. Now, when silicon is burned in this way, it makes a solid, and most rocks and sand are made of this. An ordinary stone or sand is really silicon which is already burned, and so can be burned no more. But coal is made mainly of carbon which is not yet burned, and so it can be burned.

What is the Use of Our Hair ?

The hair of our heads cannot be said to have a " use," but long ago, before primitive man began to wear any kind of clothing, the hair that grew thickly over most of his body was very useful in protecting him from changes of temperature. As he evolved, man learned to do without this protective overcoat of natural hair, and it may eventually happen that hair will disappear even from our heads. It has not done so already because we have observed, whenever possible, the fashion of keeping it looking nice by taking care of it.

Why Does a Face in a Mirror seem Crooked ?

We think that the two sides of our faces are just like each other, but every clever photographer knows that they are not. Ordinarily we notice nothing, but when we see anyone's face reflected in a mirror, then we see the left side of his face as if it were the right, and the right as if it were the left; and as our eye is accustomed to the other thing, his face looks crooked. If you had never seen the person before, you would notice nothing. You have never seen your own face except in a mirror, and if now it were possible for you to see your face as everyone else sees it, your face would look as crooked to you as the faces of your friends look when they are seen in a mirror. Of course, if the two sides of the face were exactly alike, the face would look just the same, whether seen in a mirror or directly.

What is Meant by a Blue Stocking?

Blue stocking is used to mean a learned and very studious woman. There were societies of clever women in Paris and Venice whose members used to wear blue stockings, hence the name.

What is the Freedom of a City?

We sometimes read that a town has granted its Freedom to a distinguished native or benefactor. It is usually an honorary freedom, which is a compliment and does not include any constitutional privileges.

Before the Corporations Act of 1835, in which local government was reformed, the freeman of a city did have certain valuable privileges. He could vote for the town's representative in Parliament and he did not have to pay local tolls and dues.

London is the only town in England which was exempt from the provisions of the Corporations Act. A man becomes a Freeman of London by becoming a member of a City Company of which his father was a member or by being bound as an apprentice to a member of a City Company. Only the freemen can nominate aldermen for the Court which elects the Lord Mayor.

What are the Low Countries?

The name Low Countries was formerly applied to the Netherlands or Holland (Hollow Land), of which Belgium once formed a part. It indicates the low-lying nature of the land, which is chiefly a delta formed by the Rhine, Meuse, Waal, and Schelde, which flows through it into the North Sea. Before England was separated from the Continent nearly all Holland and part of the east of England were under water, making a great bay of the North Sea. As the sea gradually retreated northward the Rhine flowed as far as Cromer to meet it. The hand of man has pushed the sea yet farther north, till now a quarter of the whole of Holland is below what was high-tide level at Amsterdam before the sea was banked up; and another eighth is less than 40 inches higher. The sea has been pushed back by the building of dykes. Dykes, too, enclose the rivers and lakes, and marshy lands are gradually being reclaimed by their use and turned into fertile fields. The same sort of thing on a much smaller scale has been done at the other end of the old " bay " in Lincolnshire, part of which is still called Holland.

What is the Nobel Prize?

Five prizes, worth thousands of pounds each, are awarded, annually as a rule, under the will of Alfred Nobel, a Swedish chemist, inventor of dynamite and other high explosives. He made a fortune from the manufacture of these and, with his brothers, out of the Baku oilfields. Yet he was a lover of peace, and the most celebrated of the five prizes, the one people are chiefly thinking of when they speak of the Nobel Prize, is given to the person or society which in any year does the greatest service in the cause of international brotherhood, in reducing or ending standing armies, or in promoting peace. He died in 1896. Of the remaining prizes, one is for the most remarkable piece of idealist writing, and the other three are for eminence in physical, chemical, and medical science respectively.

Why have the People of Washington no Vote?

The people who live in the national capital of America have no franchise from their residence there, though, of course, they may vote in other States if they have a legal residence in them.

The reason for this is that Washington stands on an area which is known as the District of Columbia, and the Constitution safeguarded the Federal Government by laying it down that the Federal capital should form part and parcel of no State. The idea was that the Federal capital should know no local politics lest the local authorities should influence the Federal authorities. Washington, in fact, belongs to all America and not merely to those who happen to reside in it.

Now the privilege of voting is given to its citizens by the States in which they live, so that those who live in Washington belong to no State and have no vote.

Who were Castor and Pollux ?

In Greek mythology Castor was famed as a tamer of horses and Pollux as a great boxer. They reigned as joint kings in Sparta and had many heroic adventures. One legend makes Castor mortal and Pollux immortal, so that when Castor was killed and went to Hades and Pollux wanted to join him there, Zeus permitted him to spend alternate days in Olympus and in Hades. Their brotherly love was rewarded by their being made stars, and they figure still as the Heavenly Twins in the constellation of Gemini.

What is Physiotherapy ?

Physiotherapy is the treatment of disease or infirmities by physical means and not by medicines. Such means include the use of heat-lamps (infra-red rays) ; light-lamps (ultra-violet rays) ; short-waves (radio-waves) ; X-rays and atomic radiations ; shock-treatment (passing electric currents through the brain) ; massage ; baths, including swimming (to help cripples to regain the use of muscles) ; and exercises.

One important branch is occupational therapy, which means giving patients work to do to restore movements or to distract their minds from their illness.

How Does a Ship's Stabiliser Work ?

Spinning very fast, a top will remain upright on its axis and will resist any pressure which tries to tip it. If you push it sideways it will bob up again despite the force of gravity. That is the principle of the gyroscope—a fast-spinning wheel which will maintain its direction against forces which try to upset its balance.

Taking advantage of this counter-resistance of the gyroscope, engineers can use it to control movements of mechanical parts, like the rudders and ailerons of aircraft. Thus the gyroscope is used as an automatic pilot.

Installed in the bottom of a ship, a huge gyroscope can stop the rolling of the vessel, that rolling which can so easily cause sea-sickness. When the waves tip the ship in one direction, the gyroscope "leans" against the movement. Thus the two movements counteract each other and the ship remains on even keel.

For a big ship the spinning wheel of the gyroscope has to be very big and heavy, thus taking up a lot of space. This difficulty has been overcome on some ships by using smaller gyroscopes and making them control motors which operate stabiliser fins on the outside of the hull—as the aircraft gyroscope operates the ailerons.

Who Started Sunday Schools ?

Though there were schools for boys and girls in monastic buildings, the first Sunday School on modern lines was born when Hannah Ball taught a little group of children at High Wycombe in the year 1769. Hannah was an enthusiastic disciple and friend of John Wesley, who encouraged her in her task.

An even more famous name is that of Robert Raikes, who was a printer at Gloucester. He came under the influence of Thomas Stock, Rector of St. John's in that city, and with his co-operation founded four Sunday Schools within the years 1780 and 1781.

Who Was Brahma ?

Brahma, in Sanskrit, means the longing of the soul to rise to God through prayer. In a broader sense it is applied to perfection itself—or God. Brahminism is not a fixed creed born at a certain time; it is the slow evolution of the several beliefs of India towards a certain religious and social organisation.

Like all primitive peoples, the natives of India first worshipped Nature, and especially light, which they called Indra. Later they came to the conclusion that there must be a creative power, and they called it Brahma. This notable advance took place about 1000 B.C. Then, after the belief in Brahma, the creator, came the belief in Vishnu, the preserver of the world, and in Siva, the destroyer. This triple god forms the Indian Trinity. That is why we never see Brahma, Vishnu, Siva, represented as three separate persons on statues and pictures, but in one body with three heads.

Brahma had four sons, who were regarded as the fathers of the four hereditary castes of India. Outside those social divisions there are but the impure and the worthless. During the first centuries of our Christian era Buddhism, born about 500 B.C., triumphed over Brahminism in a great part of India. The worship of the god Brahma is not widespread, but Brahma as the one reality is a power in the religious life of the country.

What is the Boat Race ?

This is the name given to the annual challenge race on the River Thames between two crews representing the universities of Oxford and Cambridge. It is normally held at the end of March or the beginning of April.

The first boat race was rowed in 1829 at Henley, but in 1845 the stretch of water between Putney and Mortlake was chosen for the race and it has been held there ever since, although not until 1856 did it become an annual event. (The 1855 race could not take place as the River Thames was frozen over.)

Just under 4¼ miles long, the course has several bends, and the two crews take these bends into consideration, as well as wind direction, when deciding which station to choose in the event of winning the toss.

Of the 100 races up to 1954 Cambridge had won 54 times and Oxford 45, and there had been one dead heat—in 1877—when one of the Oxford crew broke his oar and became a " passenger." The record for the course is 17 minutes 50 seconds, set up by Cambridge in 1948.

What Happens When our Foot Goes to Sleep ?

This question concerns one of the most mysterious and most wonderful things in the human body—the nervous system.

Our muscles, as we call the bands of flesh which move the different parts of our bodies, can only move when directed to do so by our motor nerves, which may be roughly described as telegraph wires between our nerve centres and our muscles. But before the mysterious order is sent from the nerve-centre along the motor nerve to the muscle, directing it to move, the nerve centre has to receive a message from another and quite different nerve called the Sensory Nerve. Scientific men call this *reflex action*.

From the brain, or from the spinal cord (the big nerve which runs up the backbone), motor and sensory nerves are connected to every part of the body. If a motor nerve is cut we lose all control of the part of the body it serves, but sensation remains. If a sensory nerve is cut we lose sensation in the part which it serves, but retain the power of movement. If both are cut we lose both sensation and the power to move.

Fortunately for us, serious damage to a nerve does not often occur, but not infrequently we experience what undue pressure on a nerve can do. If we sit on a chair so that a sharp edge presses the nerves of our leg we may easily find that our foot goes to sleep, as we say. What has happened is that pressure has affected the nerves serving the foot and, by compressing their fibres, has made them incapable of transmitting impulses. On attempting to rise we cannot feel our foot because the sensory nerve has been pressed, and we cannot direct the foot to act because the motor nerve has been pressed. The foot is numb. Gradually the nerves recover as the pressure is removed, and we get the tingling we call " pins and needles " as the power returns.

What is Daylight Saving ?

In all civilised countries for years past people have been gradually keeping later and later hours, with the result that for half the year at least they have missed much of the daylight. In the bright hours of the morning they have been in bed asleep, and for hours after darkness has fallen in the evening they have been going about their business or pleasure in artificial light.

It was impossible to get the nations to change their social habits and rise and go to bed earlier; but an Englishman, William Willett, thought of the brilliant idea of changing the clocks during the summer months, and making us all get up an hour earlier, so as to seize another hour of daylight, while we imagined we were rising at our usual time.

The question was much discussed in Parliament, but it is doubtful if the plan would have been adopted had not a war made it imperative to economise in artificial light. In the spring of 1916, the British Parliament adopted the scheme, and it has been repeated each year since. On a certain day, by Act of Parliament, all the clocks are overnight put forward one hour, so that people get up the next morning at what appears to be the same time, but is really an hour earlier. This artificial time, which gives an extra hour of daylight during the waking hours at the end of the day, remains in force about six months, and then, on a given night, all the clocks are restored to Greenwich time by having their hands put back one hour.

The Story of the Beautiful Things in the Treasure-House of the World

Antwerp Cathedral

THE GOLDEN YEARS IN EUROPE

THE growth of northern Europe during the Gothic centuries—the twelfth to the fifteenth—makes a most interesting story. But if we think we could say, after a summary of the ringing years wherein whole kingdoms changed hands, and new ideas rose in men's minds, that " a number of cathedrals were also set up," we should be putting the case wrongly.

France grew up round the feet of her cathedrals like a family about its nurse's knees. Up to the very doorways welled the life of the little townships—tiny houses huddled together in the shadow of the high-flung roofs.

The first group of these great buildings was due to an extraordinary wave of creative energy and zeal that overran northern France in the twelfth and early part of the thirteenth centuries. It lasted for about two generations, and was something like a religious revival whose expression was rather in setting up houses of God than in saving souls. It is difficult for us, a fully developed nation, with our growing years long forgotten, and, moreover—regretfully we must say it—living in an age when relatively few people practise the Fine Arts, to understand that fine flowering of the youth of the French nation.

The grand old abbey churches of Romanesque times had been built by monks and belonged to the monasteries. As the various States of France were being drawn into one kingdom, with Paris more and more the centre of government, a new spirit arose and a new power, the power and the spirit of people united by the interests of their own towns.

Each town, it seemed, cried out for a cathedral. Some of the northern architects —no one will ever know at what minute in time's history or in what place in France the door opened on Gothic architecture— someone had somewhere found that the pointed arch could be flung up to any height, and that roofs set on intersecting pointed arches or vaults could soar like clouds above the plain.

This new kind of architecture exactly suited the ardent, adventurous people of young France. The men of a town said : " We must have a cathedral. And we do not mind if people say that buildings of the new kind will totter and fall. We will take the risk. And our cathedral shall be the loveliest in France."

An architect was summoned, and all he had to do was to build, and to master constructive problems. There was none

PICTURES · STATUES · CARVINGS · BUILDINGS · IVORIES · CRAFTS

of that tiresome estimating of costs to be thought of; the people saw to that. Stone in plenty, of a fine quality, was there to be quarried. Those who could not give money gave labour. " Whenever the great blocks of stone were hauled up by cables from the quarry, the people of the district, and even those of the neighbouring regions, nobles and commons alike, harnessed themselves to the ropes by arms, breasts, and shoulders, and drew the load like beasts of burden."

THE SPIRIT OF THE OLD CATHEDRAL BUILDERS

We are reminded here of a Bible story. Helpers came and encamped there, by the rising cathedral walls, and every now and again the masons laid down their tools, and a great company joined in prayer that this cathedral which they were raising to the honour and glory of God should be worthy of its purpose. They worked in season and out, giving service that was like good measure, pressed down and running over.

In such a spirit did these first Gothic cathedrals rise on the barren shore of French towns. A flame of ardour so generous must needs burn itself out. A century after these people prayed among their stones, cathedrals were being set up by men who were summoned to work; some of them were built by forced labour.

But in the meantime, while their first cathedrals were building, the townsfolk watched eagerly for such part as might be finished in their lifetime. Additions were made later, an extended choir here, a chapel, a transept, there. The decorating with sculpture kept hundreds of people eager and happy. But as soon as the bones of the cathedral were put together, so to speak, as soon as the house of God had roof and walls, doors, and an altar, it was opened with joy unspeakable. The townsfolk remembered to their dying day the first time praises were sung under those great echoing arches, which seemed themselves to hold up their pointed hands to pray, to catch the benediction.

THE STORY OF THE BIBLE IN THE WINDOWS OF OUR CATHEDRALS

To the people, unlettered, superstitious, their cathedrals were more than the centre of town life, their pride and joy, the thing that they had made. They were like huge religious story books which the most ignorant could read. On the outside of the fabric they could see numberless figures of saints and holy persons, and learn from their attitudes and their emblems something of the reward of goodness. There were also figures of less happy individuals to whom a just punishment had been meted out.

Inside the buildings the lovely golden light of stained glass drew their eyes; and there, rank upon rank, was painted the heavenly company. The whole story of the Bible peeped out as men passed from window to window.

No peasant ever forgot the Old Testament tales and the Gospel lore learned from the cathedral pictures, and we may be sure that boys and girls growing up in those days, with no ideas in their minds got from books, were quite clear about the doom that lay in wait for the wicked, and the reward of piety. They were as sure on that point as on the number of pinnacles and decorations added to the cathedral since they themselves were three or four. They listened, grouped round the skirts of their elders in the Place, or Cathedral Square, to rare travellers who had come in from one of the highways of Europe and had met with many adventures and had seen great abbeys and churches. The little ones stared up at their own buildings and knew no other could be so fine.

THE CHANGE WHICH CAME OVER THE OLD CHURCH OF ST. DENIS

While in various places in northern France these monuments of the new art were rising, some very memorable work was being done in Paris, both in the precincts of the old Romanesque abbey of St. Denis, and in the cathedral of Paris, known all over the world as Notre Dame. In the hands of the builders, St. Denis slowly changed from Romanesque to Gothic form. Its Gothic was very simple, as nearly akin to Romanesque as two different styles could be. We are very thankful that the lovely old Romanesque crypt was left, with its pure round arches.

One of the grudges we have against Gothic builders was their inability to let well alone. They had wonderful ideals for new buildings; it was a pity they thought that nothing which was not in accord with their new ideals was fit to exist. Therefore they callously pulled down the Romanesque churches, sometimes to use stone for the new buildings, sometimes because they were weak, and

BEAUTIFUL ARCHITECTURE INDOORS AND OUT

THE NAVE AND CHOIR OF
ANTWERP CATHEDRAL

DETAILS OF THE FRONT OF
SIENA CATHEDRAL

THE CHOIR AND ORGAN IN THE
GREAT CHURCH, HAARLEM

THE SOUTH ENTRANCE TO CHARTRES CATHEDRAL

THE GATE OF THE KING
IN SEVILLE CATHEDRAL

THE AMBULATORY IN
CHARTRES CATHEDRAL

THE LOVELY WINDOWS OF
SAINTE-CHAPELLE IN PARIS

needed strengthening, sometimes out of sheer egotism. The result is that only here and there can we see the work of some of the earliest Christian builders of Europe. But this scant reverence for the work of the immediate past is a human trait we are constantly meeting.

THE GREAT PARIS CHURCH WHICH WAS A CENTURY IN BUILDING

In 1163, very soon after the Gothic choir was consecrated in the abbey church of St. Denis, the foundation stones of Notre Dame were laid. The building of this cathedral covered about a hundred years. It shows something of the simplicity of the Gothic work in St. Denis. It is sturdy, like the Romanesque, as if builders had still not forgotten, in spite of themselves, the tenets of their old faith. They were afraid to fling their arches too high. They set them on enormous pillars, carried them up to the blind-story, rested in solid masonry, then threw up more arches, rested again, and finally reached the vault lines.

This early vigour has happily not been lost in succeeding generations, and at the hands of numerous restorers who worked on Notre Dame in the nineteenth century. The foundation of the cathedral strikes into the roots of a very old Europe. It was built on the site of a heathen shrine which in the fourth century became a Christian altar.

The façade, or chief front of Notre Dame, is one of the noblest productions of early Gothic art. It has the same solidity and clearness of arrangement that marks its interior. Romanesque architects, we know, had derived much of their art from classical buildings; these, in turn, had sprung from the Greek architecture, which was so measured and logical that if one only saw the base of a column one would know the proportions of the whole building.

THE SEVERITY AND SIMPLICITY WHICH GIVE CHARM TO NOTRE DAME

From this rock foundation of style, Gothic architecture was destined to take a very wide leap. As we noted in our talk on English Gothic, no two cathedrals are exactly on the same plan or proportion. It happened sometimes that two resembled each other; but, generally speaking, from the end of the first period each Gothic building was a separate adventure.

The façade of Notre Dame is in form nearly a pure letter H. Its severity and simplicity has great charm. We feel very glad that the twin towers which finish off that part of the roof covering the side aisles have never, in the fever of a later period, been decorated or added to. They are just right; the architect who ended the towers in that uncompromising, horizontal line had a very fine taste. The apse was thrown out, chevet form, a French characteristic we have already noted, with very strong flying buttresses. At a later period the spaces between these buttresses were used for the building of little chapels.

The cathedrals of Lens, Laon, Senlis, Noyon, all begun about the middle of the twelfth century, have something of the simplicity of Notre Dame, Paris. They mark that period of early French Gothic which is generally called Lancet, and ends about the close of the twelfth century. The windows of buildings of this style are simple, with geometric tracery.

The work of the thirteenth century, marked by a development in height and general grandeur, was called Rayonnant. This name was taken from the huge circular windows with wheel-like traceries that marked the cathedrals of the period. In the fourteenth and fifteenth centuries Flamboyant Gothic ran its course in France, characterised by the flame-like, wispy traceries of the windows.

THE WONDERFUL CATHEDRAL AT BEAUVAIS WHICH IS STILL UNFINISHED

It seemed that when the early twelfth-century cathedrals were in course of construction, architects began to think how much further they could go on the same lines, developing the Gothic idea. They began to have a yearning for tremendous height in the naves and choirs. In some cases, like that of Beauvais, the builders were too daring; their choir just dropped in. The choir was restored, but the cathedral remains unfinished to this day, is but a glorious fragment consisting of a choir and a transept. It has, nevertheless, a very wonderful south doorway, with a great rose window, and the carven doors are a miracle of beauty.

The maker of the cathedral of Chartres succeeded in setting up a very lofty building on more sturdy lines. The nave is an interesting development from that of Notre Dame, but the outside gives an effect of rather tumultuous strength ; there are too many buttresses.

From the façade of the cathedral we can see at a glance that the building was begun in Romanesque times. Curiously over its round-headed porches is set the wheel window of Rayonnant Gothic. At a later period the Romanesque towers were carried up into Gothic spires. The north and south porches of Chartres are among the finest pieces of Gothic work in France.

WHY GOTHIC IS CALLED A RESTLESS STYLE OF ARCHITECTURE

Bourges Cathedral, remarkable for its heavily sculptured façade, with five doorways flanking each other, is a development of another kind. There are no transepts, and thus the building makes a long, unbroken line. In Le Mans Cathedral the architect seemed to think more of the chancel than the rest of the church. It has double aisles, and from them open out thirteen chapels. So that inside, the eye can find no rest, no final lines, and outside, the body of the church seems dwarfed behind the monstrous flying buttresses and the projecting masses of the chapels.

We need only look at a photograph of the apse of Le Mans Cathedral to see all that Gothic architecture might be, and all that it is not. And we can quite understand why it is called a restless architecture.

In the nave of Amiens Cathedral, which is one of the loveliest in France, the architect succeeded in realising his dream of height. It is a very wonderful feat of constructional skill, with scarcely a line to break the soaring pillars and arches. When we look at it we can understand why at one period the ignorant folk of France, terrified at such audacity in the way of building, made up stories about architects being in league with the evil ones, and having sold their own souls as a price for their cathedrals' amazing height and slenderly balanced interiors.

THE GENIUS OF THE SCULPTOR IN THE FAÇADE OF RHEIMS CATHEDRAL

The cathedral of Notre Dame at Rheims, for so long the coronation church of French kings, is one of the most powerful productions of medieval Europe. It has a huge, broad nave, where immense crowds could gather on great days. It was planned more or less on the lines of Notre Dame, and its façade somewhat resembles the Paris cathedral. But Rheims grew up, so to speak, in the more florid days of French Gothic, and the simple grandeur of its structure is hidden.

Although each cathedral was different from the other, there was a certain unity in the work of the architects of northern France. Some façades are more gorgeous in adornments than others. The front of Rheims is one great glory of the sculptor's genius in those days, and its pillared, bodyless towers and dainty wheel window give an ethereal look to a very powerful structure. In other façades, notably that of Bourges, the sculpture clings round the great doorways, and the upper part is barer. In several cathedrals a curious look is given to the façade by the towers of different periods and varying form and height that adorn the same building. Rouen Cathedral looks as if all its parts do not belong to each other.

As we noted in our study of English Gothic, the French cathedrals were generally carried so high that they could not support the weight of a tower at the crossing of the nave and transepts, as in the case of the British cathedrals. Sometimes they had a short spire—the highest is the slender shaft of Amiens, added in the early sixteenth century. In some of the churches of Normandy, which were nearest akin to the English, there were central towers, like the one in Rouen Cathedral. For the most part French architects concentrated their interest in towers and spires to the chief front of the cathedral.

THE BEAUTIFUL LITTLE CHURCHES IN THE TOWNS OF FRANCE

The Norman buildings strike a severer note than those in the rest of northern France. At Coutances, Bayeaux, Mont St. Michel on the Brittany border, at Quimper, churches and cathedrals are marked by plainer, more soaring lines. Mont St. Michel is especially famous for its magnificent monastery buildings set within its fortress-like walls. In a great many towns of France smaller churches appeared, some of great beauty. The finest of them all is the Sainte Chapelle of St. Louis, in Paris.

In Northern France, the cradle of Gothic architecture, the new art grew and expanded, changed its form, was enriched and made complex as the taste of its builders dictated. It had next to no opposition in the way of established architecture. As we go south we see a curious change. The Loire was the northern boundary of the stronghold of Romanesque art, and here pure Gothic has not complete sway. Indeed, faced by that glory, the abbey church at Cluny, one wonders that the people of southern France tolerated Gothic architecture at all.

The cathedrals and churches that were set up south of the Loire were a compound of Gothic and Romanesque. The most famous are the cathedrals of Albi and Carcassonne. Poitiers Cathedral is an interesting specimen of Gothic-Romanesque; that of Bordeaux shows more Gothic than any other—one of the few cathedrals with flying buttresses in the south of France.

THE UNFINISHED CATHEDRALS WHICH WERE STARTED CENTURIES AGO

Bayonne Cathedral, built in part on the ruins of an earlier erection, and still unfinished, shows some northern Gothic work, and has the remains of a fine thirteenth-century cloister. The cathedral of Toulouse is a strangely hinged-together church, and this also is unfinished, though the nave dates from the same period as the Bayonne cloisters. But, however skilfully finished, it can never have the same merit as St. Sernin's, the Romanesque church in the same historic old town, built and finished and its period rounded up before the Gothic cathedral, St. Stephen's, was thought of. Rodez is another wonderful church of the south, its naked-looking walls making a kind of huge pillar support for the sculptured towers of various periods surmounting it.

The farther south one goes, the plainer, more restful is the architecture. The builders disliked flying buttresses and disliked the idea of the nave being so much higher than the side aisles. They, therefore, carried them up almost the height of the whole building, and broke their walls with long, slender windows. The roofs were almost flat, and generally beautifully finished with parapets and small pinnacles; there was often a simple tower reminding one of the campanile of the earlier century. The result was a mixture of dignity and severity. Albi Cathedral is called a fortress church.

THE SOMETHING HUMAN AND VERY CHILD-LIKE IN FRENCH GENIUS

When the last phase of Gothic architecture appeared, it pleased one of their builders to add to this grand, majestic old church at Albi a most delicate Gothic porch, full of dainty lines and the chasings of the Flamboyant period.

There was always something very human, and a little child-like, in the French Gothic genius. When once its first spiritual ardour was sped, when it no longer flung itself skyward, it wandered about very happily, making beautiful things. And it seemed that no later architect could view the work of an earlier generation without wanting to make his mark on it, too.

By its nature it was an elastic art. There could always be another chapel added to a cathedral, another set of pinnacles, or a doorway, with its scope for limitless sculpturing; or the head of a tower could be taken off and its body carried higher, or another tower added.

Before the fifteenth century expired, architects seemed no longer capable of the long " drive " necessary for setting up a big cathedral or church. They were content to work, in unending elaborations, on a piece of one. They were so engrossed in making a porch or a tower look like lace work that a building as a huge scheme was impossible to them.

THE TREASURE-HOUSES OF THE ART OF THREE RICH CENTURIES

This same decorative rather than constructional skill had always found scope in the interiors. Long books could be written about French cathedrals, without once mentioning structure of walls and roofs, and the problems of architecture. They became treasure-houses of the art of three rich centuries. Their little and big images and statues, their tombs, their rood screens, grilles, and beautiful doors with wrought hinges, their chancel stalls and bishop's thrones, their altars and side altars—on all these a minute and wonderful skill spent itself.

Gothic art ran its course throughout civilised Europe, in Spain, Italy, Germany, the Netherlands, Austria, touched Sweden and Hungary, but nowhere had it such a magnificent field as in France and England.

Strasbourg, one of the finest of the French cathedrals, was built in the second half of the thirteenth century, and added to in later periods. Its erection coincided with the rise of Gothic architecture in Germany. Thus, a hundred very wonderful years had sped after the beginning of Notre Dame, before churches in the new style were set up east of the Rhine. Romanesque architecture had a hold there, and Gothic was not welcomed.

For a long time buildings were a mixture of the two styles. Limburg Cathedral and the Liebfrauenkirche, Treves, are fine specimens of the work that was done in transition from Romanesque to Gothic. The most interesting church of the two styles is St. Gereon, Cologne, which is built on an ancient round tomb-house.

THE STYLE THE GERMAN PEOPLE LIKED IN THEIR CHURCHES

The German people kept their love for the many-apsed churches, and they also, in some cases, adopted the French style of the chevet. Their churches were variously planned, the work of each province differing a little from the next. Like the southern French, they often preferred aisles and nave of the same height, and consequently many of their churches have no clerestory and no blind-story, and are of the type known as the " hall " church.

In northern Germany brick was mainly used, but, in whatever medium, the workmanship was good, in many cases atoning a little for poor design. The grand western façades so usual to French Gothic never became a feature of German cathedrals and churches. Their porches are often set north or south, and are rarely imposing.

St. Elizabeth, Warburg, built in the thirteenth century, is an excellent example of the hall churches with many apses. The Frauenkirche, Nuremberg, built a century later, is a fine old hall church with a quaint two-storied porch, in which is set the famous clock that starts the figures of the seven Electors in movement about the king when the noon hour strikes. Munich Cathedral is also of this hall type, and many churches, like St. Stephen, Vienna, with its fine spire.

THE BEAUTIFUL GERMAN CATHEDRAL BUILT IN THE FRENCH GOTHIC STYLE

The cathedrals of Freiburg, Ratibor, and Ulm were all built in the thirteenth and fourteenth centuries and added to later.

Cologne Cathedral is the finest example of French Gothic in Germany, and it is the largest cathedral in northern Europe. It is imposing, but not great, because its proportions are wrong. The French Gothic builders knew by instinct how wide a church should be in relation to its length, and just how much weight should go into the transepts and aisles. Here the German architects, building in the French style, were at fault.

They made their double side aisles as wide as the nave, so that the cathedral has far too much width to carry for its length. They also made their twin towers too huge and too high, five hundred feet, so that they overbalance the rest of the building. And in the decoration of the towers their artistry was at fault. They lacked the dainty ingeniousness of the French sculptor.

The secret of the failure of Cologne Cathedral, imposing as it may be, is that it was built by a people to whom Gothic architecture did not really appeal. They obeyed its rules, but knew not its spirit. Their art did not express itself in that way. To them Gothic architecture was a music for which they had no ear.

The technique of their workmanship was excellent. As craftsmen they were hard to beat. They must have carved lovingly their woodwork and stonework, so closely imitative of nature's form. But they lacked the free fling of the Frenchman's chisel.

THE GERMAN FEELING EXPRESSED IN THE CHURCHES OF THE LOW COUNTRIES

The feeling for width that marked the German churches, particularly Cologne Cathedral, was shared in the Low Countries. Antwerp Cathedral, the finest church in Belgium, is very wide, with three aisles on each side of the nave, which is carried high and has deep windows in the clerestory. A lofty fifteenth-century tower rises from the west end, and at the crossing of the transepts is a curious little turret, reminding one of Saracenic architecture, set up when Spain was the ruling power in Flanders.

Antwerp Cathedral was built in the Flamboyant period, and is covered with the profuse ornament of the last Gothic style. By accident or most wise design, the second western tower was never carried up more than one storey; otherwise the cathedral, like that of Cologne, would have been sadly dwarfed.

St. Gudule, Brussels, a much earlier church, has good western towers, in excellent proportion. There is very beautiful stained glass in the choir chapels. It is perhaps in Notre-Dame Cathedral at Tournai that one sees most of the passage of the architectural periods in the Low Countries, whose complicated and changing history and internal rivalries crushed out any great creative spirit like that which has made France wonderful for ever. More genius went into the guild halls and town halls than into the sacred buildings of these Flemish cities, whose wealth was a byword in Europe.

THE CHARM OF SPIRES AND BELFRIES IN BELGIAN ARCHITECTURE

There is a distinct charm in Belgian architecture, with its spires, belfries, towers, and ridged gables. Bruges Cathedral rises very finely over the peaceful old town. The churches and cathedrals of Ghent and Dinant fit happily into their place and show the influence of changing periods. The cathedrals of Holland—Utrecht, Haarlem, Dordrecht—are simple, with very bare interiors, but their shapes are made attractive by the level water light flooding the walls and by the immense and tranquil skies of the Dutch landscapes.

In certain parts of Italy pure Gothic architecture never appeared. The Gothic spirit was part of the miracle of the Italian Renaissance, as we remember in our earlier chapters on painting and sculpture, but its expression was altered by existing forms and traditions. Rome, the stronghold of Classic art, closed her doors against this northern invader; there is only one Gothic church, St. Maria sopra Minerva, in the whole great area of the eternal city.

Elsewhere in Italy the resistance of Romanesque and Byzantine traditions was great. The high-flung vaults of northern France were not suffered to rise; there were few flying buttresses and pinnacles, roofs were kept flat, windows small. The main feature of French Gothic had been upward soaring lines; this the Italian architects counteracted by insisting on horizontal courses. The result is a most interesting group of buildings, but they can hardly be called Gothic.

THE SPLENDID MARBLE PILE WITH THE DELICACY OF A PIECE OF LACE

The nearest in spirit to the buildings of the north, and the exception to several of the rules of Italian Gothic, is Milan Cathedral, and it is more German than French in plan. This great marble pile, which took a hundred years to build and absorbed the energies of half a hundred architects, is one of the most wonderful creations of a wonderful period.

It is the second largest cathedral set up in medieval times. But the merit of the building is something not measurable by square feet; nor is it flawless in style and proportion. Its numberless pinnacles and points, surmounted by statues, seem as if they were stalagmites flung upward from a fairy grotto. The long, horizontal lines of the building are only broken by long, narrow windows and unobstrusive buttresses, the whole formation delicately sheathed in a web of vertical strands. Huge as a fortress, it seems delicate as a lace shawl.

Florence Cathedral, also called St. Maria del Fiore, is a building of a very different kind. It was erected in the Gothic period, from about the end of the thirteenth century to the middle of the fifteenth, but in spirit it is Italian Romanesque. It is a remarkable structure, in plan a long cross of an unusual type. The nave leads up to a great domed octagonal space, and from this three apses, each domed, break out, one in the eastern end in the usual way, and twin apses in place of transepts. Five chapels cluster round each apse.

THE FAMOUS ARCHITECTS WHO BUILT THE CATHEDRAL AT FLORENCE

To pass from the nave into this great area of radiating shapes is to receive an unforgettable impression of majesty and dignity. A quaint clerestory of circular lights in set high in the nave walls. The general effect of the exterior, with its coloured marble panels and small windows, is horizontal—long lines following each other round the entire building, and all leading on to receive the weight and insistence of the massive dome. The decorating of the west front was begun in the thirteenth century, and left untouched till late in the nineteenth.

Round this cathedral much ambition and pride and many lives have gathered. We know something of the immense pride of the Florentines in their city and their art from our earlier chapters, and the cathedral, with its campanile and the baptistery standing close by, is the large monument of their heroic spirit. Famous names run in and out of its story. The first architect was Arnolfi di Cambio. Some time after his death Andrea Pisano and Francesco Talenti took up the work. The crowning labour, in more ways than one, was the huge dome set up by Brunelleschi when Renaissance architecture was developing in Italy.

The baptistery is a Romanesque building to which Arnolfi di Cambio made alterations in the late thirteenth century. It is octagonal in shape and faced outwardly with black and white marble. All over the world this building is famous because of its marvellous bronze doors, the work of Ghiberti and Andrea Pisano.

The campanile was designed by Giotto, a truly Italian erection of great beauty. As in the case of most Italian towers, like those at Siena, Mantua, Lucca, and Verona, the contour is unspoiled by

two Dominican monks, and Or San Michele planned by Taddeo Gaddi. Or San Michele possesses some particularly lovely statuary by some of her famous sculptors, like Donatello and Ghiberti.

When we think of Italian churches we think first and foremost of the historic St. Francesco at Assisi, set up in the middle of the thirteenth century. It is built on a hillside in two storeys. The style is simple; there are no aisles, and both the

THE INTERIOR OF THE CHURCH OF SAINT MARIA SOPRA MINERVA IN ROME

buttress projections; the square walls rise cleanly from the ground. Its fine vertical mass is a lovely pattern of coloured marble panels and sculptured reliefs. This tower, contrasting with the horizontal lines of the cathedral, and balancing the heavy mass of the dome, finishes one of the finest groups of medieval architecture in Europe.

In addition to the cathedral, Florence possesses some very fine churches—St. Croce, planned by Arnolfi di Cambio, St. Maria Novella, whose architects were

upper and lower church end in an angular apse. It is not only a most interesting architectural work, but a monument to a man whose story is eternally bound up in the early years of the Italian Renaissance. We know from our chapters on painting of the frescoes that adorn the dim, vaulted interiors of the upper and lower church.

The cathedral at Siena, set up as a kind of stepped platform on the sloping ground, is a fine and imposing building marked, like most of the Italian Gothic cathedrals, with a dome over the wide space at the crossing. All the artists of the town helped to set up and adorn this their chief church, and their pride in it was immense. It was planned on a huge, ambitious scale. The actual building took from 1245 to 1380, but the proposed second nave, a continuation of a transept, has never been finished. On floor and walls, outside and inside, the art of Siena has stamped her cathedral. One of its most renowned features is the pulpit carved by Niccola Pisano.

THE BEAUTY OF THE WORK OF GOTHIC YEARS IN ITALY

In the cathedrals of Orvieto and Palermo, and in churches like St. Antonio, Padua, St. Giovanni and St. Maria Gloriosa, Venice, St. Anastasia, Verona, and St. Petronio, Bologna, the art of Gothic years in Italy produced wonderful and memorable work. The farther south we go the more remote from pure Gothic is the style. Palermo Cathedral is built on the plan of the old basilican churches and reminds us more of Saracenic architecture than Gothic. In almost every Italian church there is sculpture and adornment by great artists. Some were built by monks out of love of God; some by citizens out of pride in their city.

We spoke just now of Milan Cathedral as the second largest in medieval Europe. The first in point of size is the cathedral of Seville, which, except for St. Peter's, Rome, is the largest church in the world; and this brings us into that strange and attractive world of Spanish art where the genius of the so-called Moors had left an ineradicable strain of beauty. Some of the most delightful work of Europe hides in odd corners of Spain; doorways which make one think, curiously, of some haunting song that is native to no one country or period, walls that strike a dreaming silence, as if the world had forgotten to pass that way.

THE INFLUENCE OF THE MOORS IN THE GOTHIC BUILDINGS OF SPAIN

In the north of the peninsula, naturally, in Catalonia, the influence of Gothic was most felt. But pure French Gothic is almost unknown. The architects threw up great vaulted buildings, and nestled little chapels between the buttresses, so that the walls seem flat outside. Horizontal rather than vertical lines mark the structures. Windows are not huge, as in the north of Europe; cloisters of great beauty, as at Barcelona, Segovia, Toledo, and Lerida are ornamented in a style natural to the inheritors of Saracenic art. The style of the horseshoe arch, the endless geometric wall-decoration, and the open stonework of Moorish times passed on through the short Romanesque period—whereof few traces remain—and allied itself naturally with Gothic, making a different architecture from the rest of Europe.

Seville Cathedral was built in the fifteenth and early sixteenth centuries on the site of a Mohammedan mosque. Its great masses are grouped unfamiliarly, but the structure nevertheless achieves a distinction which hugeness alone is incapable of. Its lovely stained glass throws shafts of colour across the great aisles, each as wide as the nave of Westminster Abbey, and makes even richer the rare carvings and ornamentations. In a smaller place the adornments would be too heavy, but the cathedral adjusts its proportions very happily. Were the exterior as graceless as a barn it would still be saved by the Giralda, one of the loveliest towers in the world, of which we have already spoken.

THE VARIETY OF STYLES SEEN IN THE BUILDINGS OF SPAIN

All the medieval cathedrals and churches of Spain are intensely interesting. One feels continually that history no less than the architect has been planning and shaping here. Of no one building could it be said that it is purely such and such a style. The cathedrals of Valencia and Leon, set up in the thirteenth century, remind one suddenly of France; Barcelona is a little Italian in shape. Toledo, Avila, and Gerona are, like the rest, marked by rich interior carvings.

Burgos is perhaps the most romantic and Spanish of all the cathedrals in the peninsula. One of the loveliest doorways in Europe is that of St. Pablo, Valladolid. It might be classed as Gothic, but the long dead Saracens guided the builders' hands.

Spain was too conservative, for all her upheavals, to allow herself the fine, undivided enthusiasm of early France. As we think of her sacred buildings we wish perhaps that she had expressed herself singly and loudly in some one great way. Then when we look at her work again and see here the Saracen, here the Romanesque, here the Gothic, and everywhere the sense of Spanish art, we would not have her story changed.

THE WEST FRONT OF THE BEAUTIFUL CATHEDRAL AT ROUEN

WEST FRONT OF STRASBOURG CATHEDRAL

THE HALLES WITH THE FAMOUS BELFRY AT BRUGES

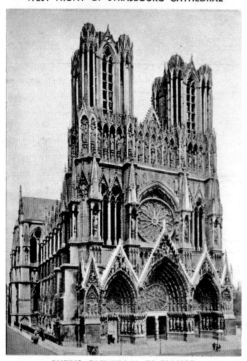

RHEIMS CATHEDRAL IN FRANCE

BURGOS CATHEDRAL IN SPAIN

THE CATHEDRAL OF ANTWERP

ULM CATHEDRAL IN GERMANY

NOTRE DAME AT LAON

AMIENS CATHEDRAL

THE BEAUTIFUL CATHEDRAL OF NOTRE DAME IN PARIS, SHOWING THE APSE

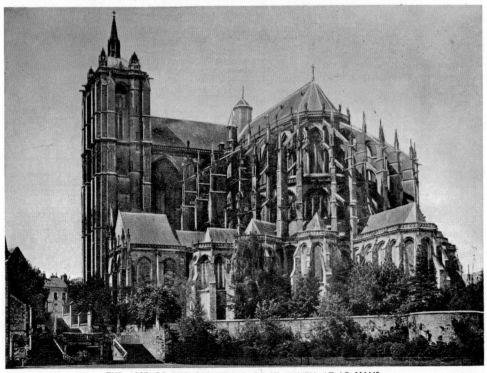

THE APSE OF THE CATHEDRAL OF ST. JULIEN AT LE MANS

THE NORTH SIDE AND WEST FRONT OF CHARTRES CATHEDRAL

THE FRONT OF THE WONDERFUL CATHEDRAL OF MILAN

COLOGNE CATHEDRAL

SIENA CATHEDRAL

THE SAINTE CHAPELLE IN PARIS

RATIBOR CATHEDRAL IN GERMANY

THE CHURCH OF ST. FRANCESCO AT ASSISI

THE CHURCH OF ST. ANTONIO AT PADUA

THE HÔTEL DE VILLE AT COURTRAI

THE OLD CATHEDRAL AT CARCASSONNE

ST. STEPHEN'S CATHEDRAL IN VIENNA

BURGOS CATHEDRAL, SHOWING THE LANTERN

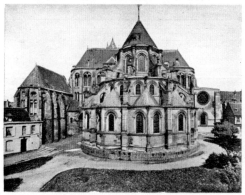

NOYON CATHEDRAL IN FRANCE

SENLIS CATHEDRAL IN FRANCE

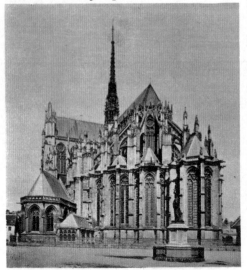

THE APSE OF AMIENS CATHEDRAL

ALBI CATHEDRAL IN FRANCE

THE GREAT CHURCH AT HAARLEM IN HOLLAND

THE CATHEDRAL AT SEVILLE

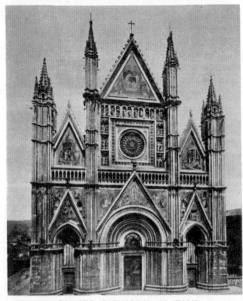

ORVIETO CATHEDRAL IN ITALY

NOYON CATHEDRAL. THE WEST FRONT

The pictures in these pages are reproduced by courtesy of Messrs. Alinari, Anderson. E.N.A., Neurdein, York & Son, and others

The Wonderful House We Live In, and Our Place in the World

The historic British Empire Exhibition at Wembley in 1924 and 1925 — Reproduced from The Times

RESOURCES OF THE COMMONWEALTH

IF we look at a map of the world we see that the greater part of our globe is covered by water. The next thing we notice is that most of the land is in the northern hemisphere. If the countries of the British Commonwealth are coloured red, we see that there is red everywhere— in Europe, in Asia, in Africa, and in America, while the only great pieces of land in the southern seas, Australia and New Zealand, are entirely red.

The British Commonwealth consists of Great Britain and a group of other countries. Some of these are colonies under British rule. Others were once colonies, but are now Dominions, which means that they are completely independent and self-governing, but still have especially close relationships with Great Britain and with each other. The Dominions are free to leave the Commonwealth at any time, but they do not want to. The Commonwealth is united, not by force, but by the common interests of its members.

The older Dominions of Canada, Australia, South Africa, and New Zealand have been joined since the Second World War by India, Pakistan, Ceylon, Ghana (formerly the Gold Coast), and the Federation of Malaya. The colonies are advancing steadily towards becoming Dominions, and the future of the British Commonwealth is clearly that of a group of independent nations, linked by mutual interests.

What a contrast there is between the area of the United Kingdom and that of the widespread Dominions overseas ! In the home country, about 50 million people live on an area of only 94,000 square miles, so there are roughly 530 persons to each square mile. Except for a few mountains, moors, woodlands, and heaths, every square yard has been worked over, cultivated, mined, or built on.

The Commonwealth covers a quarter of the land surface of the entire world, and is peopled by about a quarter of the world's inhabitants. The total population of the world is not accurately known, but it is estimated at 2500 million people. Of these, over 600 million inhabit the British Commonwealth. In the self-governing Dominions there are about 500 million people, 50 million live in Great Britain, and the rest live in Colonies or Dependencies.

The Republics of India and Pakistan have the biggest populations, with about 450 million inhabitants between them according to a recent estimate. Most of their people are very poor, but their terri-

BODY, MIND, AND SOUL · CITIZENSHIP · ECONOMICS · GOVERNMENT

tories possess opportunities for industrial development, which has already begun on a large scale. Great plans are also being made for improving their agriculture, on which most of their people depend for a living. These newly independent countries have a great future once they have overcome their initial difficulties.

WHITES FORM LESS THAN ONE-EIGHTH OF COMMONWEALTH PEOPLE

The British Commonwealth includes men of every colour, and of many different races. They speak hundreds of different languages, and belong to many religions.

The white people in the Commonwealth form a small proportion of the whole. There are over 16 million people in Canada, nine million in Australia, and more than two million in New Zealand. Some three million out of practically 14 million people in the great Union of South Africa are white. When these and the white men from other British countries are added to those in the Homeland, we find that there are about 80 million white people in the Commonwealth, or less than one in eight of its total inhabitants.

Two-thirds of British white people are at home in the British Isles, but the greater proportion of the Commonwealth's resources are over the seas. The British Isles are rich in coal and iron, but poor in all other raw materials of industry.

We produce copper, zinc, lead, tin, gold, and silver in small and negligible quantities. Copper and zinc are among the most valuable of the metals, and together they make that splendid alloy, brass, which is used for so many different purposes. Of these ores the British Isles have a very small production.

THE COLOSSAL POWER OF THE RIVERS NOW WAITING TO BE DEVELOPED

The countries in the British Commonwealth of Nations produce very large quantities of these metals, and they are also rich in lead, tin, and aluminium. They also produce something like one-half of the world's gold and about one-fifth of the world's silver.

With regard to coal and iron, the Commonwealth does not appear to have the exceptional resources of the United States and China ; nevertheless, it has a great and increasing production of both of these valuable products.

As we have seen elsewhere in these pages,

a very important way to produce mechanical power is to utilise waterfalls. In the United Kingdom we have very poor water-power resources, but in the Commonwealth, especially in Canada, New Zealand, and South Africa, there is enormous water-power to develop. For example, on the great River Zambesi, in the south of Africa, the Victoria Falls are 5000 feet wide and 350 feet high. This means that the Victoria Falls can supply energy for an enormous industrial area stretching for hundreds of miles all round the Zambesi, and probably some day this area will be one of the finest workshops of the world. The Canadian water-power resources are no less remarkable. In New Zealand there is enough water-power to carry on all the manufacturing needed by scores of millions of people.

Canada, Australia, and South Africa already possess rich industrial regions as well as being great food producers, and there is no doubt that New Zealand will follow them. As they expand, they will become the home of hundreds of millions of people, working happily and prosperously under better conditions than we in the home country have ever known. The children born in New Zealand in the years to come will enjoy wealth and comfort such as few people in Europe know today.

THE FOOD THAT COMES INTO THE MOTHER COUNTRY FROM ABROAD

Food producing is the first essential of the Commonwealth's existence, and here again we see how much the Mother Country differs from its Dominions.

At home, so far as wheat is concerned, we grow only a fraction of what we need ; the remainder has to be shipped from overseas. Then again many valuable foods, such as rice, tapioca, tea, coffee, cocoa, bananas, oranges, and so on, Nature does not allow us to produce at all. Sugar, processed from sugar beet, we cultivate on a big scale, but we import enormous quantities.

Of the meat we eat we produce about one-half, and we produce nearly all the milk, potatoes, and green vegetables we need. Butter and cheese we import in big quantities. If we had to live on the food that we can produce in these islands, at least half the population would have to leave the country, or else starve.

How very different is the position in the

Commonwealth outside these islands ! As a whole it produces far more food than its people require, just as it produces far more raw materials than its factories require. While the British Isles import food, the Commonwealth exports food.

Of many important foods, the Commonwealth produces ten to fifteen times as much as the British Isles. It is capable of much more expansion in food production, so the Dominions can not only continue to export food to the Mother Country but can sustain much larger populations.

As with food and metals, so with raw materials in general.

A very large part of the Commonwealth's area is suitable for the growing of the cotton plant. In Australia, in Africa, and elsewhere in the British Dominions a cotton production can be aimed at fully as great as has been realised in the United States, which now contains the world's greatest cotton fields.

Then there is wool. We have a good many sheep here in Britain, but all their wool would not keep the British people warm in the winter time. We have to get millions of pounds of wool from abroad to clothe ourselves, and also to make woollen and worsted yarns and cloths for the export trade.

THE SOUTHERN SHEEP THAT HELP TO CLOTHE THE WORLD

Fortunately, the Commonwealth is as rich in wool as the British Isles are poor. Australia and New Zealand are so rich in sheep that they are among the chief wool producers in the world. In other materials, hides, skins, asbestos, and so on, the Commonwealth is as naturally rich as the British Isles are naturally poor.

The great Dominion of Canada is reclaiming the wilds from the Atlantic to the Pacific, and building what will in time become one of the most powerful nations of the world. The Dominion's 16 million people will become 60 million or more, sustained by her splendid prairies, forests, fisheries, mines, and water-power.

She sends to market wheat and meat, fish and fruit, butter and cheese, hides and skins, timber, minerals, and the products of her factories.

Turning to the south, we see the Union of South Africa. Her chief exports so far are wool, copper, gold, iron and steel, diamonds, fruit, and sugar. Her industries are growing, and her resources ensure her a great industrial future.

Far away at the Antipodes, where our Great Bear is replaced as a familiar object in the heavens by the beautiful Southern Cross, lie those great territories, the Commonwealth of Australia and the Dominion of New Zealand. These are rich in all men need to build up prosperity and comfort. There are splendid fertile areas, good coal, and much water-power.

RICH MINERAL DEPOSITS WHICH WILL GIVE AUSTRALIA AN INDUSTRIAL FUTURE

Australia, it is true, has a large desert area, but vast schemes of irrigation and ambitious railways are reclaiming ever more of the land of the island continent for human maintenance. Fed by her rich deposits of iron ore, a great industry is growing, smelting and manufacturing iron and steel. Oil promises to provide much more wealth. Australia loads her argosies with wheat, mutton, beef, butter, cheese, fruit, and jam, wool, hides, skins, leather, copper, lead, tin, zinc, gold, silver, and steel.

New Zealand is still mainly an agricultural country. From her flocks of sheep come wool, mutton, and lamb for export; from her herds of cattle come beef, butter, and cheese. Her industries are developing, and the value of her exports increases every year. The day may come when ten million New Zealanders will enjoy prosperity in one of the most beautiful lands of the earth.

Over eight million people live in the Republic of Ceylon, which is tropical, and so produces different sorts of things from the countries mentioned above. Her chief export is tea, and next to this in importance is rubber. Cocoa, cinnamon, copra, and jewels are other items which she sends to the rest of the world.

THE NATURAL RICHES OF MANY OF THE COLONIES

There are also the British territories in the tropics, or in sub-tropical regions. They are important producers of raw materials. Malaya is the second most important rubber-growing country in the world, and she also produces about one-third of the world's tin supplies.

The West African countries have nearly 40 million inhabitants, and are great sources of tropical products. Ghana alone produces more than one-third of the world's supply of cocoa beans.

The four countries of West Africa are important suppliers of vegetable oils, and of nuts from which these can be extracted. From these oils are made margarine, soap, and other commodities. From Nigeria comes tin ore, from Ghana gold and manganese, and from Sierra Leone iron ore. From the forests of West Africa comes mahogany.

On the east side of the vast continent of Africa are other British colonies. Kenya exports coffee, tea, and maize, sisal for making ropes, and hides and skins. Uganda sends out cotton, coffee, and hides and skins. From Tanganyika come sisal, coffee, cotton, and diamonds, while Zanzibar supplies the bulk of the world's cloves.

TOBACCO AS THE GREATEST AGRICULTURAL EXPORT OF THE RHODESIAS

Farther south is the Federation of Rhodesia and Nyasaland. Northern Rhodesia is one of the world's most important copper producers. Southern Rhodesia also has mineral resources, and exports asbestos, chrome iron, coal, tungsten, and gold. For both, tobacco is the most important agricultural export. In Southern Rhodesia industry is developing, and the output of electricity from her water supplies is expanding. Within her territories are the Victoria Falls. Nyasaland exports on a smaller scale than the others, mainly tobacco, tea, maize, and cotton.

Near the continent of America are the colonies of the West Indies. They produce much sugar, and also export cotton, cocoa, coffee, bananas, and other agricultural produce. In Trinidad, petroleum is produced, and the island is also an important source of asphalt.

Other colonies, in the Pacific and elsewhere, have each their own contribution to make to the wealth of the world.

The glorious thing about all these developments within the British Commonwealth is that between these many and varied nations the possibility of serious differences arising is remote. The growth of the British daughter nations is one of the biggest factors making for the peace of the world. It is all for good that we can see in the free Constitution of the British Commonwealth of Nations how States, great and small, may keep their own special pride and responsibility in being, while joining with each other in common respect, in mutual aid, and in common pride of unity.

There is everything to hope for in such a development and in such a splendid example. Peace between hundreds of millions of people, constituting a host of different races and States, is seen to be not only a thing to hope for, but a thing which can be amicably achieved.

THE TRAFFIC WHICH IS FOR EVER SAILING ACROSS THE SEAS

And this matter of which we speak is closely concerned with the state of society and conditions of life in the Mother Country. Again and again we have to remind ourselves of how we live in this little country—by virtue of the trade done in the tall ships which ply unceasingly across the narrow and the deep seas. Amazing it is to think of the big vessels steaming out with goods of all sorts made in our factories, and returning with good things from every corner of the world.

Will this process of shipping out and shipping in continue? Shall we be always able to find customers abroad to buy our manufactured wares, so that we may get in exchange what we require?

The growth and development of the British Commonwealth will have much to say in answer to these questions.

The markets of the British Commonwealth of Nations, it is not too much to say, are now worth more to the British trader than the markets of all the world were worth one and a half centuries ago. It is true that other countries besides Britain have become manufacturers and big traders, and the competition between sellers will be bigger and ever bigger as time goes on. Against this we can put the confident hope that the world will need to buy very much more than in the past, and that the Britains beyond the seas will offer increasing opportunities.

WHY WE SHOULD ALL REJOICE IN THE PROSPERITY OF OTHERS

All that we have stated about the future prospects of the British Dominions makes for the advantage of the Mother Country. It is a case of mutual advantage. A nation like ourselves, which must either trade with places overseas or disperse most of its people to seek a livelihood elsewhere, has cause to rejoice in the prosperity of overseas customers, and not least in the progress of those other members of our great Commonwealth.

The Story of the Marvellous Plants that Cover the Earth

Marsh Sedge   White Water-Lily   Marsh Woundwort

FLOWERS OF THE STREAM

We cannot walk much by the side of a river or a stream without becoming conscious of the fact that the plants of inland waters are of two main kinds. Those growing by the margins of streams are generally tall, and have narrow leaves. They grow in great numbers and their narrow leaves enable them, like the grasses, to thrive by catching the sunlight. They do not need broad leaves to collect moisture, as they receive all they require by means of their roots.

On the other hand, plants actually growing in the water, floating or spreading their leaves on the surface, have broad leaves, rounded or lobed, and their upper sides are covered with wax, so that water does not settle on them, but rolls off. The reason for this is that their upper surfaces bear stomata, or air-mouths, and it would be bad for the plants if these were to be clogged with water. The floating leaves have the same structure as ordinary land-plants, but the submerged leaves are usually long and strap-shaped, and bear no air-mouths, as they do not need them. These under-water leaves get their salts, oxygen, and carbon dioxide directly from the water, and not from the air, the water containing the salts and gases passing into the leaves and being assimilated by the plant.

A submerged plant obtains its food easily and therefore grows and spreads rapidly. In tropical regions rivers become blocked, for the water plants grow continuously all the year round. While in temperate regions the winter acts as a brake on plant growth, nevertheless, in spring, summer, and autumn, when conditions are genial, they multiply with very great rapidity.

Perhaps the most characteristic and beautiful flowers of the stream are the yellow and white water-lilies. The yellow is, perhaps, the more showy, although it remains more or less ball-shaped, its five or six large yellow sepals enclosing about twenty small and narrow petals. Some leaves are submerged and are narrow, but those that float are heart-shaped, thick, and leathery. The plant has a thick, fleshy rootstock, which contains much tannic acid, and is sometimes soaked in milk to be used as a lure to cockroaches. The Turks prepare a cooling drink from the flowers. These smell much like brandy, hence the name of " brandy bottle," often used in the country for the plant. The fruit, which ripens above the water, is in the shape of a flask, and the seeds lie buried in the pulp.

If less showy, the white water-lily is more beautiful. It belongs to a different species, and its flowers spread widely when fully open. The leaves, from five to ten inches across, are all floating, and the plant is frequently found on large sheets of water. While in the middle of the day the flowers rise and expand, towards evening they close and sink.

Though called lilies, they are not lilies at all, but belong to a family which goes by the somewhat difficult name of Nymphaeaceae, so-called because they are found growing in the places the nymphs were supposed to haunt. A real lily of the stream is the snake's head, or fritillary, a beautiful plant a foot high, with a drooping flower shaped like a tulip and curiously chequered with pink and dull red or purple. This marking, and the shape of the unexpanded blossom, have given the plant its popular name of snake's head, and the other name is from the Latin fritillus, a dice-box; not that the plant is like a dice-box, but the pattern of its flowers is like that of the chequered board on which dice were formerly thrown.

The snake's head has a small bulb, and long, narrow leaves on its rounded stem, much like those of the bluebell, but not quite so wide. The plant is about a foot high.

THE HANDSOME CORN FLAG WHOSE SEEDS ARE USED IN PLACE OF COFFEE

Another plant that grows abundantly along the banks of rivers and streams is the corn flag or yellow iris, a stout plant with large, handsome yellow flowers, bigger than those of the fetid iris, or gladdon. The yellow iris has a creeping rootstock that is very acrid and yields a good black dye. In some parts of the country and in Russia, where the plant grows freely, the seeds are said to be roasted as a substitute for coffee.

The arrowhead is easily distinguished from all other plants of the stream by its distinctive arrow-shaped leaves. It is a member of the water-plantain family and is often found in rivers and ditches. A tall, leafless flowering stem rises from the midst of the arrowhead leaf-stalks, and at regular intervals this sends off short branches in threes, each branch ending in a large, delicate white or pink flower. The lower flowers, smaller than those above, have no stamens, while those above have many stamens but no pistils. The flowers with pistils develop into large round fruits. From the swollen base of the plant, runners are sent out in all directions, and at the ends of these, before the winter sets in, tubers form, and next year each tuber forms a separate plant. The tuberous roots contain much farinaceous matter, and may be eaten either raw or boiled. They grow immediately beneath the surface of the mud, and seldom exceed the size of a walnut.

THE FLOWERING RUSH WITH NARROW LEAVES LIKE SWORDS

Belonging to the same family is the water-plantain itself, which is no relation of the plantain of the fields. It is a stout herbaceous plant, growing two or three feet high along the margins of rivers, lakes, and ponds, and is quite common in England. The white, pink, or pale lilac flowers resemble those of the arrowhead, but are smaller and soon fall off.

The flowering rush is another member of the same family, its only likeness to the true rushes being in its leaves, which are long and narrow, and its leafless flower stem. This stem, rising from two to four feet high, bears a large umbel of handsome, rose-coloured flowers. The plant has a thick, creeping rootstock. It is sometimes called the common butome, from its scientific name butomus—a term made up of two Greek words: bous, an ox, and temno, I cut—which reminds us that cattle were once supposed to cut their mouths with the sword-shaped leaves.

The rose family is represented by two plants, the meadowsweet and the water avens. The first of these is abundant and its foam-like masses of small white flowers are anything but rose-like in appearance. When examined separately, however, these flowers will be seen to be much like those of the blackthorn, or sloe.

THE FRAGRANT FLOWERS OF THE QUEEN OF THE MEADOWS

The flowers are very fragrant and the popular title, queen of the meadows, often given to the plant, is not undeserved. It grows three or four feet high, and the astringent roots have been used in the tanning of leather. In Iceland a durable black dye is obtained from a decoction of the whole plant, and formerly in England the meadowsweet was used for medicinal purposes. The foliage is eaten by goats, sheep, and pigs, but not by horses or cows.

The other rose of the streams, the water avens, is a sister plant of the common avens, or herb benet, of the hedgerow. It is a handsome plant with drooping,

FLOWERS THAT BLOOM BY THE STREAM

WATER DROPWORT

ARROWHEAD

GREAT VALERIAN

MEADOWSWEET

WATER FIGWORT

WATERCRESS

BUR-REED

WATER CROWFOOT

LOOSESTRIFE

SNAKE'S HEAD

HEMP AGRIMONY

REED-MACE

SULPHUR-WORT

GIPSY-WORT

GIANT DOCK

reddish-brown flowers, and abounds in some parts of the country by riverside and in marshy fields. It was formerly used as a disinfectant, and was put into ale to prevent it turning sour, just as oil of cloves is put into paste to preserve it.

The great wild valerian is still used in medicine as a stimulant. It grows three or four feet high, and has leaves much divided, the leaflets numbering from nine to 21, and being coarsely toothed and hairy underneath. The small white flowers grow in clusters and are tinged with pink.

The most interesting thing about the great valerian is its attraction for cats and rats. It is scarcely possible to keep a plant where these animals abound, if the leaves or roots have once been bruised so as to give out their familiar scent. Cats seem to be thrown into a kind of intoxication by the scent, and will dig up the roots. Rats do the same, and in the country traps are often successfully baited with valerian. To Europeans the scent is not pleasant, but some Asiatics prize it, and use it in the preparation of various perfumes.

THE SPIKENARD WHICH WAS USED FOR ANOINTING THE FEET OF JESUS

The order to which the valerian belongs is small, but one of its most notable members is the spikenard of the New Testament. This was regarded as very precious by the ancients and it will be remembered that Judas estimated the value of the spikenard used in anointing the feet of Jesus at " three hundred pence."

Several members of the primrose family thrive in marshy places, one of the commonest being the yellow loosestrife, which is not really a loosestrife at all. It is a stout, branched plant two or three feet high, more or less downy, with oval, lance-shaped leaves, growing three or four in a whorl, and rather large, bell-shaped flowers dotted with orange.

Another primrose of the stream is the water violet, which is not a violet. It is a floating plant with large, handsome lilac flowers, each having a yellow eye, and these are arranged in whorls round a smooth succulent stem that is quite leafless. This flower stalk rises high out of the water.

Still another riverside primrose is the moneywort, or herb twopence, more commonly known in some districts as the Creeping Jenny. It is a pretty plant, quite destitute of hairs, with creeping stems that often grow more than a foot

long, and egg-shaped shining leaves. The large, cup-shaped yellow flowers grow in the axils formed by the leaves, and the whole plant drapes the river bank in a most graceful manner. It is often cultivated in rock gardens and in pots which are suspended, the leaf and flower stalks drooping gracefully all round. The leaves sometimes turn pink in autumn.

THE PURPLE LOOSESTRIFE USED IN SOME COUNTRIES AS A MEDICINE

The purple loosestrife is a real member of the loosestrife family, and in no way related to the yellow loosestrife already described among the primroses. It is an erect plant, two or three feet high, with square stems terminating in long spikes of purple flowers, arranged in whorls, with leaves beneath. It is common in ditches and marshy meadows as well as by riversides, and flowers late in the summer. In Ireland it is used as a medicine by the countryfolk, being very astringent. On the Continent, too, it is used as a remedy for dysentery, intermittent fevers, and so on.

Everybody knows the buttercup of the stream, the water crowfoot, a plant so variable that some botanists have divided it into at least nine or ten different species. Its stem either floats in water or creeps along the mud, and the lower leaves and, indeed, sometimes all of them, remain under water and are divided into many fine segments. Any leaves spread on the surface of the water are rounded and cut into a varying number of lobes. The flowers, unlike those of the bulbous buttercup of the meadow, are white. The varieties with floating leaves occur in standing waters, and those without generally in running streams. The last mentioned varieties are the plants described by Tennyson as " long mosses in the stream."

THE PLANT THE SWEDISH FARMER KEEPS NEAR HIS BEEHIVES

Of the great composite family the common butterbur spreads at a great rate in marshy meadows and on river banks. The large kidney-shaped and downy leaves are often three feet in diameter. They open after the blossoms, which form in a many-flowered head on a short, fleshy stalk. These flowers are a dull lilac in colour. Swedish farmers often plant the butterbur near their beehives on account of its early flowering, the blossoms opening as early as January. The hemp agrimony is also a composite. It is sometimes six feet high, with a reddish stem and heads of dull lilac-coloured flowers.

Another familiar plant in the edges of streams and pools and in watery ditches is the great water dock, sometimes called the giant dock. It is a picturesque plant growing sometimes as high as six feet, with sharp lance-shaped leaves often more than a foot long. The flowers, which are green, grow in crowded whorls and form a large branched raceme. The docks are closely related to the sorrels and to buckwheat.

A STREAMSIDE RELATION OF THE HEATHS THAT GROW IN DRY PLACES

Although the heaths favour dry places as a rule, one heath, the common wintergreen, is often found flowering by stream and pool. In the south it is rare, but in Scotland, the north of England, and Ireland, it is frequently seen. The pale pink, globular flowers grow on short stalks and are almost closed, and the round or egg-shaped leaves grow in tufts of three or four on rather long stalks.

The labiate family, which includes the mints and the hemp-nettles, has several members growing by the stream. One of these is the greater skull-cap, a handsome plant, about a foot or eighteen inches high, with long, lance-shaped leaves and large bright-blue flowers growing in the axils. Another is the common gipsy-wort, which has a creeping rootstock and runners, deeply cut leaves, and tiny white flowers dotted with red, growing in crowded whorls in the axils of the upper leaves. Still another labiate is the hairy mint, the commonest of all the mints. It grows in dense masses by the banks of rivers and wet ditches and varies greatly. Often it reaches a height of four feet, and the pale lavender flowers are very conspicuous. The whole plant has a strong and not unpleasant smell. One more labiate may be mentioned here. The marsh woundwort grows two or three feet high, is a hairy plant with long, lance-shaped leaves, and dull, light red flowers in a long spike. It is quite common in marshy land in the neighbourhood of ponds and streams.

WHY THE FISHERMAN DOES NOT LIKE THE WATER FIGWORT

Among the figworts of the stream is the water figwort, a tall, herbaceous plant, three to five feet high, with a square stem, smooth, heart-shaped leaves, and chocolate-brown flowers in branched racemes. The stems are hollow and succulent, but when the plant dies they become rigid. Anglers find them a great nuisance, for their lines become entangled with them. When fresh, water figwort gives out a strong, disagreeable odour, and its taste is bitter and nauseous. Goats feed on the plant, but other animals reject it. The plant has become famous by its use at the siege of La Rochelle in 1628, when, other remedies being absent, the soldiers applied water figwort to their wounds, and, it is said, were speedily healed.

Another figwort is brooklime, a near relation of the water speedwell and a very similar plant, though smaller. It is often found growing in brooks and ditches with the watercress and water parsnip. The flowers, which are of a bright blue colour, grow in racemes.

The yellow monkey-flower, another of the figworts, is really a North American plant, cultivated in water gardens, but in many places it has escaped and established itself as a wild plant by the riverside. The flowers are large and funnel-shaped, and in the wild variety are yellow, but the cultivated varieties have blossoms blotched with red or brown.

THE SMALL CREEPING MUDWORT WHICH GROWS IN MUDDY PLACES

The name of the common mudwort indicates the situations where it is found. This applies equally to its botanical name limosella, which is derived from limus, the Latin word for mud. It is a small, creeping plant with long, narrow, spoon-shaped leaves and tiny white or pale pink flowers on short stalks.

Another figwort found in the banks of rivers and streams in Cornwall, and occasionally in other southern counties, is the Cornish money-wort. It is a dainty little plant with slender stems that creep along the ground in tangled masses and have small, round, downy leaves of delicate green, and tiny pink and yellow flowers.

The common comfrey, a familiar plant of the riverside, is a member of the borage family. It is a large and handsome plant, reaching three feet, and has pointed, elliptical leaves and flowers which may be white, pink, or purple, and form in drooping clusters. Though attractive in the wild, the comfrey is a great nuisance in the garden, for, as in the case of the bindweed, the roots are brittle and the smallest piece will grow into a plant. It is hard to get rid of once it has taken hold.

Another borage is the tufted water scorpion grass, a sister plant of the forget-me-not, which it somewhat resembles. It is a light green plant with a much branched downy stem and long, slender racemes of sky-blue flowers.

Common by streams and ponds is the water bedstraw, a weak, straggling plant about a couple of feet high, with narrow, blunt leaves, four or six in a whorl, and loose panicles of white flowers. The great willow herb, sometimes called codlins and cream, a plant familiar by rivers and ditches, belongs to the family which includes the evening primrose and the enchanter's nightshade. It is a handsome plant, very downy, growing from three to six feet high, and having lance-shaped leaves with saw-like edges, which clasp the stem closely. The deep rose-coloured flowers measure nearly an inch across and are very fragrant. One of the sedges found in marshy places, near the sea, is the marsh sedge or carex, a plant two or three feet high, with long, narrow leaves and crowded spikelets of flowers. The sedges are much like the grasses, but differ in having solid, angular stems, and are of very little use to man or beast.

THE REED-MACE WHICH IS SOMETIMES MISTAKEN FOR THE BULRUSH

The small reed-mace family consists entirely of aquatic plants among which the reed-mace and the bur-reed are typical. The great reed-mace, or cat's-tail, sometimes reaches a height of eight feet, and its club-like spike of flowers causes it often to be mistaken for the bulrush, the large rush-like scirpus. The branched bur-reed is a plant three or four feet high with sword-shaped leaves and male and female flowers in separate heads.

Several members of the parsley family are found growing by the stream-side. There is the water dropwort, a plant with a fleshy, fibrous root, a stem that sends out runners, hollow leaf stalks, leaves partly submerged, and umbels of white flowers. The plant was formerly much used as a medicine in cases of consumption and asthma. It is poisonous, and if the fruit be eaten giddiness and other symptoms of narcotic poisoning follow. Even horses have been poisoned in this way.

Another of the parsley family is sulphur-wort, sometimes called pepper saxifrage. It is a smooth plant a foot or so high, with an angular stem and umbels of dull, pale yellow flowers. The plant gives out a fetid smell when bruised, and is said by some country people to give a bad flavour to milk and butter.

The procumbent marsh-wort is abundant in rivers and ditches, growing often with watercress, for which it is sometimes mistaken. It has, however, a hollow stem and leaves with a saw-like edge that enable it to be easily distinguished from watercress. The flowers are small and white.

Still another parsley of the stream is the narrow-leaved water parsnip, much commoner than its sister plant the broad-leaved water parsnip. It has feathery leaves, with saw-like edges to the leaflets, and crowded umbels of small white flowers.

WHY THE WATERCRESS WAS HELD IN HIGH ESTEEM BY THE GREEKS

Of the cabbage family among stream plants, the watercress is abundant in most parts of the country where there is running water, and often forms extensive beds near the margins of shallow streams and pools. It rarely rises more than eight or nine inches above the surface of the water. The succulent stems and rounded leaflets are too well known from its use as a salad plant to need any description here. The small white flowers open in June.

The watercress contains a pungent oil present in every part of the plant, and in addition it contains much common salt and sulphur, and also some iodine. It was probably one of the first green plants to be eaten in Europe and northern Asia, and was highly esteemed by the ancient Greeks, not only as a salad, but as a medicine. It was supposed to be particularly useful in disorders of the brain, and in speaking of the half-witted the Greeks had a popular saying, " Eat cress." Xenophon recommended the Persians to give it to their children as a means of adding to their strength and stature.

AN IMPORTANT PLANT FOR THE MARKET GARDENER NEAR THE TOWN

For centuries it has been eaten in England, but only in the nineteenth century was the plant cultivated, and now the growing of watercress is an important branch of market-gardening in the neighbourhood of most of our large towns.

A sister plant is the marsh yellow-cress, which, as its name implies, has not white but yellow flowers.

Pictures in colour of Flowers of the Stream appear on pages 6129-30.

The Story of the Peoples of All Nations and Their Homelands

Some of the beautiful buildings in the Kremlin at Moscow

RUSSIA IN OUR TIME—THE U.S.S.R.

Russia, which is now known as the Union of Soviet Socialist Republics, stretches from the Baltic on the west to the Pacific Ocean on the east. On the north she looks over the Arctic seas; southward her boundaries are the great Asiatic mountains and tablelands, the homes of the ancestors of the European nations, the Caucasus, the highlands of Asia Minor, the coast of the Black Sea.

The territory under her control decreased after the First World War. She lost Russian Poland, Bessarabia, Finland, Estonia, Latvia, and Lithuania. But since the Patriotic War— as the Russian people describe the Second World War— she has regained all but Finland. Even here she has gained the part of Karelia which is now the Karelo-Finnish S.S.R. or 12th Republic of the Union, and includes the important Petsamo nickel deposits. She also governs the north-eastern part of East Prussia, with its capital and seaport Kaliningrad (formerly Königsberg), and Ruthenia, ceded by Czechoslovakia. Her frontier with Poland may be taken as the " Curzon Line," the rough nationality frontier first suggested by Britain in 1920. As regards Latvia, Lithuania, and Estonia, Britain has never recognised Russia's right to take these so-called " Baltic States."

In Asia, Russia has taken the Kurile Islands from Japan, while the nominally independent State of Tannu-Tuva, north-west of Mongolia, has been incorporated in the U.S.S.R. as an autonomous province.

All this adds up to over 8,500,000 square miles, nearly a sixth of the world's land area, with a population, in round numbers, of 195,000,000, a population which is growing rapidly. Russia lost many millions of men in the Hitler War, but promptly planned public health services, the raising of the standard of living, and expansion of agriculture and industry, to repair the damage.

While the northern regions, with their long, bitter winter, their poor soil, and their vast areas of coniferous forest, scrub, and marsh, will always remain sparsely peopled, throughout much of the rest of Russia the population is becoming more evenly distributed as industry spreads eastwards. We shall later consider this great eastward march of industrial Russia, the pace of which quickens from year to year.

Why is it that this huge area, with its 190 nationalities speaking 150 languages and dialects, hangs together politically in spite of all the storms of revolution and wars that have burst over it? A relief map

THE FIVE CONTINENTS & 100 NATIONS & RACES THAT INHABIT THEM

gives part of the answer. The U.S.S.R. cover the great northern plains of Europe and Asia, and in these plains there is no real break but the Ural Mountains, which rise gently, offering no serious barrier to road or rail. These barely perceptible mountains do not extend as far as the Caspian Sea, but leave a large gap where the River Ural runs through the steppes to the south.

The slightly elevated plateau forming what we know as European Russia has a foundation of granite over which the ages have spread a coating of sand and chalk and clay; in huge areas of Southern Russia it is covered with what is called " black earth," largely composed of the remains of vegetable matter. This soil is so rich that wheat grown here needs little or no manuring and all sorts of crops grow luxuriantly. The wide steppe country in the southern basin of the Volga and stretching eastward across the Ural River into Southern Siberia is practically tree-less. East of the Caspian the salty plain is almost desert.

THE CANALS THAT JOIN ONE RIVER TO ANOTHER

Everywhere the watershed slopes are gradual and the river currents are slow, except at the time of the melting of the snow, when the volume of water in the rivers is enormously increased. One result of the evenness of the land is that it is easy to build canals from one river to another, and river transport is as important in Russia as rail transport. Siberia's enormous rivers run northward to the Arctic Ocean, like the Yenisei, the Ob, and the Lena, or, like the Amur, eastward to the Pacific. A summer sea route brings the riches of Siberia to the countries of the west by way of the Yenisei and the Kara Sea.

The climate of Russia is a climate of extremes. The great central plain offers no barrier to the winds that sweep across Asia; there are no mountains here to help the fall of rain, and, except in the far east, Russia does not feel the moderating influence of the sea. In winter the snow lies thick down to the shores of the Caspian. In north-eastern Siberia the cold is almost incredibly intense, Verkhoyansk having an average January temperature of more than 90 degrees of frost. This area has actually registered 122 degrees of frost! Spring comes with sudden splendour, and by June it is so hot over the central and southern regions that one wonders how there could ever have been snow.

Winter in the western districts is less severe. In the north the winter days are short, the shortest in Archangel being but 3 hours and 12 minutes long. Reward comes in summer, of course, with its extremely long days. Even Leningrad has its " white nights," when it hardly grows dark at all; and as far south as Moscow the summer nights are quite light, so that at ten in the evening the gilded domes of the Kremlin's churches still shine in the afterglow like the back-drop for some magnificent grand opera.

MIGHTY PEAKS ON THE SOUTHERN BORDERS OF RUSSIA

Though there are no big mountains in the middle of Russia, there are mighty heights on her southern borders, where Mt. Stalin (24,590 ft.) and Lenin Peak (23,680 ft.) rear their snowy crags among the Pamirs. The Caucasus range in the south-east contains Mt. Elbruz, 2700 feet higher than Mont Blanc, and the average height of the passes here is 11,000 feet. There are several good roads over the passes by which the traveller enters Georgia, and services for motor-cars pass over them. In Transcaucasia, to the south, there are other great ranges stretching down into Russian Armenia. In the far east the Verkhoyansk and Stanovoi ranges cut off the north-eastern tip of Siberia between the Sea of Okhotsk and the Arctic Ocean.

Before we consider some of the different peoples of the U.S.S.R. and how they are governed, let us see how the country, the " multi-national State," as the Russians call it, is divided up for purposes of administration.

THE SIXTEEN EQUAL REPUBLICS WHICH FORM THE SOVIET UNION

Altogether, the Soviet Union comprises 16 voluntarily federated and equal Republics. They are Soviet Russia, Ukraine, Byelo-Russia (White Russia), Azerbaijan, Georgia, Armenia, Turkmenistan, Uzbekistan, Tadzhikistan, Kazakhstan, Kirghizia, Karelo-Finnish, Moldavia, Estonia, Latvia, and Lithuania. Within the framework of several of these, too, there are autonomous Republics, national areas, and autonomous regions.

By far the biggest of the main republics,

TYPES OF THE PEOPLE OF RUSSIA

A JOLLY AGRICULTURAL
WORKER

WORKERS ON A STATE FARM
IN TURKMENISTAN

A TYPICAL UZBEK
PEASANT

A GROUP OF COLLECTIVE FARMERS TAKING A COURSE AT AN AGRICULTURAL COLLEGE

REAPING BARLEY ON A FARM
IN TURKMENISTAN

GOING TO THE HARVEST
FIELDS

A COSSACK HORSEMAN
MASTERING HIS STEED

accounting for three-quarters of the whole area of the U.S.S.R. and half of its population, is the Russian Soviet Federal Socialist Republic (the R.S.F.S.R. or Russia). This vast area, containing more than 100 nationalities, stretches from the Baltic to the Pacific and the Bering Sea, and from the Arctic to the highlands of Central Asia, and includes almost all Siberia, and the chief industrial regions except those of the Ukraine. The Ukraine is the second Republic in importance for population and economic development, and contains the huge coal and iron ore deposits of the Donets Basin north of the Black Sea.

THE RUSSIAN PEOPLE WITH WHITE SKINS, BROAD HEADS, AND WAVY HAIR

Now let us look at some of the different types of people. The chief national group—one cannot define the people of the Soviet Union as distinct races—are the Russians themselves, Slav in tongue and comprising Great Russians, White Russians (or Byelo-Russians), and Ukrainians (or Little Russians). In general these people are stocky, with white skins, broad heads, and wavy hair. Great Russians, who speak their own dialect, are square-faced and sometimes red-haired. The Moscow area was their original home.

White Russians, whose home is in the Pripet Marshes region of the Upper Dnieper basin, are the fairest, and are of medium height. The word " White " is used simply to distinguish their dialect from that of the " Great " and " Little " Russians, and has nothing to do with colour of skin, nor, of course, with the " White " Guards who fought the Bolshevik " Reds " in Revolution days.

THE SHORT, DARK PEOPLE WHO LIVE AMONG THE STEPPES

The Ukrainians live among the steppes above the Black Sea, with Kiev as their chief centre. Their history and environment has been different, and they are shorter and darker, with an artistic bent. On the other hand the Latvians (Letts) and Lithuanians of the Baltic area are often of Nordic type, blond and blue-eyed people.

Then there are the people in Karelo-Finnish and Estonia, and also in the Volga and Ural regions, whose language-group is known as Finnish-Ugrian. These broad-headed people are believed to be descendants of immigrants from the steppes of Asia 1000 years ago.

Let us here give some special attention to the three Baltic Republics—Lithuania, Latvia, and Estonia. These Republics have much in common. They adjoin each other on the almost land-locked Baltic. They all became independent of Russia at the end of the First World War, and all, after some twenty years of precarious but energetic sovereign existence, were reabsorbed by the Soviet Union, as the 14th, 15th, and 16th Republics.

The eyes of many of their menfolk—and even of their womenfolk—turn westward to the sea. The Estonians, or Ests, are renowned as a seafaring people, but Latvians and Lithuanians, too, sail the oceans in pursuit of trade. All of them are hard-working people, and they play a considerable part in the great industrial drive which, as we shall see, is the mainspring of Russian effort today. Mainly, however, they are farming people, growing their rye, barley, oats, wheat, flax, and potatoes, and rearing their livestock.

THE FACE OF THE WESTERN OUTPOSTS OF MIGHTY RUSSIA

Lithuania is the southernmost of the three, and has Byelo-Russia to the south and East Prussia to the west. To north and east lies Latvia, with its busy port of Riga on the Gulf of Riga and its second and third ports, Liepaja and Ventspils, on the Baltic. Above this again, Estonia—which has a strangely humid climate—looks mainly north across the Gulf of Finland, where its port of Tallinn faces Helsinki, capital of Finland, across fifty miles of water. The face of these western outposts of mighty Russia is generally speaking the same—pleasant, well-forested, well-watered land, where such hills as there are rarely rise above 500 feet. Latvia, which is slightly the biggest of the three, has an area about three and a half times as large as Wales. Lithuania, however, has a population—nearly three million—almost as big as those of Latvia and Estonia combined.

To return to the peoples of the older Republics of Russia. The Turkic peoples, living mostly in the southern parts of Central Asia, are another mainly (but not entirely) Mongoloid type, yellow-skinned and slant-eyed. Among these are the old nomadic shepherd-horsemen, the Kazakh-Kirghiz, chiefly Mohammedan in religion, and retaining many old customs. The "party clothes" of many of the men are gorgeous robes of silk or velvet, adorned with gold or silver; the women wear a kind of white cotton turban.

Kazakhi means "horsemen," and from the same root comes the name Cossack, and so we are reminded of the roving plunderers who broke away from serfdom in the 16th and 17th centuries and made a name for themselves as daredevil riders. The Cossacks are not in themselves a people, but are united by their mode of life and their habits. The Kazakh-Kirghiz are a people full of music and folklore, and so are the Uzbeks to the south-west of them. There are about 6½ million of these in an area about as big as the British Isles, and they dress strikingly in dark, striped, cotton robes, and high sheepskin caps.

Farthest south, in the Pamir fastnesses, are the Tadzhiks, who speak dialects akin to Persian. These are darkish, but far less Mongol in appearance owing to their high foreheads and prominent noses. West of the Uzbeks and bordering part of the Caspian are Turkmenians, tall, lean, brown people, whose womenfolk are gaily attired in silk blouses and tight-fitting trousers and silver bracelets.

THE BACKWARD PEOPLE WHO NOW HAVE THEIR OWN DOCTORS AND TEACHERS

Thousands of miles to the east we find another Turkic-speaking type, the Yakuts of North-Eastern Siberia. These are very Mongoloid to look at, with flat noses, prominent cheekbones, and slit eyes. They were practically illiterate before the Revolution, but today they have their own doctors and teachers, and even their own theatre of drama. Yet another Turkic-speaking group are the Tatars, whose chief city is Kazan on the middle Volga, but who are scattered throughout the land, in the Northern Crimea, in the Northern Caucasus, to the west of the Altai Mountains (Altai Tatars, or Oirots), and in parts of Western Siberia.

Typically Mongoloid are the tiny Evyenki group, 16,000 reindeer-breeders living east of the River Yenisei in an area nearly twice as large as England. In the north-eastern tip of the continent live people sometimes called Old Asiatics, with strong Eskimo and American (Red) Indian characteristics. As the Bering Sea was once a land-bridge between Asia

and America, this is not surprising. These backward people, whom the Soviet Government have rescued from extinction, are also reindeer-hunters, and the name of one of the tribes, the Chukots, means "those rich in reindeer." On the Bering coast itself are 2000 real Eskimos. How far we have travelled from the Nordic Letts and the Muscovites in this stupendous multinational State!

Two peoples of the U.S.S.R. are definitely Mongol in type and speak Mongol tongues. These are the Buryats in the far eastern Lake Baikal area and the Kalmyks between the northern ends of the Caspian and Black Seas.

THE MAZE OF PEOPLES FOUND IN THE CAUCASUS REGION

In the Caucasus region is found a maze of peoples, with differing language and religion, chief among whom are the Georgians, kinsfolk of Stalin. With their broad heads, dark hair and eyes, round faces and "hawk" noses, these mountaineers of the Western Caucasus are perhaps the most striking physical type found anywhere in the Union. The girls here have been famed throughout history for their beauty. In this region, too, are the swarthier Armenians, who, though they are not Jews, have many Jewish characteristics. There are now over a million Armenians under Soviet rule. Another group, the Azerbaijanis, lie close to the northern frontier of Persia. Part of Azerbaijan, in fact, is Persian.

Scattered throughout the Union are something like two million Jews. There is a national home for Jews in the Birobidjan area, almost on the Pacific coast, but only 50,000 of them have chosen to live there. The Jews of Russia differ widely in appearance—some dark, some fair, some broad of head, some narrow. But all are Soviet citizens first.

As in every other country, there are wandering Gypsies, the men being mostly horse-dealers and blacksmiths, and the women handicraft workers.

WHEN THE COMMUNISM OF MARX WAS PRACTISED IN RUSSIA

All these peoples in the Soviet Union are equal. Colour, language, and religion make no difference to the status of any citizen. We must now see how they are governed, and what part they take in the State's affairs.

We speak of Communist Russia, but

we must realise that pure Communism as preached by Karl Marx scarcely exists in the Soviet Union. It was practised only for the first three years after the Revolution, when workers actually controlled the factories, wages were fixed independently of work, private trading was forbidden, all land, including church land, was confiscated and declared to be national property, and world revolution was the great ideal.

Lenin began his New Economic Policy (N.E.P) or " retreat from Communism " in 1921, and since then Russia has been ruled, as one writer puts it, " by Communists but not necessarily according to Communist principles." One firm principle remains—national ownership of the means of production—but otherwise the system has been modified little by little, and in particular the ideal of world revolution has been put on one side. Nationalism has become the new ideal. As the Roman's pride was in saying " Civis Romanus sum "—" I am a citizen of Rome "—so would the young Russian say (if he were taught Latin at school) " Civis Sovieticus sum." Universal military service, too, is looked upon as an honourable duty.

JOSEPH STALIN, THE GREAT LEADER OF A GREAT PEOPLE

It was under the leadership of Joseph Stalin that Russia developed into the mighty Power that she is today. It was he who first devised the Union of Soviet Socialist Republics, and it was he who in 1936 remoulded the constitution in its present form. The Five-Year Plan, which we shall examine, was Stalin's plan.

Joseph Stalin became the supreme head of the State, invested with almost unlimited powers, and when he died, at the Moscow Kremlin on the evening of March 5, 1953, just tribute was paid to him as one who, like Lenin, had devoted his entire life to the selfless service of his people.

" Farewell, our teacher and leader, our beloved friend ! " said his successor, Mr. George Malenkov, in the closing passage of his funeral oration.

According to the Constitution, Soviet Russia is governed by the Supreme Council of the U.S.S.R., with its seat in the Kremlin, Moscow. This is elected by universal, direct, equal, and secret vote, and is divided into, first, the Council of the Union, comprising one member for each 300,000 of the population of the constituent Republics, and, second, the Council of Nationalities, representing Republics, Regions, and National Areas.

But the Council of Ministers (formerly Commissars) is the chief executive authority. In March 1958 Mr. N. S. Khruschev became Prime Minister in place of Marshal Bulganin, who had succeeded Mr. Malenkov in 1955. Altogether there are about 70 Ministries.

THE SOVIETS THAT ARE CONCERNED MAINLY WITH LOCAL GOVERNMENT

The system of " Soviets," or " councils of workers by hand and brain," operates throughout the Union, down to the humblest village, and finds its culmination in the Presidium of the Supreme Soviet, the President of which is President of the Union. Soviets are elected by all citizens of 18 years old and upwards, whatever their sex, race, religion, or social position.

The work of the Soviet, however, is mainly in the realm of local government. We have seen how the federal Republics contain " autonomous " Republics and Regions, but we must remember that such autonomy does not imply self-government except in local matters. All policy of national importance is framed in Moscow and the Republics are bound by this policy. It is true that the Republics can enter into direct relations with foreign States, but they must conform to the central foreign policy.

THE COMMUNIST PARTY IS THE ONLY LEGAL ONE IN THE UNION

Behind all government is the Communist Party. This is the only legal Party in the Union, although only a small minority of the population belong to it. There can be no candidates other than Communists in elections, and consequently the Party is all-powerful. Policy is discussed by the Central Committee of the Communist Party, which reports to the ten-member council or Presidium which early in 1953 replaced the Politburo (or Political Section) as supreme decision-maker of the Party.

Russia's former international policy, the policy of converting the world to her ideas, has not been dropped so much as remodelled. World revolution, which was one of the first ideals of pure Communism, is not mentioned nowadays. The Comin-

CHILDREN OF RUSSIA TODAY

A SCHOOL IN THE MODERN CITY OF MINGECHAUR IN AZERBAIJAN

THE GAMES LENDING ROOM OF A YOUTH MOVEMENT CENTRE IN MOSCOW

tern—or Communist International—which sowed revolutionary propaganda in all countries, was disbanded in 1943. Four years later there came the Cominform (Communist Information Bureau). This organisation nominally " informed " Communists everywhere of Moscow's policy, but actually had the task of spreading Communist ideas, and particularly ideas for the reorganisation of industry on Communist lines. But in 1956, shortly before the visit to Britain of Marshal Bulganin and Mr. Krushchev, Cominform, too, was disbanded.

The idea of Russia as the " Classless State " still holds good. There are people who " live well " and people who do not live so well, but the former are always people who, in the Government's opinion, have served the State well. For instance, if there is a three-roomed flat to be let in a new block of flats in Moscow it may be given to an important engineer or a general. Nobody grumbles about this, for it was Stalin's wish that everyone should realise that a great Russia was his ideal, and that such rewards as there are should go to those who, provided they are workers by hand or by brain, help to make Russia great.

THE DIGNITY OF CITIZENSHIP WHICH THE TSARS FAILED TO GIVE THE PEOPLE

So there are no class conventions or class distinctions. All are equal, and the professions are open to women. Education is equal for all, except of course where specialised studies are concerned ; the standard of dress varies little; and people address one another in the same way. There are no " Yes, sirs " or " No, sirs " in the Russia of today. People are learning rather to have that " dignity of citizenship " which the Tsars failed to give them. They are striving to reach, in as short a time as possible, that sense of their own importance and dignity that the people of Britain took long centuries to acquire.

We might think that, with this new " religion " of a great Russia set in front of them, the people would have no time for religion in the accepted sense. But this is not so. The official cold attitude to religion has decreased the power of the Orthodox Church but has by no means destroyed it, and many other religions, such as Roman Catholicism, Lutheranism, Buddhism, Tibetan Lamaism,

Mohammedanism, and the Jewish faith, have their adherents.

The Government no longer try to stamp out religion by the drastic methods they used during and after the Revolution. During the Second World War, indeed, Stalin revived the Patriarchate, which had lapsed, except for one short period, since the days of Peter the Great. But religion may not be taught in the schools. The Church may not advertise itself—though anti-religious propaganda is allowed—and there must be no religious activity except worship. The majority of churches are closed, or have been turned into museums or storehouses. As for Christmas trees, nothing can destroy the love that Russian children have for these, but in the eyes of the Government they are now " New Year " trees.

RELIGION IS STILL VERY MUCH ALIVE IN RUSSIA

Nevertheless, such churches as are open are filled to overflowing on important church occasions, and the services are beautiful and moving, and the worshippers sincerely devout. In spite of former persecution, then, religion is still very much alive in Russia—and not only among the older people. On a week day, when able-bodied people are at work, we should find only old men and old women in church, but on Sundays or on a great feast day there might even be more young people than old.

But the main interest of the young Russian, when he is not at work, is in sport, which the Government encourage to the fullest extent. More than half a million Russians take part every year in track and field athletics. " What we want to do," stated the late President Kalinin, " is to develop our people in every possible way, teach them to run and swim well, to walk smartly and easily, see that their physical well-being is maintained. In a word, we want to develop normal healthy citizens, trained to labour and to defence, with their physical and mental qualities developing parallel to one another."

SOCCER, THE NATIONAL GAME PLAYED IN SUMMER MONTHS

So the millions of Russian workers are brought together under the banner of sport. The Government have made, and have paid for, 600 large sports grounds, 14,000 playing fields, nearly 50,000 volley-ball and basket-ball courts, 6000 ski tracks, and more than 500 swimming pools.

Football (" soccer ") is the Russian national game. The Russians think it strange that we play football in winter. They cannot understand why the ground is not too hard, and why we do not slip about on the ice. In Russia, summer is the football season, and matches are played in the late afternoon, when the heat is waning. The game is taken very seriously, a very famous team being known as the Moscow Dynamos. The Georgians especially are good footballers, and they also excel as gymnasts.

Skating is of course a popular sport. Children learn to skate from the age of four or five, and they find it hard to realise that we in England have not enough frost for skating throughout the winter. Ski-running is naturally popular, too, in the hilly districts. More than a million and a half of the young people of the collective farms take part every year in ski competitions. Boxing, wrestling, and weight-lifting are encouraged because such sports and feats mean sheer physical strength. The Armenians are particularly noted for these " muscle " sports.

HOW INDUSTRY AND SPORTS GO HAND IN HAND

Each industry has its own sports society, membership of which is open to workers and their families. One finds the Electric Sports Society, and the Medical, Motor, Power, Rubber, Woolworker, Tractor, Builder, and Locomotive Sports Societies, and many more. Outstanding in the number of members are the Wings of the Soviets, for aircraft workers, and the Torpedo, for motor workers.

It may seem strange that, with all their outdoor sports activities, the Russians are also keen chess-players. But Russians have always been among the greatest masters of the chess-board, and the modern Russian worker is no exception. Mikhail Botvinnik, the electrical engineer, is a recent example of Russian chess-players who have gained world fame.

We have referred to the Russian Government's attitude towards religion—and how there is no place for this in education. But when we consider education in general we must realise that the Russians are enthusiasts. Education is free, and compulsory between the ages of 7 and 17, though there are exceptions towards the latter age. The majority of the most backward peoples of the Union have learnt to read and write, and the advance since pre-Revolution days, when only 24 per cent. of the population was literate, has been truly remarkable.

The number of children now attending elementary and secondary schools is about 40,000,000. Many children go on to specialised education, and there are about 3000 trade schools and nearly the same number for those who are learning railway and factory work.

NEARLY 900 UNIVERSITIES AND TECHNICAL COLLEGES OF UNIVERSITY LEVEL

Until recently boys and girls were educated together, but now separate schools are established in the towns, though the children meet together for play and recreation. This system is thought to make for better discipline.

There are nearly 900 universities and technical colleges of university level, ranging from Riga in the west to Vladivostok in the east, with 40,000 professors and instructors. Leningrad has a university founded by Peter the Great in 1703. The Empress Catherine founded Moscow's Imperial University about fifty years later ; but Moscow also boasts one of the biggest universities in the world, with over 1000 classrooms, a library of 1,200,000 books, and 800 acres of grounds.

It is the Estonian Republic, however, which possesses Russia's most revered university. Here, in tree-lined Tartu—better known to scholars all over the world as Dorpat—is a foundation more than three hundred years old and built on the site of a university founded in 1030. There could be no greater claim to distinction than Dorpat's claim to be the " Oxford of the Baltic."

THE TRAINING IN PRACTICAL MATTERS OF RUSSIA'S YOUNG CITIZENS

More than two million students are at work in technical schools. The Government's chief idea in education is to make the people " citizen-minded," to give them the training in practical matters that will equip them as citizens with Russia's great industrial and economic future in mind. So Russian children are taught science, including biology, which they have always loved to study.

In the early days of the Revolution children were taught that the family was unimportant, that it was the individual and his efforts that really mattered; but you cannot root out the love of family in Russia, and so family relations are once more encouraged, as they are in our own country.

RESPECT FOR THE GREAT MEN AND WOMEN OF RUSSIA'S PAST

Another good thing that has come back is the regard for such outstanding figures of pre-Revolution history as Peter the Great. In the Revolution everything was new. The old was dead, and only the new mattered. But today it is realised that the great men and women of old Russia have contributed to the making of today's Russia, and their stories are told and taught, and their achievements praised.

As with education and sport, so with literature, art, music, and so on, the goal is good citizenship, as the Russians understand it. Russians are eager readers, but today all printing is in the hands of the Government, who print only what they think will help the Russian to be a better citizen. There is a " Party Line " on literature, and prizes, including a Stalin Prize, are given for the " best " novels and other literary works. But no one could possibly win a prize if his or her book did not praise the Russian way of life, and the importance of the actual hard work the Russians are doing. One very gifted writer, Sholokhov, has published scarcely anything for many years, and may not do so until the " Party Line " changes, because he wants to take his own line. " Character-forming " and " citizen-forming " literature is the only kind that is thought good for Russians today.

ARTISTS WHO MAY NOT EXPRESS THEIR OWN IDEAS

Painters and sculptors also must conform to the general rules if they are to attain fame. The marks of good painting or sculpture are firstly subject-matter (something Russian and showing the value of strength), and secondly a photographic likeness. A new painting or bust of Stalin or Lenin stands a very good chance of success.

It is the same with music. Certain of the Russian composers whom the western world regards as important, and even great, are not acceptable, because they want to follow their own ideas of theme and treatment. They may want to compose an " idea " rather than something in the accepted " form," but the Soviet Minister who is responsible for music insists that music shall be " popular " and capable of being understood by everyone.

It may seem very strange to us that Russian writers, painters, and the like may not express their own ideas, or rather cannot express their own ideas if they want to be successful, but we must understand how Russian culture today, in every form, is part of the whole plan, which is to weld the Soviet Union into one great, uniform people. We may not agree with all this, but we must at least admit that the ideas of the rulers of Russia are sincere.

So we come to the central purpose of Stalin in moulding modern Russia—to make the Union the greatest industrial Power in the world. He aimed at doing this by successive Five-Year Plans, in which agriculture, industry, education, and social institutions are developed to the fullest extent possible—and particularly heavy industry. The first Plan was put into operation in 1928, and to date there have been six successive Plans.

A QUARTER OF A MILLION COLLECTIVE FARMS COVERING 900 MILLION ACRES

Agriculture, essential because it provides food and many raw materials for the workers, has made enormous strides, and this is largely due to the success of State farms and Collective farms. There are about 250,000 Collective farms, covering over 900 million acres, and about 4000 State farms, covering about one fifth of this area. On State farms men and women work like factory hands for wages. The Collective farm might more properly be called a village, since community life in every detail is organised on a village basis, with cottages, plots, school, health centre, club, and theatre. The peasants own their cottages and kitchen gardens, poultry, and varying numbers of live-stock. Some produce must be sold at fixed prices to the State, some may be sold through co-operative markets, some must be given to the local machine-tractor station, which supplies farm equipment. The rest, after allowing for reserves, is distributed among the Collective farmers.

The use of scientific methods of farming,

and of the latest types of farm machinery in ever-increasing numbers, has brought about a great increase in crop yield; the average grain harvest alone has shown an increase of between 50 and 100 per cent. over the figure reached at the time of the Revolution. By a process known as seed-vernalisation, evolved by the scientist Lysenko, the time of crop production is being steadily reduced, and this is of great benefit in those regions where frost binds the soil for the greater part of the year.

VAST AREAS WON FOR CROPS BY IRRIGATING THE LAND

Particular attention is being paid to irrigation and drainage, an increase of 1,650,000,000 acres for irrigated land being aimed at in the fourth Five-Year Plan and nearly the same increase for drained land. Farming and market gardening is also being intensified in the new industrial centres of the Urals, the Donets Basin (Donbas), the Kuznetsk Basin (Kuzbas), and farther east in Siberia, to assure the workers a good supply of local produce.

But the most spectacular planning is seen in the field of heavy industry. Here we find the essence of Russia's Five-Year Plans—to intensify the great switch of industry eastwards, to the Urals, to Siberia, to the Far East. The new industrial cities in the eastern foothills of the Urals, such as Magnitogorsk, Cheliabinsk, Sverdlovsk, Lipetsk, and Zlatoust, some of them mere villages in the 1920's or 1930's, or not even existing, are growing year by year. Great new iron and steel mills have gone up at Cheliabinsk, and in the Kazakh Republic, and similar works have been set going in Central Asia.

THE CITY OF YOUTH BUILT BY THE KOMSOMOLS

One of the most interesting industrial centres in all Russia, because it shows more clearly than anywhere else the energy and enthusiasm of Young Russia, is Komsomolsk, the " City of Youth," in the Khabarovsk region of the Far East. This centre of 300,000 inhabitants is dedicated to the Youth of the U.S.S.R. It has been built entirely by the Komsomols, or Young Communist League of the Soviet Union. Sixty per cent. of its population are under 30 years old. This centre of steel mills, shipbuilding ways, and oil refineries is something of which the young Russian is rightly proud.

New coalfields are being opened in the Urals, and in Southern and Eastern Siberia. The fourth Five-Year Plan alone called for the survey of 765 sites, including 250 in the Urals region and beyond, to produce in time a total annual output of 361,000,000 tons, or almost three times the total U.S.S.R. coal output of 1937! New heavy machine-building plant has been installed in the South Urals. Siberia and the Far East have created their own supplies of iron ore, deposits of 100,000,000 tons having been surveyed in Western Siberia alone. Kuzbas, in the Upper Ob valley, is already the second coalfield of the Soviet Union and one of the greatest industrial areas. The cotton industry is also moving east, new mills being started in many Siberian areas.

But the west is not being neglected. Donbas, north of the Black Sea, is the " coal-scuttle " of the Union, defying the rivalry of Kuzbas. Tremendous development is going on here in and around such cities as Stalino, Voroshilovsk, Mariupol, and Taganrog. A little to the west, the Dnieper Basin is humming louder than ever. The Lenin Power Station, with the mighty Dnieper Dam, has been rebuilt, and thirty new hydro-electric stations newly-built or planned. The fourth Five-Year Plan in itself called for an output of electric power in Russia 70 per cent. above that of 1940.

RUSSIA'S INLAND WATERWAYS AND HER PORTS FOR OVERSEAS TRADE

Moscow and Leningrad, too, are being ever more fully developed. In Leningrad, concentration is on shipyards, gasworks, and coalpits, and in the Moscow region on coal, hydro-electric works, and textiles. Rebuilding of Russia's railways has gone hand in hand with extension of its vital inland waterways, now estimated to total a quarter of a million miles in length, or nine times more than in late Tsarist days. Restoration of the 140-mile Stalin White Sea–Baltic Canal has been completed, and these northern seas linked with the Black Sea by the Don–Volga Canal opened in 1952.

Important as are Russia's inland waterways, we must not suppose that the Union is behindhand in the larger maritime sphere. Nor, when we see the Baltic peoples as men with seafaring in their blood, must we forget that many another area of Russia has produced its great sailors. The Union indeed conducts a considerable sea traffic in such wares as timber, flax, furs, oil, coal, grain, and fish, and this is constantly increasing. Ports on the Baltic and Black Seas, on the Arctic and Pacific Oceans, at one time poorly equipped, have been improved out of all recognition by the construction of new docks, cold storage plants, grain elevators, warehouses, and so on, and by the installation of the most modern loading and unloading devices.

Of the northern ports, Leningrad and Archangel are icebound in winter, though strenuous efforts are being made to lessen their period of idleness. Murmansk, however, where so many of our gallant British convoys came through with vital supplies for Russia during the Second World War, does not fare so badly. New ports, such as Igarka (which did not exist until 1929), along the Arctic sea route between Murmansk and Vladivostok, are in regular use every summer. Vladivostok itself, the former wooden village which is now Russia's most important export city in the Far East, Pacific naval base of the Union, and terminus of the Trans-Siberian Railway, is kept open by icebreakers all the year round.

RUSSIA'S EXTENSIVE SEARCH FOR OIL IN THE AZERBAIJAN REGION

But generally speaking the most important ports lie around the Black Sea, and deal with shipments of oil and grain, timber and tobacco. Such are Odessa, Nikolaiev, Kherson, Novorossisk, Tuapse, and Sukhum. Odessa, chief seaport of the Ukraine, and one of the biggest cities in Russia, has a long and rich maritime history. Today it is concerned to a considerable extent with traffic in oil, the extraction and refining of which is becoming one of Russia's most important industries. The oil industry is centred chiefly in Azerbaijan, where work has been going on towards the location of petroleum resources at no fewer than 2660 new well-sites. The Kazakh and Uzbek Republics are also fairly big oil producers, and Georgia, the state in which Stalin was born and brought up, is entering the field. Georgia, incidentally, finds time to be the health resort of the entire Soviet Union. Coal-mining and oil-refining

may burden the air in some regions, but in others there are mountain sanatoria and splendid medicinal waters, while the Black Sea coast is studded with " the seaside."

The magnitude of all Russia's industrial development, backed by the enthusiasm of the people, and linked and quickened by roadway, canal, sea-lane, and airway, almost defies imagination. To put it in a practical way, the fourth Five-Year Plan alone called for an increase in industrial output of almost 50 per cent. over the 1940 figure, at a total cost of 250,300,000,000 roubles.

THE KREMLIN SETS THE TARGETS AND THE PEOPLE CARRY THEM OUT

The policy-makers in the Kremlin in Moscow set the targets, and the Russian people carry them out. That is the secret of Russia's great and growing strength—abounding energy, ably and fearlessly directed. Added to these, there is one thing which the Tsars did not know—did not need to know—and which the revolutionaries of 1917 stupidly forgot. The revolutionaries said, " From each according to his capacity; to each according to his need." Stalin's motto was, " From each according to his capacity; to each according to his *work*."

So it was that when, in 1935, a coal-miner of the Donets Basin named Alexei Stakhanov found how to hew much more than the normal amount of coal in one shift, Stalin set him up as a model. " Stakhanovites," or record-breakers, had their names displayed on factory boards and were rewarded with extra pay. The system spread to peasant labour, and today it is general throughout Russia, with prizes and medals, and honours such as " Hero of Socialist Labour."

THE GREAT OPPORTUNITY WHICH LIES AHEAD OF RUSSIA

The Russia of history had her great men and women, and her great moments; but she now has the opportunity of becoming and remaining one of the greatest peoples the world has ever seen. The material well-being of her citizens, and the fullest development of her vast riches, are not in themselves enough. A truly great Russia is a Russia which keeps before herself, and before the whole world, the ideal of universal brotherhood and mutual understanding.

PICTURES OF U.S.S.R.

MOSCOW, CAPITAL OF THE VAST SOVIET UNION, AND ITS RIVER AS SEEN FROM THE KREMLIN

THE SUKHAREV TOWER IN
MOSCOW

THE PLANETARIUM AT
MOSCOW

THE CATHEDRAL OF ST. ISAAC
IN LENINGRAD

THE RAILWAY STATION AT STALINGRAD, THE GREAT PORT ON THE RIVER VOLGA

THE BRIDGE ACROSS THE RIVER NEVA IN THE GREAT PORT OF LENINGRAD

THE VILLAGE OF BALACLAVA, ON THE SHORES OF THE BLACK SEA

HEADQUARTERS OF THE STATE BANK AT
KHARKOV IN THE UKRAINE

AN APARTMENT HOUSE NEAR THE MOSCOW
RADIO STATION

A SPLENDID SUSPENSION BRIDGE OVER THE DNIEPER RIVER AT KIEV

YALTA, IN THE CRIMEA, WHERE CHURCHILL, ROOSEVELT, AND STALIN MET IN FEBRUARY 1945

THE NORTH RUSSIAN SEAPORT
OF ARCHANGEL

THE YENISEI RIVER BRIDGE ON THE
TRANS-SIBERIAN RAILWAY

A SQUARE IN BAKU

A STREET IN TIFLIS

THE CITY AND HARBOUR OF GORKI, ONCE KNOWN AS NIJNI NOVGOROD

PUBLIC GARDENS IN IVANOVO

A BROAD STREET IN VORONEZH

LENIN SQUARE IN THE TOWN OF SVERDLOVSK, FORMERLY KNOWN AS EKATERINBURG

WORKERS' DWELLINGS IN MOSCOW

THE MAXIM GORKI THEATRE IN STALINGRAD

A COLLECTIVE FARMERS' CLUB IN KUBAN

THE POST OFFICE IN RIGA,
CAPITAL OF LATVIA

THE OLD TOWN GATE IN TALLINN, FORMERLY
KNOWN AS REVAL, CAPITAL OF ESTONIA

A GENERAL VIEW OF KAUNAS, FORMERLY KNOWN AS KOVNO, THE CAPITAL OF LITHUANIA

THE RIVER FRONT AT RIGA

A GENERAL VIEW OF TALLINN

A SCHOOL, AT ONE TIME USED AS THE
PARLIAMENT HOUSE, AT KAUNAS

THE CATHEDRAL AT RIGA
IN LATVIA

One Thousand Poems of All Times and All Countries

THE PIED PIPER OF HAMELIN

Hameln, or Hamelin as the poet calls it, is a town in Germany, and it is said that a strange man once charmed all its rats away, in the Middle Ages. Legend also says that he charmed the children away because the Mayor and the townsmen did not keep their promise to pay him. Here is the old story put into splendid verse by Robert Browning.

Hamelin Town's in Brunswick,
  By famous Hanover city;
The river Weser, deep and wide,
Washes its wall on the southern side;
A pleasanter spot you never spied;
  But, when begins my ditty,
Almost five hundred years ago,
To see the townsfolk suffer so
  From vermin was a pity.

Rats!
  They fought the dogs, and killed the
    cats,
  And bit the babies in the cradles,
And ate the cheeses out of the vats,
  And licked the soup from the cooks' own
    ladles,
Split open the kegs of salted sprats,
Made nests inside men's Sunday hats,
And even spoiled the women's chats,
  By drowning their speaking
  With shrieking and squeaking
In fifty different sharps and flats.

At last the people in a body
  To the Town Hall came flocking;
" 'Tis clear," cried they, " our Mayor's a
    noddy;
  And as for our Corporation—shocking
To think we buy gowns lined with ermine
For dolts that can't or won't determine
What's best to rid us of our vermin!
You hope, because you're old and obese,
To find in the furry civic robe ease?

Rouse up, sirs! Give your brains a
    racking
To find the remedy we're lacking,
Or, sure as fate, we'll send you packing! "
At this the Mayor and Corporation
Quaked with a mighty consternation.

An hour they sat in council;
  At length the Mayor broke silence:
" For a guilder I'd my ermine gown sell;
  I wish I were a mile hence!
It's easy to bid one rack one's brain—
I'm sure my poor head aches again,
I've scratched it so, and all in vain.
Oh, for a trap, a trap, a trap! "
Just as he said this, what should hap
At the chamber door but a gentle tap?
" Bless us! " cried the Mayor, " what's
    that? "
(With the Corporation as he sat,
Looking little though wondrous fat;
Nor brighter was his eye, nor moister
Than a too-long-opened oyster,
Save when at noon his paunch grew
    mutinous
For a plate of turtle green and glutinous)
" Only a scraping of shoes on the mat?
Anything like the sound of a rat
Makes my heart go pit-a-pat! "

Come in! the Mayor cried, looking
    bigger:
And in did come the strangest figure!

POEMS · SONGS · BALLADS · VERSES AND RHYMES WITH MUSIC

His queer long coat from heel to head
Was half of yellow and half of red;
And he himself was tall and thin,
With sharp blue eyes, each like a pin,
And light loose hair, yet swarthy skin,
No tuft on cheek nor beard on chin,
But lips where smiles went out and in;
There was no guessing his kith and kin:
And nobody could enough admire
The tall man and his quaint attire.
Quoth one: " It's as my great-grandsire,
Starting up at the Trump of Doom's tone,
Had walked this way from his painted
    tombstone! "

He advanced to the council-table:
And, " Please your honours," said he,
    " I'm able,
By means of a secret charm to draw,
    All creatures living beneath the sun,
    That creep or swim or fly or run,
After me so as you never saw!
And I chiefly use my charm
On creatures that do people harm,
The mole and toad and newt and viper;
And people call me the Pied Piper."
(And here they noticed round his neck
    A scarf of red and yellow stripe,
To match with his coat of the self-same
    check;
    And at the scarf's end hung a pipe,
And his fingers, they noticed, were ever
    straying
As if impatient to be playing
Upon this pipe, as low it dangled
Over his vesture so old-fangled.)
" Yet," said he, " poor piper as I am,
In Tartary I freed the Cham,
    Last June, from his huge swarm of gnats;
I eased in Asia the Nizam
    Of a monstrous brood of vampire-bats:
And, as for what your brain bewilders,
If I can rid your town of rats
Will you give me a thousand guilders? "
" One?   Fifty thousand! " was the ex-
    clamation
Of the astonished Mayor and Corporation.

Into the street the Piper stept,
    Smiling first a little smile,
As if he knew what magic slept
    In his quiet pipe the while;
Then, like a musical adept,
To blow the pipe his lips he wrinkled,
And green and blue his sharp eyes twin-
    kled,
Like a candle flame where salt is sprinkled;
And ere three shrill notes the pipe uttered,
You heard as if an army muttered;

And the muttering grew to a grumbling;
And the grumbling grew to a mighty
    rumbling;
And out of the houses the rats came
    tumbling,
Great rats, small rats, lean rats, brawny
    rats,
Brown rats, black rats, grey rats, tawny rats,
Grave old plodders, gay young friskers,
    Fathers, mothers, uncles, cousins,
Cocking tails and pricking whiskers,
    Families by tens and dozens,
Brothers, sisters, husbands, wives—
Followed the Piper for their lives.
From street to street he piped advancing,
And step for step they followed dancing,
Until they came to the River Weser,
    Wherein all plunged and perished,
Save one who, stout as Julius Caesar,
Swam across and lived to carry
    (As he the manuscript he cherished)
To Rat-land home his commentary:
Which was, " At the first shrill notes of
    the pipe
I heard a sound as of scraping tripe,
And putting apples, wondrous ripe,
Into a cider-press's gripe:
And a moving away of pickle-tub boards,
And a leaving ajar of conserve-cupboards,
And a drawing the corks of train-oil flasks,
And a breaking the hoops of butter-casks:
And it seemed as if a voice
    (Sweeter far than by harp or by psaltery
Is breathed) called out, ' Oh rats, rejoice!
    The world is grown to one vast dry-
    saltery!
So munch on, crunch on, take your
    nuncheon,
Breakfast, supper, dinner, luncheon! '
And just as a bulky sugar-puncheon,
All ready staved, like a great sun shone
Glorious scarce an inch before me,
Just as methought it said, ' Come, bore
    me! '
I found the Weser rolling o'er me."

You should have heard the Hamelin people
Ringing the bells till they rocked the
    steeple.
" Go," cried the Mayor, " and get long
    poles!
Poke out the nests and block up the holes!
Consult with carpenters and builders,
And leave in our town not even a trace
Of the rats! "—when suddenly, up the face
Of the Piper perked in the market-place,
With a " First, if you please, my thousand
    guilders! "

A thousand guilders! The Mayor looked
     blue;
So did the Corporation too.
For council dinners made rare havoc
With claret, moselle, vin-de-grave, hock;
And half the money would replenish
Their cellar's biggest butt with Rhenish.
To pay this sum to a wandering fellow
With a gipsy coat of red and yellow!
" Beside," quoth the Mayor with a know-
     ing wink,
" Our business was done at the river's
     brink;
We saw with our eyes the vermin sink,
And what's dead can't come to life, I think.
So, friend, we're not the folks to shrink
From the duty of giving you something for
     drink,
And a matter of money to put in your
     poke;
But as for the guilders, what we spoke
Of them, as you very well know, was in
     joke.
Beside, our losses have made us thrifty.
A thousand guilders! Come, take fifty! "

The Piper's face fell, and he cried:
" No trifling! I can't wait, beside!
I've promised to visit by dinner-time
Bagdat, and accept the prime
Of the head cook's pottage, all he's rich in,
For having left, in the Caliph's kitchen,
Of a nest of scorpions no survivor:
With him I proved no bargain-driver,
With you, don't think I'll bate a stiver!
And folks who put me in a passion
May find me pipe to another fashion."

" How? " cried the Mayor, " d'ye think
     I'll brook
Being worse treated than a cook?
Insulted by a lazy ribald
With idle pipe and vesture piebald?
You threaten us, fellow? Do your worst,
Blow your pipe there till you burst! "

Once more he stept into the street
     And to his lips again
     Laid his long pipe of smooth, straight
     cane;
And ere he blew three notes (such sweet
Soft notes as yet musician's cunning
     Never gave the enraptured air)
There was a rustling that seemed like a
     bustling
Of merry crowds justling at pitching and
     hustling,
Small feet were pattering, wooden shoes
     clattering,

Little hands clapping and little tongues
     chattering,
And, like fowls in a farmyard when barley
     is scattering,
Out came the children running.
All the little boys and girls,
With rosy cheeks and flaxen curls,
And sparkling eyes and teeth like pearls,
Tripping and skipping, ran merrily after
The wonderful music with shouting and
     laughter.

The Mayor was dumb, and the Council
     stood
As if they were changed into blocks of wood,
Unable to move a step, or cry
To the children merrily skipping by,
And could only follow with the eye
That joyous crowd at the Piper's back.
But how the Mayor was on the rack,
And the wretched Council's bosoms beat,
As the Piper turned from the High Street
To where the Weser rolled its waters
Right in the way of their sons and
     daughters!
However, he turned from South to West,
And to Koppelberg Hill his steps addressed.
And after him the children pressed;
Great was the joy in every breast.
" He never can cross that mighty top!
He's forced to let the piping drop,
And we shall see our children stop! "
When, lo, as they reached the mountain-
     side,
A wondrous portal opened wide,
As if a cavern was suddenly hollowed;
And the Piper advanced and the children
     followed.
And when all were in to the very last,
The door in the mountain-side shut fast.
Did I say all? No! One was lame,
     And could not dance the whole of the
     way;
And in after years, if you would blame
     His sadness, he was used to say;
" It's dull in our town since my playmates
     left!
I can't forget that I'm bereft
Of all the pleasant sights they see,
Which the Piper also promised me.
For he led us, he said, to a joyous land,
Joining the town and just at hand,
Where waters gushed and fruit trees grew,
And flowers put forth a fairer hue,
And everything was strange and new.
The sparrows were brighter than peacocks
     here,
And their dogs outran our fallow deer,

And honey-bees had lost their stings,
And horses were born with eagles' wings;
And just as I became assured—
My lame foot would be speedily cured,
The music stopped and I stood still,
And found myself outside the hill,
Left alone against my will,
To go now limping as before,
And never hear of that country more ! "

Alas, alas for Hamelin !
  There came into many a burgher's pate
  A text which says that heaven's gate
  Opes to the rich at as easy rate
As the needle's eye takes a camel in!
The Mayor sent East, West, North, and
    South
To offer the Piper, by word of mouth,
  Wherever it was men's lot to find him,
Silver and gold to his heart's content,
If he'd only return the way he went,
  And bring the children behind him.
But when they saw 'twas a lost endeavour,
And Piper and dancers were gone for ever,
They made a decree that lawyers never
  Should think their records dated duly
If, after the day of the month and year,
These words did not as well appear:
" And so long after what happened here
  On the twenty-second of July,
Thirteen hundred and seventy-six ";
And the better in memory to fix
The place of the children's last retreat,
They called it the Pied Piper's Street,
Where anyone playing on pipe or tabor
Was sure for the future to lose his labour.
Nor suffered they hostelry or tavern
  To shock with mirth a street so solemn;
But opposite the place of the cavern
  They wrote the story on a column,
And on the great church window painted
The same, to make the world acquainted
How their children were stolen away;
And there it stands to this very day.
And I must not omit to say
That in Transylvania there's a tribe
Of alien people who ascribe
The outlandish ways and dress,
On which their neighbours lay such stress,
To their fathers and mothers having risen
Out of some subterraneous prison,
Into which they were trepanned
Long time ago in a mighty band
Out of Hamelin town in Brunswick land,
But how or why, they don't understand.

So, Willy, let me and you be wipers
Of scores out with all men—especially pipers !

And, whether they pipe us free from rats or
    from mice,
If we've promised them aught, let us keep our
    promise !

ON LOOKING INTO CHAPMAN'S HOMER

No sonnet has been quoted more frequently than this by John Keats. The realms of gold are bookland. The simile of Homer's breadth of outlook amazing the discoverer as the expanse of the Pacific amazed the first Spanish pioneer is as apt as it is picturesque, but Keats made a mistake here. That pioneer was not Cortez but Balboa.

MUCH have I travelled in the realms of
    gold,
  And many goodly states and kingdoms
    seen;
  Round many western islands have I
    been
Which bards in fealty to Apollo hold.
Oft of one wide expanse had I been told
  That deep-browed Homer ruled as his
    demesne;
  Yet did I never breathe its pure serene
Till I heard Chapman speak out loud and
    bold:
Then felt I like some watcher of the skies
  When a new planet swims into his ken;
Or like stout Cortez when with eagle eyes
  He stared at the Pacific—and all his
    men
Looked at each other with a wild surmise—
  Silent, upon a peak in Darien.

TO MY MOTHER'S MEMORY

The standpoint of this poem, by Sir William Watson, is a Pennine summit, looking westward toward the Lakeland mountains and eastward over the Yorkshire dales. It is the lowlier dales that command the poet's eye, for there, he tells us, was born his mother, from whom he inherited his poetic vision. This poem is quoted from Hodder and Stoughton's edition of a hundred poems by Sir William.

THIS is the summit, wild and lone.
    Westward the loftier mountains
      stand.
Let me look eastward on mine own
    Ancestral land.

O sing me songs, O tell me tales,
Of yonder valleys at my feet!
She was a daughter of those dales,
    A daughter sweet.

Oft did she speak of homesteads there,
And faces that her childhood knew.
She speaks no more; and scarce I dare
    To deem it true

That somehow she can still behold
Sunlight and moonlight, earth and sea,
Which were among the gifts untold
    She gave to me.

THE MULBERRY BUSH

Here we go round the mul-berry bush, the mul-berry bush, the mul-berry bush,

Here we go round the mul-berry bush On a cold and frost-y morn-ing.

This is the way we clap our hands, we clap our hands, we clap our hands:
This is the way we brush our hair, we brush our hair, we brush our hair:

This is the way we clap our hands, on a cold and frost-y morn-ing.
This is the way we brush our hair, on a cold and frost-y morn-ing.

LITTLE VERSES FOR VERY LITTLE PEOPLE

HEAVEN KEEP MY GIRL FOR ME

Brown eyes, straight nose;
  Dirt pies, rumpled clothes;
Torn books, spoilt toys;
Arch looks, unlike a boy's;
Little rages, obvious arts
(Three her age is); cakes, tarts;
Falling down off chairs;
Breaking crown down stairs;
Catching flies on the pane;
Deep sighs—cause not plain;
Bribing you with kisses
For a few farthing blisses;
Wide awake, as you hear,
" Mercy's sake, quiet, dear! "
New shoes, new frock;
Vague views of what's o'clock
When it's time to go to bed,
And scorn sublime for what is said;
Folded hands, saying prayers;
Understands not, nor cares;
Thinks it odd, smiles away;
Yet may God hear her pray!
Bedgown white, kiss dolly;
Good-night! that's Polly.
Last asleep, as you see;
Heaven keep my girl for me!

William Brighty Rands

KINDNESS TO ANIMALS

Little children, never give
  Pain to things that feel and live.
Let the gentle robin come
For the crumbs you save at home;
As his meat you throw along
He'll repay you with a song.
Never hurt the timid hare,
Peeping from her green grass lair,
Let her come and sport and play
On the lawn at close of day.
The little lark goes soaring high
To the bright windows of the sky,
Singing as if 'twere always spring,
And fluttering on an untired wing;
Oh! let him sing his happy song,
Nor do these gentle creatures wrong.

Anonymous

THE LITTLE GENTLEMAN

Make your meals, my little man,
  Always like a gentleman;
Wash your face and hands with care,
Change your shoes, and brush your hair;
Then, so fresh, and clean, and neat,
Come and take your proper seat:
Do not loiter and be late,
Making other people wait;
Do not rudely point or touch;
Do not eat and drink too much;

Finish what you have before
You even ask or send for more;
Never crumble or destroy
Food that others might enjoy;
They who idly crumbs will waste
Often want a loaf to taste!
Never spill your milk or tea,
Never rude or noisy be;
Never choose the daintiest food,
Be content with what is good;
Seek in all things that you can
To be a little gentleman.

Anonymous

HOW THE LEAVES CAME DOWN

I'll tell you how the leaves came down.
  The great Tree to his children said:
" You're getting sleepy, Yellow and
    Brown,
  Yes, very sleepy, little Red.
  It is quite time to go to bed."

" Ah! " begged each silly, pouting leaf,
  " Let us a little longer stay;
Dear Father Tree, behold our grief!
  'Tis such a very pleasant day,
  We do not want to go away."

So, just for one more merry day
  To the great Tree the leaflets clung,
Frolicked and danced, and had their way,
  Upon the autumn breezes swung,
  Whispering all their sports among:

" Perhaps the great Tree will forget,
  And let us stay until the spring,
If we all beg, and coax, and fret."
  But the great Tree did no such thing;
  He smiled to hear them whispering.

" Come, children, all to bed," he cried;
  And, ere the leaves could urge their
    prayer,
He shook his head, and far and wide,
  Fluttering and rustling everywhere,
  Down sped the leaflets through the air.

I saw them; on the ground they lay,
  Golden and red, a huddled swarm,
Waiting till one from far away,
  White bedclothes heaped upon her arm,
  Should come to wrap them safe and
  warm.

The great bare Tree looked down and
    smiled.
  " Good-night, dear little leaves," he said.
And from below each sleepy child
  Replied, " Good-night," and murmurèd,
  " It is so nice to go to bed! "

Susan Coolidge

Imperishable Thoughts of Men Enshrined in the Books of the World

Shakespeare's Comedies

WE have given examples of the tales told by the first great English poet Chaucer, and also by Spenser in his Faerie Queene; and now we come to Shakespeare, the greatest of all the poets. Many of his songs and fine passages are found in our poetry pages, but in this section we glance at his great plays, the Comedies, Tragedies, Histories, and Fantasies. Here we outline the stories of ten of his Comedies. A poet can only be known by reading him in his own words, but first it may be well to tell each story briefly as an introduction to the poet's own manner of telling it. A Comedy is a picture of human life that leads brightly to a happy ending. The Comedies summarised here are arranged in the order in which Shakespeare wrote them. That is the best way, because the poet's skill as a writer grew as he wrote more plays. The earliest plays depend chiefly on their plots, and on the clearing up of a tangle of difficulties. It is so in The Two Gentlemen of Verona and The Comedy of Errors. But later, as in The Merchant of Venice and As You Like It, Shakespeare displayed a wider view of life and character and a deeper thought.

THE TWO GENTLEMEN OF VERONA

THERE were two gentlemen in the town of Verona, named Valentine and Proteus, who were friends and close companions, until one of them fell in love with a lady of Verona named Julia. It was Proteus who had fallen in love, and that was quite a good reason for his refusing to accompany Valentine on his travels, though perhaps not so good a reason for Valentine to make fun of him. So Valentine set out on his travels alone, going first to Milan.

Meanwhile, thanks to an uncle of Proteus, the father of that young gentleman had been urged to send his son away, so that, when he grew old, Proteus might have no reason to regret that in his youth he had been a stay-at-home, and had neglected to see the world. His father, Antonio, therefore, sent his son after Valentine to Milan, that he might have the company of his friend, which he had before refused.

When Proteus reached Milan the comedy had begun, for, behold Valentine, who had scoffed at his friend for being in love with Julia, now himself deeply in love with Silvia, the bewitching daughter of the Duke of Milan. And his case was worse, for, being poor, he could not hope that the Duke would let him marry his daughter; whereas Proteus was at least in love with a lady of his own station in life. Like Romeo with his Juliet, Valentine's only plan was to marry his Silvia without her father's consent, and he had quite made up his mind to climb to her window and carry her away when Proteus overtook him in Milan.

Valentine's scheme was quickly upset, for no sooner had he disclosed it to his friend than Proteus, on seeing the lovely Silvia, also fell in love with her, and began to forget his Julia left in Verona. Nay, worse ; he betrayed Valentine's intention to the Duke.

The Duke now wished to convict Valentine of his intention to abduct Silvia, without disclosing to him how he had come by the knowledge of the plan. So, pretending that he himself was in love with a widow of Milan, he asked Valentine what he would advise him to do—rather a foolish question, one might think, for a duke who had already been married to ask a young man who was still unwedded. But the wisdom of the Duke lay in the fact that he knew none to be so foolish as a young man in love.

Judge if the Duke was wise or foolish when Valentine innocently advised him to do exactly what he had himself

ROMANCE · HISTORIES · DRAMAS · ESSAYS · WORLD CLASSICS

purposed doing—to carry away the lady. He even lent the Duke his own coat as a disguise, and in the pocket of the coat the Duke found a letter from Valentine addressed to his own daughter.

This discovery gave the Duke an excuse for banishing Valentine from Milan, and he now set about his own plans to marry Silvia with all speed to a foolish young nobleman named Thurio; but he enlisted the services of Proteus to help forward the match, little thinking that Valentine's friend was in love with Silvia.

Proteus was expected to give so poor an account of Valentine to Silvia, and so glowing an account of Thurio, that the maiden could not but decide to forget Valentine in favour of the foolish nobleman. But, of course, Proteus did nothing of the kind. He made his own suit to the lady, and plainly showed her that he was in love with her.

One night, Proteus, with Thurio and some musicians, came beneath the lattice window of Silvia in the court of the palace, and sang a love-song to her.

But Silvia was not the only lady who heard this love-song. Julia, no longer able to endure the absence of her lover, had left Verona disguised as a page, and, following Proteus to Milan, she had overheard this song.

When Proteus thinks himself alone, he declares his love to Silvia, who comes to the window; but she chides him for his faithlessness to his friend Valentine, to whom she declares herself betrothed; and he tells her that both the lady he loved at Verona and Valentine are dead, and pleads to have Silvia's portrait. This she promises him, saying that she is loth to be worshipped by him, but as she believes him false he is the better fitted " to worship shadows and adore false shapes," meaning that he can admire her portrait, but need not admire herself, as she does not care for him. All this is overheard by Julia, hidden in the shadow.

Next day Proteus sends Julia—who, disguised as a boy, has applied to him to be employed as his page—for the portrait, and gives her a ring to take to Silvia, the very ring Julia herself had given him before he left Verona. She is comforted to find that Silvia rejects his suit, and that she is displeased with him for his faithlessness.

Silvia, true to Valentine, has determined to escape from Milan, and by the aid of a courtier named Eglamour she sets off towards Mantua. But in a forest they meet with outlaws, and Silvia is captured.

Happily, when Valentine had been banished from Milan he too had fallen in with these very outlaws, who spared his life on his promising to become their leader, as they would be honoured by having a nobleman for their chief. So Silvia had fallen into the hands of her own true love!

Her escape from Milan led to the Duke and the others following in pursuit, Julia going with the party as page to Proteus; and they too were attacked by the outlaws, the Duke and Thurio being captured and brought before Valentine. There they saw Silvia, and the foolish Thurio exclaimed: " Yonder is Silvia, and Silvia's mine." But Valentine dared him but to breathe her name, and the cowardly Thurio, seeing the bold lover angry, and knowing his own life to be in danger, forthwith changed his tune.

The Duke, admiring the boldness of Valentine as greatly as he detested the cowardliness of Thurio, was at once won over to his daughter's side, and gave her to Valentine, who took the opportunity of securing a free pardon for his fellow outlaws, while Julia had meanwhile disclosed to Proteus how her love for him had brought her after him from Verona, and he was once more at her feet.

So the return to Milan meant happiness for all; even for the foolish Thurio, for if he had lost the Duke's daughter he had saved his own cowardly neck, which he valued more highly.

THE COMEDY OF ERRORS

THERE was a rich merchant of Syracuse, named Aegeon, who had twin boys, and these he christened with the one name Antipholus. It so happened that at the same place there were two other twin boys, whose mother was very poor, and Aegeon conceived the idea of buying these poor children, who had both been named Dromio, to bring them up as servants to his own twins. But when returning to his home by sea a great storm arose, and the merchant himself, together with one of his own children and one of the Dromios, was rescued and taken to Syracuse, while, unknown to him, his wife, Aemilia, and the other two children were

SCENES FROM THE MERCHANT OF VENICE

PORTIA AND NERISSA LEARN FROM BASSANIO THAT ALL ANTONIO'S SHIPS HAVE BEEN LOST

BASSANIO AND LORENZO MEET SHYLOCK'S SERVANT LAUNCELOT AND HIS BLIND FATHER, OLD GOBBO

rescued and taken to Ephesus, Aemilia, however, being separated from the children.

Time went past, and the twin children grew to manhood without ever hearing of each other. When Antipholus of Syracuse and his attendant Dromio were nearly twenty years of age they set out to search for their brothers, but Aegeon, thinking the searchers lost as they had not returned after some years, himself went forth to seek for them. At length Aegeon, his money all spent, found himself in Ephesus, where, admitting that he was a merchant of Syracuse, he was thrown into prison by the Duke of Ephesus, because the Duke of Syracuse had recently killed a merchant of Ephesus who had been unable to ransom himself.

Now, we must know that the son whom Aegeon had lost in the shipwreck, together with the other Dromio, had lived all this time in the town of Ephesus, while Aegeon's wife, Aemilia, had become the head of a priory. Antipholus of Ephesus was a favourite of the Duke. We can therefore see how the errors would begin when Antipholus of Syracuse, of whom Aegeon was in search, together with his particular Dromio, also arrived in Ephesus. As Antipholus of Ephesus had married a charming lady of that town, and his Dromio had married also, while both their brothers were still unmarried and knew nothing of each other, the newcomers to Ephesus had not been there long before everything was in a muddle. The one Antipholus mistook the other's Dromio for his own servant. Dromio of Ephesus mistook Antipholus of Syracuse for his master; while Antipholus was mistaken by his brother's wife for her own husband. And so on, until none of them knew whether he stood on his head or his heels.

Out of the last " error " came the explanation which put all things straight again. For Antipholus of Syracuse, naturally denying to Adriana, the wife of his brother, that he was her husband, and behaving so strangely (as she thought), had to take refuge from her and her friends, who would have had him bound as a madman, by running into the priory of which, unknown to him, his own mother was the prioress.

Adriana appealed to the Duke, who was passing the priory at the time, and he was asking for an explanation when her own husband and his attendant came up to complain of a jeweller who was charging him for a debt which he had not incurred, the debtor really being the Antipholus who was inside the priory.

At this very moment Aegeon, too, was being taken round the town as a prisoner held at ransom, and when he saw Antipholus and Dromio of Ephesus he thought they were the son and attendant of whom he was in search, though they, of course, denied all knowledge of him; but when Aemilia herself appeared she asked the aged prisoner if he was indeed the father of the twins named Antipholus. This he acknowledged, and she then told him that she was their mother and his wife, but, being parted from the children by some fishermen of Corinth after they were rescued, and believing herself alone in the world, she had entered this priory, of which she was now the head.

The tangle was soon made straight after this explanation; old Aegeon was released, and the family united after so many years and so many " errors." The bond of friendship, too, was strengthened when Antipholus of Syracuse became the husband of Luciana, sister of Adriana.

THE MERCHANT OF VENICE

ANTONIO was the name of a very rich and generous man who lived in Venice long ago, and whose merchandise many ships carried over the seas to distant lands. Though Antonio was so rich, his greatest friend, Bassanio, was a comparatively poor man.

Now, this Bassanio loved very deeply a lady, both beautiful and rich, named Portia, who lived in a distant place called Belmont, and, when once he desired to visit her, he confessed to Antonio that he could not go there for lack of money. So Antonio began to arrange for Bassanio to get the necessary gold.

Unfortunately at that time Antonio's ships were all at sea, so that his wealth was on the waters, and for that reason he had no ready money. At length he determined to borrow from an old Jew, who was a regular money-lender. Shylock was his name, and he hated Antonio because that kind merchant would always lend his money without charging interest,

SHYLOCK REFUSES TO BE MERCIFUL

JESSICA, DAUGHTER OF THE RICH JEW SHYLOCK

GRATIANO, A FRIEND OF BASSANIO

ANTONIO AND HIS FRIEND SALARINO, GUARDED BY THE GAOLER, PLEAD WITH SHYLOCK, WHO REFUSES TO HEED THE REQUEST THAT HE BREAK THE BOND

thus injuring Shylock's trade. He also knew that Antonio despised him; and, above all, he disliked Antonio because he was a Christian. So when his enemy, as he regarded Antonio, came to borrow money from him, thoughts of revenge passed through the Jew's mind.

THE STRANGE AND TERRIBLE BARGAIN THE JEW MADE WITH ANTONIO

If only Antonio's ships were wrecked, or if pirates would steal from them, Antonio would not be able to repay the loan, said Shylock. But the cunning Jew pretended to make a bargain in jest, and offered to lend the money on condition that Antonio repaid it in three months' time, or else forfeited a pound of his own flesh! Antonio did not doubt that his ships would return in time, so agreed cheerfully to this strange bargain, and got the money which enabled Bassanio, accompanied by his friend Gratiano, to go on his visit to Portia, the rich heiress.

It was known that when Portia's father was dying he gave her three caskets—one of gold, one of silver, and one of lead. On each of these was an inscription. " Who chooseth me shall gain what many men desire," was written on the gold one; " Who chooseth me shall get as much as he deserves," on the silver one; and on the lead one were the words, " Who chooseth me must give and hazard all he hath." Inside one of these caskets was a portrait of Portia, and whichever one of the men who professed to love her should choose that casket was to wed her.

THE WORDS OF MOCKERY WHICH GREETED THE FOOLISH SUITOR

Various suitors came to try their fortune in this strange lottery of love, and those who were conceited chose the gold or silver caskets. The suitor who chose the golden casket was mocked with these ominous words:

All that glisters is not gold;
Often have you heard that told:
Many a man his life hath sold
But my outside to behold:
Gilded tombs do worms infold.
Had you been as wise as bold,
Young in limbs, in judgment old,
Your answer had not been inscrolled:
Fare you well; your suit is cold.

But now came Bassanio, whom Portia really loved, and she and her maid Nerissa trembled as he made the fateful choice, and this dainty song was heard:

Tell me where is fancy bred,
Or in the heart or in the head?
How begot, how nourished?
    Reply, reply.
It is engendered in the eyes,
With gazing fed; and fancy dies
In the cradle where it lies.
    Let us all ring fancy's knell:
    I'll begin it—Ding, dong, bell.

But of course he chooses the leaden casket which contains the portrait.

In the midst of all their joy at this happy choice, Bassanio receives a letter from Antonio, who says that all his ships are lost, and Shylock is demanding his pound of flesh; but adds that he would gladly die for his friend if Bassanio were only there to bid him farewell.

Bassanio told his lady the unhappy story, and she bade him haste away to be with his friend; but as soon as he had gone she sent to her cousin, a famous lawyer, Doctor Bellario, to borrow his robes, and with these for herself, and the dress of a lawyer's clerk, which she had borrowed for Nerissa, Portia and her maid set out for Venice.

THE WISDOM OF PORTIA IN HER GREAT DEFENCE OF ANTONIO

Assembled in the Court of Justice there were all those interested in the strange case—Antonio, Bassanio, Shylock, Gratiano, the Duke of Venice, and many others—when Nerissa, dressed as a lawyer's clerk, entered and read a letter from Doctor Bellario, in which he wrote that he was ill; but his young friend, Doctor Balthazar, from Rome, would defend the case ably, and that he had never known " so young a body with so old a head." Thus was Portia, disguised as a lawyer, announced.

Now, Portia was as wise as she was beautiful, and in her speech she first of all raised the hopes of Shylock until he praised her for " a Daniel come to judgment." He was entitled to the pound of Antonio's flesh, she argued. But she made two conditions—first, he must take exactly one pound in weight, not the weight of a hair more or less; secondly, he must not take one drop of blood, as that was not mentioned in the bond.

Of course these conditions were impossible, and Shylock, now seeing where his blind hatred of " the fool that lent out money gratis " had led him, was willing to leave the court without his money, for to take his bond would have led to his being condemned to death himself. But Portia stayed him, saying:

"There is a law whereby, if any foreigner in Venice shall scheme against the life of a citizen, his money shall be forfeited, half of it going to the State, the other half to his intended victim, and his own life will rest with the mercy of the Duke."

Thus Shylock lost his bond and might have lost his life; but that was spared on condition that he willed his fortune to his own daughter, Jessica, whom he had ill-treated, and to her lover Lorenzo, and also that he renounced his old religion and became a Christian. In his delight at the happy issue of events

Bassanio offered the pretended doctor of laws anything he might ask; but, to his dismay, a ring which Portia had given him on his departure from Belmont was required of him. The lawyer's clerk also demanded Gratiano's ring, which Nerissa had given to him.

When Bassanio returned to Belmont, bringing with him Antonio to see Portia, she and Nerissa asked for their rings, which neither of the men could produce. After pretending to be very angry with their lovers, Portia and Nerissa showed the rings on their own fingers. Antonio then knew whose wise speech had saved his life; and his joy was complete when Portia gave him a letter stating that three of his ships had safely come to port.

ALL'S WELL THAT ENDS WELL

BERTRAM, the young Count of Rousillon, in the south of France, bade farewell to his widowed mother before he left their castle for the Court of the King at Paris. His mother was not alone in her sorrow over his departure, for no sooner had he gone than Helena, a lady whom the Countess had brought up as if she had been her own daughter, was overwhelmed with grief. She mourned because she loved Bertram, yet dared not let it be known, as she, the daughter of a physician, could not hope to marry a nobleman of the Royal blood of France.

In the midst of her grief a daring idea came to Helena's mind. The King of France was then so ill that all his learned men despaired of his life. He was suffering from a disease which her dead father had been able to cure, and the remedy for which Helena knew. "Why," thought she, "should I not also go to the Court of the King?" Her thoughts she spoke aloud, thinking herself alone; but she was overheard by a servant, who told the Countess.

Instead of being angry, the Countess told her that she had discovered the real cause of her tears, and even said she would welcome Helena as her daughter-in-law, promising to aid her in her mission.

When, in due time, Helena came before the ailing King, he was unwilling to allow her to try to cure his disease; but she persisted, saying that if she failed she was willing to suffer any punishment. As her reward on his recovery, she demanded that he should give her a nobleman of the

Royal blood of France as her husband, to be chosen by herself. To this he agreed.

After the King recovered he called together a number of his courtiers, explained the terms he had arranged with the fair physician, adding that he would give her wealth and raise her rank in gratitude for having cured his disease. When Helena went forward to Bertram and signified him as her choice, the young Count hotly refused thus to be forced into marriage; but his sense of loyalty overruled his pride, and he at length agreed to marry Helena. No sooner was the ceremony over, however, than he arranged secretly to go to the wars in Tuscany.

Poor Helena, the unconscious messenger of evil tidings, brought back to the Countess at Rousillon a letter from her son, in which he vowed never to return. He also told Helena he would never see her again until she had obtained a ring which he wore constantly on his finger.

Helena, gentle and timid in most things, was not to be repulsed in this disdainful fashion; so, dressed as a pilgrim, she set out for Florence, in the country of the wars.

In Florence there lived a widow and her daughter Diana. Often had Bertram told Diana of his love for her, though she had always refused to listen ; he even wished her to promise to be his wife when Helena should die. But Helena, unknown to Bertram, had come to stay in Florence with this widow and her daughter, nor did she ask for their help in vain. Diana now showed more friendliness to Bertram, and begged him to give her his ring, saying she would give him one in return.

In the darkness of the night, at the appointed place, without saying a single word, according to the agreement, rings were exchanged between Bertram and, not Diana, as he supposed, but Helena, whom he could not see.

Meanwhile, in France it had been given out that Helena was dead, as she had disappeared from Rousillon; and in Bertram's absence it was arranged that he should marry for the second time, but to a bride of nobler birth. Bertram, however, discovered a sudden love for the wife he supposed lost, and on returning to his ancestral castle he refused to marry again.

The widow from Florence came to Rousillon, where the King was on a visit, and with her were Diana and Helena, both disguised.

Diana told a strange story to the King; and everyone was completely mystified by Diana declaring that the ring had been given to her, yet not to her; that Bertram had met her at midnight, yet that it was not she. The riddle was solved by bringing forward Bertram's still living wife, who had actually got the ring from him, and for whom the erring Count had now conceived a real affection.

So Helena and Bertram were, after many trials and misunderstandings, happily united, and " all's well that ends well."

THE TAMING OF THE SHREW

A SHREW is a woman whose temper is fiery; who is never satisfied with things as they are; nagging, peevish, always finding fault.

We are to suppose, then, that Katharina, the elder daughter of Baptista, a rich gentleman of Padua in Italy, was so ill-tempered that she could be described as a shrew. Perhaps at heart she was neither selfish nor ill-feeling; but possibly, being spoiled by her parents as a child, she had grown into these unfortunate habits, which made her so unpleasant a companion that there seemed little likelihood of anyone marrying her.

Quite the opposite to Katharina was her younger sister Bianca. Charming in appearance, gentle and winsome in character and beloved by all, we may be sure there was no lack of gallant gentlemen who would willingly have married Bianca. To some of her suitors Baptista announced that he would not allow Bianca to be married until her elder sister had found a husband. In the meantime he intended that the young ladies should have the best possible teaching in the accomplishments of the time, and asked that any good tutors might be recommended to him.

At this time there had come to Padua, famous for its colleges, a young gentleman of Pisa named Lucentio, son of a rich noble of that town. His purpose in Padua was to study, but he had no sooner set eyes on Bianca than he fell in love with her, and thoughts of study were soon dismissed.

On learning that Baptista wished to engage tutors for his daughters, Lucentio planned with one of his own servants, Tranio, that he should impersonate him as a rich gentleman come to Padua to pay court to Bianca, while he himself would contrive to be engaged as tutor to the two ladies. It was so arranged, and before long Bianca was in love with her handsome and agreeable instructor.

But in the meantime one of Bianca's other suitors, a gentleman named Hortensio, had enlisted the aid of a merry friend from Verona, who undertook no less a task than to marry Katharina, and thus leave Bianca free to marry Hortensio. This was Petruchio, who was at once clever, masterful, high-spirited.

Petruchio began his love-making to Katharina by addressing her as Kate, in order to annoy her; when she scolded he pretended to find her " passing gentle "; and, finally, when she struck him he promised her as good as he had got, assuring her that he meant to marry her. When her father came on the scene, the dashing Petruchio calmly informed him that the wedding would take place next Sunday.

When Sunday came, and Petruchio arrived for the wedding, he presented an extraordinary figure, wearing a new hat, an old coat, shoes that were not neighbours, a rusty sword, and mounted on a horse so old and skinny that it was of no more value than the rubbishy harness it wore.

Baptista was thoroughly ashamed of the bridegroom, but Petruchio refused to change his clothes, as this was a part of his scheme for " taming the shrew."

TOUCHSTONE AND AUDREY IN THE FOREST OF ARDEN : A SCENE FROM AS YOU LIKE IT

In the church he behaved quite scandalously, insulting the priest, and kissing Katharina so loudly that the building echoed with the sound. Nor would he wait for the wedding feast, but set out at once with his wife for Verona.

Their journey was one series of misfortunes, and the bridegroom behaved as if he cared nothing for his bride. The last part of the way they had to walk, owing to their horses taking flight when Petruchio was thrashing his servant; and they arrived, footsore and weary, at his residence, where he made matters worse by complaining about everything, throwing the food on the floor and beating his attendants.

In this way Petruchio behaved for a time, and was always in so bad a temper that Katharina had no chance to show how bad her own temper was. Hortensio came to see them, and Petruchio decided they would return with him to Padua, promising that they should both go there dressed according to their rank. But when costumes for Katharina and himself were brought in to choose, he declared them all unsuitable, throwing them on the floor, and when at last they did set out he was still wearing his odd clothes.

At Padua, meanwhile, Baptista had promised that Bianca would be wedded to her richest suitor, and this was Tranio, who was playing the part of Lucentio, while the other pretended to be merely the teacher of Greek and Latin. Tranio arranged with an elderly man to impersonate the father of Lucentio, and got him to give his consent to the wedding, inviting Baptista to his house to arrange the matter, while Bianca was to follow with a servant.

Bianca did follow, but with the pretended tutor Lucentio, who took her to church on the way and married her. When Lucentio arrived at his own house at Padua, his real father from Pisa had just come to visit him, so that Lucentio was in time to kneel at his feet and ask at once his pardon and his blessing.

The journey of Petruchio and Katharina back to Padua was conducted in the strangest way, Petruchio insisting on his wife agreeing to his most ridiculous statements, and making her kiss him publicly in the street under threat that they would return to Verona if she were ashamed to do so.

Indeed, by the time they reached Lucentio's house there was no more obedient wife in all Italy. Katharina was actually so " tamed " that she even made a little speech to the other ladies present on the virtue of a wife's obedience.

MUCH ADO ABOUT NOTHING

WHEN returning from battle with some of his principal followers, Don Pedro, Prince of Arragon, an ancient kingdom of Spain, broke his journey at the town of Messina to rest for a time as the guest of its governor Leonato.

This Leonato had a daughter, as gentle and good as she was beautiful and clever. Her name was Hero, and she and her cousin Beatrice, who was witty and merry, more lively, but not quite so even-tempered as Hero, made the home of Leonato bright and happy. It so happened that in the train of Don Pedro there was a young and brave gentleman of Florence named Claudio, a favourite of the Prince.

Claudio was very happy in going to Messina, as he was in love with Hero, whom he had seen before, and he now rejoiced that the Prince had promised to advance his suit.

There was another gentleman of the Prince's train, named Benedick, a young nobleman from Padua, who was also a favourite of Don Pedro's; and he too was brave and manly, but more moody than Claudio, sometimes liking to read a book rather than to make himself agreeable to the ladies. All went smoothly so far as Hero and Claudio were concerned, for not only was it clear they loved one another, but, Leonato having given his consent to their marriage, preparations for that happy event were soon in progress. Meanwhile, every time that Beatrice and Benedick had met they found occasion to quarrel, though they seemed to like each other's company.

Now, when a couple are engaged to be married they are usually so happy that they like to see others happy also; and so it was with Hero and Claudio. Together with the Duke and Leonato, they agreed on a little plan to make Beatrice and Benedick cease their bickering and love each other.

One day, when Benedick had withdrawn to a shady arbour in the garden, the Prince, Leonato, and Claudio seated themselves near to where he was and began to talk, so that Benedick might hear them in his arbour, about the way in which poor Beatrice was dying of love for him! They pretended that she was deeply in love with Benedick, and yet Hero had said: " Beatrice would die ere she made her love known."

This, you will see, was the beginning of their little scheme, and it is no wonder that Benedick, overhearing their remarks, began to regret his behaviour to Beatrice.

Meanwhile, Hero had her part to play in this pretty comedy of love, and, sending one of her attendants to tell the unsuspecting Beatrice that Hero and another lady in the garden were talking about her, it was not many minutes before that lively and inquisitive lady had stolen out to overhear what they might have to say. Their talk was all about Benedick being deeply in love with her. They also spoke in so much praise of him that Beatrice forthwith became as tender in her thoughts towards him.

But into this happy comedy the figure of a mischief-maker now steps. This is Don John, half-brother of the Prince, whom he hates so much that he would do anything to annoy him. For the moment he can think of nothing better than to stir up the feeling of jealousy between the Prince's young friend Claudio and the unsuspecting Hero. Assuring the lover that Hero had really given her heart to another gallant, and inducing both Claudio and Don Pedro to hide with him in the garden on the eve of Hero's intended wedding day, a lady was seen by them at Hero's window bidding farewell to an unknown man. This was merely one of Hero's lady companions saying goodnight to her own sweetheart, a follower of Don John, but Claudio and the Prince were both misled into thinking it was Hero herself.

Claudio, mad with rage, swore to renounce the innocent Hero at the altar next day. This cruel threat he actually fulfilled, and the poor lady, utterly at a loss to understand the cause, almost died of grief. Her cousin Beatrice, of course, would not believe her capable of any dishonourable action, and made Benedick, now in love with herself, undertake to fight a duel with Claudio.

In the meantime it was pretended that Hero had really died; and Benedick had challenged Claudio to the duel, just when Dogberry and Verges, two comically stupid officers of the watch, brought in two of Don John's followers whom they had arrested at night, scheming of some plot, as they believed. To save himself, one of the prisoners at once confessed that he had visited his sweetheart that night, so that when she came to the window the watchers in the garden might mistake her for Hero. This he had done at the instigation of Don John.

Claudio, on hearing this, was overwhelmed with grief, and, believing the innocent lady to have died, he was in despair; but Leonato told him his brother had a daughter the very image of the child he had lost, and if Claudio would marry her he would forgive him the sorrow he had caused by his folly in listening to slanderous tongues.

When this new bride came to meet her bridegroom her features were masked; but judge of Claudio's surprise when she uncovered her face, and he looked again into the dear eyes of Hero!

The threatened duel between Claudio and Benedick had now no excuse, for all were friends again; and not only do we see Hero and Claudio ready for their wedding, but Beatrice and Benedick also.

AS YOU LIKE IT

THERE was a kind and peace-loving Duke against whom his brother Frederick successfully rebelled, usurping his dominions. Withdrawing into the great and wild Forest of Arden, this Duke, with a number of faithful followers, lived in his exile a happy and peaceful life.

One of his old friends had been Sir Rowland de Boys, who died, leaving three sons, Oliver, Orlando, and Jaques. To the first-named, who was the eldest, he left all his money and estates, except one thousand crowns for Orlando. Oliver was charged to give his brothers a good upbringing, but, though he provided Jaques with ample schooling, he had a hatred of Orlando, whom he kept idly at home. As Orlando grew up he could not endure his idle life, and at length demanded the money which his father had left him, so that he might leave his brother's house.

Oliver, wishing to keep the money, arranged with a great wrestler, who was a servant of Frederick, the usurper, to challenge Orlando to a match, believing his brother might be killed if he fought.

THE BEAUTIFUL ROSALIND LEAVES HER CRUEL UNCLE'S PALACE

The match was duly arranged, and among the spectators were Frederick's daughter Celia, and her fair cousin Rosalind, whom Frederick allowed to live at the palace, though she was the daughter of the exiled Duke, the two girls being inseparable friends. When Rosalind saw that so young a man was to fight the champion wrestler she begged of him to refuse. Orlando, however, was not afraid; and, to the surprise of all, he overthrew the usurper's champion.

Frederick, who witnessed the combat, was about to congratulate the victor, when he heard that he was the son of his old enemy, and the praise on his lips changed to anger. But Rosalind, in admiration of Orlando's bravery, gave him a chain she was wearing. This action so annoyed Frederick that he now banished her from the palace. Perhaps he had been waiting for the excuse, as Rosalind was so beautiful in person, and so witty in mind, that his own daughter Celia, though comely and pleasant, suffered by contrast with the bewitching daughter of the banished Duke.

Celia dearly loved her cousin Rosalind, and had not the least jealousy of her charms, so that when her companion was banished from the palace she did not hesitate to share her fate, and they went away together, taking with them the witty jester Touchstone, whose comic sayings would cheer them on their way.

ORLANDO SEEKS SANCTUARY IN THE FAMOUS FOREST OF ARDEN

They did not go, of course, in the rich dresses they wore in the palace. Rosalind, who was " more than common tall," dressed herself like a shepherd, while Celia put on the clothes of a shepherdess. Their destination was the Forest of Arden, where the banished Duke held his rustic court.

Now, when Orlando was returning to the house of his brother he was met by an old servant of the family named Adam, who loved the youth so much that, knowing Oliver meant to kill him, he had brought all the savings of his life, some five hundred crowns, and urged Orlando to go away with him. They, too, set out for the safe seclusion of the famous forest.

Rosalind and Celia in due time gained the shelter of the forest, where at length they found a lodging in a little cottage; but what perplexed them greatly was to discover little verses written on paper and placed in the trunks of trees, expressing great love for Rosalind. Who could the unknown rhymer be? Celia undertook to find out, and traced him at length to Orlando, whom Rosalind, still pretending to be a man, promised to cure of his love if he would come each day and make love to her in the name of Rosalind.

A friend of the Duke, another Jaques, is used to infuse grave thought into the play, as a contrast to its holiday feeling in the forest. He it is who reminds his companions of the drama played in each of their lives, from childhood to old age.

HOW SHAKESPEARE DESCRIBED THE SEVEN AGES OF MAN

All the world's a stage,
And all the men and women merely players:
They have their exits, and their entrances;
And one man in his time plays many parts,
His acts being seven ages. At first, the infant,
Mewling and puking in the nurse's arms.
And then the whining schoolboy, with his satchel,
And shining morning face, creeping like snail
Unwillingly to school. And then the lover,
Sighing like furnace, with a woful ballad
Made to his mistress' eyebrow. Then a soldier,
Full of strange oaths, and bearded like the pard,
Jealous in honour, sudden and quick in quarrel,
Seeking the bubble reputation
Even in the cannon's mouth. And then the justice,
In fair round belly with good capon lined,
With eyes severe, and beard of formal cut,
Full of wise saws and modern instances;
And so he plays his part. The sixth age shifts
Into the lean and slippered pantaloon,
With spectacles on nose, and pouch on side,
His youthful hose well saved, a world too wide
For his shrunk shank; and his big manly voice,
Turning again toward childish treble, pipes
And whistles in his sound. Last scene of all,
That ends his strange, eventful history,
Is second childishness, and mere oblivion,
Sans teeth, sans eyes, sans taste, sans everything.

The flight of the two ladies from the palace had led Frederick, the usurper, to accuse Oliver of sheltering them and Orlando, little knowing how Oliver had tried to rid himself of his younger brother.

So Oliver too was banished from Court, and, in common with the other exiles, made for the forest, where he would have been killed by a lion had not Orlando rescued him at the cost of injury to himself.

This noble action so shamed Oliver that he took his brother to his heart; and since Orlando, being injured, could not visit Rosalind's cottage as usual, Oliver went there to explain his absence, and, seeing Celia, dressed as a shepherdess, fell in love with her forthwith.

It was arranged that the wedding of Oliver and Celia should take place at the Duke's encampment, and as Orlando protested that he still loved the lady who gave him the chain, Rosalind promised she would bring her to him at the wedding of Celia; which she did, of course, by putting off her disguise and appearing there as her own delightful self, not only to the joy of Orlando, but also of her father the Duke.

Oliver was now so happy that he promised to give Orlando his estates; but presently news came that Frederick himself was on the way to kill his brother, the banished Duke. By a strange chance, however, he met a good old man who spoke to him of the evil life he was leading, and so changed his mind that he determined for the future to give his thoughts to religion, and surrendered to the Duke the dominions which he had unlawfully usurped. Thus happiness was restored to all.

TWELFTH NIGHT; OR WHAT YOU WILL

FANCY Shakespeare at a loss for a title! It seems absurd that one whose mind was so full of fancies, so rich in thoughts, should ever have been at a loss for a title for a play he had written. Yet such was the case with the comedy which we know as Twelfth Night; or, What You Will. It is said to have been christened Twelfth Night for no better reason than that it was first performed on January 6, which was observed as a festival in Shakespeare's day, and long afterwards, being the twelfth day after Christmas.

Illyria was the name of a country on the Adriatic Sea, and, while sailing thither, the twin son and daughter of a gentleman of Messaline were wrecked. The youth's name was Sebastian, his sister was called Viola.

Both of them had the good fortune to escape from drowning during the shipwreck, but they did not reach the land together, and each was ignorant of the other's fate. Viola was saved by a sea captain, by whose help she contrived to dress up as a page, and made her way to the Court of Orsino, Duke of Illyria. It was safer for her to assume this disguise than to travel as an unprotected girl in a strange land, and she had no difficulty in getting accepted as a page to the Duke, for she looked a handsome boy!

Now, the Duke was in love with a young and rich lady of his land, the Countess Olivia, and wished to marry her. But Olivia had rejected his proposals, refused to see him, and even spoke of shutting herself up for seven years to mourn for a dead brother. The Duke thought that his handsome young page would be a good messenger to send to Olivia on his behalf, and so Viola was sent by Orsino to plead with the fair countess on behalf of her princely lover. But, greatly to Viola's embarrassment, instead of softening Olivia's heart towards the Duke, the messenger had spoken so sweetly that Olivia fell in love with the pretty page.

A new and unpleasant actor now came upon the scene, in the person of a drunken old courtier named Sir Andrew Aguecheek, who had the audacity to consider himself a rival for the hand of Olivia. This Sir Andrew, noticing that the Countess was so favourably disposed to the engaging young attendant of the Duke, challenged Viola to a duel.

Viola's disguise had thus brought her into a strange adventure, and she had no idea what the issue would be. But three months had now passed since the shipwreck, and her brother Sebastian, in company with his friend Antonio, who was so devoted to the young gentleman that he had even given him all his money, was on his way to the palace of Orsino. Antonio, having been at the time in arms against the Duke, was afraid to accompany Sebastian to the palace, and thus their ways had to separate, to their mutual sorrow.

Soon after leaving his friend, Antonio was surprised to come upon two persons about to engage in a duel, and thinking the younger of them to be none other than Sebastian, he promptly interfered on his behalf. The duellists, however, as we may guess, were Sir Andrew and Viola, the notorious old coward having forced the young page to draw her sword, much against her will, just at the moment of Antonio's timely arrival. The immediate result of Antonio's interference was not only to stop the fight, but to bring some of the followers of the Duke on the scene, and then, recognising him as a former enemy, put him under arrest. Hereupon he turned to Viola, and asked her—thinking her Sebastian—to give him back some of his money, knowing he might have need of it; but Viola showed her natural astonishment at this request.

While Viola's adventures are thus increasing, Sebastian too is having his share of misunderstanding, for Sir Andrew Aguecheek, baulked of his revenge on the timid page, comes upon Sebastian in front of Olivia's house, and, mistaking him for Viola, draws his sword upon the youth; but the coward has soon excellent cause to regret having forced the boy to fight. The Countess, having witnessed what she supposes to be the manly conduct of the Duke's page in the encounter with Sir Andrew, is more than ever charmed with him, and, inviting Sebastian into her house, frankly declares her love for him.

Here is, indeed, the strangest of Sebastian's adventures; but as the lady is young and lovely he accepts the situation gallantly, and a priest being at hand the wedding ceremony is not delayed. Olivia is in entire surrender; she no longer dreams of seven years of mourning for the dead! The next scene in this comedy of errors takes us to the audience chamber of the Duke, whither Antonio has been brought by his captors before Orsino. There Antonio, seeing Viola with the Duke, and still mistaking her for her twin brother, chides her for the way in which she has repaid his constant friendship of the past three months.

The Duke, of course, was mystified by Antonio's words, as Viola had acted as his page for three months; but confusion became worse confounded when Olivia arrived, and, seeing Viola there, addressed her as "husband." The Duke was enraged that his attendant should, as he now thought, have betrayed his trust and made love to the lady; nor were matters improved when Viola denied Olivia's statement that they were married, and the priest who performed the ceremony was called to bear witness to it! Sir Andrew Aguecheek added a further touch to the confusion by appearing and stating that the Duke's page had but recently in a quarrel broken his head, and that of his boon companion Sir Toby Belch, Olivia's uncle, for whom he sought the services of a surgeon.

When matters were thus at their worst all was suddenly made clear by the appearance of Sebastian himself, who, after explanations, discovered that the Duke's page was none other than his own sister, whom he had believed dead. As Sebastian had so quickly become the husband of Olivia, who, while refusing to become the wife of the Duke, was nothing loth to be his " sister," Orsino chose the true romantic ending for this comedy of the twins by offering his hand to Viola.

MEASURE FOR MEASURE

In olden times there was a Duke of Vienna whose good-natured treatment of his people had not been to the advantage of his State. The laws of the city not being strictly enforced, as all laws should be, people stood in no fear of them. The Duke saw that for his people's good the laws would have to be kept, but at the same time he did not wish to appear suddenly to change from a kind ruler into a tyrant. He had, therefore, to think of some way to carry out his reform without appearing to have lost his kindly interest in his subjects.

Among the noblemen of Vienna was one Angelo, a stern, severe, and cold-hearted man. The Duke, thinking that Angelo would be just the man to enforce the laws, appointed him Lord Deputy, and gave out a report that he himself was leaving for a time to visit another country. Instead of going away, however, he assumed the habit of a monk, and, thus disguised, remained in Vienna to see how Angelo conducted himself.

As chance would have it, the first case to call for Angelo's judgment was that of Claudio, a young gentleman who had secretly married a young lady named Juliet. In those days, and still in many parts of Europe, a bride had to bring her husband a marriage dower, a gift of money or land, presented by her parents or relatives. Claudio and Juliet were keeping their marriage secret until it was known what fortune her relatives would fix for her dower. For this Claudio was condemned to death, a sentence which was an outrage; but Angelo was keen to exercise his new power, like all persons " drest in a little brief authority."

Claudio had a sister who, when this misfortune befell her brother, had but newly entered a convent, and on news of the impending execution of her brother reaching her, retiring and gentle though she was, she took courage to go forth and intercede with Angelo on behalf of Claudio.

Although the Lord Deputy was a cold and cruel man, he was not insensible to the winning beauty of Isabella, as Claudio's sister was named, and her appeal seemed to soften him; but that was only because a selfish desire to possess the beautiful creature had been awakened in him. If she would consent to marry him, he promised to pardon her brother, thus ready to add one injustice to another. The idea was horrible to a young lady who had just given up the thought of marriage, and of all men Angelo would have been the last she could have cared for. So she indignantly refused him, and when she visited her brother in prison he too approved of her refusal; but, as he thought the more of his impending doom, his courage failed, and he begged her to submit for his sake.

The talk between the brother and sister in the prison had been overheard by a supposed friar, who was none other than the Duke in disguise, and he was filled with anger to find that Angelo was abusing his trust. In a flash he thought of a clever way to outwit Angelo and bring happiness where so much sorrow threatened.

There was a lady, he told Isabella, named Mariana, whom Angelo, five years before, had vowed to marry, but did not do so, as her marriage dower was not forthcoming; yet Mariana loved him still. Isabella was to make pretence af agreeing to Angelo's proposals for the sake of her brother, but she had to arrange with this Mariana that she would take Isabella's place at the wedding, wearing a veil, so that the bridegroom would not discover the ruse till too late. Mariana was also to say to Angelo when she came before him veiled: " Remember now my brother."

All this was carried out accordingly; but a pirate having died in prison, whose hair and beard resembled those of Claudio, the Duke managed to get the head of this dead man sent to Angelo with the intimation that it was the head of Claudio! Meanwhile Claudio himself had been, thanks to the Duke, taken out of danger.

Now was the moment for the Duke to complete the discomfiture of his unfaithful deputy; so, withdrawing from the city, and dressing again in his proper clothes, he sent forward news that he was returning from Poland.

Angelo came to the city gate to meet him, and the usual friendly speeches were made, the Duke appearing ignorant of all that had happened. Then came forward Isabella, pretending to appeal to the Duke to punish Angelo for having murdered her brother. Angelo was indeed dismayed when the veiled lady he had but newly wedded also came forward and disclosed herself as his old sweetheart.

The Duke threatened to visit upon Angelo the fate which had been designed for Claudio; but both Isabella and Mariana begged that he might be pardoned, and this the Duke agreed to. Nor did Isabella refuse the offer of the kind-hearted Duke to make her his own wife. And so the comedy ended with happiness for all. We can see why it is called Measure for Measure, as Angelo was made to feel himself in much the same position as that in which he had placed Claudio.

THE COMEDY OF THE WINTER'S TALE

THERE were two Kings who had been brought up together and grown to like each other so well that they were almost as brothers. The one was King of Sicilia, his name being Leontes; and the other, who was called Polixenes, reigned over the kingdom of Bohemia.

Once when Polixenes was on a visit to Leontes, Leontes had so enjoyed his society that he begged his friend to stay longer. But Polixenes seemed bent on returning to Bohemia, until Hermione, the tender and loving Queen of Leontes, joined her entreaties to those of her husband, when Polixenes yielded to her gentle persuasion and decided to prolong his visit.

Unhappily, Leontes, though in the main a good and kind king, must have been of a jealous nature, for though he had asked his wife to urge Polixenes to stay, when his old friend did, for her asking, what he had not seemed ready to do for him, Leontes suddenly became foolishly jealous. In his folly he told his servant Camillo that he believed Polixenes and Hermione had fallen in love; but Camillo knew this was not true. He humoured the jealous King, however, by promising to poison Polixenes if what Leontes said was true. But what he did was to tell the King of Bohemia of the madness that had afflicted his old friend, and that night both Polixenes and Camillo fled from Sicilia.

THE JEALOUSY THAT BROUGHT LEONTES TO THE DEPTHS OF DESPAIR

Nothing would persuade Leontes of his folly, and he accused his poor Queen of acts and thoughts of which she was entirely innocent. He even refused to look on their newly-born daughter Perdita, and ordered that the child should be taken and left to die in a desert.

Naturally Hermione denied the unjust charges brought against her, and in this she was supported by the famous oracle at Delphi. This oracle was supposed to be the voice of the gods, which in pagan times could be consulted on matters of difficulty through the priestess in the great temple of Delphi. It was, of course, entirely superstition; but the answer that came from Delphi as to Hermione's conduct said she was entirely innocent, whereas Leontes was a jealous tyrant, who would not have an heir " if that which is lost be not found."

Soon the words of the oracle seemed to be coming true, as the King's only son, the young Prince Mamillius, died of grief at his mother's woes; and Hermione herself became so ill that it was openly declared she too had died.

Too late, the jealous King realised his folly; and now that he believed both his wife and son to be dead, he declared he would visit their grave each day and spend his years in mourning.

THE KINDLY SHEPHERD WHO RESCUED THE LITTLE PRINCESS

But Leontes did not know that, while the officer who had taken little Perdita to a desert part of Bohemia had himself been killed by a bear, the child had been rescued by a shepherd, who knew from certain jewels and other things the officer had with him that the child was of royal birth.

Still, the shepherd took no steps to seek out the parents, but brought her up as his own daughter, and watched her with joy and delight as she grew into the loveliest shepherdess that ever was.

Sixteen years thus passed by, and Perdita found herself beloved by a brave and handsome youth, who often came to visit her as she tended her sheep; but whence he came she did not know.

After all these years, too, Camillo, who had lived with Polixenes since they fled from Sicilia together, had a great longing to return to his native country. But the King of Bohemia was loth to let him go, as he wished that they should go together in disguise to discover why the young Prince Florizel was so often absent from Court and loved to spend his time in the quiet of the country.

This Camillo agreed to, and their discovery was indeed a surprise to the King, for Florizel proved to be none other than the sweetheart of Perdita, the shepherdess, whom he wished to marry. The King, of course, sternly forbade him, and threatened to have Perdita removed if she ever saw Florizel again. But Camillo now carried out his wish to return to his native land, and took with him, in disguise, both Florizel and the lovely shepherdess.

THE HAPPY ENDING OF YEARS OF SORROW FOR LEONTES

Leontes gave a warm welcome to the son of his old friend, whom he had so greatly wronged; and the old shepherd, having followed the runaways into Sicilia, disclosed the parentage of Perdita, to the joy of her father.

Then came the happiest event of all, when Paulina, a dear friend of Hermione, and widow of the officer who had taken Perdita away, invited Leontes to see a beautiful new statue of Hermione. When he did see it, so lifelike it seemed that he could scarce forbear to touch it; and lo! the figure descended from the pedestal and laid her head on his breast. It was Hermione herself.

Leontes, now happier than his folly gave him any right to be, was friends again with Polixenes; and, of course, Florizel and Perdita were married in due course, thus uniting the fortunes of the two kingdoms.

And so ends The Winter's Tale on a happy note. The tangled skein is straightened out, and the course of true love gives promise of henceforth running smooth.

The Story of the Most Beautiful Book in the World

The road to Jerusalem along which Paul went to meet Peter

PAUL AND PETER MEET

IF we think of the proud place that Saul of Tarsus had occupied in Jerusalem we shall be able to understand the feelings of Paul the Apostle as he drew near the Holy City, footsore and weary, after the long journey from Damascus.

Of all the Jews in that sacred city he had been the most zealous for the Law. Famous for his learning, marked out for the highest honours by his passionate energies, a man stamped with the seal of power and dominion, he had exercised a unique spell upon the multitude of Jews, both in the temple and in the street.

He had been, perhaps, the most famous Jew in Jerusalem. His friendships were among the proud and powerful Pharisees. His fame was the fame of a master man, a leader, a ruler of the most shining and distinguished qualities. And now he was returning on foot, as an outlaw, a friendless, homeless, penniless wanderer on the earth—worse than this, as a traitor.

But one great aspiration upheld him in this difficult hour. Hidden away in some mean house in one of the poor back streets of the city was a Galilean fisherman who had lived with Jesus, who had heard his voice, looked into his eyes, broken bread with him, sat with him on the Mount of Olives, and asked him concerning the kingdom of heaven.

To reach this Galilean fisherman was now the desire of the once proud Pharisee. His intense and bitter loneliness could only be supported by the company of one who had known Jesus, who could tell him all he desired to know about that wondrous revelation of High God. And so, through the humiliation and bitterness of his return, Paul felt the joy that was before him, and hastened his steps toward the city in which Peter lived.

It seems that he met with Barnabas, a friend of his, one who had known him in the past, who believed in him, and knew the story of his conversion. By this good and excellent man, destined to be the companion of his life, Paul was led to the house where Peter the fisherman lodged.

We could well sacrifice some of the chief books in the world for a single chapter describing to us the meeting of Peter and Paul. No meeting could be more dramatic.

The characters of the two men seize our imagination. Peter was the most impulsive and headstrong of Christ's followers; Christ had upbraided him on one occasion with a swift rebuke, and on another occasion had warned him that he would deny his Master; yet all through had shown him a love and confidence which lifted him above the heads of the other disciples.

GREAT FIGURES OF THE OLD TESTAMENT · THE LIFE OF JESUS

Paul, for his part, was equally impetuous, headstrong, and reckless; but his impetuosity was of the intellect, not of the heart. He was the impulsive zealot of the Law, with a quick brain for argument, a fierce and haughty contempt for the loose ideas of ignorant men.

These two men, the provincial and unlearned fisherman and the brilliant and accomplished Pharisee, came face to face in a house in Jerusalem, long ago forgotten, and for fifteen days discussed the character and the works of Jesus of Nazareth.

THE FIFTEEN DAYS PAUL SPENT IN JERUSALEM WITH PETER

" After three years," says Paul, " I went up to Jerusalem to see Peter, and abode with him fifteen days. But other of the apostles saw I none, save James, the Lord's brother." That is all we know of this great interview.

But we have another glimpse of Paul's general reception at Jerusalem. However kind may have been the greeting of the warm-hearted, noble-natured Peter, from the rest of the Nazarenes at Jerusalem Paul received the coldest welcome. " They were all afraid of him, and believed not that he was a disciple."

He was met on every side (says Dean Farrar) by cold, distrustful looks. At one stroke he had lost all his old friends ; it seemed to be too likely that he would gain no new ones in their place. The brethren regarded him with terror and mistrust ; they did not believe that he was a disciple at all. The *facts* which accompanied his conversion they may, indeed, have heard of ; but they had occurred three years before.

The news of his recent preaching and recent peril in Damascus was not likely to have reached them ; but, even if it had, it would have seemed so strange that they might be pardoned for looking with doubt on the persecutor turned brother—for even fearing that the asserted conversion might be only a ruse to learn their secrets, and so entrap them to their final ruin.

PAUL'S VISION OF THE LIGHT OF THE WORLD THAT WAS TO COVER THE EARTH

But Paul, however hurt he might be by this cold distrust of the brotherhood, was at least exalted by what Peter had to tell him. Everything the simple fisherman said became charged with spiritual meaning to the greater soul of this greatest of men. He listened to Peter's narrative, questioned and cross-examined, fastened the whole story into his heart, and at the end rose up and went boldly out to preach Jesus to the Jews and to the Greeks.

And now once more we see the same tragedy that we witnessed at Damascus. As the Gadarenes implored Jesus to depart from their coasts, so the timid Nazarenes in Jerusalem begged Paul to go from them, lest his bold preaching should bring ruin on the brotherhood. There is no question that Peter and the rest of the apostles conceived of Christ's Church—not then called a Church, and by Peter himself never called a Church to the end of his days—as something existing for a very few, to which other people should be wooed in secret even if they were to be wooed at all.

But to Paul the vision was grander and more sublime than that. He perceived in the mists of the future a Church embracing humanity and transforming human character. Such a Church was not to steal secret and ashamed through the ages, but was to lift itself high into all men's view and challenge the soul of the nations with its purity and its unanswerable holiness.

HOW PAUL WAS ONCE AGAIN DRIVEN INTO EXILE

Therefore it was that his bold preaching stirred the muddy waters at Jerusalem and once more revived the storm of anger and persecution. Paul, with his clear vision, could not hide Christ's light under a bushel. He wanted all men to see the Great Light. So he preached with the fearless energy of his soul, and presented Jesus to Jerusalem as the Son of God, Saviour of all mankind.

He was marked down for death. Such preaching was unthinkable in Jerusalem. As he had been marked down at Damascus for stirring up strife, so he was marked down in Jerusalem; and now, as then, he was saved by flight. He had to be hurried out of the city. Once more we find him, on the threshold of his burning purpose, driven into exile, a homeless man, frightening his friends and rousing his enemies to fury. He went to Tarsus, and the chronicle says, significantly: " Then had the Churches rest throughout all Judaea and Galilee and Samaria."

Rest! Yes, they rested, and the nations of the Earth continued to live as if the Son of God had never existed. Yet Christianity was to spread in a wonderful way throughout the world.

(Next chapter in this group, page 6171)

The Interests and Pleasures of Life for All Indoors and Out

LEARNING TO SAIL A BOAT

SAILING is one of the most fascinating of all pastimes. But before you learn how to sail a boat you should know how to handle a dinghy.

It is quite impossible to teach rowing and sailing from books; they must be learned from actual experience. However, you need not be entirely unacquainted with boats when you go afloat for the first time. You can be familiar with the seaman's vocabulary, and with the principles of rowing and sailing, and you can memorise certain rules.

Let us first consider rowing. The drawing below shows the construction of a small dinghy and the names of its principal parts. These names are common to all boats so far as they apply.

It is fairly easy to row after a fashion, and you will soon learn not to splash. Hold the oars with thumbs underneath, one hand slightly below the other to avoid knocking as the oars pass. Keep the head and back erect but slightly forward, and stretch the arms to the fullest extent. Begin to pull immediately the blades are in the water, with elbows in. As the oars come out, drop the wrists, and turn the back of the hands towards the body to bring the blades of the oars flat to the surface of the water. The blades should remain flat during the return stroke, and just clear of the water. This is called feathering.

The tendency to pull the boat in a circle can be avoided by keeping a distant, fixed object in line with some part of the stern of your boat. Take long strokes and keep a steady rhythm, not too fast. Do not allow the oars to plunge deep in the water, so that you cannot complete the stroke. This is called catching a crab. The oars should not be dipped below the blades, and they should not be lifted high out of the water during the return stroke.

When getting into or out of a boat, be careful to step near the centre line. Stepping to one side would cause the boat to tilt. Draw the boat against the bank to steady it. To trim the boat properly if you have a passenger, you will probably need to row from the forward thwart instead of the centre one.

When coming in to the shore, approach, if possible, against the direction of the tide or stream. If on a beach with breakers, the boat will tend to come in sideways to the waves. This must be avoided or the boat

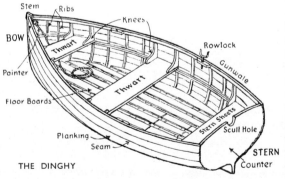

THE DINGHY

Stem · Ribs · Knees · BOW · Thwart · Rowlock · Painter · Gunwale · Thwart · Floor Boards · Stern Sheets · Planking · Scull Hole · Seam · STERN · Counter

CRAFTS · GAMES · NEEDLEWORK · PUZZLES · SCIENCE EXPERIMENTS

may fill with water and get bumped on the shingle. Use a clove hitch, shown below, to tie the boat to a pile or stake.

It sometimes happens that an oar or a rowlock is lost overboard. In that case you can get along by paddling with the other oar; but if there is a scull hole in the counter, as seen in the dinghy on the previous page, an expert will scull with the oar over the stern. This knack is well worth learning, although it is difficult, and will need much practice.

All boats except small dinghies are steered by means of a rudder. This is hinged vertically on its front edge so that it can be turned from side to side by means of the tiller, or, on a rowing boat, by steering lines. Small dinghies are steered with the oars, by holding water with one oar and rowing with the other.

If you are using a dinghy as a tender for a sailing boat, the oars should be shipped smartly before coming alongside, and the rowlock in the side next to the yacht should be pulled out. Always approach with your bow in the same direction as the yacht's bow, and round up to her from astern. If there is a tide running, approach from the leeward side. The correct place to land is abaft midships, not forward of midships.

A dinghy towed behind a sailing boat should be given enough scope of the painter, the correct term for the bow rope, to allow her to travel on the forward side of the second following wave.

The illustrations on the opposite page show the names of the important parts of a sailing boat. Imagine you are in a sailing boat, and the wind is blowing from behind you as you face her bow. The wind will send the boat along by pushing on the sails ; and they are correctly trimmed when, allowing for their curvature, they are as nearly as possible at right angles to the direction of the wind. This is achieved by slacking off the main sheet until the boom, which is hinged at the mast, swings outwards nearly at 90 degrees to the boat. Note that a sheet is a rope, *not* a sail. You are now said to be sailing, or running before the wind, If you turn the boat, by pushing the tiller away from you, or the wind veers, there will come a

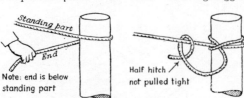

SAILING DIAGRAM. THE BOAT MARKED A HAVING RIGHT OF WAY IN EVERY CASE

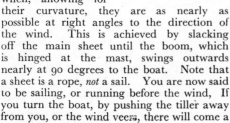

Note: end is below standing part

Half hitch
not pulled tight

THE CLOVE HITCH, SHOWING HALF HITCH, ADDED FOR EXTRA SECURITY

time when it is blowing sideways on to the boat. This is called a beam wind; and the sails will now be flapping, so to keep the boat moving, the sheets must be hauled in just enough to stop the sails from flapping. Sailing like this is called reaching.

If the wind veers still further, or the boat is turned still more, until the wind is approaching as shown by the arrow in the plan of the sloop, it is possible to keep the boat sailing by tightening the sheets still more. The sails are now behaving like the wings of an aeroplane, and the forward thrust propelling the boat, apparently against the wind, is derived from the suction caused by the flow of the wind over the curved back of the sails. You are now sailing to windward. The boat can be pointed more towards the wind, until her keel makes an angle of about 45 degrees with the direction of the wind. The main sheet should then be hauled in until the boom is over the point where the side joins the stern. The sheets are now trimmed as flat as practicable, and the boat is therefore said to be sailing close-hauled. If you point still closer to the direction of the wind, the sails will begin to flap and the boat will lose its way. She is said to be luffed. This is the only way to stop a sailing boat.

From the above you will now see that if you wish to go in the direction from which the wind is coming, you must sail at an angle of about 45 degrees in one direction and then turn the boat 90 degrees and sail at an angle of 45 degrees to the wind in the other direction. This zig-zagging is called tacking, as already described on page 3277, and the process of turning from one tack to another is called going about. When the wind is blowing over the starboard bow, and the sails are over the port side, as in the sloop plan, you are said to be on the starboard tack, and vice versa. The terms starboard, meaning the right-hand side, and port, the left-hand side, of a boat or ship, apply to all craft, irrespective of size or type.

When reaching or sailing closehauled, the boat will lean over according to the strength of the wind, and you should balance her by making the crew sit on the windward side. An extra strong puff of wind might still blow her over, and when she begins to heel too much, you quickly luff, to let the wind blow on both sides of the sail at the same time. In that position you cannot be knocked down. Practically all sailing boats are built so that they tend to luff if allowed to, and this has to be resisted with the helm. If you let go of the sheets the sails will flap because the wind is blowing on both sides at the same time, so you cannot go wrong if you remember to let go of every-thing—the tiller and the sheets— if you think you are going to be blown over. Get the boat sailing again as quickly as possible, in case the next squall comes from a different direction. If that happens, and you have not steerage way— which means the boat is not moving quickly enough to respond to the rudder—you can-not turn towards it, and you may still be blown over.

A lot of experi-ence is required in steering a boat so that she sails to windward at her best, and in judging how quickly she will turn when going about or luffing up to her moorings. A sensitive touch is needed for good helmsmanship.

When you are running with the wind dead aft (that is over the stern), and you turn the boat slightly, or the wind changes until it is blowing over the quarter on which the sail is carried, the danger of a gybe arises. The wind gets behind the main sail and slams it over to the other side very violently. This is an accidental gybe, and on a windy day the boom gathers terrific momentum and might hurt someone, or damage the rigging, or even capsize the boat. The controlled gybe whereby the boat is turned so that the wind passes from one quarter to the other, past a point directly astern, is not at all dangerous, but requires a lot of practice.

There are certain rules of right of way which sailing boats should keep; but always avoid an accident rather than stick to your course when you have right of way and the other boat does not recognise it.

A boat that is closehauled has right of way over a boat that is not closehauled. If two boats meet, both of them closehauled, but on opposite tacks, the boat on the starboard tack, with the wind over the starboard side, and the boom over the port side, has right of way. If two boats are converging on the same tack, the one that is to leeward and sailing closer to the wind, has right of way. If neither is close-hauled, and the sails are on opposite sides of the boat, the boat with its boom over the port side and the wind over the starboard side, has right of way. If neither is close-hauled, but they are converging with booms on the same side, the boat that is to leeward has right of way. These rules are illustrated in the diagram on the facing page.

Sailing boats have right of way over power craft, but it is as well to keep out of their way, and to know what is meant when they toot their sirens. One toot means, " I am directing my course to starboard " ; two means, " I am directing my course to port "; three means, " I am going astern."

Seamen use knots that hold fast yet are easily undone. The clove hitch, reef, and bowline will serve practically every purpose you come across. The method of tying the clove hitch is shown here, and the bowline and reef are on pages 4463 and 4464.

1. Head
2. Luff
3. Tack
4. Foot
5. Clew
6. Leech
7. Battens

DIAGRAM OF HALF DECK CENTRE-BOARD BERMUDIAN SLOOP WITH PRINCIPAL PARTS NAMED

PLAN OF SLOOP ON STARBOARD TACK WITH PARTS MARKED

THE GAME OF WHAT-ARE-THESE-THINGS?

HERE are descriptions of a number of things mentioned in this book. It will be a good game to see who can first guess the correct answers, which are given on page 6177.

1. What is this round prickly ball, covered all over with spines like a hedgehog? It comes from the south of France, where the natives take off the prickly coat, and are in the habit of boiling the three brown things inside and using them for a nourishing food. In England, too, we eat this article—baked, boiled, or made into puddings, but not into bread. It is hard and sweet when baked, soft and flowery when boiled. If Devonshire were only dry as well as warm, we should get fine specimens from that county; but as no large ones will grow in any quantity in Britain we have to rely on the warm countries bordering the Mediterranean for our supply.

2. For weeks at a time hundreds of boats are busily at work in the North Sea, hauling in treasures of the deep, which the small steamer takes away to the London market. In fine weather or boisterous gales the work of casting and hauling the drift-nets goes on. Altogether these boats take many millions of the silvery treasures from the sea around our coast. A lot of people are glad to have this wholesome, cheap, and nutritious food, which is appetising and satisfying, whether eaten fresh or salted.

3. We have various uses for leaves. Sometimes we use them in making clothing; more often we eat them. This pointed, laurel-shaped leaf grew on a plant in a country of Southern Asia. A girl picked it, and put it with others on a round tray to dry in the sun, until it became spotted and gave out a peculiar odour. It was then roasted, and rolled by hand or roller to squeeze out any moisture remaining. Next it was put in a sieve over a fire. Soon it turned quite black, and now looks like a dried-up, useless bit of black stuff. But it is so valuable that it has been sent hundreds of miles by sea to us. In it there is a stimulating property which makes people who use it feel no longer tired.

4. A tiny egg weighing the one-hundredth part of a grain is hatched in a little bag worn round someone's neck. The little creature is fed on leaves, and, as it grows big, splits its skin, and wriggles out of it. Three times more it casts its skin like this. When it is large, fat, and about three inches long, it works together two little streams of a sticky fluid that comes from its body, so that this forms a nice, cosy covering for it. From two

to five days this busy work goes on, the little head seeming to do all the work of pressing the sticky fluid into a thick substantial coat— so thick, indeed, that the creature becomes quite invisible. No person can make such a wonderful thing as that coat, nor can any plant produce it. The thread composing it is soft and smooth, and we make it into all kinds of things—hats, shoes, gloves, umbrellas, and dress materials. This wonderful product is in demand all over the world.

5. Some plants like brilliant sunshine and blue skies; but there is one plant, of great value to mankind, which flourishes best in a land where summer is cool, and the rain frequent. What the botanist calls the fruit grows on a spikelet, and has a tough husk to protect it. If the husks are eaten in large quantities they are rather indigestible; and the difficulty is to get rid of the indigestible husk, and yet keep all the nutriment of the inside. The plant is a most valuable food, and the vigour of mind and body characteristic of the Scottish race is attributed to its use.

6. Nature provides us with many delicious things to eat. One that most people like is made by the skill and intelligent work of a tiny creature that loves the sunshine, blue skies, and brightly-coloured flowers. On a fine summer day it flies miles to find food for itself and the young ones at home; and it stores up what is not wanted in regularly-shaped cells that are made by itself and its companions. Being prudent, it thinks of future needs, and stores a big supply of food for the dark, frosty, winter days to come. But people, even babies, like that food, and so artificial storage places are arranged for its reception. This product, which is eaten with bread and butter, may also be put into cakes or used as medicine.

7. Thousands of miles away from England men are hard at work picking something off trees. The harvest from the trees is quickly packed in boxes, thousands of which arrive in England about Christmas-time. Some of the fruit will be eaten raw, some made into puddings, some into jam or jelly, some into sauce, and some of it, grown at home, will be made into a drink. The fruit is pretty in appearance, and very wholesome, for it contains a good deal of iron. It may be that specimens in the same dish have come from not the other side of the globe or from Canada, but from our own garden; if so, we shall probably find that these have thinner skins, and a much better flavour.

ANSWERS TO THE GAME OF WHAT-ANIMALS-ARE-THESE?

ON page 5934 are some descriptions of animals, and we have to guess what they are from the descriptions that are given.

These are the names of the different creatures:

1. Spider	3. Giraffe	5. Bat
2. Tortoise	4. Amoeba	6. Porpoise

The Story of the Boundless Universe and All Its Wondrous Worlds

Point reached by
the Sound Waves
through Air

Point reached by
the Sound Waves
through Steel Rails

Point reached by
the Sound Waves
through Water

This picture shows us how far the sound waves made by the ringing of bells would travel through air, steel, and water in a certain given time if the bells were all struck at exactly the same moment.

THE WAVES OF SOUND

IN order to have light it is necessary that there shall be not only something outside our bodies, but also an eye to see that something. All Nature is in darkness except where there are eyes to see.

In the same way, " the silence that is in the starry sky " is never broken on the Earth except where there are ears to hear. We are now going to study the something outside ourselves which the ear responds to. We may call that something Sound, but it is not really sound till there is an ear to hear it.

As light is a wave motion, so is sound, and certain facts which are common to all kinds of wave motion are therefore true of both light and sound. But otherwise the differences between these two kinds of wave motion are very great. Anything that carries, or conducts, or conveys, we may call a *medium*, which really means the " thing in the middle." Sound, then, unlike light and radiant heat, is a wave motion in a material medium. This medium is very often air, but it may be a gas or mixture of gases; it may be such a liquid as water, or it may be a solid body.

Where there is no matter there can be no sound, for sound is not otherwise conveyed. It follows that no disturbances on the Sun or the Moon could ever produce

a noise that we could hear, because beyond the limits of our atmosphere there is nothing between us and these heavenly bodies, and though empty space conveys light, it cannot convey sound.

When we say that sound is a wave motion, or a vibration, we make a statement which anyone will agree is true who has seen or felt what happens when sound is produced. For instance, we may hold a piece of string tightly, one end in each hand, and then suddenly pull it. It will actually be seen to vibrate as it produces a little musical note.

The same is true of a piano wire. If we touch a bell that has been sounded we can feel that it is vibrating; also we know that, in such a case as that of a tumbler which has been struck, the finger which stops the vibrations stops the sound at the same time, proving that the vibrations are the cause of the sound. Every time the string or the bell moves it gives the air a little kick, and so there is produced a series of waves which reach our ear, and then become sound.

It is easy to prove that the air conveys these waves. We may put an electric bell in a transparent vessel and set it going, and then we may start to draw the air away by means of an air-pump. As we reduce the amount of air surrounding

ASTRONOMY · GEOLOGY · GEOGRAPHY · CHEMISTRY · PHYSICS · LIFE

the bell, our sight of the bell is not affected, because we see it by light which travels through space; but the sound of the bell gradually becomes fainter, until at last it ceases. The bell itself is vibrating as it was before, but if there is no longer any air round it, it cannot create the waves we call sound. Then, if the air is gradually admitted again, the sound will return. This simple experiment teaches us not only what it is that conveys sound, but also that the loudness of sound depends largely on the state of the air.

WHY SOUND TRAVELS MORE QUICKLY AT ONE TIME THAN ANOTHER

When we compare the speed of light and sound we find a great difference. We see the puff of smoke from a distant cannon some seconds before we hear the report of the explosion. Light travels so fast that, however distant the gun is, we see the flash in fractions of a thousandth part of a second. But sound travels comparatively at a very slow speed, and this speed can easily be reckoned.

The speed of light and of radiant heat is always exactly the same in any circumstances, so far as we can discover. This, however, is not at all true of sound, the speed of which varies considerably with different circumstances.

We may notice at once that, fortunately for the art of music, the speed of sound varies only in very small degree with its pitch or with its loudness. It would be a very serious matter for the hearing of music if, when we were listening to an orchestra, the sound of the flutes reached our ears a beat or two before the sound of the double basses, when the composer meant us to hear them together; or if a tune, being loudly played by one part of the orchestra, and softly accompanied by another part of it, reached our ears before or after the accompaniment.

WHY A NOISE WILL TRAVEL FASTER THROUGH IRON THAN THROUGH AIR

The ordinary speed of sound through air is about 1100 feet a second. As the temperature of the air rises it becomes slightly more elastic; it rebounds better when struck, so to speak, and therefore the passage of sound through it—which entirely depends on the elasticity of the air—is made easier. The speed of sound, therefore, increases somewhat with a rise in temperature of the air, so long as the air is of the same density. If we under-stand this principle of elasticity, we shall see why it is that sound passes more rapidly through liquids than through gases, such as the air, and still more rapidly through solids.

Such a metal as iron, in the solid state, has much greater elasticity than air, and sound will travel through it about seventeen times as fast as through air. This means that waves of the same shape which pass through air pass in and through the solid iron. It is possible to make a confusion here about speed, and therefore we must just explain that the pitch of a musical note depends on the number of waves striking the ear in a second. This is quite a distinct question from the rate at which the waves travel through the air or anything else.

A given sound conveyed through iron will reach the ear about seventeen times more quickly than when conveyed through air, but its pitch will be the same in both cases, because the number of vibrations occurring in each second is the same in both cases, though they get through the iron so much more quickly.

WHY WE HEAR WELL ON A CLEAR AND FROSTY NIGHT

When we come to study the loudness of sound we find that the first law about it is the same as the law of other wave motions, such as radiant heat or light.

In the exact language of science, the law is that *the loudness of sound varies inversely as the square of the distance.* This is simply a neat and quick way of saying that, if we walk three times as far away from the source of the sound as we were before, its loudness will be not one-third of what it was, but one-ninth of what it was, nine being the square of three. The square of a number is the number multiplied by itself.

That is all there is to say about the power of such things as light and gravitation; but in the case of sound other things come in, for the density of the medium which conveys it is very important. On a frosty night the air is very dense. One consequence of this is that a motor-car runs better, because the engine gets a better supply of oxygen. Another consequence is that sounds are heard more loudly.

At the seaside, when we watch the waves rolling up against a breakwater or a cliff, we know that they may be reflected, or bounced back. Often the waves may be broken up, and what exactly happens will depend on the kind of surface they strike against. But if it is a smooth, flat surface, we see that the waves are reflected from it, almost as a ball is from a wall. Now, if sound is really a wave motion, we should expect that it could be reflected as the waves of the sea may be; and this is indeed the fact, as we shall soon see.

All wave motions can be reflected. What is true of sound is as true of radiant

the other hand, we throw it slantwise, it comes off the wall slantwise.

This is equally true of sound and radiant heat and light. One of the points to notice is that the level, or plane, as we say, in which the wave approaches the surface is the same as that in which it comes off. For instance, suppose the sound were running along on the level of this paper, and then struck obliquely (or slanting-wise) a wall at the edge of the paper, it would come back not only at the same angle at which it approached the

IN THE DOME OF ST. PAUL'S—LISTENERS TESTING SOUND IN THE WHISPERING GALLERY

heat and light as of the waves of the sea. There are certain laws which apply to these very different cases. The first, stated in scientific language, is that *the angle of incidence and the angle of reflection are equal.* This means that the angle at which the wave approaches the surface is the same as the angle at which it will leave the surface. The same applies to a billiard-ball striking the cushion of a billiard-table or to throwing a ball against a wall. If we throw the ball straight at the wall, it comes back straight, except for the influence of gravitation; if, on

wall, but still travelling on the level of the paper—not bent upwards or downwards so as to travel either above or below the level of the paper.

This is true also of light and radiant heat. We all know that sounds seem different in the open air when compared with sounds in a closed room; we know how different our voices sound in different places. All this is a question of the reflection of sound. The most striking way in which we can prove to ourselves that sound is reflected is in hearing an echo.

One of the ways in which we can test for ourselves the rate at which sound moves is to make a sound at a certain distance from an echoing surface, and then notice how long it takes the echo to reach our ears. There are echoes in Nature besides those we make ourselves, and the best instance of reflection of sound causing an echo is a peal of thunder.

Thunder is a disturbance in the air forming a sound, made by the passage of lightning from cloud to cloud, or from cloud to earth. If there is no echo we simply hear a single clap of thunder. When we hear a peal we simply hear that clap of thunder echoed again and again from cloud and earth.

THINGS THAT MUST BE REMEMBERED AT GREAT MEETINGS AND CONCERTS

In places made for speaking or for music, echoes are often a great nuisance. All our pleasure in listening to music depends on the absence of any echoes that can be noticed. In one of the most famous halls in London it was almost impossible to hear music with pleasure because of the echoes from its great round wall.

Thus, when a player struck a single chord on a piano, it sounded throughout the hall like a quickly repeated chord.

The case is still worse in listening to a speaker, because everything depends on our hearing each syllable apart from any echoes of words previously spoken. Many devices have to be adopted in order to prevent, as far as possible, the reflection of sound in such cases. Tapestries and hangings, and so on, are bad reflectors of sound, and may be of service; wires stretched across the hall above the heads of the audience may often help to break up the sound waves, so that they are, at any rate, not reflected from the roof.

SOUND PROPERTIES IMPROVED BY THE PRESENCE OF AN AUDIENCE

The people themselves, by their mere presence, improve the properties of a hall for speaking and singing, because their bodies form a broken surface for the floor of the hall, and the sound waves are broken up as the waves of the sea are broken up when they strike an irregular cliff as compared with a flat breakwater.

When the surfaces are far away from the speaker or the musician, time is taken in the reflection, and so a distinct echo is heard. But if the sound is produced close to a curved surface, as in the case of many churches, the echo occurs so quickly that, instead of being heard by the ear as an echo interfering with everything, it blends with the sound of which it is an echo, and simply makes it more clear.

The Whispering Gallery of St. Paul's Cathedral is really an illustration of the same thing. The principle of echoes, or the reflection of sound, is invaluable in every case where we employ anything in the nature of a trumpet. The use of the outer ears of animals depends on the reflection of sound, as do the artificial ear-trumpets made for deaf people. Sound is reflected from side to side of the ear or the ear-trumpet until it reaches the place where it is to be heard.

We know that light may not only be reflected but also bent, or *refracted*. That is what happens when we concentrate the light of the Sun by means of a burning-glass on a piece of paper ; and it also happens in many other cases. Now, it is very interesting to discover that sound can be refracted in its course, as light can.

AN EXPERIMENT WITH A SWINGING BALLOON AND A WATCH

If we take a big bag or balloon, and fill it with carbon dioxide, we find that this bag acts towards sound as a lens acts towards light. The sound waves will be bent by the gas in the balloon, and they will be brought to a focus on the other side of the balloon.

Thus, as in a well-known experiment made by Lord Rayleigh, a great student of sound, we may stand opposite a watch at such a distance that we can hear nothing. But if a balloon filled with carbon dioxide is made to swing slowly from side to side between us and the watch, and if we are just at the right distance, then, when the balloon is in the middle of its swing, and focuses the sound waves, we shall hear the watch ticking.

We still have things to learn about sound waves, because just as there are ultra-violet waves of light which the eye cannot see, so there are sound waves of such high frequency that the ear cannot detect them. A whole new science is developing in the use of these supersonic waves, as they are called. They have the power to kill bacteria and to cause chemical changes in a substance.

(Next chapter in this group, page 6179)

The Story of Immortal Folk Whose Work Will Never Die

Edward John Eyre   Ludwig Leichhardt   John McDouall Stuart

THE MEN WHO MADE AUSTRALIA KNOWN

Down in the great South Sea of the old traveller's dreams there is an island continent of three million square miles and a young British nation of just over seven million people. The continent is one of the oldest land masses in the world; the nation is one of the youngest.

The history of this nation is as strange, as romantic, as stirring, as anything to be found in the annals of mankind. "What are you, my good woman?" said Sir Walter Scott to an aged woman who begged of him.

"Your honour, it's a poor old struggler I am—just that," she answered.

If we ask the people of the Australian nation what they are they may proudly answer : "We are just young strugglers, honourably that." They have had one of the hardest tasks ever set a people, and they have done marvels.

In a nutshell the story is this. We sent the first of them out to this great land saying, *Go and possess it*, and they did not know what they were to possess. They settled down at Sydney on less than twenty square miles of land, called it New South Wales, and declared it British. They were landed on an unknown sea-coast, and for a quarter of a century they never got more than fifty miles inland. Australia was a closed book to them.

The Blue Mountains, towering behind the coastline, kept them prisoners for 25 years. All that time they were trying to find a way through or over, and they failed; route after route led them to Castle Despair. But at last, after a quarter of a century, Gregory Blaxland went boldly up the mountain face and over, and, cutting his way through dense scrub for sixteen days, looked down on the Land of Promise.

There before him, over the mountains, was land smiling like an English meadow, pasture for herds and flocks, life for human beings. It was emancipation from that terrible prison-house on the storm-wracked coast.

It was emancipation in more senses than one, for of the 1163 people who reached Australia on the seventh of February in 1788 no less than 565 men, 144 women, six girls, and five boys had gone from our prisons.

We had just lost one nation in America, and so we were founding another; and it was founded on prison wrecks. Our ancestors of those days were not more cruel than we are now, but they had inherited ideas as to how crime should be punished. There were scores of small offences for which death was the penalty, and still more punished by transportation

EXPLORERS · INVENTORS · WRITERS · ARTISTS · SCIENTISTS

overseas. So hundreds of men from our prisons were sent out with this batch of emigrants who were to begin the history of Australia.

It is not necessary to assume that every man among them was a perfect gentle knight, as Chaucer says, but it is true that most of them were mild offenders. Many of them became splendid characters, tradesmen, lawyers, doctors, schoolmasters; the really bad continued bad and became worse.

THE TOWN SET UP AMID COPPER AND SILVER AND GOLD

Well, there they were, with one sheep and a little herd of cattle, which at once ran away and was lost in the bush for the next six years. Blaxland's discovery was the first way out from the little area in which they were settled.

The new land was at once possessed, and in the year of Waterloo—which finally convinced Napoleon that he was not to have either Little Treasure Island or this wondrous continent he had also coveted—the first inland town was established. It was Bathurst, set amid gold and silver and copper and slate, though of these things nothing was to be known for another generation. But, once there, the enterprise of these people bore its fruit, and rivers were found, the great Liverpool plains were revealed, with a way out to the sea at Port Macquarie, and the twenty square miles of colony was found to be only the gate to 120,000 square miles.

Gradually some sense of the realities was grasped, and the Australians found that they were in a land where it is summer when winter has the northern half of the world in its grip, a land whose climate is largely tropical, where enormous deserts of sand and stone are sandwiched between vast areas of prickly scrub and multitudes of eucalyptus trees; where all the animals are strange to the rest of the world ; where rivers are few and for the most part, instead of running to the sea, flow inland and lose themselves in the desert, yet where land is fair and good to stock and for purposes of cultivation.

THE PRIMITIVE PEOPLE OF THE GREAT ISLAND CONTINENT

Then there was the problem of the natives, the strangest and most primitive of peoples—savages, cannibals, wielding a marvellous weapon in the boomerang, and able to make fire by rubbing wood on wood, yet too ignorant to build a hut; matchless as climbers and trackers, but generally beast-like in their habits, and filled with superstitions and terrors.

The natives, indeed, played their part with us in the opening-up of this mighty land of which they had made not one particle of use. Escaping convicts treated them with fearful cruelty at times, and so kindled a vengeful spirit in them. We read of one man cutting off a native's finger to make himself a pipe-stopper.

Yet these poor creatures could be affectionate and faithful. All the big exploring trips included natives, and great things these poor people did at times; terrible things, too, often. To some of them a white man was a meal; to others he was a god, and some would face him as Caliban on his island faced Trinculo in Shakespeare's Tempest, when he said:

> Hast thou not dropped from heaven? I'll show thee every fertile inch of the island? I'll kiss thy foot; I'll swear myself thy subject. I'll shew thee the best springs; I'll pluck thee berries. I'll fish for thee, and get thee wood enough. I with my long nails will dig the pignuts; show thee a jay's nest, and instruct thee how to snare the nimble marmozet.

Services of this kind the Blackfellows often rendered the early settlers, though many a brave heart was stayed in midjourney with a native spear through it.

JOHN OXLEY AND HIS DISAPPOINTING JOURNEYS ALONG THE RIVERS

Even an Australian Caliban would have been esteemed by John Oxley, the first of the great adventurers into the interior, who, in 1817, traced the way of the River Lachlan, was led into a world of swamps wherever he turned, and went back to Sydney believing an inland sea to be beyond the point at which he failed. A second trip brought to light stretches of the Macquarie River and the existence of many others. His, indeed, was a rare haul of waters in name, but little, alas, in reality; for Australia is a land of disappointing rivers. One of the rivers he found was the Brisbane, on which the city of that name stands. But the next great discovery was that of an adventurous botanist, Allan Cunningham, who, breasting the Liverpool Range, came upon that dreamland of the shepherd, the Darling Downs, an unrivalled pasture of six thousand square miles in an unbroken piece. What hope and courage must have

A SAVAGE HERO COMES BETWEEN HIS TRIBESMEN AND THE GREAT EXPLORER STURT, AND BY HIS BRAVE
ACTION SAVES THE WHITE MAN'S LIFE

come to the young colony with this discovery! The year was 1827, and in 1828 the new land began to make true history.

Captain Charles Sturt reached Australia as a soldier, but, resigning his commission, he led an expedition from Sydney in search of the inland sea which Oxley had imagined. So hopeful was he that he took a little boat on wheels. With him was Hamilton Hume, a rare spirit; and they had two soldiers and eight convicts to keep them company.

There are wet seasons and dry seasons in Australia. Oxley had explored in a wet one; here was one of the opposite kind. The land was parched so that it split the hoofs of the horses. The great ostrich-like birds stood gasping with the heat, which caused even the native dogs to totter like phantoms.

Where he had hoped to find a sea Sturt found a wilderness of reeds, but after miserable sufferings, borne with firmness and dignity, the party were gladdened by the sight of a river, eighty yards wide and alive with water fowl. The delighted men rushed down the steep banks to drink, only to find the water *as salt as the sea!*

THE LITTLE RAFT WITH WHICH A GREAT RIVER WAS DISCOVERED

It was what we have ever since known as the Darling River. The party retraced their steps, wandered on, and touched the same river ninety miles farther inland, but still it was undrinkable. They found and named the Bogan, and then went back to Sydney. In his next expedition, in 1830-31, Sturt followed the course of the Murrumbidgee River. He reached the river 200 miles from Sydney, and traced it for a week, when he saw that he could not take his whole troop with him. They had a whale boat on wheels and vehicles for their goods; and he caused a little raft to be made. On this he placed such goods as could not be carried in the boat, roped the two craft together, took six men with him, sent the remainder back, and boldly struck out on the river.

The river ran faster and faster, and when his raft smashed they swirled along for days. Then, to their great delight, they were swept from this narrow and forbidding waterway out on to the bosom of the magnificent highway now known as Murray River, the greatest river of the southern continent.

Along its broad surface they sped for nearly a month, not uneventfully. There was a moment when hundreds of natives menaced them from the shore, when, as a host of spears was about to be cast at them and Sturt was about to fire, a native of commanding manner emerged suddenly from the jungle, leaped into the water, approached the leader of the attacking natives, pulled down his spear, covered him with his own body in front of the white man's gun, and restored peace.

THE TERRIBLE JOURNEY OF AN EXPLORER AND HIS STARVING CREW

We should like to know the history of that noble savage, but we never shall. A truly splendid deed, it saved these dauntless seven. On they went, until their river ended in a swampy lake, which they called the Alexandrina. They were near the sea, where Adelaide now stands, but there was no hope in that direction. They had no ships; they had little food; the only course was to row back the way they had come, and once more face the natives.

For two months this little crew urged their reluctant boat against the stream. Day by day they suffered from heat and famine, day by day they grew weaker; day by day they were in peril from the natives. But they did this great journey at last, though there was madness in the boat for the last few days. They reached the old camping-ground from which they had set out, and there they divided their last ounce of food. Then, in the nick of time, up came a rescue party with stores, and they returned in triumph to Sydney, having travelled over 2000 miles.

THE EXPLORERS IMPRISONED FOR SIX MONTHS BY THE HEAT

It may be said that Sturt by his discoveries had created South Australia. The province was founded five years later, and in 1838 he was appointed its surveyor-general. But the spirit of the adventurer was always his, and in 1844 he headed a new expedition, which included John McDouall Stuart, to see what lay at the back of the beyond in the new territory; the purpose of this expedition was to examine the heart of South Australia.

Leaving Lake Torrens on their left, they passed up the Murray and the Darling Rivers and struck due north. It was winter time, so water held for a while, but they reached the desert region associated with the Barrier Range and the Grey

THE LAST DAYS OF TWO HEROES

THE AUSTRALIAN EXPLORERS BURKE AND WILLS, HALF-STARVED AND EXHAUSTED, ON THEIR TRAGIC
HOMEWARD JOURNEY AFTER HAVING CROSSED THE CONTINENT.

Range. All was dry. The earth was split on the surface, and wounded the feet of the pack animals. Travelling was an agony. At last they came to a place where water welled up from a rock. Sturt called it Rocky Glen, and stayed there.

For six terrible months they were imprisoned by the heat. They explored from this centre, but found nothing but sterility. To make life bearable they made a dug-out in the earth in which to shelter from the sun, but the temperature in the shade was 130 degrees. It dried the ink on their pens before they could write; it caused the screws to fall out of their boxes; it made metal so hot that it blistered their hands; it split their combs and knife-handles into fragments, made the lead fall out of their pencils, rendered their nails as brittle as glass, and prevented the hair of man and the wool of sheep from growing.

THE BEAUTIFUL SIGHT WHICH MET THE EYES OF COLLET BARKER

Slow starvation in such heat brought on scurvy, and at last there was nothing left to do but to turn home. They discovered Cooper's Creek, an important water-course; but when they reached Adelaide they were far spent, and Sturt's eyes were almost blinded by the glare of the sun.

Captain Sturt's efforts have carried us ahead of the true calendar of events. We must turn back a moment to note the bitter end of Collet Barker of Sturt's old regiment, who went to seek a connection between the sea in St. Vincent's Gulf and Lake Alexandrina. He climbed the steep ascent of Mount Lofty, and was the first known man to look out across the lovely plains where Adelaide now stands; he found the narrow channel by which the Murray River enters the sea, and with a zealot's ardour he threw off his clothes and swam across to make sure of its width.

THE TRAGIC FATE OF A MAN IN HIS HOUR OF TRIUMPH

He was never seen again. There were natives hidden in great numbers on the opposite side of the river, and his companions saw the smoke of fires ascend, and wondered why. When a search was afterwards made the truth was made known by a native woman. The blacks said they had thrown the body into the sea, but the truth is that they were cannibals; the smoke had come from their fires when they killed the Englishman, and they had held a horrible feast that night in 1831.

Now came the terrific journeys of Edward John Eyre, son of a Yorkshire clergyman, in 1840.

None of the records of the endurance of explorers surpasses his. He first made the overland journey across the desert to the north of the Australian Bight, where the telegraph line now runs between South Australia and Western Australia.

Eyre was descended from the notable Eyre family of the Derbyshire Peakland. After experience as a sheep farmer in New South Wales he became a magistrate in South Australia and official protector of the native tribes, over whom he had great influence. In this capacity he explored the country to the north of Spencer Gulf, found Lake Torrens, and reached, across 200 miles of desert, the lake that bears his name. He spoke in his Journal of this expedition as a failure, but no one thinks it a failure now. This was in 1840. In February 1841, he decided to attempt the journey of 850 miles from Fowler Bay to Albany, across wholly unexplored country. The most sheltered part of Fowler Bay, from which the dangerous part of the journey began, is now known as Port Eyre.

THE DESERT EXPLORERS WHO DUG IN THE SAND FOR WATER

The intrepid explorer had with him one white companion, Baxter, who had been his overseer, and three natives. They had a little cavalcade of nine horses, a pony, a foal, six sheep, and nine weeks' supply of flour, tea, and sugar, with some water. It was the height of summer. The first 135 miles did not produce a drop of water, and the whole party would have perished but for the water carried by the pack-horses. The horses went five days without water, and the sheep six days, and were so exhausted that all the baggage except such as was essential to life had to be abandoned. On the fifth day enough water was found to save the horses, but it had to be dug for, and was found at a depth of five feet.

The white men and the strongest of the natives walked all the way, and the two younger natives rode the strongest horse alternately. The next waterless stretch was 160 miles. When, at the end of this parched desert, they were in utter despair, they reached a patch of moist sand, and found fresh water six feet below the surface.

All their stores, except two guns and a small quantity of tea, sugar, and flour, had now been abandoned or used. The pony and two horses were dead, and only two sheep were left. They had no water, and were only saved by a heavy fall of dew in the night before they reached the underground water. Eyre had collected in the night with a sponge enough dew to fill a quart pot. Eyre stayed by the underground water while Baxter went back 47 miles to recover some of the stores. He took three horses with him, but returned with only one of them.

They were now half-way on the journey, with no hope of more water for 150 miles. Some of the abandoned stores were retrieved by Eyre going back with one of the natives, and the two carried the stores between them. At the place where the town of Eyre now stands they stayed 28 days to regain strength, the natives eating the horses and the white men the sheep.

THE FAITHFUL BLACK BOY WHO REMAINED TRUE TO HIS MASTER

Then the worst calamity of all befell the dauntless travellers. Leaving the camp one night to attend to the remaining horses, Eyre heard a gun fired behind him, and when he rushed back he found Baxter dying, shot by two of the natives, who had deserted with guns, nearly all the ammunition, and part of the stores. Only four gallons of water were left. The black boy Wylie remained faithful, and Eyre struggled on for seven more days and nights, with the two murderers tracking him at a distance through the desert. Then again they reached water, six feet below the surface, and rested, Eyre now being desperately ill. This was at the part of the coast now called Point Malcolm. They had waited there for a week, and almost reached the end of their supply of food, when a French whaling ship, with an English captain, came into the bay. For ten days Eyre was the guest of the captain, and then, refreshed and provided with fresh supplies, he renewed his journey, and in another month reached Albany.

A MAN'S LONG AND TERRIBLE JOURNEYS ACROSS A CONTINENT

Afterwards Eyre became Lieutenant-Governor of New Zealand, Governor of St. Vincent, and finally Governor of Jamaica, where he was a centre for violent controversy because of the stern decision with which he suppressed a Negro rising.

Notwithstanding the strain he endured in his pioneering days, and the anxieties of his later career, he died in peace at 86, after 35 years of retirement.

The next name looming large is that of the ill-fated Ludwig Leichhardt. He set out from Sydney in 1844 to cross the continent to Port Essington in the north. He had with him five Englishmen and two natives, and expected to make the journey in about eight months. It took 17 months. He had a frightful experience, one of his companions being killed and two terribly wounded by natives. All his stores were gone and his equipment quite worn out when at last the survivors staggered to their destination.

A ship took them back to Sydney, where Leichhardt had a public reception and a handsome reward. Leichhardt made other expeditions, both with the purpose of crossing from east to west, but ill luck dogged him all the way. When he was last heard of, in April 1848, he had seven companions, 50 oxen, 20 mules, and six horses. He wrote " All well " from Macpherson's station on the Cogoon River, and then, with all his little host, vanished as if the earth had swallowed him.

Between 1851 and 1865 five expeditions went out in quest of him, and in 1861 an explorer found his old camp and a tree with L marked on it. But never has Leichhardt been seen or heard of since.

Now we come to Jacky Jacky, whose fame should live as long as Australian history is remembered.

HOW JACKY ESCAPED FROM HIS ENEMIES BY WALKING IN A RIVER

Jacky's master in 1848 was a fine fellow named Edmund Kennedy, who did excellent work in tracing a river to Cooper's Creek, and then set out, with Jacky and nine men, to explore the great Cape York Peninsula in the north of Queensland. Toiling through dense jungles and prickly shrubs, which tore the clothes from their backs and the skin from their hands, the party was in dire straits, so that Kennedy split the troop, and, in company with three white men and Jacky, pushed on for the peak of the peninsula.

One of the three was fatally injured, and Kennedy left him to the other two while he and Jacky hurried to the coast for assistance. But the chapter of disaster was near an end. Savages attacked and killed him. Jacky kept his head in this bitter hour, and frightened the wretches away with his gun. Then he dug a grave and buried his master. Kennedy had kept precious journals, and these Jacky took away with him.

In order to get through the ranks of his enemies he plunged into a river, and, walking miles with only his head above the water, he reached the sea and was carried by a ship back to Sydney, where he delivered the treasured journals of his lost master. Of the others of the party only two survived; six of them died of starvation.

The m a n y expe-ditions sent out in search of Leichhardt added much to com-mon knowledge of the land, and the attack had by this time been made from each coast in turn. Now we come to a period in which great spirits worked at the same time on the s a m e plan. The travels of John McDouall Stuart, begun in 1859, map-ped t h e continent from south to north, but in the meantime two other explorers, Robert O'Hara Burke and William John Wills, succeeded in crossing the contin-ent, only to die of starvation on their way back. It was for this expedition that camels were first brought to Australia. McDouall Stuart had only horses.

EYRE, WITH A NATIVE, ON THE LAST STAGE OF HIS GREAT JOURNEY

The first attempt Stuart made to cross the continent began with cold; then rains soaked his stores and caused a horse to sink to death in a morass; then came days of thorny scrub, which tore his clothes and his horse's harness to pieces; then blindness threatened in Stuart's right eye. Still on he went, and he planted the British flag in what seemed to him to be the very centre of the continent.

The way grew worse and worse. At times the horses had to go for a hundred hours without water. Two of them went

mad, a third dashed away with him into the bush and smashed his right hand. His gums grew so sore that he could swallow only fluid; his hands festered and the muscles showed through his skin. But it was only the murderous attacks of natives which finally turned him back, when he was within 400 miles of triumph. Within four months of reaching Adelaide he was off again. Though he did not know it, Wills and Burke, taking a more easterly route, were bound for the same goal, and actually beat him. He pur-sued his former route and passed his far-thest north, naming creeks and wells and mountains as he went on his way.

One curious thing he found was as pathetic in its way as anything revealed in Egypt's Valley of the Kings. Propped up in the branches of a tree was a beautiful small canoe 30 inches long. It had been made with great skill, with native carving on the sides, and in it lay the body of a little native child.

The way was in-creasingly difficult. Nettles grew fifty feet high, stinging with a deadly poison; scrub with fierce thorns grew so long that a horseman could not be seen five yards away; and this, coupled with shortage of water, at last drove them back when they were within 150 miles of the coast they were seeking.

On reaching Adelaide Stuart heard that Burke and Wills were dead, but he set forth a third time, and now he conquered. Heat, privation, native attacks, long de-tours made to avoid the prickly jungle, accident, injury, thirst, were all borne with a noble fortitude. Natives, when they did not openly attack, fired the bush around him day after day, but the patient valour of this great man overcame all obstacles and all enemies.

He sought the ocean as eagerly as Columbus sought the land, and at last, on July 24, 1862, one of his party cried, in an ecstasy of exultation, *The sea, the sea!* In that moment of his happiness, after years of effort and suffering and privation, Stuart was dumb. He stooped down to the waters, and dipped his feet and washed his hands in the sea, " as I promised Sir Richard Macdonnell I would do if I reached it."

He left on the shore of Van Diemen's Gulf a flag and a notice announcing the name of his party, their route, and the date; and then he turned home. The way he went, so slowly and in such pain, is the route by which communication is now as fast as light, for Stuart's great march laid down the path by which the continental telegraph runs.

The story of Australia's pioneers does not end with the explorers who travelled through desert and jungle. As the great new continent was opened up by settlers and graziers, and as new townships came into being, the great problem was that of communications.

HOW THE AEROPLANE CAME TO AUSTRALIA

The communities were so scattered and the distances so vast, that it was impossible to build railways or even good roads to serve the whole population. The greater part of Australia became known as the outback, where travelling was slow and difficult and where business was hindered by postal delays and lack of transport.

In these conditions it was natural that when the flying machine was invented, Australians looked to it as a possible solution to their problems.

Towards the end of the 19th century a tall, shy, bearded Australian, Lawrence Hargrave, pondered the question: How do birds fly? He built a workshop near Sydney to carry out experiments to find the answer to that question. That was in 1884. For nine years he experimented. He produced model monoplanes that eventually flew 384 feet. He experimented with miniature engines and invented the rotary motor. He contributed articles to the journal of the Royal Society and in this way Hargrave's ideas reached America.

What is generally regarded as the first aeroplane flight in Australia was made by Harry Houdini, at Digger's Rest, Victoria, on March 18, 1910 with a Voisin biplane. On his third flight, which lasted $3\frac{1}{2}$ minutes, he covered about two miles and reached a height of 100 feet.

In 1910, J. L. Duigan built the first aeroplane to be made in Australia, and flew it for a distance of 196 yards. Experiments still went on, but before any more ideas could be followed up the great war of 1914 overtook the world. During the war years many Australians became aviators, and acquired skill and experience in military aircraft.

THE PRIZE THAT WAS WON BY TWO FLYING BROTHERS

After the war a prize of £10,000 was offered by the Australian Commonwealth Government for the first flight from England to Australia. The prize was won by two brothers, Captains Ross and Keith Smith, as pilots, with Sergeants J. M. Bennett and W. H. Shiers as engineers. They left Hounslow, near London, in their Vickers Vimy aircraft on November 12, 1919, and landed in Darwin a month later. The brothers were knighted for their achievement, and a memorial to the flight has been built on the sand which was their landing strip.

Australia wanted air services, and in 1920 a company was registered under the name of Queensland and Northern Territory Aerial Services Ltd., which soon became familiar by its initials, QANTAS, which Australians pronounce Kwantus, as though it were a word.

" THE MOST AIR-MINDED COUNTRY IN THE WORLD "

Other Australian aviators quickly achieved international fame, among them Bert Hinkler, Kingsford Smith (later Sir Charles Kingsford Smith) and C. P. T. Ulm, so that Australia soon laid claim to being the most air-minded country in the world.

When the time came to open an air-mail service between the United Kingdom and Australia, QANTAS co-operated with Imperial Airways in pioneering the route across the eastern hemisphere. In 1934 QANTAS gave up its routes within Australia and, as Qantas Empire Airways Ltd., took its place among the International Airlines.

In 1958 Qantas became the first airline to fly right round the world through both hemispheres.

A READY-MADE GENTLEMAN AT HOME

AN AMUSING PICTURE OF MR. JOURDAIN SHOWING HIS WIFE HOW TO FENCE—FROM THE PAINTING
BY CHARLES R. LESLIE. See story on page 6079

MR. JOURDAIN IS INTRODUCED TO A NOBLE LADY—FROM THE PAINTING BY W. P. FRITH
The lower picture is reproduced by courtesy of the Corporation of Preston

The Great Stories of the World That Will Be Told for Ever

THE EMPEROR'S NIGHTINGALE

THE palace of the Emperor of China was the most magnificent in the world. It was made entirely of fine porcelain, extremely costly, but at the same time so brittle that it was dangerous even to touch it. The emperor's garden extended so far that even the gardener did not know the end of it.

Whoever walked beyond it, however, came to a beautiful wood with very high trees, and beyond that to a lake. The wood went quite down to the lake, which was very deep and blue; and among the branches dwelled a nightingale, who sang so sweetly that even the poor fisherman, who had so much else to do when he came out at night-time to cast his nets, would stand still and listen to her song.

Travellers came from all parts of the world to the emperor's city; and they admired the city, the palace, and the garden; but if they heard the nightingale they said: " This is best of all." And they talked about her after they went home, and learned men wrote most beautiful verses about the nightingale of the wood near the lake.

These books went round the world, and one of them at last happened to reach the emperor.

" What in the world is this? " said he. " The nightingale! I do not know it ! Can there be such a bird in my garden without my having heard of it? " So he called his gentleman usher.

" There is said to be a very remarkable bird here called the nightingale," said the emperor. " Her song, they say, is worth more than anything else in my dominions. Why has no one told me of her? "

" I have never before heard her mentioned," said the gentleman usher.

" I wish her to come and sing before me this evening," said the emperor. " Seek her! "

But where was she to be found? The gentleman usher ran up one flight of steps, down another, through halls, and through passages; not one of all whom he met had ever seen or heard of the nightingale.

At last he met a poor little girl in the kitchen, who said: " Oh, yes, I know her very well! "

" Little kitchen maiden," said the gentleman usher, " I will procure for you a sure appointment in the kitchen if you will conduct me to the nightingale."

So they went together to the wood where the nightingale used to sing, and half the Court went with them.

The little girl stopped before a tree.

" There she is! " said she, pointing to a little bird up in the branches.

IMAGINATION · CHIVALRY · LEGENDS · GOLDEN DEEDS · FAIRY TALES

"Most excellent nightingale!" said the gentleman usher, "I have the honour to invite you to a Court festival which is to take place this evening, when his Imperial Majesty will doubtless be enchanted with your delightful song."

"My song would sound far better among the green trees," said the nightingale. However, she followed willingly when she heard the emperor wished it.

At the palace she sang so sweetly that she touched the hearts of all who heard her; and the emperor was so delighted that he said: "The nightingale shall have my golden slippers and wear them round her neck."

But the nightingale said: "I have seen tears in the emperor's eyes. That is the greatest reward I can have."

Yes, indeed, the nightingale's success was complete. She was now to remain at Court and to have her own cage, and all the city talked of the wonderful bird.

One day a large parcel arrived directed to the emperor.

Inside was a little piece of mechanism, lying in a box—an artificial nightingale, which was intended to look like the living one, but was covered with diamonds, rubies, and sapphires. When this artificial bird had been wound up it could sing one of the tunes that the real nightingale sang; and its tail, glittering with silver and gold, went up and down all the time. A little band was fastened round its neck, on which was written: The Nightingale of the Emperor of China is poor compared with that of the Emperor of Japan."

"That is famous!" said everyone; and he who had brought the bird obtained the title of Chief Imperial Nightingale Bringer. "Now they shall sing together; we will have a duet."

And so they had to sing together: but it did not succeed, for the real nightingale sang in her own way, and the artificial bird produced its tones by wheels.

"It is not his fault," said the artist; "he keeps exact time, and sings quite according to method."

So the artificial bird had now to sing alone. He was quite as successful as the real nightingale, and then he was so much prettier to look at; his plumage sparkled with jewels, silver, and gold.

Three-and-thirty times he sang one and the same tune, and yet he was not weary; everyone would willingly have heard him

again. However, the emperor now wished the real nightingale to sing something. But where was she? Nobody had noticed that she had flown out of the open window, flown away to her own green wood.

"What is the meaning of this?" said the emperor; and all the courtiers abused the nightingale, and called her a most ungrateful creature. "We have the best bird, at all events," said they. And for the four-and-thirtieth time they heard the same tune; but still they did not quite know it.

The real nightingale was banished from the empire; but the artificial bird had its place on a silken cushion close to the emperor's bed.

Thus it went on for a whole year. But one evening, when the bird was in full voice, and the emperor lay in bed and listened, there was suddenly a noise— "bang!"—inside the bird, and the music stopped.

The emperor jumped quickly out of bed, and had his chief physician called. But of what use could he be? Then a clockmaker was fetched, and at last, after a great deal of consultation, the bird in some measure was put to rights again; but the clockmaker said it must be spared much singing, for the pegs were almost worn out, and it was impossible to renew them. So now the bird was allowed to sing only once a year.

When five years were passed away, a great affliction visited the whole empire. The emperor was ill.

Stiff and pale he lay in his splendid bed with the long velvet curtains and heavy gold tassels. Death sat at the emperor's bedside, and the emperor was afraid. A window was opened above, and the moon shone down on the emperor and the artificial bird.

"Music, music!" cried the emperor. "Thou dear little artificial bird, sing, I pray thee, sing!"

But the bird was silent; there was no one there to wind him up.

But suddenly the room became filled with such beautiful sounds that Death could not stay. The music of the real, living nightingale could vanquish Death, who, like a cold, white shadow, flew out of the window.

"Thanks, thanks!" said the emperor. "Thou heavenly little bird, I know thee well. I have banished thee from my realm, and thou hast brought me back to life. How shall I reward thee?"

"Thou hast already rewarded me," said the nightingale. "I have seen tears in thine eyes, as when I sang to thee for the first time. Those I shall never forget; they are jewels which do so much good to a minstrel's heart. But sleep now, and wake fresh and healthy. I will sing thee to sleep."

And she sang, and the emperor fell into a sweet and healing sleep.

When all the people knew that their emperor was whole again their joy knew no bounds, and the little nightingale was more popular than anyone in the land.

The emperor begged her to stay with him and live in the palace, but to this she would not consent.

"I must be free," said she. "But in the evening, when you are alone, I will come and sit by your window and sing to you of the good and evil of the world, and fill your mind with helpful thoughts."

THE RACE WITH THE WOLVES

ONE still night in the depth of winter a Russian baron set out from the little frontier town of Rob-rin.

The snow lay knee-deep in the streets, and was still falling as the baron, with his wife and child and his servant Eric, got into the sledge and started on the next stage of his journey home to Petrograd.

The landlord of the inn begged him not to attempt to travel that night, as the roads were full of snowdrifts and packs of hungry wolves were known to be in the neighbourhood. But the baron was anxious to get on to the next town, called Bolisov, and the order was given to start.

About an hour after, as they approached a great forest, the baron's wife suddenly exclaimed: "Hark! What was that?"

In the distance came a long, melancholy wailing that rose and fell on the still night air. There was no mistaking that sound: it was the howling of a pack of wolves.

The baron and his servant got ready their pistols; and none too soon, for, looking back, they saw grey, shadowy forms coming across the snow. Faster and faster flew the horses, rocking the sledge violently from side to side.

But the wolves drew steadily nearer. There was a large number of them, led by an enormous old wolf, which, as soon as he got alongside, tried to spring upon one of the horses. Bang went Eric's pistol, and the wolf sprang into the air and fell down dead. At this the others fell back for a few moments, but they were soon again in full pursuit. This time the baron and Eric fired together, and four wolves fell dead in the snow. The rest of the pack paused for a moment, but they were soon again in full pursuit.

"There is no help for it. We must turn one of the horses loose," cried Eric, desperately. "Cut the traces!"

This was done, and one of the leaders dashed aside into the forest with the whole pack of wolves after him.

"We are saved!" cried the baron.

But his servant Eric knew only too well that the hungry animals would soon come on again. Sure enough they did, and then another horse had to be sacrificed.

The carriage was now within two miles of Bolisov, and the lights of the outlying houses could be seen in the distance. The party in the carriage thought they were saved; but as they galloped along it became evident that the horses were tired out and were slackening speed, while the wolves were once more rapidly overtaking the party. Then it was that the servant proved himself a hero.

"I will get down, Baron, and keep the wolves at bay while you, with your wife and child, get away to the town. If we stay together we shall all perish. But perhaps I may manage to keep the wolves off till you return with help."

The baron could not bear the thought of losing his faithful servant in this way, but Eric was determined to risk his life to save his master.

"Now God be with you all!" cried Eric. "Fire as I jump out!"

The baron fired, and his faithful servant sprang into the midst of the wolves. The savage animals stopped for a moment with the blaze of the pistols in their eyes. Then came a fearful, savage yell, and Eric fired again at the wolves. Then there was silence as the horses dashed forward.

Eric was never seen again, but his pistols were found lying in the bloodstained snow. A stone cross now stands on the spot, bearing the name of the heroic servant on one side, and on the other the words: "Greater love hath no man than this, that a man lay down his life for his friends."

A MAD TEA-PARTY

Here is a famous episode from Lewis Carroll's immortal Alice in Wonderland. Alice, in her journey through the strange country she has found at the bottom of the rabbit-hole, comes to the March Hare's house.

THERE was a table set out under a tree in front of the house, and the March Hare and the Hatter were having tea at it: a Dormouse was sitting between them, fast asleep, and the other two were resting their elbows on it, and talking over its head. "Very uncomfortable for the Dormouse," thought Alice; "only, as it's asleep, I suppose it doesn't mind."

The table was a large one, but the three were all crowded together at one corner of it. "No room! No room!" they cried out when they saw Alice coming. "There's *plenty* of room!" said Alice indignantly, and she sat down in a large armchair at one end of the table.

"Have some wine," the March Hare said in an encouraging tone.

Alice looked all round the table, but there was nothing on it but tea. "I don't see any wine," she remarked.

"There isn't any," said the March Hare.

"Then it wasn't very civil of you to offer it," said Alice angrily.

"It wasn't very civil of you to sit down without being invited," said the March Hare.

"I didn't know it was *your* table," said Alice; "it's laid for a great many more than three."

"Your hair wants cutting," said the Hatter. He had been looking at Alice for some time with great curiosity, and this was his first speech.

"You shouldn't make personal remarks," Alice said with some severity; "it's very rude."

The Hatter opened his eyes very wide on hearing this; but all he *said* was, "Why is a raven like a writing-desk?"

Come, we shall have some fun now! thought Alice. I'm glad they've begun asking riddles. "I believe I can guess that," she added aloud.

"Do you mean that you think you can find out the answer to it?" said the March Hare.

"Exactly so," said Alice.

"Then you should say what you mean," the March Hare went on.

"I do," Alice hastily replied; "at least—at least I mean what I say—that's the same thing, you know."

"Not the same thing a bit!" said the Hatter. "You might just as well say that 'I see what I eat' is the same thing as 'I eat what I see'!"

"You might just as well say," added the March Hare, "that 'I like what I get' is the same thing as 'I get what I like'!"

"You might just as well say," added the Dormouse, who seemed to be talking in his sleep, "that 'I breathe when I sleep' is the same thing as 'I sleep when I breathe'!"

"It *is* the same thing with you," said the Hatter, and here the conversation dropped, and the party sat silent for a minute.

The Hatter was the first to break the silence. "What day of the month is it?" he said, turning to Alice: he had taken his watch out of his pocket, and was looking at it uneasily, shaking it every now and then, and holding it to his ear.

Alice considered a little, and then said, "The fourth."

"Two days wrong!" sighed the Hatter. "I told you butter wouldn't suit the works!" he added, looking angrily at the March Hare.

"It was the *best* butter," the March Hare meekly replied.

"Yes, but some crumbs must have got in as well," the Hatter grumbled: "you shouldn't have put it in with the bread-knife."

The March Hare took the watch and looked at it gloomily: then he dipped it into his cup of tea, and looked at it again: but he could think of nothing better to say than his first remark, "It was the *best* butter, you know."

Alice had been looking over his shoulder with some curiosity. "What a funny watch!" she remarked. "It tells the day of the month, and doesn't tell what o'clock it is!"

"Why should it?" muttered the Hatter. "Does *your* watch tell you what year it is?"

"Of course not," Alice replied very readily: "but that's because it stays the same year for such a long time together."

"Which is just the case with *mine*," said the Hatter.

Alice felt dreadfully puzzled. The

Hatter's remark seemed to have no meaning in it, and yet it was certainly English.

"The Dormouse is asleep again," said the Hatter, and he poured a little hot tea upon its nose.

The Dormouse shook its head impatiently, and said, without opening its eyes, "Of course, of course; just what I was going to remark myself."

"Have you guessed the riddle yet?" the Hatter said, turning to Alice again.

"No, I give it up," Alice replied: "what's the answer?"

"I haven't the slightest idea," said the Hatter.

"Nor I," said the March Hare.

Alice sighed wearily. "I think you might do something better with the time," she said, "than waste it asking riddles with no answers."

"If you knew Time as well as I do," said the Hatter, "you wouldn't talk about wasting *it*. It's *him*."

"I don't know what you mean," said Alice.

"Of course you don't!" the Hatter said, tossing his head contemptuously. "I dare say you never even spoke to Time!"

"Perhaps not," Alice cautiously replied: "but I know I have to beat time when I learn music."

"Ah! that accounts for it," said the Hatter. "He won't stand beating. Now, if you only kept on good terms with him, he'd do almost anything you liked with the clock. For instance, suppose it were nine o'clock in the morning, just time to begin lessons; you'd only have to whisper a hint to Time, and round goes the clock in a twinkling! Half-past one, time for dinner!"

("I only wish it was," the March Hare said to itself in a whisper.)

"That would be grand, certainly," said Alice thoughtfully: "but then — I shouldn't be hungry for it, you know."

"Not at first, perhaps," said the Hatter: "but you could keep it to half-past one as long as you liked."

"Is that the way *you* manage?" Alice asked.

The Hatter shook his head mournfully. "Not I!" he replied. "We quarrelled last March—just before *he* went mad, you know——" (pointing with his teaspoon

at the March Hare), "——it was at the great concert given by the Queen of Hearts, and I had to sing

> Twinkle, twinkle, little bat!
> How I wonder what you're at!

You know the song, perhaps?"

"I've heard something like it," said Alice.

"It goes on, you know," the Hatter continued, "in this way:

> Up above the world you fly,
> Like a tea-tray in the sky.
> Twinkle, twinkle——"

Here the Dormouse shook itself, and began singing in its sleep, "Twinkle, twinkle, twinkle, twinkle——" and went on so long that they had to pinch it to make it stop.

"Well, I'd hardly finished the first verse," said the Hatter, "when the Queen jumped up and bawled out, 'He's murdering the time! Off with his head'!"

"How dreadfully savage!" exclaimed Alice.

"And ever since that," the Hatter went on in a mournful tone, "he won't do a thing I ask! It's always six o'clock now."

A bright idea came into Alice's head. "Is that the reason so many tea-things are put out here?" she asked.

"Yes, that's it," said the Hatter with a sigh: "it's always tea-time, and we've no time to wash the things between whiles."

"Then you keep moving round, I suppose?" said Alice.

"Exactly so," said the Hatter: "as the things get used up."

"But what happens when you come to the beginning again?" Alice ventured to ask.

"Suppose we change the subject," the March Hare interrupted, yawning. "I'm getting tired of this. I vote the young lady tells us a story."

"I'm afraid I don't know one," said Alice, rather alarmed at the proposal.

"Then the Dormouse shall!" they both cried. "Wake up, Dormouse!" And they pinched it on both sides at once.

The Dormouse slowly opened his eyes. "I wasn't asleep," he said in a hoarse, feeble voice: "I heard every word you fellows were saying."

"Tell us a story!" said the March Hare.

"Yes, please do!" pleaded Alice.

"And be quick about it," added the

Hatter, " or you'll be asleep again before it's done."

" Once upon a time there were three little sisters," the Dormouse began in a great hurry; " and their names were Elsie, Lacie, and Tillie; and they lived at the bottom of a well——"

" What did they live on? " said Alice, who always took a great interest in questions of eating and drinking.

" They lived on treacle," said the Dormouse, after thinking a minute or two.

" They couldn't have done that, you know," Alice gently remarked; " they'd have been ill."

" So they were," said the Dormouse; " *very* ill."

Alice tried to fancy to herself what such an extraordinary way of living would be like, but it puzzled her too much, so she went on: " But why did they live at the bottom of a well? "

" Take some more tea," the March Hare said to Alice, very earnestly.

" I've had nothing yet," Alice replied in an offended tone, " so I can't take more."

" You mean you can't take *less*," said the Hatter: " it's very easy to take *more* than nothing."

" Nobody asked *your* opinion," said Alice.

" Who's making personal remarks now? " the Hatter asked triumphantly.

Alice did not quite know what to say to this: so she helped herself to some tea and bread-and-butter, and then turned to the Dormouse, and repeated her question. " Why did they live at the bottom of a well? "

The Dormouse again took a minute or two to think about it, and then said, " It was a treacle-well."

" There's no such thing! " Alice was beginning very angrily, but the Hatter and the March Hare went " Sh! sh! " and the Dormouse sulkily remarked, " If you can't be civil, you'd better finish the story for yourself."

" No, please go on! " Alice said. " I won't interrupt again. I dare say there may be *one*."

" One, indeed! " said the Dormouse indignantly. However, he consented to go on. " And so these three little sisters—they were learning to draw, you know——"

" What did they draw? " said Alice, quite forgetting her promise.

" Treacle," said the Dormouse, without considering at all this time.

" I want a clean cup," interrupted the Hatter: " let's all move one place on."

Alice did not wish to offend the Dormouse again, so she began very cautiously: " But I don't understand. Where did they draw the treacle from? "

" You can draw water out of a water-well," said the Hatter; " so I should think you could draw treacle out of a treacle-well—eh, stupid? "

" But they were *in* the well," Alice said to the Dormouse, not choosing to notice this last remark.

" Of course they were," said the Dormouse; " well in."

This answer so confused poor Alice, that she let the Dormouse go on for some time without interrupting it.

" They were learning to draw," the Dormouse went on, yawning and rubbing its eyes, for it was getting very sleepy; " and they drew all manner of things—everything that begins with an M——"

" Why with an M? " said Alice.

" Why not? " said the March Hare.

Alice was silent.

The Dormouse had closed its eyes by this time, and was going off into a doze; but, on being pinched by the Hatter, it woke up again with a little shriek, and went on: " —that begins with an M, such as mouse-traps, and the moon, and memory, and muchness—you know you say things are ' much of a muchness '—did you ever see such a thing as a drawing of a muchness? "

" Really, now you ask me," said Alice, very much confused, " I don't think——"

" Then you shouldn't talk," said the Hatter.

This piece of rudeness was more than Alice could bear: she got up in great disgust, and walked off; the Dormouse fell asleep instantly, and neither of the others took the least notice of her going, though she looked back once or twice, half hoping that they would call after her: the last time she saw them, they were trying to put the Dormouse into the teapot.

" At any rate, I'll never go *there* again!" said Alice as she picked her way through the wood. " It's the stupidest tea-party I ever was at in all my life."

THE READY-MADE GENTLEMAN

Mr. Jourdain is one of the characters of the great French writer Molière in his play of Le Bourgeois Gentilhomme, from which this is retold.

MR. JOURDAIN was a squat, short little man. His round head was the shape of a globe, his eyes grey and frank. But the bright colours of his cheeks and his shortness of breath proved that Mr. Jourdain belonged to that class of men who lead too inactive a life. In fact, for forty years you might have seen Mr. Jourdain behind his counter, busy measuring cloth; or at his desk, reckoning up his expenses and checking big registers. Indeed, during forty long years this business man had not left his shop for a single day.

And now, at fifty, Mr. Jourdain had a good little income, and he intended to enjoy it. Enjoying his income meant to him to wear silk and velvet instead of the good cloth he had been selling all his life; he longed to show himself in a gilded coach and " to be among the fine folks."

But Mr. Jourdain was not quite his own master. There was Mrs. Jourdain.

Mrs. Jourdain, a respectable middle-class dame, full of good sense, but a little masterful, was what we call strong-minded. Living in a splendid house, she remained the same Mrs. Jourdain as of old. She did not blush at being greeted by the friends of other days; she gladly remembered them and recalled her working days, and the foolish excuses and stupid pretensions of her husband greatly displeased her—all the more because their daughter Lucile was now old enough to be provided with a worthy husband.

One morning Mr. Jourdain, parading in a sumptuous dressing-gown, awaited his dancing master—for " Is one a man of fashion with no airs and graces ? " Another morning he would expect his music master or his fencing master—" For when you are not acquainted with the arts you must learn them." Then he would call in masters of philosophy and literature. He learned that all that was not verse was prose, and what was not prose was verse. " Then I speak in prose all day without any effort ? " Mr. Jourdain would say: " how learned I am! "

The tailor was brought in to clothe Mr. Jourdain in sumptuous garb: satin and brocade, feathers and wig—nothing was left out.

" You have gone crazy, my good man," sighed Mrs. Jourdain.

" My dear, you know nothing about elegance," her husband would reply. " Suppose I ask you what are the words you utter ? "

" Words of good sense, sir," his wife would say.

" That is not the question. Take the words I speak: what are they ? "

" Nonsense! " said the good wife.

" Oh, dear! You don't understand! The way in which you speak, I speak, is called—what is it called ? —prose! "

Such was the goings-on in Mr. Jourdain's house, a life ridiculous, bringing in due course ridiculous consequences.

One day a neighbour introduced himself and declared to Mr. Jourdain: " I love your daughter. May I have the honour of being accepted as your son-in-law? "

To which, of course, Mr. Jourdain immediately replied: " Only one word, sir: do you go to the Court? "

" Bless you, sir," said Cléonte, " I am the son of good people who have left me enough money to figure at the Court, but, to tell the truth, I am not a nobleman."

" Then let us be friends," said Mr. Jourdain, " but you will not be my son-in-law."

Now Cléonte and Lucile loved each other, and Mrs. Jourdain approved of the young man. How could Mr. Jourdain be persuaded? They talked over many plans, and at last resolved upon an innocent and gentle trick, in which the mania of our would-be nobleman would serve the cause of reasonable folk.

" Trust me, sir," Cléonte's faithful man, Covielle, had declared, full of sympathy with his master's disappointment. " Trust me. That man is mad. He likes to make himself a laughing-stock. Let us foster his inclination. Let us encourage him in his foolishness. We will play our parts. Costumes and actors are easy to find! Ah! you were honest enough to tell Mr. Jourdain of your condition. Well, I am certain that he will now believe you are the son of the Grand Turk! "

Thus it came about one day that Mr. Jourdain found himself face to face with a Cléonte so cleverly disguised as a Turkish prince that the foolish man did not know him, and greatly honoured so illustrious a visitor. Covielle played the part of a disguised interpreter.

" Sir," Covielle began, " I have the honour of introducing to you the son of the

Grand Turk. The prince wishes me to say that he knew your father, who was a gentleman of the best blood."

"Ah!" exclaimed the proud peacock Mr. Jourdain; "and would you believe that there are silly people, my own wife among them, who pretend that my father was a merchant!"

"A merchant? Nonsense! It is just this. Your father knew a great deal about cloth, and had a lot sent from all parts. Being most kind, he used to provide his friends with it.

"But, sir," Covielle went on, "we have called to tell you the best news in the world. My master, the Grand Turk's son, is in love with your daughter."

"A prince in love with Lucile!"

"Yes, and he wishes to marry her. The prince comes to ask for your daughter in marriage, but in order to have a father-in-law worthy of himself he wishes to make you a mamamouchi."

"Mamamouchi?" burst out the bewildered Mr. Joudain, overcome with pride.

"Yes, mamamouchi; that is to say, a sort of knight. There is no higher title in all Turkey, and you will rank among the greatest lords in the world."

"All this would be splendid," concluded Mr. Jourdain, "but the difficulty is that my daughter has fallen in love with a certain Cléonte and will not consent to marry anybody else."

"How do you know?" said Covielle. "She may change her mind at the sight of the prince; he is a fine man."

It is so easy to believe a thing is possible when you wish it to be so that Mr. Jourdain thought to himself: "Of course she may alter her mind. Ah! to be the father-in-law of a prince!"

Mrs. Jourdain and Lucile had not up to now been told of this scheme, and, thinking Mr. Jourdain was going out of his mind, they nearly lost their heads at the sight of this Turkish prince, so that when her father told Lucile what he expected she replied:

"No, no, Father; I will never marry anybody but Cléonte!"

Happily the wise Covielle was there, and whispered a word of warning, so that Lucile could add in time: "However, you are my father, and I must obey you."

"I shall have to give in too," Mrs. Jourdain said, and, being a woman of action, she added: "Let us send for a lawyer, and let the marriage be performed today lest the prince change his mind!"

And so Lucile married Cléonte, and we may hope that they lived happy ever after.

THE TREASURE AND WHERE IT LAY

LITTLE Joris was the son of a poor widow who lived in a small cottage on the edge of a great forest. He had no brothers or sisters to speak to—only the trees and flowers and birds.

When the cold days of winter began, and oatmeal and flour became dearer and dearer to buy, Joris thought he would like to go into the woods and try to find a great treasure to give to his mother.

So the very next time he was sent out to gather fuel for the fire he went deeper into the wood than he had ever done before. He was not a bit frightened. He talked all the time. "Hullo, tree," he would say, "how old are you? Do you know where the treasure is?" Or he would part the long grass where a little wood violet lay hid, and say, "Ah, you thought I didn't see you!"

So he wandered on and on until suddenly he caught sight of a little man with a long red cowl on his head, looking round the stalk of a very large mushroom.

"Can you tell me where I can find a treasure for my mother, please?" cried Joris. "She is very poor, and——"

"A treasure! Ha, ha!" laughed the little man. "Why, your mother has a treasure already!" And he vanished quickly between the tall reeds that lined the banks of the little stream.

Poor Joris was very puzzled indeed. Why had his mother not told him of this treasure? The little man must certainly be mistaken.

Joris turned sadly homeward, and, following the stream, found his way safely back to the cottage door.

His mother ran out to meet him.

"Where have you been, my darling?" she cried, putting her arms round his neck. "I was so afraid you were lost."

Joris told his mother all about his wanderings, and what the little man had said.

"He was quite right, my dear son," said his mother, hugging him closer to her bosom. "*You* are my treasure."

LE LOUP DANS LA NUIT

This is a French translation of the story told in English on page 5958

Au milieu du siècle dernier un avocat français, le Baron de Monthyon, légua une grosse somme d'argent pour la fondation d'un prix annuel à donner " à la personne, en France, qui pendant l'année aurait commis les actions les plus vertueuses."

La liste de ces prix constitue une série merveilleuse de nobles actes; mais il est douteux qu'elle contienne une histoire plus héroïque que celle de Madeleine Saunier, une jeune fille, dont l'âme était toute de charité, et qui s'appliqua à aider autrui d'une façon admirable.

Une pauvre veuve aveugle habitait avec sa fille souffrante, à trois kilomètres de sa demeure, et pendant quinze ans Madeleine ne manqua jamais d'aller, à pied, chez elles, de les nourrir, de mettre leur maison en ordre, et de leur donner de la joie; elles attendaient impatiemment son retour le lendemain.

À une distance égale, mais dans une autre direction, vivait, dans une maisonnette isolée, une pauvre fille atteinte de la lèpre, et abandonnée de ses amis. Pendant dix-huit mois Madeleine la visita deux fois par jour, pour lui donner le peu de nourriture qu'elle pouvait manger et pour panser ses plaies atroces, jusqu'au jour où la pauvre lépreuse mourut entre ses bras.

En 1840 Madeleine fut presque noyée en tâchant de traverser une rivière grossie par les pluies, qui la séparait d'une personne qu'elle visitait journellement, et quand on lui reprocha sa témérité, elle répondit simplement: " Je n'ai pas pu m'en empêcher; ne pouvant aller la visiter hier, j'ai senti que je devais aller la voir aujourd'hui."

Pendant un rigoureux hiver elle eut une dangereuse aventure: Elle soignait une mourante, appelée Mancel, qui habitait au flanc d'une colline dans une cabane qui ressemblait davantage à la tanière d'une bête sauvage qu'à la demeure d'un être humain.

Vers la fin d'une longue nuit, Madeleine avait allumé quelques brindilles vertes, pour essayer de remédier au froid intense, lorsque la porte vermoulue fut poussée du dehors, et elle vit un loup prêt à bondir dans la chambre.

Elle sauta contre la porte et la tint solidement, s'aidant de tout ce qu'elle pouvait atteindre pour la maintenir fermée, tandis que l'animal se ruait contre les planches. Et elle criait de toutes ses forces, dans l'espoir d'éloigner le loup en l'effrayant. Mais durant tout le reste de cette nuit terrible elle eut à maintenir la porte contre lui.

THE BOY WHO SAVED A CREW

In the year 1798, during a terrific storm, a French ship, La Tribune, was wrecked one evening off Halifax, Nova Scotia, and a number of men belonging to the crew managed to climb into the rigging, where they remained all night.

When daylight dawned the poor men were still in the rigging, almost exhausted by their terrible experiences of the night. The sea, however, was still rising in angry waves, and beating like a torrent upon the wreckage and the shore, so that none of the strong men on the beach dared venture out to rescue the shipwrecked mariners.

It was then that a deed of amazing courage and splendid heroism was performed by a boy of thirteen, whose name, unfortunately, we do not know.

This lad had been watching the wreck for hours and listening to the talk of the spectators, expecting that some of them would, at any rate, make an effort to save the wrecked sailors. When at last he found that no one dared to make the attempt he determined to see what he himself could do to reach the vessel.

Jumping into a small boat, he rowed with all his might for the wreck, and, though the wind and the waves were almost too strong for him, he managed at last to reach the ship and get his little boat near enough to take off two of the men. They were too exhausted to assist in rowing to the shore, but the plucky boy, by great exertions, landed them safely.

Then he started for the wreck once more. But his strength was exhausted and he had to return to the shore.

The brave example set by so young a lad, however, bore good fruit, for the men were shamed into making an effort, and several boats went out to the wreck, finally saving every one of the men who had taken refuge in the rigging.

A SWARM OF FLIES

WARBLE-FLY

HESSIAN-FLY

THE SHEEP KED, A WINGLESS FLY

AN EGG RAFT OF THE COMMON GREY GNAT

BLUEBOTTLE-FLY

GIRDLED DRONE-FLY

NOONTIDE-FLY

THE HOVER-FLY GRUB, THE FLY, AND A HOVER-FLY JUST EMERGED FROM ITS CHRYSALIS

HORSE BOT-FLY

SPOTTED MOSQUITO CHRYSALIS

NASAL BOT-FLY

The pictures on these pages are by Mrs. M. H. Crawford, Messrs. Collins, Ward, and others

Nature's Wonderful Living Family in Earth and Air and Sea

A gnat emerging from its cocoon

GNATS AND FLIES

PEOPLE often ask why such pests as flies and mosquitoes were made, and expect that in some way these insects can be caused to justify themselves or plead guilty to their misdoings.

But Nature never apologises, is never penitent, never pitiful to the incompetent. Her ancient plan was to endow various Orders in various ways. She has expended the nicest care over the equipment of a mosquito which carries the seeds of death into human blood, but she has fostered in the human skull a brain which, rightly directed, enables us to avert this peril that flies by night.

Not all mosquitoes are deadly. We have many British species which inject a mild poison into our blood to inflame but not to destroy. The mosquito which does kill is only the medium, not the cause. It is itself the victim of a parasite, and that parasite is the instrument of destruction.

The insects of which we go most in fear are taskmasters without mercy, but by attention to hygiene, by the employment of specifics against infection, we can make our lives secure and sweet at home, and little by little, as civilisation advances, we shall carry the same methods into the wilds, and make them also safe for human life.

Ice and snow, chilling rains, and bitter winds were in the world when we came into it, to deprive us of life; fire and flood, raging torrents, and deep swift seas were there to burn or drown us. We descend from ancestors who learned to bridle, to circumvent, these lawless forces and reduce them to our service. The insect problem is not more difficult, though not less deadly.

We can track the death-dealing mosquito and defy its ravages, and, taking the malarial enemy captive, now make it bite to our advantage. For one of the newest marvels of science is that inoculation, in a mild form, by the malaria-carrying mosquito, is a cure for general paralysis of the insane.

Not all mosquitoes are ministers of death. Unless they are themselves infected they cannot transmit disease to us. The germs of malaria and of yellow fever, of which mosquitoes are the carriers, are parasites which pass one stage of their lives in the blood and stomach of the mosquito, and the other stage in the blood of man or other mammal.

We cannot suppose that gnats thrive on their infection. They would be better without it. They themselves are victims, and victimise us in turn if we come within their orbit. As a fact we have more than one species of the Anopheles mosquitoes, the malarial ones, in Great Britain, but they are entirely harmless, save for their irritating bites, unless a person or animal

PREHISTORIC LIFE · MAMMALS · BIRDS · REPTILES · FISHES · INSECTS

affected with malaria chances to be bitten by them.

If that happens then the parasite passes from the blood of the man into the body of the gnat, multiplies there, and is passed on into the system of the next person bitten. That man thus becomes a carrier of the affliction and can infect numerous other mosquitoes, all of which, when they drink their succeeding meals of blood from new human victims, continue to spread the disease.

WHEN MALARIA WAS WIDESPREAD IN BRITAIN

That was why there was a danger of malaria reviving in Britain after the First World War, when soldiers came home with the organism of malaria in their blood. It was feared that if these men were bitten by Anopheles mosquitoes the poison would be passed on to others.

There is little doubt that in bygone centuries malaria was a widespread scourge in our own land. We read hundreds of references to ague in the history of what we call Merrie England. That ague was malaria. Almost unconsciously we defeated the dreadful malady by the cultivation of the soil. We drained fen and bog and marsh, and turned them into fields and gardens and towns. At each intake of such reclaimed lands we dried up the source of the mosquito life.

Malaria itself tells the tale of the old belief as to the disease which it describes. Men thought that marsh air was ill to breathe, and that it was this air which brought malaria. The word malaria means simply bad air; as a fact, however, air had nothing to do with the matter.

CLEANLINESS AS THE GREAT ENEMY OF DISEASE

It was the water, the marshes, the sodden banks of rivers and lakes, the puddles and muddy pools of filthy cities and villages, that were the breeding places of the fatal gnats. Malaria and mosquitoes vanished together from a district when cleanliness took the place of neglect, and bog was converted into dry land. Apparently the supply of malarial parasites died out in our midst in face of this campaign, for the malarial gnats that we now have are, if uninfected from external sources, as innocent, though as irritating, as the black midges, which torment us with their poisoned bites on the damp tennis lawn and on the rivers where we float and loll.

The tracking down of the germs of malaria and yellow fever is a triumph of our own time and the achievement of our own heroes of science, a dazzling story, of which we have read in other pages.

The building of the Panama Canal was one of the grandest engineering achievements the world has seen, but the conquest of the little mosquito which had so long kept it back was a performance of even greater significance. That conquest has its echo in every tropical land to which civilisation spreads. Beat the mosquito by cleanliness and common prudence, and the tropics become health resorts, where formerly a white man was doomed.

What did the mosquitoes do for their blood supply before man appeared among them as a reservoir? They lived, we suppose, on vegetable juices. The deduction is based on the fact that mosquitoes deadly to man and animal teem in billions in great areas of tropical country where man has never yet established himself, and where big mammals have not gained a foothold.

THE CHILDREN OF NATURE WHO SEEM TO HAVE TAKEN THE WRONG TURNING

If the dreaded gnats are vegetarians there today, they must always have been, and it is reasonable to assume that the same rule governed the attitude and appetite of the ancient mosquito. Another line of inquiry has led science to the belief that the bacteria now so deadly to other forms of life were once equally innocuous, and lived lives of innocence, guiltless of their fellow creatures' blood.

If this be granted, then how nonsensical it is to charge Nature with the guilt of her insect children. They do ill where we permit their existence, but they are simply fresh examples of groups of life which have taken what seems to us the wrong turning, like the kea parrot, which has become a murderer of sheep, and the gull which has turned inland from the stormy sea to garner into its crop the grain that man hoped to harvest for himself.

We invite disaster at the instance of this great order of two-winged insects, the Diptera, as they are called, to which the mosquitoes, midges, and the rest belong. A stride from the mosquito, and we are in the midst of those long, brown-bodied flies with prodigious straggling limbs, flies which we call daddy-longlegs or crane-flies.

They look like mosquitoes as we might

see a mosquito under a magnifying lens, but they have none of the sawing and piercing implements of the smaller and more formidable insect. Their mouth parts are framed only for the harmless occupation of sucking up surface moisture. The adult crane-flies are harmless, though the spear-like projection at the rear of the female's body suggests a lusty sting. Indeed, it is but that marvellous contrivance the drill with which she bores, and through which descend the eggs she deposits in the ground.

The mosquito larva is hatched in water and is harmless there; but the baby of daddy-longlegs is hatched in the earth, in the lawns, the pastures, the flower borders. And this does mischief enough to grass, the roots of flowers, and so on, to make up for all the engaging helplessness of the swarming adults, drifting in brown clouds in the air of a summer night.

That we are plagued by these leather-jackets, as the larvae are called, is one of the penalties we pay for the indiscriminate slaughter of rooks, starlings, and other hunters after the leather-jacket.

THE TERRIBLE PROCESSION OF WORMS WHICH EAT THE GROWING CROPS

We cannot always trace cause to effect in the multiplication of our insect foes; as, for example, when enormous hosts of the army worm appear and devour pasture and corn like a moving fire. But, as corn cannot be damaged save where man has sown it, we may be right in assuming that the hand which scattered the grain scattered also the natural foes of the army worm which eats the crop.

The parent of the army worm is a small black fly which lays some hundred eggs in the earth. The larva is a maggot and is about a quarter of an inch long. Normally little groups keep to themselves, but in the great years, when numbers are outrageous, swarms meet swarms. The innumerable larvae form themselves into long columns and march as an army, not all in orderly procession, but when one part of the line halts the others crawl above it, and the sinuous mass winds its slow length along, feeding, fattening, clearing all before it like locusts.

Perhaps because supplies grow short, perhaps because maturity in the larval form is attained, the great mass contracts, thickens, becomes an enormous ball, and disappears slowly into the earth.

Much mystery is made of this vanishing into the ground where mystery does not exist. The underlying strata of army worms excavate and sink the whole mass of life, as a burying beetle sinks the dead bird or mouse on which it intends to live.

A NATURAL EXPLANATION OF AN APPARENT MYSTERY

The obvious reason for this tunnelling and engulfing of the host is that their hour for change into the pupal state has arrived, and the larvae know it as well as a caterpillar instinctively knows when it must spin its cocoon and change.

Leaving the army worms to their crawling, we glance into the air to espy the hateful little midges which bite and cause intense irritation to all, and genuine illness to people who are susceptible to their not very terrible venom. We have not to see them; a good ear catches the high note of their wings and humming as they fly. They are not mosquitoes, though closely related to them; and their bite is never fatal.

It is inflicted by lancet and saw, after which a fluid is injected by the insect to render the blood thinner and capable of being drawn up. The effect of British mosquito and midge is much the same on us in its irritation, but only the mosquito can carry the germ of fever; though the midge bite, when administered by a swarm of insects, can drive away sleep and happiness from all but those fortunate people whose blood is impervious to the effect of the little drop of virus.

HOW THE PLUMED MIDGES PAY FOR THEIR FIERY SPLENDOUR

Midges, which are among the minor inflictions of summer life in the open, have their troubles not less grave than those they inflict. Enormous swarms of plumed midges, like our own kind, have been observed in Russian Asia to be apparently on fire with splendour, luminous and lovely. But this phosphorescent brilliance seems to be the product of harmful bacteria, which so enfeeble the victim that it is reduced to crawling, quite deprived of the power of flight.

Now, are we to assume that such a condition of luminosity can become habitual and harmless in a group? It would almost appear so, for among the fungus midges two or three genera are known in which the power to light a lamp in the living body is accompanied by no more hurt than in the glow-worm. In Europe there is the *Ceroplatus sesiosides*, and in New Zealand, where it is called the glow-worm, the *Boletophila luminosa;* both put forth an astonishing radiance, but to what end we cannot yet say.

To us only the beauty appears, but as the larvae possess the radiance as well as their parents, and employ it as a lure to tempt prey to their gummy webs, there seems to be some such purpose in it as that which lights the lanterns of the deep-sea octopus and those of the great-jawed hungry fishes of the ocean abysses.

THE FILTHY CONDITIONS IN WHICH THE FLIES COME INTO LIFE

There is not much mystery remaining for us in the life history of the flies which haunt our homes, unless it be the mystery as to why we tolerate them. The flies which infest our homes are not born there, but are cradled in corruption and horror, in dunghills, in deadly, disease-breeding dumps.

It is there that the adult female lays her eggs, there that the eggs hatch into the maggots which fishermen use as bait, calling them gentles. Egg, larva, pupa stage, are all passed in these horrid surroundings. The fly bursts from its pupal case, and has to crawl through filth to the daylight. Its feet and its hairy body bring with them crowds of deadly microbes. In they come to the house, straight to the food and milk, to foul them, to cause fatal illness to babies, sickness, and possibly eventual death, to adults.

Practically all the abominations which used to poison the food of our ancestors and make their lives melancholy and brief have been swept away by modern sanitation, yet the fly, deadly as any, is still suffered through ignorance or indifference.

WHY WE MUST ALWAYS KEEP FOOD AWAY FROM FLIES

Harold Maxwell Lefroy, the 20th-century entomologist, had the great patience to work out the life history of the fly as devotedly as the men who lead romantic expeditions into the tropics to study creatures whose mysteries are endowed with that glamour and fascination which distance and unfamiliarity impart, and he found a terrible tale to tell the world of this common foe of our domestic peace and comfort.

The fly carries living corruption about its body; it carries corruption in the food which it has eaten, and, when it meets a more attractive diet, it throws up this poison on the fresh food in order to fill itself with the more alluring diet. Especially is this the case when it finds a supply of milk. Into it goes the poison which will kill a baby, and, indeed, was once responsible for the deaths of great numbers of children in our islands.

Lefroy showed that the house-fly keeps the germs of typhoid alive in its body for 28 days, and that for another 23 days after this deadly parasite leaves the body of the insect it retains its life and virulence. In addition, the fly could bring into our homes cholera, enteric, and dysentery. By attacking the face it could cause ophthalmia, the loathsome affection which mars the beauty and use of myriads of bright eyes in the East. Probably the germs of tubercular consumption also find a carrier in the fly.

Yet this slayer of our children and poisoner of our adults is tolerated. The refuse heaps in which it breeds are permitted to remain uncovered and untreated, at the cost of innumerable little human lives every year.

THE SMALL BLACK HOUSE-FLY WHICH DRAWS ITS VICTIM'S BLOOD

We have more than one species of house-fly. The majority merely moisten and suck; but the little black house-flies draw blood. These are not undersized members of the ordinary fly tribe, but fully developed examples of their kind— for flies are full-sized at birth, and never grow after quitting the chrysalis form. Care and cleanliness will some day banish the fly from our houses, but till then we have a potential minister of death or violent illness in every one that alights on our food.

But all the flies are a problem. There is the bluebottle, which we rather admire because of its breezy, tempestuous dash and hum. Yet it is a horrid creature, depositing its ravenous maggots not merely on meat, but on living flesh, on open wounds, even in the nostrils of sleeping infants and invalids. Civilisation ought not to endure this little monster.

But there are worse flies than ours, as any Italian will tell us who, with natives of other warm countries, has had experience of the sand-fly. It is a minute fly, difficult to discover; but, now that it is known to inject into its victim the bacilli from which pellagra arises, it is one of the most dreaded of insects.

Pellagra is a terrible source of suffering to human beings, ending after many years in madness and miserable death. Who will rid the world of sand-flies ? Within

dismal discovery that a sand-fly is born with an inheritance of infection. Sand-flies bred from eggs brought with great care to London and reared in scrupulously sterilised conditions have been permitted to bite volunteer students, and have set up the fell malady in them for which the

GRUBS OF THE HOUSE-FLY

THE HOUSE-FLY

PUPAE OF THE HOUSE-FLY

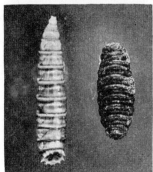

THE GRUB AND PUPA OF THE
BLUEBOTTLE-FLY

LARVAE OF THE PEAR MIDGE
INSIDE A PEAR

THE MAGGOT, PUPA, AND EMPTY
PUPA CASE OF THE APPLE MAGGOT

THE DADDY-LONGLEGS, OR
CRANE-FLY

THE GRUB AND PUPA CASE
OF THE CRANE-FLY

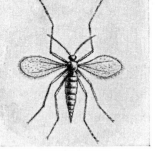

BRITISH WHEAT
MIDGE

recent years this insect has been proved even more frightful than was supposed. We had all imagined that the sand-fly, like the mosquito, must be individually infected by bacteria, of the parasites of which it is the host, before it could cause pellagra in a human being.

Scientists have, however, made the

breed is infamous. Thus the risk of the spread of pellagra is lamentably greater than any of us had dreamed, possibly not in England, but in warmer lands of the British Commonwealth, especially now that swift aeroplanes course the skies and carry the insects of one place across an ocean to another land.

With ways less terrible to ourselves, but dreadful to animals, there are many flies which keep to the open air. Among these are various bot-flies. One of these the Gastrophilus equi, is a plague to horse life. Irritated by the attentions of the fly the horse licks itself and transfers the larvae to its mouth, whence they are swallowed. The larvae, on hatching, hook themselves to the stomach or intestines of the horse, and there complete their larval growth.

THE HORRID WARBLE-FLY AND THE DISCOMFORT IT CAUSES TO CATTLE

We do not know that the process is injurious to the horse, but it must cause discomfort. There is unfortunately less doubt as to the warble-fly, which cattle fear as we fear angered hornets.

In the blazing heat of a summer afternoon, when the cattle should be chewing the cud in the shade of the trees, we may see them madly rushing about their pastures. The cattle are clumsily seeking to flee from a dreaded enemy.

The fly deposits its eggs on the hide of the animal. There these hatch for the maggots to eat their way into the flesh and cause hideous wounds beneath the skin. As many as 400 of these gnawing parasites have been found beneath the hide of a single cow. The poor animal is miserable; it loses flesh, its milk is insufficient and inferior, and when the end comes, and its hide is to be converted into leather, immense damage is found to have been caused. The British leather trade suffers from this cause a loss of millions of pounds a year, to say nothing of the sufferings that the unfortunate cattle have to endure.

THE DELIBERATE PERSECUTION PRACTISED BY THE FOREST-FLIES

The so-called sheep bot-fly is another horror, which penetrates the flesh of the sheep's nose with disastrous effect. But the name of this fly is too restricted in its implication, for the insect attacks man, birds, frogs, toads, and other amphibians.

We have noted the love of cattle for shade, a passion which horses share, but there are winged enemies for them there too, various species of strange forest-flies. A more deliberate career of persecution than that of the forest-flies could not be imagined. They attack the horse, the cattle, the deer, even birds, and, beginning as winged couriers, bite off their wings when they alight on their prey, just as queen ants bite off theirs after their marriage flight, and settle down to drink blood drawn from those parts of the flesh least protected by hair.

There are infinitely more terrible forest-flies than these, however, the tsetse-flies which haunt the forests deeply fringing the great waterways of Africa. There are many species of tsetse-flies, some harmful to domestic animals and not to man, others as terrible enemies as human beings have to confront.

These flies are parasitic on the great game of the Dark Continent, and, fashioned to take their blood supply from animals with tough hides such as antelopes and zebras, they are furnished with potent piercing and sucking implements, though in themselves generally resembling in size and outline our own blow-flies.

THE BARRIER OF FLIES THAT KEEPS THE STRANGER OUT

Now, in the blood of the game which these flies attack swarm myriads of low organisms, eel-like in outline, called trypanosomes, which undergo one stage of their growth in the original host, are then sucked up in the blood drawn by the fly, to remain dormant in the interior of the insect and renew growth and attain maturity in the body of the mammal which the tsetse next bites.

The range of the tsetses is widespread, but not continuous. They abound in what are known as fly belts, areas of great size which have their definite beginnings and endings. Into these belts no domestic animal can penetrate and live. The fly injects its poisonous parasites into horse, ox, donkey, dog, and these sicken and die a horrible death. That disease, peculiar to animals, and not extending to man, is called nagana, and cannot develop in human blood.

That is terrible, and a hindrance to colonisation in the fly-infested country, for we are entirely dependent on animal service in such conditions. But it is from the tsetse-fly that that dread malady, sleeping sickness, is carried to men. The name conveys the character of the ailment, and is not to be confused with sleepy sickness.

The actual sleeping sickness is as fatal to white men as nagana is to white men's animals, as terrible in its course, as deadly in its issue. Natives whose ancestry has for generations lived among tsetse-flies are as immune as zebras and lions are to nagana; but when new areas are opened up between tsetse country and non-tsetse country, the flies, advancing through the cleared ways, produce frightful havoc among the non-immune natives.

HOW THE RAILWAYS IN AFRICA HELPED TO SPREAD DISEASE

Possibly no malady has run through Africa with such frightful rapidity as sleeping sickness since railways, during our own lifetime, have created long corridors through forest land along which the disease could be carried; and there have been times when the black sons of Africa have died from sudden onslaughts of sleeping sickness by the hundred thousand. That is what a puny fly, to whose attacks man is unaccustomed, can do for humanity.

Flies of many species have yet to be studied, and there are a host already described for the student who can seek their story in science manuals; but we may repeat that not all the flies in our midst are harmful. The bee flies are a boon to us, for whereas the adults restrict themselves to the nectar of flowers which they help to fertilise, their larvae are great devourers of caterpillars and of ground insects which harm our crops. The drone-fly's larvae eat decaying vegetation which makes wayside waters noisome, and also consume carrion when the eggs are laid in the carcase of a dead animal.

The humble-bee flies closely resemble the bees after which they are named, but they puzzle us. Some place their eggs in the nests of honey-bees, some in those of wasps. It is not certain whether the larvae eat the young of the bees and wasps or whether they merely act as scavengers and consume waste matter.

A USEFUL LITTLE ALLY AND ITS FINE POWER OF FLIGHT

The second supposition seems the more probable, for we cannot imagine that creatures so sagacious as bees and wasps would sanction the presence of slaughterers of their larvae.

We are on more certain ground with the hover-flies, and can welcome them with delight unqualified. As they dart and dash among our sunlit flowers, first with the speed of a dragon-fly, then pulling up short as though halted by the most marvellous of brakes, then rising straight on a level keel, next darting sideways, then backward, then down, fast as the sunbeam they follow, we see the perfection of flight.

More grace and enterprise in flight, greater suggestion of rapturous enjoyment, no creature shows. We welcome them for their merry grace and avidity, but we accept them as unsworn, uncontracted allies, for their larvae grow up among the rose-gorging green-fly, and devour the vital juices of those hateful parasites with an appetite like that of a hungry donkey introduced to unlimited carrots.

Even if we had no green-fly to ruin our roses we should still retain the hover-fly in our affections for its grace and beauty, but there are some flies which we value for service without regard to their appeal to our sense of the artistic. There is in northern Africa, for example, a fly as much like our house nuisance as the tsetse-fly, the Idia fasciata, which is worth far more than its weight in gold. It is to the devouring locust what the monitor lizard is to the crocodile; it eats the locusts' eggs.

A FLY OF NORTH AFRICA AND ITS SPLENDID WORK FOR MAN

The parent fly has no direct part in the service, except a wonderful instinct for finding where the eggs lie. She is more determined than even the ichneumon, which pierces a tree to lay her eggs, for this little fly burrows down three or more inches into the hard and burning soil to reach the place where the great powerful locust has hidden its store of eggs.

There the Idia fasciata lays *her* eggs, and the young ones, when hatched, live entirely on the locust eggs, which they devour in great quantities. How much they save us by this beneficial destruction of the foes of our crops is not to be estimated, but our debt to them must be very great.

Flies in the past must have rendered great service merely as devourers of carrion and in the destruction of vegetation which would have rankly overgrown the earth. The parasites which they then collected did not matter to us, for we and our animals were not there to be afflicted by them. Now, however, we have overrun their ancient territory, and by our own neglect have conduced to their multiplication, to our serious disadvantage.

We have taken weeds and converted them into cultivated growths indispensable to human life and health. The parasites have come in with the vegetation which we have seized and improved. There is not a thing we cultivate which has not its special parasite or parasites, pests which have to be combated as anxiously as frost on summer nights.

There are flies peculiar to celery, to carrots, to onions, to apples, and so forth, all laying eggs from which maggots emerge to devour either the foliage, the fruit, or the root of the growth to which their lives are committed.

PESTS OF THE COUNTRYSIDE AND HOW WE MAY DEFEAT THEM

The number of pests increases where neglect makes multiplication easy. There is a treatment for each if we will take the trouble to apply it. A few pence may bring to any of us admirable publications prepared by the greatest living experts, under the direction of the Ministry of Agriculture. It is our own fault if we do not meet these scourges of the fields, pasture, and garden forearmed with the knowledge that may make us triumphant.

Human population is constantly growing; indeed it is slowly overtaking food supplies, so we shall in time have to fight the insects scientifically or starve. For they are marvellous in their methods of maintaining a hold on life and of extending their sphere. There are flies which do not depend on the hazard of reproduction of separate generations by successive batches of eggs.

Some are borne alive, devouring the body of their mother before entering the world as larvae, ready immediately to turn into chrysalises. More wonderful, we have baby flies giving birth to other baby flies. That is to say, the larvae, without ever attaining perfect insect form, produce larvae like themselves.

THE STRANGE CASE OF THE FLIES THAT HAVE LOST THEIR WINGS

The new generation of larvae devour the old larvae of which they are born, and they themselves, remaining babies, become parents, for they also, without growing up, evolve other larvae from their own bodies.

It seems marvellous, but is it primitive, or a tremendous feat of specialisation? Probably it is the first, for we find salmon when not nearly mature becoming parents; we find amphibian larvae becoming parents, and any of us can grow an entire begonia from a single leaf of such a plant.

Yes, the flies can make as great changes, in time, as we can, though there is not a notable brain among the lot of them. The hateful flea is merely a fly of other days. It is one of the two-winged insects which have lost their wings.

Some time ago Dr. Karl Absolon, curator of the Brunn Museum, found flies in the Balkan caves and underground water-courses which have lost their wings as completely as the fleas. Let us hope that their future may be less disastrous to man than that of the flea.

The subject is so unpleasant as to be banned, with that of other human vermin, in polite society. But we ought to discuss these things ; for the flea has slain millions of human beings, and although it no longer kills people in our country, it is still a menace in Eastern lands.

For this detestable flea, which has given up its wings in order to batten on the blood of mammals of all sorts, is the demon of the plague tragedy. He it is who carries the fatal germ that has mowed down more millions of human beings in Asia and Europe, England not excepted, than all the wars ever fought. When a plague-stricken rat dies, its fleas leap on a human being, bite him, and he dies of the plague.

NATURE'S REPROOF OF THOSE WHO DISOBEY HER LAWS

Happily our ports are so well guarded against rats that there is little likelihood of plague returning to the England which it has so often scourged.

Although fleas in Britain are comparatively harmless, they are hateful creatures still. To us they are a symptom of dirt, idleness, and slovenliness. For fleas infest people who do not wash and do not change their clothing frequently, or keep their homes clean.

Fleas also attack some of our domestic animals, irritating them intensely, and it is our duty for our pets' comfort as well as for our own, to keep them free of the pests by using some kind of disinfectant.

Fleas do persist, therefore we are not what we should be. Man's flea-borne afflictions are a reproof and scourge from Nature. His sins find him out; the innocent suffer for the guilty. The insects which we hold in detestation seem to be Nature's incitement to Man to scorn sloth, indifference, and ignorance, and to ensure cleanliness, care, and decency of life, as becomes the highest of God's creatures.

PICTURE-STORY OF A PIECE OF SILK

A glorious robe of silk is the work of an insignificant insect called by man a worm. The silkworm is the caterpillar of an unattractive cream-coloured moth, seen on the left with eggs that it has just laid. These eggs hatch out into black larvae, which grow into whitish-grey caterpillars (right) about three inches long.

After feeding voraciously on mulberry leaves, the caterpillar spins an oval cocoon of very fine silk, about the size of a pigeon's egg, as seen in the left-hand picture. The silk is generally yellow, but sometimes white. Each fibre is double and is spun from a viscid fluid that comes from two tubes in the body. The middle picture shows an opened cocoon with the chrysalis inside, and on the right is silk wound from the cocoon.

The left-hand picture shows a bundle of cocoons waiting for the silk to be wound off, and on the right are a number of chrysalids removed from the cocoons. About 1600 silkworms produce one pound of silk.

MOTHS' EGGS, SILKWORMS, AND COCOONS

The eggs of the moths are hatched in an incubator, as in the left-hand picture, and when the silkworms have hatched out they are placed on frames arranged in tiers, and fed day and night with a plentiful supply of fresh mulberry leaves, as shown in the picture on the right.

The cocoons from which the raw silk is obtained are completed by the silkworm in seven days. The best are set aside for carrying on the race of silkworms, and the others are graded and then sent to the workshop.

REELING THE SILK OFF THE COCOONS

In order to soften the cocoons so that the silk thread can be withdrawn, they are boiled.

When this has been done, the cocoons are shaken down and the leading threads are found for reeling.

Here the silk is being withdrawn from the softened cocoons and passed on to a reeling machine.

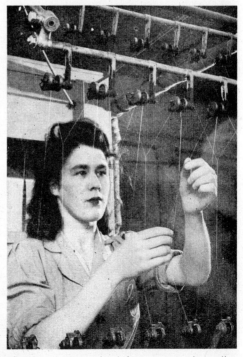

The threads are twisted into one on the reeling machine. This helps to dry and polish the silk.

PREPARING THE SILK FOR THE WEAVERS

From the reeling machines the threads are wound on to spindles. Here an assistant is seen mending a break in one of the threads.

Here a finished skein of raw silk is being carefully examined, layer by layer, to ensure that there are no breaks or flaws in it.

Before the raw silk is passed on to the throwsters and weavers, the skeins of silk are examined, weighed, and pressed. These pictures were taken at a silk farm at Lullingstone Castle, in Kent.

PICTURE-STORY OF RAYON

Rayon is made from cellulose, which forms the walls of the cells of plants and trees. Canadian spruce is largely used, and here we see the bark being removed. The logs are then reduced to pulp.

The pulp is dried and made into sheets which, on arrival at the factory, are steeped in a caustic soda solution and become alkali cellulose. Here we see the sheets being removed from the steeping press.

SHREDDING AND DISSOLVING THE PULP

The alkali cellulose sheets are next ground into crumbs by the shredding machine shown here, then stored for a time to allow the caustic soda to complete its chemical action.

The crumbs are then emptied into the large churns shown above and treated with carbon bisulphide. This dissolves the crumbs into a soluble orange-red substance called cellulose xanthate.

The cellulose xanthate is then placed in mixers such as the one shown in this photograph to be dissolved in a weak caustic soda.

The solution is then filtered in these machines and stored. After ripening into viscose (looking like a clear brown honey) it is ready for spinning.

In this spinning machine the viscose is pumped into an acid bath through a nozzle with holes only one-five-hundredth of an inch wide. The tiny jets of viscose are transformed by the acid into fibres which are drawn together to form a thread of rayon. After various treatments the thread is ready for processing or coning.

FROM SPINNING MACHINE TO WEAVERS

This great machine combines the work of spinning, finishing, and drying, leaving the yarn ready to be coned. The viscose is pumped through the acid baths at the top and the thread is led out and travels downwards onto a series of reels which wash and dry the yarn.

Here we see the rayon yarn being wound onto cones ready for dispatch to the mills.

Here in the mill we see the process of warping—assembling the lengthwise threads of fabric.

Plain Answers to the Questions of the Children of the World

CAN A BRAIN EVER GET FILLED UP?

A T one time it would have been said that after a certain age our brains completely stop growing, but that is not quite true, because it has now been found that in almost all of the brains of the higher type of people there are a certain number of cells which have not fully developed so as to do any work, and which may develop even after we are fully grown up.

All this, however, is a mystery; and it is certain that in the case of many people there is no real limit to what the brain can do and hold. Robert Browning made a great scholar in one of his poems say, " No end to learning "; and this is a motto the wisest men have always believed in. It is also certainly a motto which keeps people young, young at any age, and helps to prolong their lives.

What this question means is whether the brain can become so filled up with knowledge that it can remember no more; whether it can be so full that new facts packed into it must displace old ones.

Before we can consider that as a possibility we must ask what memory consists of and how the brain is affected by memory or thought. The brain consists of unnumbered cells, some of which are certainly storehouses of memory, others being connected with cells which set in motion

nerves that give orders to the body's muscles. Every time we have a thought, every time we make a movement, there must be thousands of brain cells in action to register the thought that produces the movement; and every time there must be some wastage of them. But the body is always renewing the brain cells, and the brain as a whole wears out perhaps less than any other part of the body.

In the brain there is a wonderful division of labour. There are brain cells for receiving sensations, brain cells for giving orders to the muscles or the organs of the body, and besides these there are what are called association nerve cells (or *neurones*), which are far more numerous than all the rest put together and are the connecting link between the others. They are all found in one portion of the brain, and may be described as the nerve cells of experience. They register and keep a record of experiences and impressions conveyed to them by the other nerves, and they may, indeed, be regarded as the storehouse of impressions.

What they have done once they will remember partially to do another time, and when they have done it a great many times they do it very readily. If, on the other hand, they do not have practice in

FIRE · WIND · WATER · LIFE · MIND · SLEEP · HOW · WHY · WHERE

doing things they forget them. So, by the growing old of the association of neurones, the nerve cells of experience, the right hand may forget its cunning, or the memory may forget the year of Magna Carta or any other date.

Thus the brain may in a way get filled up, not because its experience cells can carry no more, but because new experiences, new impressions, new facts may have given them new things to do which they remember better than they remember others which went before.

Often when people grow old they remember best their childish experiences. That is perhaps because the experience cells, relieved from the pressure of new work, are able to recall their old ways.

Why Does My Face Turn White When I am Frightened ?

The skin of our faces has a certain amount of colour of its own, but the main part of the colour of the face—at any rate, in this part of the world—is the colour of the blood shining through the skin. It is the heart that drives the blood through the skin of the face. When a person is frightened the nerves running from his brain to the heart almost stop the heart from beating, so scarcely any blood whatever is sent through the skin of the face, and we see the pale colour of almost bloodless skin. Anything that interferes with the heart's beating will have the same result as fright : bad air, for instance, causing anyone to faint. When a person's face becomes extremely pale, we should understand that there is a risk of his fainting, for if not enough blood is passing through his face, it is probable that not enough blood is passing through his brain.

Where Does the Rainbow End ?

As we trace the rainbow down on each side it seems to touch the earth, and there are stories of children who have set out to find the end of the rainbow. But the rainbow ends nowhere, for it is a mere appearance in the sky, due to tiny drops of water, and it " ends," if we are to use that word, simply where the drops of water end that are so placed as to reflect the sunlight in this way to our eyes. Really no two people see exactly the same rainbow. They could not do so unless their eyes were in the same place. As we move, the bow we see moves with us.

Does Camphor Keep Moths Away ?

Camphor, like most other things that have a smell, is what we call *volatile*—that is, it gives itself off into the air in the form of a gas. Like many other volatile things, camphor is an *antiseptic*, a thing, natural or artificial, that is very bad for the lives of microbes.

Now, most things that are poisonous to microbes are poisonous to insects. Indeed, as a rule, a poison to any kind of life is a poison to all kinds. Camphor in large doses would kill a man. The camphor gives itself off into the air around it, and as it is very poisonous to moths, the moth flies away when it smells camphor. It is a great advantage when an antiseptic is volatile, and all the most useful antiseptics are so. If a thing is not volatile, it can only have its effect on anything that touches it.

But if an antiseptic is volatile it flies about in the air as it spreads, the amount of it in the air gets less; and so insects or microbes can get within a certain distance and not suffer; but they cannot go nearer, or else they would be killed. Every antiseptic we use to preserve clothes by putting it in a drawer will therefore protect all the contents of the drawer.

Why Do We Always Want to Run Down a Steep Hill ?

If we could see the Earth as a great ball, we should notice the hills as places where the surface of the ball sticks out. It is rather like an old composition cricket-ball that has got rough. Now, plainly, in such a case anything on the top of a rough place is farther from the centre of the ball than anything lying in the hollow between rough places.

The case of the Earth is the same. When we are on the top of a hill, we are farther from the centre of the Earth than when we are at the bottom of a hill. The Earth's attraction, which we call gravity, is always trying to pull us and everything else as near as possible to the centre. So when we start going downhill we do not so much drive ourselves as allow ourselves to be pulled by the Earth's power.

We notice this best, perhaps, when we coast down hill on a bicycle; but it is just as true when we are on our legs, only that we cannot roll as the bicycle wheels do. So our natural inclination is to yield to the Earth's pull and run downhill.

How Does the Earth Turn Without Shaking ?

The Earth is a huge and heavy ball, spinning with great speed and momentum through space. Its own spinning keeps it steady like a spinning top, and its only shake is a very slow wobble on its axis, like the wobble of a top. It is probable that the steady pull of the Sun, which holds the Earth in its orbit, also tends to steady it. So long as it is spinning strongly and steadily through space there is really nothing to cause it to shake, unless the Earth quakes in itself, as it does sometimes with terrible effect. The attraction of the Moon is great enough to lift the Earth's oceans and slightly to raise the Earth's crust, but even that pull is not enough to shake such a heavy and steadily spinning ball as our planet.

What was the Gordian Knot ?

The people of Phrygia, an ancient country of Asia Minor, had been so tried for a long time that they thought their troubles would have no end; but the gods declared that everything would come right if they chose as a king the first man they met on his way to Jupiter's temple. The peasant Gordius passed by, driving a wagon, and, hailed as king, he consecrated his wagon to the god Jupiter.

But it is not as a king that Gordius has remained famous; he is remembered simply for a knot, the knot by which he fixed his wagon to the temple. So cleverly was it tied that no end could be perceived in the cord, and it came to be predicted that whoever could untie the Gordian Knot would win the whole of Asia.

The conquering Alexander happened to pass that way, and, puzzled with the famous knot, he cut it with his sword. This daring act much impressed his subjects, who then regarded Alexander as the future conqueror of Asia—as he was.

We now speak of any complex problem that can only be solved in a drastic way as a Gordian Knot.

Why is Tight Clothing Bad for Us ?

All our clothing, from head to feet, should be worn loose. Anything tight on the trunk of the body interferes with the movements of deep, easy breathing, and injures our health. Tight clothing is bad also because it interferes with the proper circulation of the blood through the body. Many foolish people suffer from cold feet because they wear boots so tight that blood is simply unable to get into them. The proper way to keep warm is by our blood, not by clothing or leather; and the way to help the blood to do its work is to give it room to flow instead of tightening the veins and stopping its circulation.

Why is an Axe-handle Curved ?

Experience has shown that more work can be obtained from an axe with a curved handle than from one with a straight handle. In the first place, the shape of a half-strung bow renders the handle stronger and less likely to snap when in use, as the double curve gives it added flexibility, enabling it to give in either direction under the strain of the woodman's blow. Then the curved handle enables the axe-head to be swung through a greater distance than if it were on a straight handle, so increasing its momentum.

Do Fish Fall from the Sky ?

Fish do not, of course, fall like meteorites from another world, but they sometimes do drop on dry land at some distance from the sea.

What has happened in such a case is that a terrific whirlwind has caught up water from the sea and carried it inland. Small fish are borne along in the water and fall to earth when the wind has spent its force.

Why Does Mustard Burn Our Tongue ?

There are a number of chemical substances which, when applied to the skin or the tender parts of the body, cause us to feel a sensation of burning; and mustard is one of them. It acts on the tongue or other sensitive parts as an irritant, causing the blood-vessels in the part to swell up and discharge some of their contents. If sufficient be applied this will form a blister. This is what happens in the case of a mustard plaster. When the mustard has been in contact with the skin a little while we find that a red patch is produced by the swelling of the blood-vessels. This causes pressure on the nerves and irritation of the endings of the nerves, with the result that there is a sensation which we describe as burning. A number of other substances besides mustard have the same effect, and some of them are employed by doctors as local irritants.

What is a Lonk ?

The lonk is an old breed of sheep whose ancestral home is the hilly country between Lancashire and Yorkshire. About a century ago Jonathon Binns, writing on Lancashire agriculture, spoke of the improved Haslingden or Lonk breed as having been known there for at least a century before.

They fell out of popularity early in this century and were allowed to get too narrow along the back and too long in the leg. Then breeders turned their attention to them again, and the lonk, large-framed and robust and shorter-legged, is now a sheep with a great reputation and a Breeders Association of its own. The rams, with massive spiral horns, have a commanding appearance and a champion among them, Summerhouse Spellbinder, weighed 397 pounds. The sheep of this breed live long and yield good clips of wool.

Who Are the Gypsies ?

The true Gypsies call their race Romany; our name for them comes from "Egyptians," for it was formerly thought that they were wandering Egyptians.

This old belief came from a tale the Gypsies themselves spread when they first appeared in Western Europe about 1417. They said they had been driven out of their own land, "Little Egypt," by the Saracens because they would not renounce their faith. The Gypsies probably made up this story to win sympathy from the nations among whom they wandered.

Where the Gypsies first came from is still something of a mystery. Some authorities have thought from India, because so many words in their language, Romany, are similar to words in Sanskrit, the ancient language of India, and to words in modern Indian tongues.

Hordes of Gypsies roamed Europe in the 15th century, but they did not reach England until about 1514. They lived by begging, fortune-telling, giving performances of music, singing, dancing, by mending pots and pans (as tinkers). They were also clever smiths and in parts of Transylvania as late as 1865 they were farriers and blacksmiths, and frequently carried out all the ironwork of a village.

They were often accused of stealing children—of which they were quite innocent—and of cheating and thieving, and were cruelly persecuted. Nevertheless they survived and handed down their way of life and their language to their descendants.

Roaming the world today are thousands of these nomads, all speaking dialects of the same language. Every continent has them, in America they are found from Canada to Brazil, and they have even found their way to the new countries, Australia and New Zealand.

In our land by no means all the van-dwellers we see are true Gypsies. The real " Romanies " are clean, cheerful, harmless, and very interesting people.

Can we Abolish Noise ?

It is not possible entirely to abolish noise while we cannot abolish air vibrations which produce it. There is at the University of Utrecht a sound-proof room from which outside noises are so well excluded by layers of cork, asbestos, and other materials in the fabric of the walls that a person inside the room can hear his own heart-beats or the creaking of his muscles and joints. But air is as rigidly excluded from the room as noise.

Similarly a measure of ensuring quiet in the rooms of modern buildings has been successfully undertaken by filling the hollow walls of the room with a special kind of prepared seaweed known as eel grass or with glass wool, but these devices are equally incompetent to shut off outside noises when the windows are opened.

The problem of silencing noises at their source is of a different kind. The most objectionable of them are such as arise from street drills, electric riveters, and the engines of motor-cars or aeroplanes. Something can be done with these, for even a pistol can be fitted with a silencer which reduces the sound of the explosion to a dull plop. Silencers of some kind have been suggested and made for street drills, and the only objection offered to them is that they reduce the efficiency of the implement. That is an objection which we believe can be overcome and it should not be beyond the powers of inventors to reduce by allied means the explosive sounds issuing from the engines of cars and aeroplanes.

Did Any of the Apostles Come to Britain ?

Although many of the Apostles are said to have travelled far and wide, there is no record of any of them having come to Britain. Still, this does not make it certain that none of them came. Britain was within easy reach of Rome, and we know Paul went to Rome, and Peter also. But it is not likely that Paul came to Britain. He tells the Roman Christians in his letter to the Romans that he hopes to go on to Spain after he has seen them, and Clement of Rome, a great and good man, in a letter he wrote to the Corinthians in A.D. 96, mentions the fact that Paul went " to the extreme of the west," or " to the western limit."

There is no doubt, however, that the Apostles literally obeyed our Lord's command, and as far as possible preached the Gospel to every creature. John settled at Ephesus; Matthew is said to have preached in Ethiopia; Bartholomew visited Asia and Arabia. Thomas is reported to have founded the Church in Persia, and Andrew to have gone to Scythia. And there is very little doubt that at a very early date the Gospel was preached as far away as India.

What is a Pot-Hole ?

A pot-hole is a cauldron-shaped cavity which may sometimes be seen in the rocks by the sea, or near a swiftly flowing river or a waterfall. In all cases the cavity starts as a slight inequality in the surface, and then the revolving in it of loose stones by the eddying water sets up a grinding action, which gradually wears away the cavity until it becomes quite a deep hole. Of course, the stones, in excavating the holes, are themselves worn down to sand or gravel, but fresh stones are washed in to take their place. On the sides of narrow gorges traces of old pot-holes are often to be seen high up above the present level of the torrent.

Why do We Shiver When We are Very Cold ?

There are more good reasons than one why we shiver when we are cold. The machinery of it, as we may say, is that cold, *at first*, rather excites and disturbs the nervous system, as heat usually soothes it. We notice these contrary effects of heat and cold in the case of a warm bath and a cold dip. This, of course, is not to say that shivering is the same thing as the feeling of activity we have after a cold dip; but in each case the cold has been what is called a stimulant. But now we have to ask whether the shivering is of any use to us, or whether it is a wholly useless and purposeless thing. Beyond any doubt it is possible to show that shivering serves the purposes of the body as hunger does. One good reason for shivering is that it makes us aware of cold as we might not otherwise be, and so we can protect ourselves.

Why Cannot We Sleep with Our Eyes Open ?

To begin with, one reason why our eyes are shut during sleep is that it needs effort to keep our eyes open. When we get sleepy we relax that effort, and our eyelids drop of their own weight. So that is one answer to the question. We cannot sleep with our eyes open because we cannot hold our eyelids up when we are asleep. But another question is, Why would it keep a man awake to hold his eyes open in the light? The reason is that light keeps us awake by exciting our brain, and when we want to go to sleep, of course, one of the first things we have to do is to shut our brain off from the outside world by darkness and by silence. So there are two answers to our question: one is that when we are asleep we cannot hold up our eyelids, and the other is that light keeps the brain active.

What is the Sorbonne ?

The Sorbonne is the seat of the faculties of science and literature in the Paris University and the chief centre of French learning. It is named after its founder, Robert of Sorbonne, a chaplain of King Louis the Ninth. The original aim was a special establishment where religious studies could be brought within the reach of poor students.

From an ecclesiastical centre of learning the Sorbonne grew in the nineteenth century to be a seat of modern learning. The first books printed in France were printed at the Sorbonne, and in the seventeenth century Cardinal Richelieu had it enlarged. The library of the Sorbonne has 600,000 books and manuscripts. Its amphitheatre is the meeting-place of all the famous scholars of France.

Why is a River Always Moving?

The water of a river, like everything else on the surface of the Earth, is always being pulled as near as possible to the centre of the Earth by gravitation. Even when a river or a stream is rushing fast downwards it still stays on the surface; but we must remember that the new part of the surface it reaches is nearer the Earth's centre. When anything falls towards the centre of the Earth it loses some energy which it had in it before it fell, and we must ask where the water got this energy from—the energy which, for instance, will turn a mill-wheel. What raised the water in the first place, and never fails to raise more water? It is the Sun. And so the answer to our question is that a river is always moving because the Sun is always shining. The Sun's power raised from the sea the water that falls as rain, and makes rivers. Therefore it is really the Sun that turns the mill-wheel, and it is the Sun that opposes us when we try to swim or row up-stream.

What is a Patent?

A patent is a document issued by the Patent Office (a Government office worked as a part of the Civil Service) to secure for inventors any profit they may be able to make, over a reasonable period, from an invention that is new and immediately useful. The period of monopoly accounted reasonable is fourteen years. If, however, the inventor can show that he has not, in that time, been sufficiently rewarded, the period may be extended. A patent will not be granted to anyone who uses his invention for purposes of profit before he patents it. The patent must be granted first, and the invention not be used for profit till the patent has been secured. The object of this restriction is to discountenance the concealment of inventions, as such concealment might lead to an invention being used for the purpose of profit for many years.

If an invention has been and remains in use unpatented, unknown to a patentee, his patent is made void by the prior discovery. A general principle cannot be patented, but only its practical application to a definite useful purpose. The granting of a patent does not ensure the patentee against an action for infringement of an earlier patent.

Why is the Sky Dull when a Storm is Coming on?

The light of day is almost all due to direct sunlight and to skylight, which is sunlight reflected from the sky—that is to say, from the air. When a storm is coming on, the clouds gather, and as these clouds are thick and dense they cut off the light of the sky, and so we say that the sky is dull. If we went in an aeroplane above the clouds we should find ourselves in brilliant sunshine.

What Makes a Whirlpool?

We make a little whirlpool when we stir our tea, and a whirlwind moving above water will set it whirling for a time. But there are great whirlpools which remain from century to century. The cause of them is the meeting of two strong currents of water. When we take a top or a ball and hold it between our hands and spin it by pushing one hand from us and pulling the other hand towards us, we really see how two opposing currents may affect the water where they meet.

There is a great whirlpool below the Falls of Niagara; another, about which wonderful stories have been told, is the famous Maelstrom off the coast of Norway; but the most famous of all is the whirlpool called Charybdis, in the Strait of Messina. We know that this whirlpool existed thousands of years ago, but the region is terribly liable to earthquakes, as everyone now knows, and it is said that the position of Charybdis has been altered in consequence. Not far from where Charybdis used to be was a great rock, dangerous to sailors; its name was Scylla. It was very difficult for small ships to pass between the whirlpool and the rock without being engulfed in the one or wrecked upon the other, and to this day, when a man has to steer his course of life very carefully between two dangers, we say that he is between Scylla and Charybdis.

What is the Cap of Liberty?

Freed slaves in ancient Rome wore the Phrygian cap in token of their freedom. The Phrygians were a race of Greek origin whose name meant freemen, and their characteristic headgear has stood for freedom ever since. The red cap which was worn during the French Revolution was called the Cap of Liberty.

What are the Dead Sea Scrolls ?

In the early summer of 1947 an Arab boy was looking for a lost goat in the desolate region of sand and rock-hills at Khirbet Qumran on the Dead Sea. He threw a stone into the opening of a cave in a hillside and his quick ear caught the sound of crashing pottery. Scrambling into the cave, he found a stack of covered jars, and inside them—preserved for over a thousand years in a good state by the fine, dry air—some inscribed rolls of parchment, or scrolls.

These scrolls were sold to a dealer in Bethlehem, and eventually went to the Hebrew University in Jerusalem, where scholars quickly saw that they were written in Hebrew, were of great antiquity, and that they were probably a very ancient version of the Old Testament.

It is now generally agreed that the scrolls are the remains of the library of a Jewish sect which had a kind of monastery at Khirbet Qumran from at least 100 B.C. When the Romans closed in on Jerusalem A.D. 66–70 this Qumran Community dispersed, having placed its library in hillside caves near the monastery. They never returned to reclaim them, and the scrolls lay hidden in the caves through the centuries.

Further extensive searches in the caves revealed about 75 scrolls, Biblical and non-Biblical. One of the most complete is of the Book of Isaiah which shows a text a thousand years earlier than the one in standard Hebrew Bibles. Dr. Frank Cross, a well-known American scholar who has compared the texts, says, " The great Isaiah scroll will have considerable value in reconstructing the ancient language, especially the ancient pronunciation of Hebrew, since its system of spelling is far more complete; to all intents and purposes the Isaiah scrolls of Cave One are simply early manuscripts belonging well inside the stream of tradition which produced the text we possess." Five caves have now been explored and the full story of the relation of the find to our present Bible has yet to be written; but scholars do not anticipate that the texts of the Scrolls will greatly differ from our present Bible text.

What is even more interesting, however, is the discussion on the Qumran Community to which the Dead Sea Scrolls belonged. This community was active all during the life of Jesus Christ. Did Jesus Himself know of them, and their belief in a " Teacher of Righteousness "? Were some of their practices such as baptism, ritual meals of bread and wine, and references to the " Holy Spirit " copied by the early Christian communities after the death of Jesus? Did Jesus Himself have contact with the Qumran Community during the early years of His life, particularly during the " eighteen silent years " about which we have such little knowledge ?

All these questions are being discussed as the Dead Sea Scrolls yield up their story through the non-Biblical texts of the Scrolls. What is agreed is that the Qumran Community was a branch of the Essenes, a party within Judaism, as important as the Scribes and Pharisees. We hear little about them in the New Testament, and it is suggested that this is largely because the early Christians were friendly with them and took over some of their practices into the new Christian community. It is even suggested that the Essenes " Teacher of Righteousness " is " Jesus of Nazareth " and that there are intimate parallels between the Essene and primitive Christian communities.

The Dead Sea Scrolls are helping scholars to understand more of the world in which Jesus of Nazareth grew up, and in which Christianity took root. These discoveries strengthen Christianity's claims to be a historical religion which developed under God in a particular part of the world at a particular time.

Did Cinderella really Wear a Glass Slipper ?

In the original story Cinderella did *not* wear a glass slipper ; the word glass crept into the story through a curious error on the part of the man who translated it from French into English. He mistook the word *vair*, fur, for *verre*, glass. At that time fur was worn only by kings and princes, so the fairy who took pity on Cinderella gave her slippers of fur fit for a princess.

The story of Cinderella is very old, and is probably of Eastern origin. It is found in almost every language in Europe. In France, Charles Perrault and Madame D'Aulnoy include it in their Fairy Tales, and Grimm has it in his Household Tales.

Who is Britannia on a Penny?

The figure of Britannia on an English penny originally represented an actual lady who, in her day, was regarded as a model of beauty. The lady was Frances Stuart, Duchess of Richmond, and it was in the reign of Charles the Second that her likeness was transferred to all the copper coinage. We can judge whether she is fairly pictured as Britannia, for her portrait was painted by Sir Peter Lely, the fashionable artist of her time, and belongs to the Barbers' Company in London. There is a copy of it in Hampton Court Palace, and in the Islip Chapel of Westminster Abbey is a wax effigy of the lady as she appeared at the coronation of Queen Anne. She was very fond of animals, and in her will left legacies to people to look after her cats, thereby giving that caustic little poet Alexander Pope an excuse for his line

> Die, or endow a college or a cat.

Does a Flower Sleep at Night?

Plants do go to sleep at night for several interesting reasons. Animals depend on plants and trees for their proper air, and plants and trees depend on animal life for theirs. Plants take in the carbon dioxide from the air, using the carbon and giving out the oxygen, thus forming material for the life of animals. Animals, that is, men and beasts, breathe out carbon dioxide, and so make a useful contribution towards keeping the air fit for the life of plants.

But when the sun is shining, or so long as light lasts, the plant is so busy taking in its store of carbon dioxide that it has not time to put forth the oxygen due from it. When the daylight dies away, the plant ceases to take in the carbon, and, while sleeping, gives off its oxygen. A flower takes its food in the day and grows at night. It becomes heavier during the day, but lighter during the night, when it is giving off and not taking in anything.

But we must not suppose that plants sleep only at night. Some sleep during the day and wake up in the evening. Pollen has to be brought to many plants by insects. Some insects sleep by day and work by night. These are they which visit the night flowers, carrying the pollen which they need.

Then there are early risers among the flowers. The crocus, for instance, wakes early and goes to sleep soon after midday.

Plants and flowers seem to know as well as the wisest of human beings what best to do. Some are so delicate that they cannot bear the glare of the hot sun, so they go to sleep before the heat becomes too great for them, closing their petals and protecting their sensitive parts. Others cannot bear much moisture or cooling, and they sleep until all is safe again.

For the most part it is at night that the plants sleep. The flowers close their petals with wonderful neatness; the leaves curl; some stalks hang limp, while the stalks of others, in order to let out the oxygen, have to keep erect, as we do when we wish to breathe deep breaths. We can learn a good deal by watching the daily life of the common wild daisy.

What is Goldbeater's Skin?

Goldbeater's skin is made from the peritoneum of an ox, a skin which protects the internal organs and acts as a wall to the abdomen. Its chief use, and indeed the use which gave goldbeater's skin its name, is in connection with the making of gold leaf. Gold leaf as used for gilding is actually real gold, or sometimes an alloy of gold and another metal, which has been treated to annealing and hammering processes till it is about only one 290,000th of an inch thick. After several preliminary processes, small, thin squares of gold are placed in a pile and between special paper, and then hammered. As the gold becomes thinner it, of course, spreads out. It is then cut into smaller pieces, piled between sheets of goldbeater's skin, and again hammered. This process is repeated two or three times, goldbeater's skin being the separating material for each successive hammering, which becomes lighter as the leaf becomes thinner, till the desired degree of thinness is reached. Goldbeater's skin is also used for the making of ballonets for airships.

Why do Leaves Change Colour in the Autumn?

In the autumn the beautiful green stuff made by the sunlight in the plant changes and goes. It is not that the plant is dying, but that it is going to rest for the winter. As it is not going to use its leaves, it takes out of them everything that will be useful. In doing this the plant or the tree changes the green stuff in the leaf, and so we get various colours produced in the autumn.

The Story of the Beautiful Things in the Treasure-House of the World

The back of the beautiful Pitri Palace in Florence

THE RENAISSANCE IN ITALY

WE were last thinking of Gothic architecture, that vast growth which seemed, during the first hundred years of its branching, to be something of a miracle. It was, we remember, a religious architecture, and as such came to its fulfilment.

There have been revivals in Gothic; one of them produced a number of buildings in England during the last century, but there have never been any developments. Nothing has been evolved out of Gothic ideally suited to municipal buildings.

The style which followed it rose in a country where the Gothic movement had found little favour—Italy. It bears the general name of Renaissance architecture; but this must not be confused with the Renaissance in painting and sculpture which happened much earlier.

When Renaissance architecture arose the Middle Ages were past. The invention of the printing press had naturally resulted in a wider reach of scholarship than had been possible when the monks were the sole tutors of Europe.

The spreading of printed books throughout the Continent had two results—the Reformation and the Renaissance in architecture and literature. Books made men think, made men rub their eyes and dimly apprehend the loveliness of Greek and Roman art and literature. In reaction, they presently turned aside from productions of medieval Europe, and found nothing worthy unless it was of the classic spirit. To this intense interest in the history and literature of the past, in the fifteenth and sixteenth centuries, was given the name of Humanism.

In addition to these internal forces there was an outside event of much significance. In 1453 Constantinople, the centre of Greek and Roman art and learning, fell to the Turks, and a great number of Greek scholars, fleeing from the new Power, settled in Italy. They came at a time when the country was sensitive to their " touch," and the effect on Europe as a whole was immeasurable.

Thus, after being forgotten for a thousand years or so, after centuries when the buildings of the old Roman Empire, containing beautiful Greek statues, had served as a quarry, classic art became triumphant in Italy, and produced, among other things, Renaissance architecture.

This new style, we must remember, which first appeared in Florence and her neighbouring towns, was born of classic ideals, but it was not classic architecture simply copied in another country. It was an architecture that used classic ideals in so far as they were suited to the needs of a race whose religion, government, and

PICTURES · STATUES · CARVINGS · BUILDINGS · IVORIES · CRAFTS

styles of living were far removed from those of ancient Greece and Rome. Therein lay its strength.

It grew slowly, like all great styles. From the outset it was as much suited to secular as to sacred buildings, and it was different from Gothic in that its construction was saner and capable of infinite development. It branched out in many directions, and to it most of the buildings of the present day can be attributed.

THE DIGNITY AND STRENGTH OF THE BUILDINGS OF FLORENCE

When Florence took the lead in Renaissance architecture she was a very queen of cities, and there were many stars in her crown. She led Europe in the matter of art; her great industry and pride had created an immense wealth and power; she was the strongest force in Italy. She was nevertheless at the mercy of the fortunes of war, within and without, and it was natural that her chief buildings should be in the style of fortress-palaces for her reigning princes, like the Medici.

There was plenty of fine stone and marble in Tuscany, and this material, being quarried in large blocks and set rough-hewn in the courses of the walls, gave at once a rugged character to the new architecture. The chief note of buildings like the Riccardi Palace and the Pitti Palace in Florence is enormous strength combined with a very fine dignity.

The architects seemed to begin these great palaces with the idea of a foursquare fortress, and made as few openings on the ground floor as possible. One can easily imagine the Riccardi standing a siege. In the higher storeys the buildings seemed to breathe a little—set with tall, rounded windows in undeviating regularity. Sun screens catch the light and make patches of shadow on the stonework. Then, surmounting all, a huge cornice ran its unbroken line round the building and seemed to frown down on the narrow street with its gaily dressed passers-by.

THE FINE FINISH A CORNICE GIVES TO A BUILDING

The Riccardi, famous for ever because of the Medici, for whom it was built about 1430–34 from the designs of Michelozzo, is the most fortress-like of these early Tuscan palaces. It was known as the palace of the Medici, and only took its present name when, in 1659, the Marquis Riccardi became its owner.

The Strozzi Palace is another of these fine rugged buildings, set up in 1489. Two architects, Da Majano and Cronaca, worked on it. Cronaca also built the Guadagni Palace. The Ruccellai Palace, erected about 1450, marks a slight change. It has no cornice—suffering a little thereby, for that frowning line finishes a building in a very fine way—and on the Ruccellai appear for the first time the classic pilasters which became such a feature in Renaissance architecture.

Among these princely houses the Pitti Palace stands as chief, famous the world over. It was begun by Brunelleschi, the first great architect of the Renaissance, in 1441, and about a hundred years later was finished by Ammanati. The palace was built for Luca Pitti—one of the powerful fifteenth-century Florentines, a great tyrant who used his power as magistrate to force citizens to find money for his palace. When the family fell on evil times the house was sold to beautiful Eleonora, wife of Cosimo I, the Grand Duke, in 1549. Eleonora caused the famous Boboli Garden to be constructed. Part of its lovely stretch faces the chief court of the Pitti, where the architect allowed himself to set up the classic columns which look beautiful in the court and would have spoiled the front of the building.

THE WORK OF CENTURIES IN THE NOBLE PITTI PALACE

The world owes a great deal to the various people, patrons and architects and artists, who during the course of three hundred years conspired together to make the Pitti Palace one of the noblest places in the world. The building stands on rising ground, overlooking the city and the river, and round it, like a great girdle, is thrown the greenery of the garden. The additions that were made in the eighteenth century, after the Pitti had become the home of the reigning king, happily did not mar its beauty. Except for the Vatican, it is the largest palace in Italy.

The Pitti Palace is one of the buildings that one can call noble—most palaces are either grand or beautiful—and this nobility is due not to its great size, but to its symmetry and perfect proportions, and the long sweep of its lines. Its weight is horizontal rather than vertical, and this strength is increased by the lines that accentuate the storeys, and not lessened by one superfluous vertical line or ornament.

THE BEAUTIFUL ARCHITECTURE OF ITALY

THE LOGGIA OF SAN PAOLO IN FLORENCE

THE CHURCH OF ST. SPIRITO
IN FLORENCE

THE CAMPANILE OF
ST. SPIRITO

INSIDE THE CHURCH OF THE
CERTOSA OF PAVIA

ON THE GRAND CANAL IN VENICE

BALBI PALACE IN VENICE

The pictures on these pages are by Mesrrs. Alinari, Anderson, Brogi, McLeish, E.N.A., and others

From the Pitti, which contains great treasures of art, a gallery runs on to the Uffizi, once a palace, and now one of the finest art galleries of the world.

When we think of our own achievements, or the work of the past century, we cannot help feeling that the world is passing through a comparatively uninspired period.

THE SPIRIT THAT IS MISSING IN THE WORLD TODAY

We have never been visited again by the fine spirit that created the Italian Renaissance. In those days a man took in his stride something that nowadays would be a separate life-work. It was quite usual for an architect to be also sculptor and painter of note. The shining examples of this wealth of genius were, of course, Raphael and Michael Angelo. But men whose names are not so honoured shared this richness and fullness of genius. The architect was naturally an artist of first quality. And, moreover, during this period the servants of architecture, the craftsmen, were persons of great gifts. The wood-carvers, goldsmiths, ironworkers, the kind of sculptors we should call now monumental masons, alone would have made the century memorable. At the end of the Renaissance the wave of golden energy ebbed away.

Many architects were at work in Florence and the neighbouring cities— men like Borgognone, Michelozzo, Filarete, Alberti, Alessi, Cronaca, and Brunelleschi, the most gifted of them all.

SPLENDID PALACES TOWERING ABOVE THE NARROW STREETS OF GENOA

The Renaissance helped to make Genoa, already marked by some fine churches of an earlier period, a most individual and distinguished-looking town. As in all the great Italian cities, palaces were built for her princes of commerce, and threw up their beautiful lines high above her narrow streets. One of the most famous, now known as Municipio, was the Doria-Tursi Palace, built at the end of the sixteenth century. Earlier than that, Alessi was at work in Genoa, and to him more than anyone else is due the guiding of the taste of persons who were so willing and glad to make their town beautiful. Under Alessi's leadership the authorities reformed their famous street which is now called the Strada Garibaldi, and almost all the palaces that make it so picturesque

are this architect's work. Others set up at a later date, like the Balbi and the Durazzo, owe much to Alessi's teaching.

One of the earliest town hospitals in Europe, the Ospedale Maggiore, rose in Milan during this period. In northern Italy most of the important works were buildings of a secular nature. Many churches and cathedrals, like those of Florence and Genoa, were altered and added to, and some new ones built. In Florence there was St. Spirito and St. Lorenzo, and the Pazzi Chapel—one of Brunelleschi's most beautiful little buildings ; and in Genoa St. Maria in Carignano, the work of Alessi. The most important church of this group, historically speaking, is St. Andrea, Mantua, as it was the first to be built in the style that has been accepted as pure Renaissance.

THE TRIUMPHAL ARCH WHICH LEADS INTO A CHURCH

St. Andrea served as a model for many later buildings of a sacred character. The Roman arch was now being used by architects for the chief entrance of a church. A good example is St. Francesco, Rimini, whose principal porch was to be a copy of the Arch of Severus. Unfortunately the façade was not finished. In St. Andrea, Mantua, the Roman triumphal arch forms a magnificent entrance.

One of the most interesting buildings of Europe is the Certosa at Pavia, the city where so many scholars found peace in the tumultuous years of northern Italy. The Certosa was planned in the fourteenth century by the chief lord of Pavia, who had determined to have " a place wherein to dwell, a garden wherein to disport himself, and a chapel wherein to worship." It was begun in the Gothic years and finished in the Renaissance. A history of architecture and Italian beauty thus exists in this group, from the Gothic cloisters up to the strange-looking Renaissance storeyed tower set at the crossing in the church, and the marvellous gleaming front. This façade of marble, added to the Gothic church by Borgognone, is one of the triumphs of the early period of the Renaissance. A wealth of art was spent on the carved doors and on the interior decoration. One of the finest of the Certosa monuments is that to Ludovico Sforza and Beatrice d'Este, by Solari.

Northern Italy during the Renaissance years was like a great forest where art lovers could wander happily for years, finding constantly new beauties, large and small.

The great main growth of the movement came to maturity in Rome and Venice. Here the personalities of two architects dominated the work—first Bramante and then Michael Angelo.

THE MASS OF TOWERS AND SPIRES IN A GOTHIC BUILDING

Bramante, who was born at Urbino in 1444, two years before the death of Brunelleschi, saw all the possibilities of the new style, and in his work we can see its development. We can also see now at a glance the difference between a town which loved the Gothic style and one which loved Renaissance.

The sky line of Gothic buildings was a mass of mounting spires and towers and pinnacles, every line in the masonry carried as high as it would go. The sky line of Renaissance is a long horizontal bar, either a heavy cornice like that of the Riccardi Palace, for instance, or an open balustrade, like that of the Capitol at Rome. The ceilings of Gothic buildings were a mass of intricate vaulting; in Renaissance we find horizontal ceilings, panelled and moulded or simply arched. The tower of the Gothic church gave place to a dome at the crossing. We can see this at once by comparing St. Paul's Cathedral with Westminster Abbey. Renaissance windows were very simple and much smaller than those of Gothic buildings; they were square-headed or round-headed, sometimes round-headed in a square frame—a feature which Bramante treated with great refinement—sometimes square-headed surmounted by a triangular pediment, a feature very common in so-called classical buildings of modern times.

THE PLACE OF THE PILLAR IN THE WORK OF THE RENAISSANCE

The use of the Orders, either as pillars or pilasters, which, we remember, are the fronts of pillars fastened to the wall as an ornament, became the strongest characteristic of Renaissance work. And the more the columns struck the simple, vertical line, the more the courses of the storeys and roof struck a powerful horizontal line. On the basis of this severe plainness of structure a great deal of ornament of all kinds was laid.

Bramante, his pupils and assistants, are responsible for a large number of buildings that rose toward the end of the fifteenth

century and in the first half of the sixteenth century. His youthful training as an artist was under Mantegna, as an architect under Alberti. Bramante's early work is at Milan; there he built the churches of St. Satiro and St. Maria delle Grazie. Two very beautiful pieces of sacred architecture by Bramante are at Rome—the cloister, with its two-storey arcade, of St. Maria della Pace, and the tiny circular church, a miracle of taste and proportion, called the Tempietto, in St. Peter in Montorio.

Of Bramante's work on St. Peter's and the Vatican we shall be thinking presently. Apart from that his most famous secular buildings are the Cancelleria Palace and the Giraud Palace, Rome. It was Bramante's assistant, Sangallo, who planned in 1534 what is probably the greatest house of sixteenth - century Renaissance — the Farnese Palace, Rome. Part of it was erected under Sangallo's supervision; Michael Angelo added the third storey ten years later. One of the chief beauties of the Farnese is its huge, unbroken cornice.

WORTHY STUDENTS WHO FOLLOWED A GREAT MASTER

The chief of Bramante's pupils and followers are Peruzzi and the great Raphael, Bramante's nephew. To these men the master handed on his scholarly tastes and his admirable restraint; most of the work they produced is worthy of the Bramante tradition. Peruzzi built, among other things, the Villa Farnesina, which Raphael helped him to adorn with frescoes. Raphael was responsible for certain parts of the Vatican, for the front of St. Lorenzo in Miranda, and the Villa Madama, Rome, and the Pandolfini Palace, Florence, which was built after his death, and is supposed to be his best architectural design. Raphael was also consulted about St. Peter's by the Pope, but it does not appear that he took any active part in the construction of the great church.

Giulio Romano, the painter, was one of Raphael's pupils, and builder as well. His finest piece of architecture is the Del Té Palace, Mantua, a wonderful one-storey building. When it was set up Giulio had the pleasure of painting some of the frescoes himself.

In the latter half of the sixteenth century some extremely interesting work was done by Barozzi da Vignola, who appears to have divided his time between Italy and

France, and also found leisure to write a book which was important to students of that century, The Five Orders of Architecture. Among Vignola's chief buildings were the church of St. Andrea and the Gesù Church, Rome, the Farnese Palace, Caprarola, and the Villa of Pope Julius, now the Etruscan Museum, Rome.

THE BIGGEST GROUP OF FINE BUILDINGS IN THE WORLD

In the Vatican and St. Peter's all the grandeur of Roman art and history foregathered; with the Piazza they make the hugest, most famous group of fine buildings in the world.

This huge edifice was not set up in any one period: centuries have gone to its forming. The first bit of the Vatican, adjoining the ancient basilican church of St. Peter, was built at the end of the fifth century. About the year 1200 this fragment was reconstructed; the first additions were made by Pope Nicholas III eighty years later.

During the fourteenth century the popes made their home at Avignon, in southern France. They built a magnificent fortress-palace there, and sent for Italian painters to decorate the walls. In 1377 they returned to Rome, and at once it seemed an interest in art and architecture was aroused in the great city. Presently one of the popes caused a passage to be built on arches connecting the Vatican with the Castle of St. Angelo, whither, during the terrible sack of Rome in 1527, Pope Clement was glad to flee.

HOW THE VATICAN GREW AND GREW THROUGHOUT THE AGES

Bit by bit the palace was added to, each ruler trying to leave his stamp on it. Pope Sixtus built the Sistine Chapel, of whose decorations we read on page 696; Alexander added the Borgia Tower. In the reign of Leo, and the warlike Julius who swung his sword, so to speak, through so many artists' lives, Bramante added his famous parts—the court of St. Damaso and the Belvedere Court; and Raphael decorated his gallery and rooms. A later pope caused Sangallo the architect to add the Pauline Chapel and other apartments. After that the palace was widened, Bramante's courtyard being added to on the eastward side. Addition after addition came, courtyards and magnificent staircases and galleries, and at last the Vatican had about a thousand rooms and was finished. It is now a treasure-house of art, containing the largest collection of classic sculpture in the world.

In 1505 Pope Julius was taken with an idea of building a tomb house for himself; from it grew the largest church in the world, St. Peter's, Rome. In order to clear the way, Julius had the old basilican church pulled down (this had been built by Constantine in 330 near the place of St. Peter's martyrdom in Nero's circus) and then he invited all architects of note to compete for the work of the new building. The drawings and sketches made for this monument are now treasured in the Uffizi, Florence, and they show, if we had no other evidence, what a wealth of art there was in Italy in those days.

Bramante's design was chosen, and in 1506 the foundation stone laid. His plan was to build St. Peter's in the form of a Greek cross with a huge dome like that of the Pantheon, and a tower, in stages, of most beautiful work, at each of the four points of the cross.

THE ARCHITECTS WHO TRIED TO UPSET THE PLANS OF BRAMANTE

Seven years later Julius died, and his successor called in Sangallo, Fra Giocondo, and Raphael, who, being also architects, had ideas other than those of Bramante. The work of the first two was finished before they could alter much of the magnificent work Bramante had begun. Raphael suggested that the Greek cross plan should become a Latin cross, which, considering the proportions and general mass of the building, was a foolish suggestion. After Raphael's death Peruzzi was then made architect, and he liked the Greek cross formation. So, one way and another, the church grew.

Troubles within and without disturbed both the building and its advisers. The work had to stop for want of money; then war cast its shadow across the climbing walls; the sack of Rome, that seven months' horror, came. Peruzzi died in 1536, and Sangallo the Younger became architect to St. Peter's in his place. It seemed that no man could go on with the plan originally accepted; each had to make his mark in some way, and build, or try to build, a St. Peter's of his own. Sangallo proceeded to work according to his plan; but before he could finally spoil the building death in turn took him. And then on to this stage of many actors strode Michael Angelo, genius, master, who had, as we know, played many parts.

The master was seventy-two, but not too old to fire guns. Slip-slap, to right and left, was shot the work of other men. Once more Bramante's plan of the Greek cross was reverted to, these two geniuses meeting on this point of taste. As such the church was carried on, but Michael Angelo added his own treatment of chapels and apse. His work was vigorous and sane, and he began constructing the huge dome in a daring manner which has been the amazement of architects ever since.

THE ONE IDEA OF BRAMANTE WHICH NOW REMAINS IN ST. PETER'S

It is impossible to read the tale of the building of St. Peter's without wishing very sadly that either Bramante or Michael Angelo could have made a finished work of it, or, at any rate, that after the architect's death his very able plans might have been carried out. There is very little left of the original, exquisite, and restrained design Bramante made now, save the idea of the dome. For in 1564 Vignola added cupolas in place of Bramante's towers, and Maderna, an architect of the early seventeenth century, for the last time contested the Greek cross plan, pulled out the nave to make it in form a Latin cross, and added the chief front.

The last architect to make his mark on St. Peter's was Bernini. He built the magnificent entrance piazza, a great, wide, circular sweep, with its fourfold arcade of huge pillars. This fine empty space before the chief façade is of the most wonderful value, as it frames and sets back the great church. St. Peter's is an awe-inspiring sight, and quite half of the effect, to the approaching visitor, is caused by the sweep of Bernini's piazza.

Everything about St. Peter's is huge. It is 435 feet to the top of the cross on the great dome. The pillars that run round the actual building are immense. The church's interior is almost oppressive in its magnificence.

THE MEN WHO COPIED THE STYLE OF MICHAEL ANGELO

Michael Angelo had done many other architectural works before he touched St. Peter's. His labours were varied, from the staircase at the Biblioteca Laurenziana, Florence, which Vasari finished from his design, to the Medici Mausoleum. His greatest civic building was the Capitol at Rome. Another work of his in the great city was the turning of a Roman bath house into the church of St. Maria degli Angeli.

After Michael Angelo another change came over Renaissance architecture in Italy. The great genius had a number of followers who imitated his restless, tormented grandeur, and could not by their smallness get at the strength that underlay it. In the seventeenth century architects began to have a horror of simple, classic lines, and they felt that the more curves a building had the better it was. To this period, that of the degeneration of Renaissance style, which corresponds in architectural history with the last eccentricities of Gothic, the name of Baroque or Rococo has been given. It is, as the reader will guess, not a good architecture. But in spite of its inherent weaknesses some interesting Baroque work was produced in Venice and the neighbouring towns.

GLORY OF VENICE IN THE FIFTEENTH AND SIXTEENTH CENTURIES

In Venice, fairy town set in the sea, palaces of dazzling beauty mark the Renaissance period. Like Florence, she was an independent power and had much wealth which she joyfully expended in the interests of art and architecture. Palaces arose in the Gothic and Renaissance period as a matter of course, just as nowadays, in a thriving English town, huge shops would appear. The standard of the Venetian was high; nothing paltry or cheap was allowed to appear; we can scarcely conceive of the glory of fifteenth and sixteenth-century Venice.

The city had of course an allure of her own, which, apart from the strong, individual taste of the Venetians, gave a distinction to her architecture. No other Italian palaces were lapped by tides which flung up an added radiance into the sun's light and drew down the lines of walls and doors in long, wavering reflections, and painted them in the richness of colour that tranquil water alone can give.

It was because sky and sea made such a glory of the marble lines that Venetian architecture in the years of wealth became so decorative. Surface ornament was peculiarly rich in the Baroque period, too rich. Balconies flung out their traceries against the gleaming walls ; cornices running the length of the storeys laid bands of blue shadow on the palace fronts.

We have already noted, in mentioning St. Mark's, how independent was the Venetian spirit. When Renaissance architecture rose in the city her artists and architects created not only this rich surface effect, but they had an art of grouping their windows which is very pleasant and sets them apart from other Italian palaces of the period. They liked a cluster of window forms in the middle of a façade, with the bare wall on either side making the group appear all the richer by contrast.

THE LOVELY CITY THAT STANDS ON A NETWORK OF CANALS

To go along the Grand Canal, which is the main street of Venice, almost lined with palaces, and across the wonderful Rialto Bridge, is to receive an unforgettable lesson in the Venetian genius.

As in other Italian towns, it was often difficult to decide whether a Venetian's work entitled him more to the description of architect than sculptor. The two arts almost always went together; many men have laid the stamp of their dual gifts on Venice. In the sixteenth century two great names stand out, the gifted Lombardi family and Jacopo Tatti, generally known as Sansovino. To Pietro Lombardo is due, among other notable works, the lovely marble church of St. Maria dei Miracoli, one of the most exquisite things the Renaissance produced in Venice. To Sansovino, again among other notable works, the city owes the Library of St. Mark, the greatest civic building produced in Italy in this period. St. Mark's School, now a hospital, was built by one of the younger Lombardi.

MAGNIFICENT PALACE WHICH USED UP THE LABOUR OF CENTURIES

Many architects were concerned in the most famous house in Venice, the palace of the Dukes, or Doges. Like the Vatican, it took centuries to grow. It was begun early in the ninth century, was twice burned down and rebuilt, and suffered many alterations. The façades date from the Gothic period (Bartolommeo Buon was responsible for some of this early beauty) and each successive generation added something. The great courtyard with its arcade is one of the most delightful things in Italy, and is unique in the architecture of its period.

The palace is built of various kinds of marble, in some parts rose and white blocks making a pattern of colour which, added to the open tracery and richly-carved columns, gives an exquisite effect. In due course Pietro Lombardo was employed on the palace, and after him Bergamasco, and, later, Scarpagnino, another architect. From the courtyard rises the famous Giant's Staircase, and here Sansovino, working in the capacity of sculptor this time, placed the fine figures of Mars and Neptune. Paul Veronese and Tintoretto painted some of the walls and ceilings of this famous palace; its doorways and chimney-pieces are wonderfully carved. At every third step, it seems, one is confronted by a great work of art. The Bridge of Sighs, its gleaming shape hung over the narrow waterway, connects the palace to the prison.

The last great architect of the later Renaissance was Andrea Palladio, a man of great gifts who has had a considerable effect on Europe from his day to our own. Some of his works were carried out in Vicenza; many were begun, but did not reach completion.

THE FINE THINGS PALLADIO MADE FROM HIS POOR MATERIAL

Palladio had often to build in poor material, like brick faced with stucco, and it was a mark of genius that out of such commonplace material he should have created works of art. He published a famous work on architecture which contained a history and description of buildings since destroyed, and also designs for his own buildings.

Palladio built many palaces in Vicenza, and added the famous arcades to the old basilica in that town. One of his best-known works was the Redentore Church, Venice.

Soon after Palladio's death buildings of the Baroque style began to be seen. Probably the most famous of all Baroque buildings is the St. Maria della Salute Church in Venice, built by Longhena. Bernini, whose piazza for St. Peter's we have already mentioned, was a Baroque architect, one of many who laboured in Italy, not altogether for its good, in the seventeenth century.

All countries and races have to pay the price of a great period in art by the poor work which inevitably follows it. And perhaps we can appreciate pure Renaissance buildings in Italy all the better because we are obliged to pass by so much that is unworthy of them.

GREAT BUILDINGS OF ITALY

THE BEAUTIFUL CHURCH OF SANTA MARIA DELLA SALUTE ON THE BANKS OF
THE GRAND CANAL IN VENICE

ST. MARIA DELLE GRAZIE, MILAN

SPINELLI PALACE, VENICE

ST. MARIA DEI MIRACOLI, VENICE

ONE OF THE SPLENDID PALACES ON THE GRAND CANAL IN VENICE

COURT OF THE MAGGIORE HOSPITAL IN MILAN

THE GIRAUD-TORLONIA PALACE IN ROME

TEMPLE IN THE CHURCH OF
ST. PETER MONTORIO, ROME

SAN BERNARDINO CHURCH,
PERUGIA

THE FAMOUS MEDICI CHAPEL
IN FLORENCE

THE CERTOSA OF PAVIA, AN OLD CARTHUSIAN MONASTERY, NOW A NATIONAL MONUMENT

THE GUADAGNI PALACE IN FLORENCE

THE PALACE OF THE DOGES IN VENICE

THE RIALTO BRIDGE ACROSS THE GRAND CANAL IN VENICE

THE FARNESE PALACE IN ROME, WHICH MICHAEL ANGELO HELPED TO BUILD

ST. PETER'S IN ROME, THE BIGGEST CHURCH IN THE WORLD

THE VATICAN IN ROME, SEEN FROM THE COLONNADED SQUARE IN FRONT OF ST. PETER'S

THE VILLA FARNESINA IN ROME

THE GREAT STROZZI PALACE IN FLORENCE

THE OLD TOWN HALL OF VERONA

A DOORWAY OF THE CERTOSA
OF PAVIA

LOOKING UP INTO THE
CUPOLA OF ST. PETER'S

A DOORWAY OF THE FARNESE
PALACE, ROME

THE BASILICA PALLADIANA AT VICENZA

A PALACE ON THE GRAND CANAL IN VENICE

THE PALACE OF THE CONSERVATORI IN ROME

GRIMANI PALACE IN VENICE

A HALL IN THE VATICAN

PISANI PALACE IN VENICE

A GALLERY IN THE RICCARDI PALACE,
FLORENCE

THE BEAUTIFUL INTERIOR OF ST. PETER'S
IN ROME

THE ARCHES OF THE PALACE OF THE DOGES AT VENICE

A COURT IN THE RICCARDI PALACE, FLORENCE

A COURT IN THE FARNESE PALACE, ROME

The Wonderful House We Live In, and Our Place in the World

These flags of the United Nations flying side by side symbolise the co-operation essential to world harmony

CO-OPERATION

ALL we have learned about the production of wealth leads to the conclusion that men, by working together, can do far more for themselves as individuals than by working against each other. This principle of working together we call co-operation.

Co-operation, while it means combined effort, does not mean the loss of individual character, initiative, enterprise, or effort. If it did it would be valueless, because it is necessary that the powers of every boy and girl, of every man and woman, should be fully developed. It would be a bad thing for industry, trade, and society if individuals merely worked like cogs in a machine, without knowing why they were at work, and without any responsibilities for their actions.

There is no better way of illustrating the true conception of co-operation than by a cricket team. As every boy and girl knows, it consists of eleven players. The eleven go into the field to play the game, as we say. It is " cricket " to play for your side and not for yourself. The game is instinct with fair play. It is a matter of concerted, combined, or co-operative effort between eleven individuals, each with brains of his own, powers of his own, and ideas of his own. Each player desires to

succeed. Each gets individual pleasure out of the contest.

How is it done ? How is it that each cricketer gets a good game as an individual while the first principle of the game is to study the interest of one's side and not of oneself ? The answer is, first, that the game has definite rules, which each player consents to obey. There would be no pleasure if there were no rules. For example, if there were no rule as to the width of the bat, a batsman might produce a bat eight inches wide, plant it in front of his wicket, and defy anybody to get him out.

Then, also, each member of the eleven, in addition to obeying the general laws of cricket, also agrees to obey the captain. This captain appoints the members of the team to their places in the field, according to their individual abilities, and decides the order in which the batsmen shall go in.

By obedience to these commands each member of the team gets his best individual chance. If he has a natural and effective break he is put on to bowl. If he is exceptionally quick of eye, and smart in snapping balls off the bat, he keeps wicket or is placed in the slips. If he is a bad fieldsman, and yet a first-class bat, he is put at mid-on, but goes in to bat

BODY, MIND, AND SOUL · CITIZENSHIP · ECONOMICS · GOVERNMENT

early in the innings. So we see each player given individual opportunity in which he can distinguish himself, and yet at the same time finding his pleasure, not merely in individual effort, but in what is truly co-operative work.

The best results in work are obtained in the same spirit of enlightened self-expression. In mutually directed efforts individuals can find the most complete satisfaction of their own working powers. Happiness, as well as fruitfulness in work, follows such co-operation. Doing his best in cricket, the player enjoys not only his own efforts, but the approval and the esteem of his fellow players. Doing his best in co-operative work, the worker can gain for himself precisely the same individual and social happiness.

TRADE THE SERVANT OF THOSE WHO ARE ITS CUSTOMERS

In analysis, all the varied occupations which are carried on within our country are co-operative so far as they are useful. In the long run, no trade or industry can survive unless it meets the need of a number of people sufficient to sustain it. Whether a man sees or not that the trade he carries on is really a servant of those who are its customers, it is nevertheless true that that trade is part of a scheme of service. It is curiously true that sometimes a man who imagines himself to be a most selfish creature, who thinks of nothing else but of looking after, as he would say, Number One, is really working hard all the time to serve others, and leaving for himself very little leisure.

Fortunately, people are becoming more and more conscious of the mutuality of work—of how one occupation is dove-tailed with another, of how trades depend on each other, and of how necessary it is for all the individuals working in a trade to have harmonious relations.

THE GREAT OPPORTUNITY THAT COMES TO THE CHILDREN OF TODAY

Thus we see the members of industries working together in trade associations, which have central offices and meeting-places where, from time to time, they discuss the progress of the trade, how to make improvements in its products or its methods, and how best the general interest of the whole of the members can be served by individual action just as at cricket.

We see also the workers in industries drawn together in trade unions, which are formed to help the whole body of workers. No doubt, as time goes on, these will be more and more closely associated with the actual governors of trades, so that an industry will become a body co-operative within itself, and a conscious servant of the public. For every industry is a public servant, and the more it is conscious of the fact, the better for it and for the nation of which it is a part.

Each working section of the nation must come to understand and appreciate the others. Here, surely, is a great idea for children to grow up with, so that, when they come to take part in the serious business of life, they may try to understand what a wonderful thing the work of a great nation is, and help to make it better, happier, and more fruitful.

Among the things in which there has been more and more co-operation in work is the effort to make occupations safer for those who work in them. So a " Safety First " campaign has arisen. More care is taken than of old in safeguarding workers from being killed or injured by faulty appliances, by bad methods, or by unguarded machinery.

MORE WEALTH CAN BE PRODUCED IF WORKERS HAVE HEALTHY CONDITIONS

There is also the question of making work-places clean, well-ventilated, and comfortable as well as safe. Good employers now provide those who serve them with fine rest-rooms, canteens, lockers, and lavatories. It is also becoming more and more widely understood that if work is done under the best conditions, in roomy places where there is plenty of light streaming in from large windows, where there is ample space in which to move about, and where the air is not too cold in winter or too hot in summer, far more wealth can be produced by the same amount of effort than in unhealthy, badly arranged, crowded work-rooms. All these things, too, are expressions of enlightened self-interest, of co-operative endeavour, of the heartening and noble conception that work, being an essential part of the daily life of the world, should be treated in terms of common humanity.

Although all manufacture is aimed at satisfying the wants of people, there is much buying and selling between firms, in the normal process of production. Every industry buys raw materials from others, and also partly finished products, such as iron bars, or small parts such as nuts and bolts, nails, and washers. Many industries sell their products to other industries. The iron and steel makers, for instance, sell their product to engineering works, and cotton spinners sell yarn to weavers.

No industry could keep going on its own if others did not exist. Most firms, for example, would be unable to continue if the coal mines closed down. The mines themselves, however, depend on the engineering industries to provide machinery and tools for the miners to use, and on wire rope manufacturers for the steel cables which hoist the coal up the shaft. Furthermore, no miner would be willing to work if he was paid in coal alone. He must be able to spend his wages on goods produced by other industries.

It is possible for an industry to be so important that the community could not get along without it, but no industry is so important that it could get along without the rest of the community.

THE MORE WEALTHY COUNTRIES THERE ARE, THE BETTER FOR ALL

It is not alone in our own country that we have to consider this important principle of co-operation.

If we remind ourselves of the history of what we now call the British Isles, we know that not very long ago our islands, small as they are, contained nations which warred fiercely upon each other. Now we are able, fortunately, to regard them as being one co-operative whole in the matter of work and trade. We do not make the mistake of thinking that if someone in Scotland gets an order for business it is bad for someone in England. We know that nothing could be better for England than that Scotland should be prosperous, and that London is not better off, but worse off, if Lancashire suffers in trade.

So it is between countries which are not united under one government, as England, Wales, Scotland, and Northern Ireland are. The more wealthy countries there are in the world, the better for everybody. Prosperity in one country has a tendency to spread. What is of especial importance to us in Britain at present is the wealth of those backward countries in the hotter parts of the world which are very poor now, but will be able to buy more of our goods if they become wealthier through developing their agriculture and local industries. Similarly, increasing wealth in the richer countries means better markets for the high quality goods which they can produce.

WE MUST ANTICIPATE THE FUTURE WANTS OF PEOPLE

Of course, as other countries develop industries to produce goods which they buy from us at present, some of our factories may have to close down. When this happens, we shall have to change over to making different things. An example of this occurred in Lancashire, where the cotton trade was badly hit by competition from new cotton mills which were set up all over the world, and especially in Japan and India. Because most countries now run cotton mills, our cotton industry will never again be as big at it once was. We have lost the advantage which we had when we were the first country to develop this industry.

However, other industries were growing up at the same time as cotton declined. The sort of goods which we export is continually changing. Radar equipment, for instance, is a completely new form of export since the Second World War. If we are to continue selling to the world we shall have to keep on developing new products to take the place of the older ones as the rest of the world begins to make them. Men's needs are continually changing, and we must keep looking ahead to see *what people will want in the future* without worrying too much about what we used to be able to sell in the past.

THE CIVILISING EFFECT OF TRADE BETWEEN NATIONS

World trade is in essence just as much a scheme of co-operation as is trade within our own borders. Individual firms within the country are constantly changing their products to suit consumers at home, just as they must do to provide what the foreign customer wants. We buy abroad and sell abroad for precisely the same reason that people in Lancashire buy and sell in London. Trade is not a one-sided affair, but a matter of mutual interest. Thus, if we buy wheat from

Australia, and sell heavy machinery there, it is to the advantage of both the Australians and ourselves.

World commerce, as it was before the war, amounted to a redistribution of goods and services all over the world, which made for the comfort and prosperity of every part of it. Nothing is more unwise or untrue than to regard trade as a sort of warfare. If a ship leaves a British port, taking railway material or cloth or motor-cars to another country, it is not a deed of cunning. They go out because they have been bought by someone to whom they will be useful, and when we export to a nation we serve that nation even while we serve ourselves.

So it is with imports. The foreign nations or British Dominions which send us goods do not injure us. On the contrary, we buy abroad what we need, and when the purchases arrive they serve us, just as our exports serve others.

THE THINGS WE RECEIVE FROM AND SUPPLY TO THE WORLD

Here is a description of part of the exchange of goods and services with the world at large by which we live :

IMPORTS	EXPORTS
THE WORLD SUPPLIES TO US	WE SUPPLY TO THE WORLD
Food, including corn, meat, dairy produce, fruit, vegetables, wine, tea, coffee, cocoa, sugar, and so on.	Manufactured articles, including iron and steel, brass goods, engines, railway material, machinery, tools, electric goods, cotton goods, woollens and worsteds, jute goods, linen, apparel, hats, chemicals, boots, ships, rubber goods, earthenware, gloves, and so on.
Raw materials, including ores, cotton, wool, jute, hemp, silk, timber, hides, skins, asbestos, india-rubber, gutta-percha, sulphur, oil-seeds, and so on.	
Manufactured articles, including copper, brass, lead, iron, machines, yarns, oils, chemicals, dyes, wood-pulp, and so on.	Ship Services (that is, our ships carry goods for oversea nations).
Tobacco.	Financial Services (our bankers work for people overseas).
	Coal.

We could not exist as a great nation without the supplies we receive from abroad, for not only should we be without food for about one-half of our people, but most of our factories would be without the raw materials which are the food of work. An account of our imports is really an account of the services which the world performs for us. An account of our exports is really an account of the services we perform for the world.

The two acts balance each other, and that is a matter of mutual benefit and an expression of co-operation.

We see how interdependent men are, and how interdependent nations are. A man trying to live for himself alone is like a boy " sent to Coventry," as we say. A nation seeking to be self-sufficing is really robbing itself of the advantage of belonging to a world which can serve it.

WHY WARS MAKE THE WORLD A MUCH POORER PLACE

The progress of the world has arisen from the extension of commercial relations. It is by no means a thing to deplore that different nations have different natural resources, and that their peoples have varying attributes. It is the very variety of different lands and different peoples which gives savour to humanity, and interest to the intelligent man who surveys the globe.

The most obvious reason why wars impoverish the world is that they cause so much physical destruction of wealth. Buildings are blown up or burnt, complicated military apparatus is manufactured and then destroyed, and ships which took thousands of men several years to build are sunk in a few minutes. Countries are therefore poorer after wars because they have had so much of their wealth destroyed.

Another reason why wars make the world poorer is because their effects last long after they have finished. Trade is dislocated, and takes time to find regular channels again. Most important of all, war destroys that mutual confidence between nations without which trade between them is impossible. This confidence takes years to regain. Thus, it is difficult to take advantage of the international division of labour which we discussed in an earlier chapter, and we are unable to benefit from the full potential wealth of the world.

THE PEACE THAT IS ESSENTIAL FOR THE MUTUAL SERVICE OF NATIONS

Thus the interdependence of nations is really the co-operation of nations, the mutual service of nations. In peace alone it can flourish, and the more fully we understand the need and value of this co-operation, the more determined we shall be to make it ever wider in its operations.

FLOWERS OF THE BOGLAND

1. MARSH MARIGOLD 2. BLUE MARSH VETCHLING 3. HORSE MINT 4. YELLOW MEADOW-RUE 5. MARSH WILLOW-HERB. 6. GREAT SUNDEW 7. KNOTTED FIGWORT 8. IVY-LEAVED BELLFLOWER 9. YELLOW MARSH SAXIFRAGE 10. MARSH PLUME-THISTLE

1. MARSH CINQUEFOIL 2. NODDING BUR-MARIGOLD 3. MARSH RED-RATTLE 4. WATER HEMLOCK 5. MEADOW CRANE'S-BILL 6. SMALL MARSH VALERIAN 7. MARSH CUDWEED 8. MARSH GENTIAN 9. MARSH VIOLET 10. MARSH ANDROMEDA 11. MARSH RAGWORT 12. PENNYROYAL 13. FLAX-SEED

FLOWERS OF THE STREAM

1. FLOWERING RUSH   2. YELLOW WATER-LILY   3. WATER MINT   4. BROOKLIME   5. GREATER SKULLCAP
6. COMMON COMFREY 7. WATER VIOLET 8. WATER BEDSTRAW 9. GREAT VALERIAN 10. MARSH YELLOW-CRESS
11. COMMON BUTTERBUR   12. YELLOW LOOSESTRIFE

I. YELLOW IRIS 2. SNAKE'S HEAD 3. LARGE-FLOWERED BITTERCRESS 4. WATER AVENS 5. MARSH WHORLED MINT 6. NARROW-LEAVED WATER PARSNIP 7. PURPLE LOOSESTRIFE 8. YELLOW MONKEY-FLOWER 9. WATER PLANTAIN 10. GREAT WILLOW HERB II. MONEYWORT 12. PROCUMBENT MARSH-WORT

The Story of the Peoples of all Nations and Their Homelands

Ulus Square, in the centre of Ankara, capital of Turkey

TURKEY, ANCIENT AND MODERN

Turkey is a bridge between Europe and Asia, with territory in both continents ; it stands on either side of the narrow waters joining the Black Sea to the Mediterranean. Of its total area, 296,500 square miles (more than three times the size of Great Britain), much the greater part occupies the Anatolian Peninsula, or Asia Minor. Only a little over 9000 square miles of Turkey is in Europe, bordering Greece and Bulgaria.

But modern Turkey is only a small part of what once was a great and far-reaching empire.

Because of its position as a bridge between East and West, Turkey has been the scene of many great movements of peoples and upheavals of nations. The famous city of Troy, of whose siege, before the dawn of written history, Homer tells us, stood near the mouth of the Dardanelles. The great Persian host of Darius marched through this land. So did Xenophon with his immortal Ten Thousand; and Alexander the Great on his conquering progress from Macedonia. It was in Asia Minor, too, that Caesar, returning from his Egyptian campaign, came and saw and conquered. And at Tarsus, St. Paul was born.

Early in the seventh century of the Christian era a young man called Mohammed was growing up in Arabia. He was a reformer, for he taught the Saracens to give up idolatry and form themselves into one nation. His new religion taught that there is but one God, that both the Jewish and Christian religions had come from God, but that he, Mohammed, was sent to teach a more perfect faith, and to force it on the world.

It is almost impossible for us to realise the force and fury with which the followers of Mohammed, catching the fire of his tremendous enthusiasm, set forth to conquer the world. They were ready to give up their lives for what they believed, for they firmly held that if they fell in battle against unbelievers they would then be sure of happiness in the world to come. Province after province fell to them, including Jerusalem. The magnificent walls of Constantinople saved that city for another three centuries, but nearly all the time the emperors of the East were engaged in fighting the followers of the Prophet.

During these years the Roman and Greek Churches were drifting wider apart. Latin ceased to be a common tongue, and the Roman element became less strong. Greek language and literature were more

THE FIVE CONTINENTS & 100 NATIONS & RACES THAT INHABIT THEM

widely cultivated and many scholars were at work in monasteries and schools, often in spots remote from the turmoil of war.

For, besides the struggle with the Mohammedan Saracens and the Turks who followed them, the empire was beset by the Seljuk Turks from beyond Persia. Having become Mohammedans, they gained Asia Minor and Palestine.

To regain Jerusalem and its holy places for Christendom the Crusades were therefore started in Western Europe, and went on for many years. But, so far from being able to rescue the land sacred to Christians from Mohammedan power, the Christian people of Western Europe were busy quarrelling with one another, and the Turks saw the opportunity for attacking Constantinople, the seat of Christian authority in the region of civilisation which drew its inspiration from Greece.

Constantinople in those days was becoming more and more a City State instead of the heart of an empire, as it had been in earlier years when it became the chief seat of Christianity in the East.

THE THRILLING JOURNEY OF A PRINCE OUT OF ASIA INTO EUROPE

At this time a fresh incursion of Turks, called Ottomans, from their leader Osman, joined in the contest between Mohammedanism and Christianity with an intense vigour, and secured a firm foothold in Asia Minor, on the opposite shore of the Bosphorus to Constantinople. From this point of vantage it was not difficult to cross into Europe.

The story of how the Turkish Crown Prince with eighty men crossed into Europe on rafts is most thrilling. At the narrowest part of the Dardanelles, no wider than a good-sized river, they succeeded in planting a fort, the foothold of the Ottoman Turks in Europe. Before many years had passed towns, villages, and valleys fell to the conquerors—even Adrianople, the second city of the empire, fell. Several causes helped. The rulers of the old empire were weak and foolish ; the Balkan Christians were fiercely destroying one another while the hour of their doom was coming nearer ; and the other peoples around, the Venetians, Genoese, Hungarians, Poles, Austrians, were too disunited, or too busy with their own affairs, to join forces against the invaders at their gates.

Sigismund of Hungary headed a force when the Turks burst through the Balkans ; but they were too strong for him, and, besides, he was much taken up with persecuting John Huss, the brave Protestant leader of Bohemia. Later the courageous John Hunyadi, with the Poles, defeated the Turks, but was afterwards in his turn defeated at Kossovo.

THE SONS OF THE CONQUERED PEOPLES WHO FOUGHT FOR THE TURKS

The Turks now determined to have Constantinople for their capital, so all the time they were increasing their ships and their army. One way of increasing the strength of the army was to make the conquered peoples give up the finest of their boys. These boys were brought up as Mohammedans, and drilled to fight against their own countries. These troops were the famous Janissaries, or new soldiers, who helped so largely to destroy the Eastern Empire, and gained so much power over the sultans.

The ruins of the walls of Constantine's city show how strong were the defences when the last emperor stood bravely in the breach against Mohammed II. He knew the end was near, and at midnight had taken the sacrament in the beautiful church of St. Sophia. Then, after a short rest in his ruined palace, he sadly mounted his horse and rode away to the post of danger, amid the sobs of the crowd.

Before long the besiegers made their entrance over his dead body. It was on May 29, 1453, that the great church of Christianity passed into the hands of its enemies.

St. Sophia still stands in its grandeur, and many of its beautiful mosaics tell of its Christian past, though for more than four centuries it has been used as a Mohammedan mosque. It is now a museum.

THE FLIGHT OF LEARNED MEN THAT LED TO THE NEW LEARNING

This conquest by the Turks of the old Greek Empire, and particularly the fall of Constantinople, caused the flight of many students and learned men, with the manuscripts they so much loved, towards the West, chiefly to Italy. The westward trek of these scholars was one of the factors that led to what was called the New Learning and the New Birth of Art—or the Renaissance, as we say.

During the years that followed the taking of Constantinople the Crescent on the Ottoman banner shone triumphantly over an immense and powerful empire from the Danube to the Euphrates, from the Caspian Sea to the Strait of Gibraltar. The discipline and unity of purpose of the Mohammedans prevailed against the jealousies and quarrels of the so-called Christian kingdoms.

Among the Turkish rulers—who came to be called sultans—were many strong and clever men. One of the greatest was

It was said of Suleiman that, while he ruled, sword and pen were never dry, so continually was he fighting, and so great was the number of writers in his day. It was he who swore he would take no rest till the prayer of the Prophet rang out from the tower of St. Stephen's Church in Vienna. But his quarter of a million Turks were obliged to retire from the gallant city, and so the spread of the Turkish power in the valley of the Danube was checked for a while.

At the great naval battle of Lepanto, a

A MODERN PRIMARY SCHOOL AT ISTANBUL, OVERLOOKING THE BOSPHORUS

Mohammed II, who had ridden over Constantine's body and up the nave of St. Sophia on that eventful day in May, 1453. He ruled for thirty years, and conquered Serbia, Bosnia, and Greece.

Another great sultan was Suleiman the Magnificent, who lived at the same time as Henry the Eighth of England.

In 1511, two years after Henry the Eighth came to the throne, came the first attempt to establish trade relations between Britain and Turkey. Seventy years later the first English ambassador to the Sultan was appointed under Elizabeth the First.

few years after Suleiman's death, a limit was set to Turkish power in the Mediterranean and on the sea generally. After this came a succession of weak and cruel rulers, and under them there were wars with the Persians, mutinies of the Janissaries (who had become a very rich and strong body), and other disasters.

Ottoman power rose again for a time under the able rule of a family named Köprülü, many of whom acted as prime ministers, or chief viziers. It was under one of these men that the Turks made an unsuccessful attempt to capture Vienna.

At this time the Turks were masters

of the whole of the Balkan Peninsula; but from that September day in 1683 the tide of Turkish power in Europe began to ebb.

The Turks were driven out of Hungary; many towns and islands in the Mediterranean were taken from them; Greece passed for a time to the Venetians before entering on its long, final struggle for freedom against the Turks. The Russians captured Azov, on the Black Sea, and by degrees its northern shore passed into their hands.

During the Crimean War (1854–56) Britain, with France, fought on the side of Turkey against the Russians. The name of Florence Nightingale, and the wonderful work she did for the allies in that campaign, are still remembered in Turkey.

With the growth of Russia's power came the right to interfere in the provinces north of the Danube, particularly Moldavia and Wallachia, which, from dependence on Turkey, became in 1878, largely through Russian influence, the independent Kingdom of Rumania.

THE STRUGGLE OF THE SMALL NATIONS AGAINST THE TURKISH POWER

The Western nations, in love with liberty, also gave sympathy and help to the oppressed Balkan peoples. The story of the two hundred years before 1918 was a story of nation after nation striving to gain freedom from its Mohammedan rulers.

At the beginning of that period Turkey held all the Balkan Peninsula, Hungary to the summits of the Carpathians, all that is now Rumania, part of the Russian Ukraine, the Crimea, the northern slopes of the Caucasian range, part of Georgia, all Asia Minor, nearly all of Armenia, part of Kurdistan, Mesopotamia, Palestine, Arabia, Egypt, Tripoli, Tunis, and Algiers, with Albania, Bosnia, Herzegovina, Dalmatia, and part of Croatia.

Two hundred years later, just before the First World War, she had lost Algiers and Tunis to France; Rumania, Serbia, Greece, and Bulgaria were independent; Egypt was only under a sovereignty that had no meaning; Bosnia and Herzegovina had passed to Austria; and only Macedonia and Thrace in Europe, and Asiatic Turkey, with Palestine, Mesopotamia, and the western part of Arabia remained Turkish; while Russia had annexed a part of Armenia and all lands once Turkish in the Circassian district.

When Germany's ambition turned the Kaiser's thoughts to the East, he saw in Turkey a possible helper, and the officers of the Turkish army who had studied the arts of war in Germany were impressed by the military efficiency of that nation, which appeared to them irresistible.

BRITISH FORCES AND THEIR THREE LINES OF ADVANCE ON TURKEY

Accordingly, when the War broke out, these men linked Turkey with the fate of Germany. There never was any reason for supposing that they represented the opinion of the average Turk ; but the German-influenced Turkish officers controlled the army, and Turkey became Germany's ally in the Near East.

All Turkey's strength was needed to ward off a British movement from India by the Persian Gulf on Baghdad, the capital of the Mesopotamian plain ; an advance from Egypt on Palestine ; and an attempt to reach Constantinople from the Mediterranean through the Dardanelles and over the Gallipoli Peninsula.

The Mesopotamia advance was finally successful. The British Gallipoli attack was repulsed after heroic bravery had been shown on both sides and terrible losses suffered ; but the blow through Palestine, under the dashing leadership of General Allenby in 1918, succeeded so completely that Turkey surrendered unconditionally.

THE DIRE STRAITS TO WHICH A PROUD NATION WAS REDUCED

The territorial losses to Turkey through her support of Germany were Mesopotamia, which was formed into an independent Arab kingdom, called Iraq ; all the parts of the peninsula of Arabia that had been garrisoned by Turkish troops ; the State now called Jordan ; Palestine, which was afterwards administered by Great Britain under a mandate from the League of Nations ; Syria and Lebanon, afterwards administered by France under a mandate ; and the part of Thrace west of the Maritza River, which was ceded to Greece.

Never has any proud and conquering nation been reduced to worse straits than the Turks were in when the First World War ended in the defeat of Germany and its mistaken allies. The Government of the Turkish Empire, as all the world knew, and educated and intelligent Turks had realised, was hopelessly corrupt under the reigning Osmanli dynasty. Bribery ruled everywhere. But this Government by the Turkish Sultans, rotten to the core, was seated on one of the world's most commanding sites, and the question as to what should take its place was of high importance to all the nations that had vital interests in the Mediterranean and the main route to the East.

THE VICTORIOUS ALLIES OCCUPY ALL OF TURKEY'S EUROPEAN TERRITORY

There would have been no doubt about who would have reigned at Constantinople if Germany had won the war. But that bubble burst, and Russia, who had been seeking dominance there by slow pressure for more than a century, was divorced from the rest of the world by her preoccupation with internal revolution. So, when the crash of Turkey came Germany and Russia were safely out of the way, and French, British, and Italian troops occupied a portion of European Turkey round Constantinople.

The Government of the Sultan was bolstered up temporarily by the Powers in possession, as his was the only authority that could be said to represent Turkey. That country seemed to be " down and out." All its European territory was occupied by the victorious allies, and Greece was encouraged to invade Asia Minor and occupy as much territory there in the neighbourhood of Izmir (Smyrna) as it could control.

Izmir was then the chief commercial city in Asiatic Turkey and had a large Greek population. A numerous Greek army crossed to Asia Minor and made extensive inroads into regions unquestionably Turkish.

THE TURKS FACE THE FUTURE IN A WAY WHICH STARTLES THE WORLD

Then came a dramatic change which upset the calculations of politicians. Turkey, driven to stand at bay, found herself by finding a leader.

One of the living wonders has been the power of the Turks, living in comparatively small minorities, to rule over wide lands that have large majorities of varied races. They ruled for centuries over Arabs, Egyptians, Armenians, Georgians, Bulgars, Serbs, Greeks, Croats, Jews, Assyrians and a medley of other races. How was it done?

The most salient characteristics of the Turk have been an indomitable courage, an implacable pride, an unwavering ruthlessness. That spirit, time after time, kept them from being overwhelmed. But a crisis had come at last when they seemed on the brink of utter defeat at the hands of the race they most despised. Their outlying lands where they were in a minority were lost, and their own lands, for the most part bleak and stern, where they were in a permanent majority, and whence they had emerged to harass Europe long ago, were being violated. They faced their dark fate with a thoroughness and a competence that startled the world.

The Turkey of the Sultanate at Constantinople, the Government, the Sublime Porte, as it was called, was hopelessly diseased and prostrate, but the Turkish people were on the verge of a new life. And now the puzzled politicians of the big European States were planning how *they* would carve up Turkey afresh to suit themselves. It was not, however, to happen so.

THE INTELLIGENT TURKS WHO SAW WHAT WAS THE MATTER WITH THEIR COUNTRY

The times of warlike activity, which were shattering Empires, were enabling educated, intelligent Turks to see clearly what was the matter with their country. It was chiefly the younger officers in the Turkish army who saw that the only hopes for Turkey were to sweep away her corrupt Government, to invite the people to form a free Republic, and to clear the foreign invaders out of the land.

Nothing could be done with Constantinople, in European Turkey, for it was held by foreign troops. A new capital was needed, far away from Europe's armies and navies, where all Turkish patriots could rally to free their country from foreign control.

So, far inland, 200 miles from Constantinople, at Ankara (or Angora as it was once called), then quite a small town on the bleak Anatolian highlands, Turkey began the experiment of freeing herself under the direction of the master-mind that appeared in her midst at the very moment when he was wanted. Or, more probably, it was the man, Mustafa Kemal (later to be universally known as Kemal Atatürk), who made the moment by having the necessary thought, personality, and genius.

The Turkish nation, men and women alike, responded to Kemal's call, and with almost incredible heroism and sacrifice swept the Greek army clean out of Asia Minor in one triumphant campaign. So he became Ghazi (" The Victorious "), saviour of his country.

With Turkish thoroughness, not only the Greek army, but nearly all the Greek population was bundled swiftly out of Turkey. The Turks formed a representative Grand National Assembly, abolished the Sultanate, and formed a Republic. This was proclaimed on October 29, 1923, with a single-chamber legislature elected for four years, and Kemal Atatürk was elected first President.

THE TREATY OF PEACE WHICH LED TO FRIENDLINESS

In a Conference of the Powers most intimately concerned, held at Lausanne between November 1922 and February 1923, a Treaty of Peace was arranged which led to a satisfactory mapping of the new Turkey and a resumption of a friendly attitude all round. The final effects were that Turkey again carried on the government of the part of European Turkey that is called Eastern Thrace; Adrianople and Constantinople (now Istanbul) were re-occupied by Turkish troops as the Allied armies gradually withdrew; and Turkey relinquished all claims to lands outside Asia Minor and Eastern Thrace except the islands Imbros and Tenedos, which guard the approaches to the Dardanelles.

The straits leading to the Black Sea were given freedom for trade. Turkish law was made the law for all in Turkey, and special legal privileges were no longer allowed to foreigners. The country became independent, without any restraints being imposed on behalf of those who were not Turks.

THE EMERGENCE OF THE NEW TURKEY UNDER A RESOLUTE LEADER

The new Republic was a singularly compact territory, easily defended, and bordering only on Greece, Bulgaria, Soviet Russia, Persia, Iraq, and Syria; thus its neighbourly relations were very greatly simplified.

The re-establishment of Turkey as an independent Power to be treated with respect was so striking in its sureness and completeness that no one can wonder at the Turkish people making a national hero of the man to whom the change was almost entirely due. Their confidence in Kemal Atatürk as a soldier was unbounded, but would he, as a statesman and the organiser of a ruined nation that had long been weltering in corruption, ignorance, and industrial inefficiency, be equal to the peaceful tasks that confronted him?

In the 15 years during which he was President, Kemal Atatürk achieved miracles, and his successors, Ismet Inönü and Celâl Bayar, have carried on his good work. No one inside or outside Turkey could have dreamed that such changes could have been brought about as those which have transformed the Turkish nation, socially, politically, and industrially, under the masterly insight and driving power of that remarkable man, Kemal Atatürk. The whole life of a nation has been shaped afresh on new patterns.

Kemal Atatürk and those who were working with him felt that the new Turkey must be built on foundations wholly different from the traditions of the past. The most cherished usages of the race must be swept away if they fettered and restrained the nation from becoming free, independent, and prosperous.

HOW WOMEN BECAME FREE TO HELP IN TURKEY'S RISE TO GREATNESS

The first — and very momentous — step in this rebirth was to set free the womanhood of the country to share with the men the work and the glory of its redemption. The Turkish women had lived their lives largely in seclusion. It was considered a shame for them to show their faces in public, and they could only walk out thickly veiled. Organised life of men and women together in free co-operation, as in education, or in any mixed industrial work, had been impossible. All this was changed by the abolition of the veil and the admission of women to public rights and duties. Now they are sharing with men in all kinds of work, in education, in qualifications for the professions, and in many forms of industry. The outlook of all womanhood in Turkey has been completely changed, and the resources of public service have been vastly augmented. Woman, too, has a new dignity through the marriage laws being brought into conformity with those of Western Europe.

In Turkey today every religion is free,

including the Islamic. Every Turk can be a Mohammedan. But he must not label himself first as a Mohammedan. He is first a loyal Turk. The wearing of the hat known as a fez was the Mohammedan sign of a Turk. The wearing of a fez by any Turk was forbidden. The Turks had to leave off wearing the fez and thus show that their first allegiance was to Turkey.

The truth is that modern Turkish education is far broader than a purely Islamic education could be. Turkey is relying on genuine education to build up a fine nation. Every Turk must learn to read and write. He is being helped in every way to do so. The Turkish language is difficult to read and write, so its lettering has been altered, Latinised, and simplified, and the Turks are fast becoming a reading and writing people. English has become the first foreign language to be taught in the schools.

Turkey is largely an agricultural country with few large towns. But there are 40,000 villages and in them the majority of people live. Providing all with modern schools has been a huge task, but when a child leaves his village school he may attend

KEMAL ATATÜRK, FOUNDER OF MODERN TURKEY

a five-year course at one of the Village Institutes. Half his time there is spent in ordinary school work and the rest in trades or crafts—house-building or furniture-making for the boys; house-keeping, first-aid, or child-care for the girls.

For those who can take Higher Education there are Middle Schools with pupils from 12 to 15 and this is followed by the Lycée, or senior school, from 15 to 19. Turkey has three universities, two in Istanbul and the third in the capital.

One other thing the Turk has done is to take himself a surname. Everybody now has an allowed surname, for greater convenience. Kemal's surname, as we have stated, by universal assent became Atatürk, which means Great Turk.

The net results of these achievements and changes in Turkey since she sprang into a new national consciousness are that she is a compact, peaceful nation with a population of about 21,000,000, of whom over one-and-a-half million are in Europe and the rest in Asia Minor. The group of towns around the Bosphorus—Istanbul, Beyoglu (Pera), and Usküdar (Scutari)—which unitedly were called Constantinople, have lost very many of their inhabitants since it was the centre of government, and now number about a million. Edirne (formerly Adrianople), the other European town, has declined too.

The capital, Ankara, has been laid out on modern lines and has a population of about 300,000.

For local government the country is divided up into provinces, much as Britain is divided into counties. Each province has its own council and provincial assembly whose members are elected by popular vote every four years. There are 66 provinces and, Turkey being a big country, each province is divided into districts which are sub-divided into groups of villages with local official bodies on about the level of our own parish councils.

There has been a great expansion in the business of the country. Manufactures are increasing. There are iron and steel and textile industries, and other manufactures are paper, glass, sugar, cement. Mining is carried on in Turkey's principal minerals of coal, lignite, chrome, cement, sulphur, and manganese ore.

Children under 12 are not allowed to be employed in industry, and those under 18 must not work underground and on night shifts. Social insurance schemes have been introduced.

More than half the population are engaged in agriculture, and their products range from wheat, tobacco, figs, nuts, silk, and olives, to hides, furs, and gum.

Before Kemal Atatürk died, the Turkish Republic had become powerful and respected, and when the Second World War began the Powers of Europe sought her goodwill, but Turkey, wisely, perhaps, in view of the calamities war had brought her in the past, remained neutral until nearly the end, when she declared war on Germany and Japan. In recent years Turkey has received much help from Britain and America, a large sum being allotted to her under the Marshall Plan.

THE FIRST DEMOCRATIC GENERAL ELECTION TO BE HELD IN REPUBLICAN TURKEY

The astonishing development of the new Turkish Republic, however, was not, during its first 24 years, carried out under a democratic form of government. Until 1946 only one party was allowed to exist, the Republican People's Party. Then this great people took another big step forward —into complete democracy. Different political parties were allowed to be formed, and in 1946 the first democratic general election since the birth of the Republic was held. The ballot was secret, all Turkish men and women over 22 were able to vote as they wished, and thus Turkey's first popularly chosen *Büyük Millet Meclisi* (Grand National Assembly) came to power.

In 1950, only 26 years after the founding of the new Republic, an opposition party came peacefully to power. This was the Democratic Party founded by Celâl Bayar, Turkey's third President, who visited England to attend the funeral of King George the Sixth. Under the new Party domestic policy laid stress on private enterprise against state operation.

THE MODERN STATE IN WHICH THE OLD AND THE NEW LIVE TOGETHER

Turkey is a land of endeavour and opportunity. Its people are fully occupied with creating a modern state in a land which, till the second quarter of this century, lagged far behind Europe. In the towns now are modern buildings and shops and the sort of clothes and cars to be seen anywhere else in Europe. And there is always a local Association football team.

But Turkey is not a country of big towns. Most of its people live in villages and in them can be seen the contrasts of the old gradually being ousted by the new—tractors on the land, but the older men still in traditional costume; new, hygienic houses only slowly taking the place of the humbler dwellings of a past age. And perhaps three out of ten village children still with no school to attend.

But everywhere instruction and help is being provided to learn new ways and better methods.

In a land pitifully short of railways a big 15-year plan is in full blast to build 1400 miles of new track. In 20 years over 14,000 miles of roads have been laid. Iron mining has been started and is going ahead fast; the coal industry has been transformed with Marshall Aid, and the old mines for copper and chrome have been reorganised. British engineers have helped in setting up steel works. Irrigation, drainage, and flood protection have been carried out far and wide and five new ports on the Black Sea, which has few natural harbours but is famous for its sudden storms, are being built.

KINDLY CLIMATE OF THE COAST IN WHICH FIGS, GRAPES, AND OLIVES RIPEN

The centre of the country is a great plateau, dry in summer and snow-covered in winter. To the east are high mountains with valleys of good pasture. On the Aegean coast, facing Greece, is the kindlier climate in which figs and grapes and olives ripen. And in the far southeast, where the coast curves round toward Lebanon and Palestine, there are groves of oranges and lemons. But half of Turkey is still pasture of varying quality, and only a quarter is cultivated. The rest is moorland or forest.

The new Republic is a founder member of the United Nations and a full member of the North Atlantic Treaty Organisation. She has thus firmly joined herself to the bulwark of western defence. When the call came she did not hesitate to send a contingent to fight in Korea, where the Turkish Brigade was described by the Supreme Commander as " The Bravest of the Brave."

So the descendants of the Turks who terrorised Europe are fast striding towards a position among the foremost civilised nations of the world.

PICTURES AND MAPS OF TURKEY

GALATA BRIDGE ACROSS THE BOSPHORUS AT ISTANBUL, A MODERN CITY WITH AN ANCIENT SKYLINE

THE BUILDINGS AND GROUNDS OF THE IZMIR ANNUAL FAIR

THE ANCIENT AQUEDUCTS OF PARADISE IN IZMIR

THE STATUE OF KEMAL ATATÜRK AT BURSA

ST. SOPHIA IN ISTANBUL, WHICH HAS BEEN A CHURCH, A MOSQUE, AND A MUSEUM

THE MOSQUE OF SULEYMANIYE AT ISTANBUL

THE ROOFS AND MINARETS OF IZMIR, WITH THE ACROPOLIS IN THE BACKGROUND

A CAFÉ BY A BRIDGE IN BURSA

A MODERN HOTEL IN BURSA

THE GATEWAY TO THE UNIVERSITY AND THE BEYAZIT TOWER IN ISTANBUL

A SNACK FOR...
AT A SCHOOL...

THE DOLMABAHÇE PALACE IN ISTANBUL,
FORMER RESIDENCE OF THE SULTAN

THE SULTAN AHMET FOUNTAIN
IN ISTANBUL

THE KEMAL ATATÜRK MAUSOLEUM AT ANKARA

STUDENTS AT A...

YUKSEK-KALDIRIM, A STREET OF STEPS LEADING
TO THE TOWER OF GALATA

THE TOWER OF GALATA
IN ISTANBUL

Children's E

THE MIN

A SUGA
N

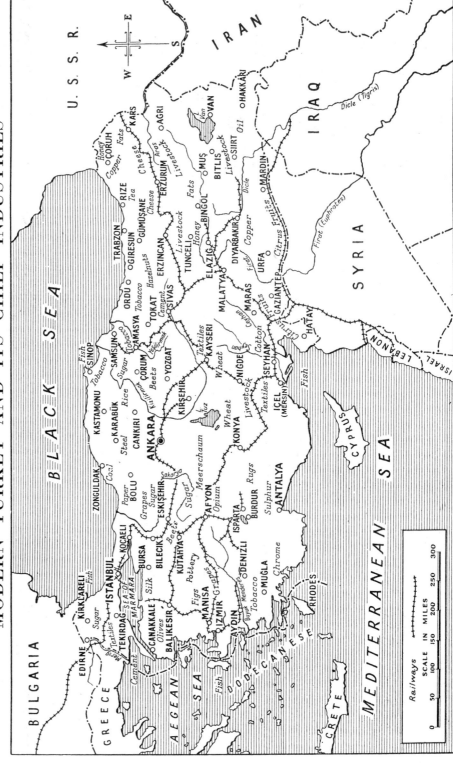

MODERN TURKEY AND ITS CHIEF INDUSTRIES

THIS MAP OF MODERN TURKEY SHOWS ITS CHIEF PLACES AND MOST IMPORTANT PRODUCTS AND INDUSTRIES

6146

Another came; nor yet bes
Nor up the lawn, nor at
    he;

" The next, with dirges due i
Slow through the church-
    saw him borne;
Approach and read (for thou
    the lay
Graved on the stone benea
    thorn."

Here rests his head upon the lap o
  A Youth to Fortune and to F
Fair Science frowned not on his h
  birth,
   And Melancholy marked him f

Large was his bounty, and his sou
  Heaven did a recompense as larg
He gave to Misery all he had—a t
  He gained from Heaven ('i
    wished) a friend.

No farther seek his merits to discle
  Or draw his frailties from their
(There they alike in trembling hop
  The bosom of his Father and h

IN THE MAKING

Arthur St. John Adcock, a notable critic of n
was himself a poet in spirit and in form. He
the thought, eternally true, that each of
changing his personality, with death and re
processes continually taking place durin

THE end is never afar
  From the hour when our li
In peace we are still at war,
  For the victories no one wins
The young speed on to the fray,
  The old go forward in fear,
Yet youth may die in a day,
  And age may live for a year.

Shaped and broken and wrough
  Anew in the world's rough str
I change in heart and in thought
  And grope from life into life;
No longer now we abide
  In the world that was ours of yo
And I have so often died,
  I dread not death any more.

The boy that I used to be
  Is naught but an old regret—
A something that sleeps, ay, me!
  In a grave that others forget:
I have changed as the years have
  I shall change as the years go b
I that was I am dead,
  And I that am I must die.

POETRY

One Thousand Poems of All Times and All Countries

GRAY'S ELEGY

Thomas Gray, the author of this beautiful elegy, was a great scholar, but he did not write many poems. The churchyard about which he wrote is that of Stoke Poges, in Buckinghamshire, of which a picture is given on the left. Gray, who was born in London in 1716, died at Cambridge in 1771, and was buried in this churchyard. The Elegy Written in a Country Churchyard is one of the most perfect poems in the English language, and it is, perhaps, more frequently quoted than any other.

THE curfew tolls the knell of parting
    day,
  The lowing herd wind slowly o'er the
    lea,
The ploughman homeward plods his
    weary way,
  And leaves the world to darkness and
    to me.

NOW fades the glimmering landscape on
    the sight,
  And all the air a solemn stillness holds,
Save where the beetle wheels his droning
    flight,
  And drowsy tinklings lull the distant
    folds:

SAVE that from yonder ivy-mantled tower
    The moping owl does to the moon
    complain
Of such as, wandering near her secret
    bower,
  Molest her ancient solitary reign.

BENEATH those rugged elms, that yew
    tree's shade,
  Where heaves the turf in many a
    mouldering heap,
Each in his narrow cell for ever laid,
  The rude forefathers of the hamlet sleep.

THE breezy call of incense-breathing morn,
    The swallow twittering from the
    straw-built shed,
The cock's shrill clarion, or the echoing
    horn,
  No more shall rouse them from their
    lowly bed.

FOR them no more the blazing hearth
    shall burn,
  Or busy housewife ply her evening care:
No children run to lisp their sire's return,
  Or climb his knees the envied kiss to
    share.

OFT did the harvest to their sickle yield,
    Their furrow oft the stubborn glebe
    has broke;
How jocund did they drive their team
    afield!
  How bowed the woods beneath their
    sturdy stroke!

LET not Ambition mock their useful toil,
    Their homely joys, and destiny
    obscure;
Nor Grandeur hear with a disdainful smile
  The short and simple annals of the poor.

THE boast of heraldry, the pomp of power,
    And all that beauty, all that wealth,
    e'er gave,
Await alike th' inevitable hour:
  The paths of glory lead but to the grave.

NOT you, ye Proud, impute to these the
    fault,
  If Memory o'er their tomb no trophies
    raise
Where through the long-drawn aisle and
    fretted vault
  The pealing anthem swells the note of
    praise.

CAN storied urn or animated bust
    Back to its mansion call the fleeting
    breath?

POEMS · SONGS · BALLADS · VERSES AND RHYMES WITH MUSIC

Can Honour's voice prov
  dust,
    Or Flattery soothe the d
    Death?

Perhaps in this neglected s
  Some heart once pregnan
    fire;
Hands that the rod of emp
  swayed,
    Or waked to ecstasy the

But Knowledge to their ey
  page,
    Rich with the spoils of ti
    unroll;
Chill Penury repressed their
  And froze the genial curre

Full many a gem of purest i
  The dark, unfathomed ca
    bear:
Full many a flower is born to
  And waste its sweetness (
    air.

Some village Hampden, that
  less breast
    The little tyrant of his fiel
Some mute inglorious Milto
  rest,
    Some Cromwell guiltless of
    blood.

Th' applause of listening sen
  mand,
    The threats of pain and rui
To scatter plenty o'er a smilir
  And read their history in a i

Their lot forbade: nor ci
  alone
    Their growing virtues, but
    confined;
Forbade to wade through sla
  throne,
    And shut the gates of mer
    kind;

The struggling pangs of consci
  hide,
    To quench the blushes of
    shame,
Or heap the shrine of Luxury a
  With incense kindled at the M

Far from the madding crow
  strife
    Their sober wishes never
    stray;
Along the cool, sequestered val
  They kept the noiseless tenc
    way.

THE FOUNTAIN

James Russell Lowell, the writer of these happy lines, which express so well the feeling that comes to us in watching the play of a fountain on a summer day, was a famous American poet and humorist. He was born in 1819 and died in 1891.

INTO the sunshine,
  Full of the light,
Leaping and flashing
  From morn till night!

Into the moonlight,
  Whiter than snow,
Waving so flower-like,
  When the winds blow!

Into the starlight,
  Rushing in spray,
Happy at midnight,
  Happy by day!

Ever in motion,
  Blithesome and cheery,
Still climbing heavenward
  Never aweary;

Glad of all weathers,
  Still seeming best,
Upward or downward,
  Motion thy rest;

Full of a nature
  Nothing can tame,
Changed every moment,
  Ever the same;

Ceaseless aspiring,
  Ceaseless content,
Darkness or sunshine
  Thy element;

Glorious fountain!
  Let my heart be
Fresh, changeful, constant,
  Upward like thee!

FATHER WILLIAM

Robert Southey, in writing this poem, sought to illustrate the blessings of living a sober, industrious, virtuous life. He makes Youth ask of Age the way to live, and this is the only wise course. We should profit by the experience of those who have travelled the road of life before us.

YOU are old, Father William, the young
    man cried,
  The few locks that are left you are grey;
You are hale, Father William, a hearty old
    man;
  Now tell me the reason, I pray.

In the days of my youth, Father William
    replied,
  I remembered that youth would fly fast;
And abused not my health and my vigour
    at first
  That I never might need them at last.

You are old, Father William, the young
    man cried,
  And pleasures with youth pass away;
And yet you lament not the days that are
    gone;
  Now tell me the reason, I pray.

In the days of my youth, Father William
    replied,
  I remembered that youth could not last;
I thought of the future, whatever I did,
  That I never might grieve for the past.

You are old, Father William, the young
    man cried,
  And life must be hastening away:
You are cheerful, and love to converse upon
    death;
  Now tell me the reason, I pray.

I am cheerful, young man, Father William
    replied;
  Let the cause thy attention engage:
In the days of my youth I remembered
    my God,
  And He hath not forgotten my age!

TO THE SKYLARK

This is one of the many poems in which William Words-worth describes with so much truth and loving observation the characteristics of the wild creatures of our land.

ETHEREAL minstrel! pilgrim of the sky!
  Dost thou despise the earth where
    cares abound?
Or, while the wings aspire, are heart and eye
  Both with thy nest upon the dewy
    ground?
Thy nest which thou canst drop into at
    will,
Those quivering wings composed, that
    music still!

To the last point of vision, and beyond,
  Mount, daring warbler! that love-
    prompted strain,
Twixt thee and thine an ever-failing bond,
  Thrills not the less the bosom of the
    plain;
Yet might'st thou seem, proud privilege!
    to sing
All independent of the leafy spring.

Leave to the nightingale her shady wood;
  A privacy of glorious light is thine,
Whence thou dost pour upon the world a
    flood
  Of harmony, with instinct more divine;
Type of the wise who soar, but never
    roam;
True to the kindred points of Heaven and
    home.

THE TRAVELLER'S RETURN

Robert Southey here describes without exaggeration the joy which comes when we return from a journey to the companionship of those we love beneath the roof of our home.

SWEET to the morning traveller
    The song amid the sky,
Where, twinkling in the dewy light,
    The skylark soars on high.

And cheering to the traveller
    The gales that round him play,
When faint and heavily he drags
    Along his noontide way.

And when beneath the unclouded sun
    Full wearily toils he
The flowing water makes to him
    A soothing melody.

And when the evening light decays,
    And all is calm around,
There is sweet music to his ear
    In the distant sheep-bell's sound.

But O! of all delightful sounds
    Of evening or of morn,
The sweetest is the voice of love
    That welcomes his return.

THREE YEARS SHE GREW

This exquisite poem, descriptive of a child who lived with Nature till she reflected its manifold beauty, refers apparently to a dream-child of Wordsworth's mind. Or there may have been a real child he had made his own by imagination and had lost, for in two other poems a Lucy is loved and dies. It was natural that Wordsworth, whose love of Nature was a passion, should picture a young life sunning itself in the pleasures that had been to him a perpetual joy.

THREE years she grew in sun and shower;
    Then Nature said: " A lovelier flower
    On earth was never sown.
This child I to myself will take;
She shall be mine, and I will make
    A lady of my own.

" Myself will to my darling be
Both law and impulse, and with me
    The girl, in rock and plain,
In earth and heaven, in glade and bower,
Shall feel an overseeing power
    To kindle or restrain.

" She shall be sportive as the fawn
That, wild with glee, across the lawn
    Or up the mountain springs;
And hers shall be the breathing balm,
And hers the silence and the calm
    Of mute, insensate things.

" The floating clouds their state shall lend
To her; for her the willow bend;
    Nor shall she fail to see
Even in the motions of the storm
Grace that shall mould the maiden's form
    By silent sympathy.

" The stars of midnight shall be dear
To her; and she shall lean her ear
    In many a secret place,
Where rivulets dance their wayward round,
And beauty born of murmuring sound
    Shall pass into her face.

" And vital feelings of delight
Shall rear her form to stately height,
    Her virgin bosom swell;
Such thoughts to Lucy I will give
While she and I together live
    Here in this happy dell."

Thus Nature spake ; the work was done—
How soon my Lucy's race was run!
    She died, and left to me
This heath, this calm and quiet scene;
The memory of what has been,
    And never more will be.

THE TORCH OF LIFE

The proper title of this stirring poem in praise of the manly game of cricket is Vitai Lampada, which means in English, The Torch of Life. The idea of the poem is that if we keep shining in our life the spirit of honour we identify with " playing the game," we shall be making the best use of our powers. The poem is by Sir Henry Newbolt (1862-1938), and is printed here by permission.

THERE'S a breathless hush in the Close
    tonight—
    Ten to make and the match to win—
A bumping pitch, and a blinding light,
    An hour to play, and the last man in.
And it's not for the sake of a ribboned coat,
    Or the selfish hope of a season's fame,
But his Captain's hand on his shoulder
    smote:
    Play up! Play up! and play the game!

The sand of the desert is sodden red—
    Red with the wreck of a square that
    broke—
The Gatling's jammed, and the Colonel
    dead,
    And the regiment blind with dust and
    smoke.
The river of death has brimmed his banks,
    And England's far, and honour a name,
But the voice of a schoolboy rallies the
    ranks:
    Play up! Play up! and play the game!

This is the word that year by year,
    While in her place the school is set,
Every one of her sons must hear,
    And none that hears it dare forget.
This they all with a joyful mind
    Bear through life like a torch of flame,
And, falling, fling to the host behind—
    Play up! Play up! and play the game!

THE CHARCOAL-BURNER

This most delightful study of an old charcoal-burner, attuned by long wont to his woodland surroundings, is from the graceful pen of Sir Edmund Gosse, whom literary people of his own time regarded with affectionate admiration, both as a poet and a critic. The charcoal-burner stands before us as a proof of the poet's quality. How perfectly the old man blends with the rural scene! Compared with him the mere visitor is an alien in the woods. And the poet's comprehension of the man is as complete as the man's comprehension of the life of Nature.

HE lives within the hollow wood,
  From one clear dell he seldom
    ranges;
His daily toil in solitude
  Revolves, but never changes.

A still old man, with grizzled beard,
  Grey eye, bent shape, and smoke-tanned
    features,
His quiet footstep is not feared
  By shyest woodland creatures.

I love to watch the pale blue spire
  His scented labour builds above it;
I track the woodland by his fire,
  And, seen afar, I love it.

It seems among the serious trees
  The emblem of a living pleasure,
It animates the silences
  As with a tuneful measure.

And dream not that such humdrum ways
  Fold naught of Nature's charm around
    him;
The mystery of soundless days
  Hath sought for him and found him.

He hides within his simple brain
  An instinct innocent and holy,
The music of a wood-bird's strain,
  Nor blithe, nor melancholy.

But hung upon the calm content
  Of wholesome leaf and bough and
    blossom:
An unecstatic ravishment
  Born in a rustic bosom.

He knows the moods of forest things,
  He feels, in his own speechless fashion,
For helpless forms of fur and wings
  A mild paternal passion.

Within his horny hand he holds
  The warm brood of the ruddy squirrel;
Their bushy mother storms and scolds,
  But knows no sense of peril.

The dormouse shares his crumb of cheese,
  His homeward trudge the rabbits follow;
He finds, in angles of the trees,
  The cup-nest of the swallow.

And through this sympathy, perchance,
  The beating heart of life he reaches
Far more than we who idly dance
  An hour beneath the beeches.

Our science and our empty pride,
  Our busy dream of introspection,
To God seem vain and poor beside
  This dumb, sincere reflection.

Yet he will die unsought, unknown,
  A nameless headstone stand above him,
And the vast woodland, vague and lone,
  Be all that's left to love him.

THE ONE CLEAR CALL

We need an ever-present guide in times of doubt and difficulty, and in this poem Harold Begbie reminds us there is such a Guide for all of us. The one safe and conquering course is to do as we feel Jesus would have done.

MY son, when you stand looking right
    and left,
  Uncertain, tortured, which way you
    should go,
So that your very soul in two seems cleft,
  Your will a leaf in all the winds that
    blow:
Then check the mill-race of your thoughts,
    and strain
  No more through tears the rightful
    course to see,
But listen, silent, with a quiet brain
  For the one faithful whisper *Follow Me.*

When you stand doubting in the storm of
    life,
  Troubled and harassed how a man
    should act,
So that your brain is nothing but a strife
  To tear away the Lie and face the Fact:
Then from the loud contention draw apart,
  No longer beat your brain for a decree,
But wait with patience and a peaceful
    heart
  For the unerring whisper *Follow Me.*

There is no darkness on His road of light,
  No doubt in hearts that follow where
    He leads;
Each step makes clearer still the True and
    Right,
  Each act prepares the way for greater
    deeds:
All's well! The lightnings and the
    thunders cease,
  The sky is fair, the stars no longer dim,
Heart, mind, and soul at last have lasting
    peace,
  And the man says, assured, *I follow
    Him.*

THE EXILE'S SONG

Robert Gilfillan (1798-1850) was a Scottish poet who, while acting as a grocer's shop assistant in Dunfermline and as a commercial clerk in Leith, gained considerable commendation for his songs. The best of them is this plaintive longing of a Scottish wanderer for Scotland. Where he is supposed to be is not easy to decide. It is a land of slavery where the bulbul sings to an Indian maid. What land, fit for a Scottish emigrant, can that be?

OH, why left I my hame?
　　Why did I cross the deep?
Oh, why left I the land
　　Where my forefathers sleep?
I sigh for Scotia's shore,
　　And I gaze across the sea,
But I canna get a blink
　　O' my ain countrie!

The palm tree waveth high,
　　And fair the myrtle springs,
And to the Indian maid
　　The bulbul sweetly sings;
But I dinna see the broom
　　Wi' its tassels on the lea,
Nor hear the lintie's sang,
　　O' my ain countrie!

Oh, here no Sabbath bell
　　Awakes the Sabbath morn,
Nor song of reapers heard
　　Amang the yellow corn;
For the tyrant's voice is here,
　　And the wail of slaverie;
But the sun of freedom shines
　　In my ain countrie.

There's a hope for every woe
　　And a balm for every pain,
But the first joys o' our heart
　　Come never back again.
There's a track upon the deep,
　　And a path across the sea;
But the weary ne'er return
　　To their ain countrie.

THE THREE BEST THINGS

In these three sonnets Dr. Henry Van Dyke, the American poet, gives a complete chart for a whole life's guidance.

WORK

LET me but do my work from day to day,
　In field or forest, at the desk or loom,
　In roaring market-place or tranquil room;
Let me but find it in my heart to say,
When vagrant wishes beckon me astray,
　" This is my work; my blessing, not my doom;
　Of all who live, I am the one by whom
This work can best be done in the right way."

Then shall I see it not too great nor small
　To suit my spirit and to prove my powers;
Then shall I cheerful greet the labouring hours,
And cheerful turn, when the long shadows fall
At eventide, to play and love and rest,
Because I know for me my work is best.

LOVE

Let me but love my love without disguise,
　Nor wear a mask of fashion old or new,
　Nor wait to speak till I can hear a clue,
Nor play a part to shine in other's eyes,
Nor bow my knees to what my heart denies;
　But what I am, to that let me be true,
　And let me worship where my love is due,
And so through love and worship let me rise.

For love is but the heart's in mortal thirst
　To be completely known and all forgiven,
　Even as sinful souls that enter heaven:
So take me, dear, and understand my worst,
And freely pardon it, because confessed,
And let me find, in loving thee, my best.

LIFE

Let me but live my life from year to year,
　With forward face and unreluctant soul;
　Not hurrying to, nor turning from, the goal;
Not mourning for the things that disappear
In the dim past, nor holding back in fear
From what the future veils; but with a whole
And happy heart, that pays its toll
To Youth and Age, and travels on with cheer.

So let the way wind up the hill or down,
　O'er rough or smooth, the journey will be joy,
　Still seeking what I sought when but a boy,
New friendship, high adventure, and a crown,
My heart will keep the courage of the quest,
And hope the road's last turn will be the best.

TO A NIGHTINGALE

John Keats was one of our greatest English poets. This poem is one of his masterpieces. It contains a number of allusions to the mythology, or fables, of ancient Greece, for Keats was steeped in the ancient lore we call " classical," and as a poet he was really more inspired and quickened by the spirit of old Greece than by that of his own time.

MY heart aches, and a drowsy numbness
    pains
My sense, as though of hemlock I had
    drunk,
Or emptied some dull opiate to the drains
    One minute past, and Lethe-wards had
      sunk:
'Tis not through envy of thy happy lot,
    But being too happy in thy happiness,
      That thou, light-winged Dryad of the
      trees,
        In some melodious plot
Of beechen green, and shadows number-
    less,
      Singest of summer in full-throated
      ease.

O for a draught of vintage! that hath been
    Cooled a long age in the deep-delved
      earth,
Tasting of Flora and the country-green,
    Dance, and Provençal song, and sun-
      burnt mirth!
O for a beaker full of the warm South!
    Full of the true, the blushful Hippocrene,
      With beaded bubbles winking at the
      brim,
        And purple-stained mouth;
That I might drink, and leave the world
    unseen,
      And with thee fade away into the
      forest dim:

Fade far away, dissolve, and quite forget
    What thou among the leaves hast never
      known,
The weariness, the fever, and the fret
    Here, where men sit and hear each other
      groan;
Where palsy shakes a few, sad, last grey
    hairs,
    Where youth grows pale, and spectre-
      thin, and dies;
      Where but to think is to be full of
      sorrow
        And leaden-eyed despairs;
    Where beauty cannot keep her lustrous
      eyes,
      Or new Love pine at them beyond
      tomorrow.

Away! Away! For I will fly to thee,
    Not charioted by Bacchus and his pards,

But on the viewless wings of Poesy,
    Though the dull brain perplexes and
      retards:
Already with thee! tender is the night,
    And haply the Queen-Moon is on her
      throne,
      Clustered around by all her starry
      Fays;
        But here there is no light,
Save what from heaven is with the
    breezes blown
      Through verdurous glooms and wind-
      ing mossy ways.

I cannot see what flowers are at my feet,
    Nor what soft incense hangs upon the
      boughs,
But, in embalmèd darkness, guess each
    sweet
    Wherewith the seasonable month en-
      dows
The grass, the thicket, and the fruit-tree
    wild;
    White hawthorn, and the pastoral
      eglantine;
      Fast fading violets covered up in
      leaves;
        And mid-May's eldest child,
The coming musk-rose, full of dewy
    wine,
      The murmurous haunt of flies on
      summer eves.

Darkling I listen; and for many a time
    I have been half in love with easeful
      Death,
Called him soft names in many a musèd
    rhyme,
    To take into the air my quiet breath;
Now more than ever seems it rich to die,
    To cease upon the midnight with no pain,
      While thou art pouring forth thy
      soul abroad
        In such an ecstasy!
Still wouldst thou sing, and I have ears
    in vain—
    To thy high requiem become a sod.

Thou wast not born for death, immortal
    Bird!
No hungry generations tread thee down;
The voice I hear this passing night was
    heard
    In ancient days by emperor and clown:
Perhaps the self-same song that found a
    path
    Through the sad heart of Ruth, when,
      sick for home,
      She stood in tears amid the alien corn;

The same that oft-times hath
Charmed magic casements, opening on
    the foam
Of perilous seas, in faery lands
    forlorn.

Forlorn ! The very word is like a bell
  To toll me back from thee to my sole self !
Adieu ! the fancy cannot cheat so well
  As she is famed to do, deceiving elf.
Adieu ! adieu ! the plaintive anthem fades
    Past the near meadows, over the still
      stream,
    Up the hill-side; and now 'tis buried
      deep
In the next valley-glades:
Was it a vision, or a waking dream ?
Fled is that music: Do I wake or sleep ?

THE CHAMBERED NAUTILUS

The nautilus is an eight-armed cuttle fish with a shell. It often floats on the surface of the sea, and the people of ancient Greece thought it raised sails and was blown along by the wind. They made a mistake. The so-called sails are its arms. As the nautilus grows it leaves the inmost recess of its spiral shell and forms a larger outer spiral chamber. Oliver Wendell Holmes in this poem refers to the ancient legend of the sails, and describes the stages of shell-building, thus leading up to the magnificent last verse, which contains one of the noblest similes to be found in all literature.

THIS is the ship of pearl, which, poets
    feign,
  Sails the unshadowed main—
The venturous bark that flings
On the sweet summer wind its purpled
    wings
In gulfs enchanted, where the Siren sings,
  And coral reefs lie bare,
Where the cold sea-maids rise to sun their
    streaming hair.

Its webs of living gauze no more unfurl;
  Wrecked is the ship of pearl !
And every chambered cell,
Where its dim dreaming life was wont to
    dwell,
As the frail tenant shaped his growing
    shell,
  Before thee lies revealed,
Its irised ceiling rent, its sunless crypt
    unsealed !

Year after year beheld the silent toil
  That spread his lustrous coil;
  Still, as the spiral grew,
He left the past year's dwelling for the
    new,
Stole with soft step its shining archway
    through,
  Built up its idle door,
Stretched in his last-found home, and
    knew the old no more.

Thanks for the heavenly message brought
    by thee,
  Child of the wandering sea,
  Cast from her lap, forlorn !
From thy dead lips a clearer note is born
Than ever Triton blew from wreathèd
    horn !
  While on mine ear it rings,
Through the deep caves of thought I hear
    a voice that sings :

Build thee more stately mansions, O my
    soul,
  As the swift seasons roll !
  Leave thy low-vaulted past!
Let each new temple, nobler than the last,
Shut thee from heaven with a dome more
    vast,
  Till thou at length art free,
Leaving thine outgrown shell by life's
    unresting sea !

TOLERANCE

This plea for generous feeling towards all who are truly religious, whatever their faith may be, but also a defence of indignation against those who make religion a cloak for wrong, is made by Sir Lewis Morris, a poet who was popular in the last quarter of the 19th century. He died in 1907.

CALL no faith false which e'er has
    brought
Relief to any laden life,
Cessation from the pain of thought,
Refreshment 'mid the dust of strife.

What though the thing to which they
    kneel
Be dumb and dead as wood or stone,
Though all the rapture which they feel
Be for the worshipper alone ?

They worship, they adore, they bow
Before the Ineffable Source, before
The hidden soul of good; and thou,
With all thy wit, what dost thou more ?

Kneel with them; only if there come
Some zealot or sleek knave who strives
To mar the sanctities of home,
To tear asunder wedded lives;

Or who by subtle wile has sought,
By shameful promise, shameful threat,
To turn the thinker from his thought,
To efface the eternal landmarks set

'Twixt faith and knowledge—hold not
    peace
For such, but like a sudden flame
Let loose thy scorn on him, nor cease
Till thou hast covered him with shame.

THE BLAME

Many people shirk blame that is their very own. Not so that firmly thoughtful Victorian poet John Addington Symonds. In these verses he braces us to face the fact that we are responsible for whatever we may do.

Blame not the times in which we live,
  Nor Fortune frail and fugitive;
Blame not thy parents, nor the rule
Of vice or wrong once learned at school;
  But blame thyself, O man !

Although both heaven and earth combined
To mould thy flesh and form thy mind,
Though every thought, word, action, will,
Was framed by powers beyond thee, still
  Thou art thyself, O man !

And self to take or leave is free,
Feeling its own sufficiency:
In spite of science, spite of fate,
The judge within thee soon or late
  Will blame but thee, O man !

A WALK IN SPRING

In these verses by M. A. Stodart, the writer imagines the thoughts that come to a boy or girl when the chill days of winter have said good-bye and the smiling days of spring have come back again. The words are childlike, because they are supposed to be spoken by a very small child.

I'm very glad the spring is come—the sun
  shines out so bright,
The little birds upon the trees are singing
  for delight,
The young grass looks so fresh and green,
  the lambkins sport and play,
And I can skip and run about as merrily
  as they.
I like to see the daisy and the buttercups
  once more,
The primrose and the cowslip too, and
  every pretty flower;
I like to see the butterfly fluttering her
  painted wing,
And all things seem, just like myself, so
  pleased to see the spring.
The fishes in the little brook are jumping
  up on high,
The lark is singing sweetly as she mounts
  into the sky;
The rooks are building up their nests upon
  the great tall tree,
And everything's as busy and as happy
  as can be.
There's not a cloud upon the sky, there's
  nothing dark or sad;
I jump, and scarce know what to do, I feel
  so very glad.
God must be very good indeed, Who made
  each pretty thing:
I'm sure we ought to love Him much for
  bringing back the spring.

THERE'S A LAND, A DEAR LAND

Charles Mackay, the song writer, though not a great poet, had the power of writing with a manly swing which every-one can appreciate, and which carries us buoyantly along. This fine song of England is one of Mackay's best examples.

There's a land, a dear land, where the
  rights of the free,
Though firm as the earth, are as wide as
  the sea;
Where the primroses bloom, and the
  nightingales sing,
And the honest poor man is as good as a
  king.
    Showery ! Flowery !
    Tearful ! Cheerful !
England, wave-guarded and green to the
  shore !
    West Land ! Best Land !
    Thy Land ! My Land !
Glory be with her, and Peace evermore !

There's a land, a dear land, where our
  vigour of soul
Is fed by the tempests that blow from the
  Pole;
Where a slave cannot breathe, or invader
  presume
To ask for more earth than will cover his
  tomb.
    Sea Land ! Free Land !
    Fairest ! Rarest !
Home of brave men and the girls they
  adore !
    Fearless ! Peerless !
    Thy Land ! My Land !
Glory be with her, and Peace evermore !

THE MILLER'S DAUGHTER

Here we have an example of Tennyson's early love songs, dainty and tender. The miller's daughter is not a real person, but an imaginary sweetheart.

It is the miller's daughter,
  And she is grown so dear, so dear,
That I would be the jewel
  That trembles in her ear:
For hid in ringlets day and night,
I'd touch her neck so warm and white.

And I would be the girdle
  About her dainty, dainty waist,
And her heart would beat against me,
  In sorrow and in rest:
And I should know if it beat right,
I'd clasp it round so close and tight.

And I would be the necklace,
  And all day long to fall and rise
Upon her balmy bosom,
  With her laughter or her sighs,
And I would lie so light, so light,
I scarce should be unclasped at night.

HICKORY, DICKORY DOCK

WARM HANDS, WARM

LITTLE VERSES FOR VERY LITTLE PEOPLE

THE FUNNY LITTLE FELLOW

'Twas a Funny Little Fellow
  Of the very purest type,
For he had a heart as mellow
  As an apple over-ripe,
And the brightest little twinkle
  When a funny thing occurred,
And the lightest little tinkle
  Of a laugh you ever heard!
His smile was like the glitter
  Of the sun in tropic lands,
And his talk a sweeter twitter
  Than the swallow understands;
Hear him sing and tell a story,
  Snap a joke, ignite a pun,
'Twas a capture, rapture, glory,
  And explosion—all in one !
Though he hadn't any money—
  That condiment which tends
To make a fellow " honey "
  For the palate of his friends—
Sweet simples he compounded,
  Sovereign antidotes for sin
Or taint, a faith unbounded
  That his friends were genuine.
He wasn't honoured, maybe,
  For his songs of praise were slim,
Yet I never knew a baby
  That wouldn't crow for him;
I never knew a mother
  But urged a kindly claim
Upon him as a brother
  At the mention of his name.
The sick have ceased their sighing,
  And have even found the grace
Of a smile when they were dying
  As they looked upon his face;
And I've seen his eyes of laughter
  Melt in tears that only ran
As though, swift-dancing after,
  Came the Funny Little Man.
He laughed away the sorrow
  And he laughed away the gloom
We are all so prone to borrow
  From the darkness of the tomb;
And he laughed across the ocean
  Of a happy life, and passed,
With a laugh of glad emotion,
  Into Paradise at last.
And I think the Angels knew him,
  And had gathered to await
His coming, and run to him
  Through the widely-opened Gate,
With their faces gleaming sunny
  For his laughter-loving sake,
And thinking, " What a funny
  Little Angel he will make! "
  James Whitcomb Riley

WEIGHING THE BABY

How many pounds does the baby
    weigh,
  Baby who came but a month ago?
How many pounds from the crowning curl
  To the rosy point of the restless toe ?

Grandfather ties the 'kerchief knot,
  Tenderly guides the swinging weight,
And carefully over his glasses peers
  To read the record, " only eight."

Softly the echo goes around:
  The father laughs at the tiny girl;
The fair young mother sings the words,
  While grandmother smooths the golden
    curl;

And, stooping above the precious thing,
  Nestles a kiss within a prayer,
Murmuring softly, " Little one,
  Grandfather did not weigh you fair."

Nobody weighed the baby's smile,
  Or the love that came with the helpless
    one;
Nobody weighed the threads of care
  From which a woman's life is spun.

No index tells the mighty worth
  Of a little baby's quiet breath,
A soft, unceasing metronome,
  Patient and faithful until death.

Nobody weighed the baby's soul,
  For here on earth no weights there be
That could avail; God only knows
  Its value in eternity.

Only eight pounds to hold a soul
  That seeks no angel's silver wing,
But shrines it in this human guise,
  Within so frail and small a thing!

Oh, mother! laugh your merry note,
  Be gay and glad, but don't forget
From baby's eyes looks out a soul
  That claims a home in Eden yet.
  Ethel Lynn Beers

BARTHOLOMEW

Bartholomew is very sweet,
  From sandy hair to rosy feet.

Bartholomew is six months old,
And dearer far than pearls or gold.

Bartholomew has deep blue eyes,
Round pieces dropped from out the skies.

Bartholomew is hugged and kissed:
He loves a flower in either fist.

Bartholomew's my saucy son:
No mother has a sweeter one!
  Norman Gale

Imperishable Thoughts of Men Enshrined in the Books of the World

Shakespeare's Tragedies

WE have already read the stories of ten of Shakespeare's plays, and five more are told here. But we must bear in mind that most of Shakespeare's comedies and tragedies were founded on stories he did not invent himself. Some of the stories had been favourites on the Continent and in England long before the poet made use of them for his plays. They might have been forgotten for ever if he had not retold them by means of the characters he created, and in his own wonderfully beautiful language. He wrote both tragedies and comedies, and he excelled all the other dramatists the world has known by being equally great in tragedy and in comedy. A tragedy is a poetic play in which the characters suffer heavy sorrow, some of the chief persons die, and the end is sadness. A comedy is a play in which all ends happily. The first plays we read were all comedies, but here we read the stories of five tragedies, Romeo and Juliet, Hamlet, Othello, Macbeth, and King Lear.

ROMEO AND JULIET

IN the ancient Italian town of Verona lived two noble families at deadly enmity with each other. One family was named Montague, and the other Capulet.

Romeo, the brave and handsome youth, heir of the Montagues, was in love with a lady called Rosaline; but she refused to have anything to do with him, which made him so sorrowful that he shunned all gaiety and lay sleepless at nights. It chanced one day, when Romeo was speaking in the street with his cousin Benvolio, that a servant came to him, asking if he could read a paper he carried, on which were the names of the guests to whom he was bearing invitations to a ball given by the great Capulet. Romeo noticed Rosaline was to be among the guests, whereon Benvolio suggested they should go to the ball masked, and that when Romeo saw the many lovely ladies who would be there he might forget the disdainful Rosaline.

The lover thought it would be impossible ever to forget Rosaline; but when, in due time, he was mingling with the dancers in his foeman's house, he saw a lady who was so fair that she seemed to be " a snowy dove trooping with crows," and he determined that he would speak to her as soon as he could. While asking a servant the name of the fair one, Tybalt, a young Capulet, recognised Romeo's voice, and wanted to challenge him; but

the lord of the house kept him back, saying that Romeo bore himself like a gentleman, and was said to be " a virtuous and well-governed youth."

Romeo had now come up to the fair lady, and, kissing her hand, had spoken a few words of admiration, and received the assurance that he was not displeasing to her. But when he knew that she was none other than Juliet, the only child of Capulet, he was very sad. For he had fallen in love with the daughter of his father's mortal enemy.

At midnight Romeo departed, but he felt that he could not go homeward and leave the place where Juliet was; so he climbed over the orchard wall into Capulet's garden, and while he was hidden by the darkness of the night he saw the lady appearing at the window. She called his name to the night air, saying:

O Romeo, Romeo! Wherefore art thou Romeo?
Deny thy father, and refuse thy name;
Or, if thou wilt not, be but sworn my love,
And I'll no longer be a Capulet.

When she had spoken more words in this strain, Romeo stepped forward and told her that his name was now hateful to himself as it was that of her family's enemies. That night they vowed their love for each other, and decided to be married at all risks.

In the early morning we next see Romeo at the cell of Friar Laurence, a priest who thought the lover had come from his usual sleepless night weeping over Rosaline's hardness. He was surprised to hear of the new love, but rejoiced to think that now, perhaps, the feud between the Capulets and the Montagues would come to an end with the union of this couple. Willingly he consented to marry them secretly.

ROMEO LEAVES HIS BRIDE AND FLEES TO MANTUA

Before long Juliet arrived, and presently the priest had made her Romeo's bride.

Soon after this Romeo's friend, Mercutio, a kinsman of the Prince of Verona, and a very quick-tempered man, engages in a quarrel with Tybalt, and Romeo appears on the scene. Tybalt immediately turns on Romeo, who, having so lately wedded a Capulet, now feels kindly towards the family, and refuses the challenge. Thereupon Mercutio draws his sword on Tybalt, who kills him.

Romeo could not let his friend's death pass unavenged, and, scarcely had he slain Tybalt, than the Prince arrived. He had long been vexed by these family feuds, and now his displeasure was so great that he banished Romeo.

Friar Laurence advised Romeo to flee to Mantua, and there to wait until he could make his marriage known, implore the Prince's pardon, and come back to Verona. Juliet's old nurse brought Romeo a ring from his young bride, and after a brief meeting with Juliet he hastened from Verona.

Juliet was plunged in sorrow, but her mother thought it was for the death of her cousin Tybalt; and when a young nobleman named Paris asked for her daughter's hand, Lady Capulet agreed that they should be married within a few days.

THE OLD FRIAR'S RUSE TO SAVE JULIET FROM COUNT PARIS

At first Juliet refused, and then she went to take counsel of the Friar, saying she would kill herself rather than be married to Paris. As a desperate plan of escape the Friar gave her a phial, from which she was to drink on the eve of the wedding her mother had arranged. It contained a drug which would make her fall into a trance with all the appearance of death, and she would then be taken to the family vault. Meanwhile, Friar Laurence was to send for Romeo, and when Juliet had awakened from her long sleep her lover would be by her side ready to take her with him to Mantua.

The strange and dangerous scheme of the Friar was carried out so far that Romeo came to the tomb after Juliet had been placed in it; but he had come thinking she was really dead, and had provided himself with poison that he might die beside her. Paris, however, was there before him, having come to strew flowers on Juliet's coffin. The two men quarrelled and fought at the grave, Paris being killed.

When Romeo had opened the vault he laid the body of Paris beside that of Tybalt, and then he gazed on the beautiful face of his wife, kissed her for the last time, and drank the poison, saying:

> Eyes, look your last!
> Arms, take your last embrace! and lips, O you,
> The doors of breath, seal with a righteous kiss
> A dateless bargain to engrossing death!
>
> . . . . .
>
> Here's to my love! O true apothecary!
> Thy drugs are quick. Thus with a kiss I die.

THE END OF THE HATRED OF THE TWO OLD FAMILIES

Romeo had been in the tomb for half an hour when Friar Laurence came to find Juliet, as it was now time she should recover. On entering the vault he saw Romeo lying near the blood-stained Paris, and called anxiously to Juliet to arise, for she was now beginning to show signs of life. She awoke, and he told her that if she would but come, he would put her " among a sisterhood of holy nuns." But, hearing the sound of approaching footsteps, he fled.

When the sight of her dead Romeo and the bleeding Paris met the awakened eyes of Juliet, she snatched up Romeo's dagger and stabbed herself.

The watchman came in, and then they summoned the Montagues and Capulets, and the Friar was brought back. He explained to the astonished company the cause of the tragedy, and when the Prince reproached them with the death of the youthful lovers on account of the feud between the families, Montagues and Capulets alike were stricken with remorse.

Montague reared to the true and faithful Juliet a statue of pure gold, and the same honour was paid to Romeo by Capulet. Thus ended the rivalry and hatred of the two families.

A SCENE FROM ROMEO AND JULIET

A SERVANT LOOKS AT THE NAMES OF GUESTS INVITED TO THE BALL IN VERONA

HAMLET, PRINCE OF DENMARK

PRECISELY as the clock struck midnight the ghost of the former King of Denmark used to appear on the walls of the Castle of Elsinore.

Scared soldiers of the guard told Prince Hamlet of this, and he determined to speak to his father's spirit the next time it appeared. For this purpose he waited through the cold, dark night until the midnight hour, when the ghost was seen beckoning to him. His faithful officers would have detained him, but Hamlet broke from them and went after the spirit.

Hamlet had been so full of love for his father that his grief for the King's death two months before had increased daily, and was now mingled with horrified anger at his own mother Queen Gertrude, and his father's brother Claudius, who had married the Queen in less than two months after the death of the King.

The young Prince's mind was full of unrest at this disgraceful conduct, and he was suspicious as to the death of his father; so that when the spirit revealed to him the fact that he had been poisoned by his brother, in order that the brother might wed his Queen and sit on his throne, Hamlet's whole thoughts turned bitterly to means of vengeance. Encouraged by his father's spirit, he resolved never to rest till the usurper had paid for his crime; and, the better to carry out his plans, he feigned madness, speaking strangely even to Ophelia, a beautiful maiden he loved.

It chanced that a company of players came to the castle, and Hamlet, looking every way for means to convict the new king of his crime, conceived that by means of these play-actors he might reveal his knowledge of his evil deeds.

HAMLET AND HORATIO WATCH THE GRAVEDIGGERS AT WORK

With this end in view Hamlet arranged that the company should perform the next day a play dealing with the murder of a Duke of Venice, and that into this some new lines which Hamlet was to write should be introduced. We can guess that these lines would refer to a king poisoned by his brother so that the brother might enjoy his possessions and wed his widow; for Hamlet exclaimed, when he had made this arrangement with the players:

The play's the thing
Wherein I'll catch the conscience of the king.

And so it all falls out. When the tragedy is performed before the King and Queen the mimic deeds enacted on the stage are, in every detail, so like the manner in which Hamlet's father had been slain, by the pouring of a poisonous drug into his ear as he lay asleep, that the guilty Claudius and Gertrude can stand it no longer, and leave the room in great excitement and disorder. The play had caught the conscience of the treacherous King!

In great agitation Claudius expressed to Queen Gertrude his wrath against Hamlet, and bade her reprimand her son for his conduct. She summoned Hamlet to her private apartment; but Ophelia's father, the aged Polonius, who was Lord Chamberlain of the kingdom, remained hidden behind a curtain, fearing lest some violence might result from the Prince's supposed madness. When the Queen reproved her son for having the play performed, he straightway told her that he would not let her go until he had set up a glass where she might see the inmost part of herself. So wild were his words that the Queen, fearing he would kill her, called for help, and

Polonius echoed the call. Hamlet, pretending that the disturbance was created by a rat behind the curtain, thrust in his sword and killed the old courtier. Then, with wild, strange words of scorn, he reproached his mother till she entreated him to speak no more.

But sad was the fate that befell the beautiful Ophelia. Believing her lover's affection to have turned to hatred, and hearing of her father's death at his hand, she could do naught but brood over her woes, till at last her mind gave way.

King Claudius, of course, had but one thought now—to be rid of Hamlet, whom he believed to possess his secret. The Prince was sent to England with a sealed letter from Claudius in which the King desired that Hamlet should be put to death on landing. But this was not to be. The ship bearing the Prince was attacked by pirates, who took all on board prisoners, eventually restoring Hamlet to Denmark. Returning to Elsinore with his faithful friend Horatio, they entered a churchyard where a new grave was being dug, and there they stood watching the gravediggers, little dreaming for whom the grave was being made. Presently appeared a funeral procession. Hamlet and his friend withdrew, but from their hiding-place they saw the corpse of Ophelia borne in the midst. That unhappy girl had been drowned while gathering flowers by the side of a brook.

Tenderly the body was laid in the grave; but Laertes, Ophelia's brother, distraught at her death, threw himself on her body and begged that he might be buried with her. Hamlet then ran forward and leapt in beside the living and the dead. A fierce struggle ensued, Laertes accusing Hamlet of his sister's death, because his conduct had turned her mind. But in the end they all withdrew, and Ophelia was left in her grave.

A duel, however, had to be fought between Hamlet and Laertes, and the whole Court assembled to watch the fateful combat. Claudius hoped it would rid him of Hamlet, and caused a cup of poisoned wine to be placed in readiness for the Prince, that he might drink it when exhausted, in case he overcame Laertes, for whose use a poisoned rapier had been provided. In the struggle Laertes and Hamlet unknowingly changed swords, but not before the Prince had received a wound from the poisoned point; and Laertes, in his turn, was next wounded with the same sword. Meanwhile, Queen Gertrude, drinking in honour of her son's clever swordsmanship, partook of the deadly wine intended for another, and died.

The death of his mother showed Hamlet the last villainy of the wicked Claudius, which had entirely miscarried and robbed him of his Queen. Laertes, dying, forgave the Prince, and seeing all clear at the last, he denounced the King as the cause of all their woe; while Hamlet, turning his steel on Claudius, made the murderer drink the deadly cup himself; and presently, Hamlet's own wound taking effect, the chief actor in this strange, sad tragedy breathed his last.

OTHELLO, THE MOOR OF VENICE

THE city of Venice, though now only one of the many beautiful towns of Italy, was formerly the scene of a great republican government that sent its ambassadors to the mighty nations of the world and ruled over many other towns as well as Venice itself, while its ships traded to far countries, and its soldiers and sailors won colonies in other lands.

In these great days a Moor, or dark-skinned man from the north of Africa, named Othello, was a brilliant leader of the army of Venice. He was a man of noble mind, despite his black skin, and so able that he was sent to be governor of Cyprus, which then belonged to Venice.

Now, in addition to all his triumphs as a soldier, Othello had the fortune to win the love of one of the most beautiful women in Venice, whose name was Desdemona, the daughter of Brabantio, a senator, or member of the Government of Venice. It may seem strange that a black man should be loved by a fair lady who had refused many rich suitors; but she thought more of his noble mind than of his looks, and all her delight was to listen to his thrilling tales of the battles in which he had fought, of his hairbreadth escapes, of the strange adventures through which he had passed by land and sea.

But her father, Brabantio, did not know

of the things she kept hidden in her heart, as she knew he would never approve of her wedding the Moor. His anger was terrible when one night he was awakened by two men, who told him that Desdemona had left him and was now married to Othello. One of these men was Iago, who long had served the Moor as one of his officers, but who now hated him bitterly, since Othello had chosen Cassio as his lieutenant when Iago thought he should have been preferred. Iago was cunning, spiteful, and capable of any villainy; while Cassio was frank and open, but easily led astray.

THE SPLENDID SPEECH OF THE MOOR IN DEFENCE OF HIS MARRIAGE

Brabantio appealed against Othello to the Duke of Venice and the senators, who at first were in his favour. But Othello answered the charge of stealing away Desdemona in so manly a way that the Duke and others were soon won to his side, especially as Desdemona herself proved that she loved the gallant Moor and was proud to be his wife.

Here is the speech in which Othello made his courteous but bold defence.

Most potent, grave and reverend signiors,
My very noble and approved good masters,
That I have taken away this old man's daughter,
It is most true; true, I have married her;
The very head and front of my offending
Hath this extent, no more. Rude am I in my
    speech,
And little blessed with the soft phrase of peace;
For since these arms of mine had seven years'
    pith,
Till now some nine moons wasted, they have
    used
Their dearest action in the tented field;
And little of this great world can I speak
More than pertains to feats of broil and battle;
And therefore little shall I grace my cause
In speaking for myself. Yet, by your gracious
    patience,
I will a round, unvarnished tale deliver
Of my whole course of love; what drugs, what
    charms,
What conjuration, and what mighty magic,
For such proceeding I am charged withal,
I won his daughter.

Her father loved me; oft invited me;
Still questioned me the story of my life
From year to year, the battles, sieges, fortunes
That I have passed.
I ran it through, even from my boyish days
To the very moment that he bade me tell it;
Wherein I spake of most disastrous chances,
Of moving accidents by flood and field,

Of hairbreadth escapes in the imminent deadly
    breach,
Of being taken by the insolent foe
And sold to slavery, of my redemption thence
And portance in my travel's history;
Wherein of antres vast and desarts idle,
Rough quarries, rocks and hills whose heads
    touch heaven,
It was my hint to speak, such was the process;
And of the Cannibals that each other eat,
The Anthropophagi, and men whose heads
Do grow beneath their shoulders. This to hear
Would Desdemona seriously incline;
But still the house-affairs would draw her thence;
Which ever as she could with haste dispatch,
She'd come again, and with a greedy ear
Devour up my discourse. Which I observing,
Took once a pliant hour, and found good means
To draw from her a prayer of earnest heart
That I would all my pilgrimage dilate,
Whereof by parcels she had something heard,
But not intVo.tively; I did consent,
And often did beguile her of her tears
When I did speak of some distressful stroke
That my youth suffered. My story being done,
She gave me for my pains a world of sighs;
She swore, in faith, 'twas strange, 'twas passing
    strange,
'Twas pitiful, 'twas wondrous pitiful;
She wished she had not heard it, yet she wished
That heaven had made her such a man; she
    thanked me,
And bade me, if I had a friend that loved her,
I should but teach him how to tell my story,
And that would woo her. Upon this hint I
    spake;
She loved me for the dangers I had passed,
And I loved her that she did pity them.

That very night the devotion of Othello to the country he had served so well was put once more to the test, as he was ordered off to defend Cyprus, which was in danger of being attacked by the Turks.

THE CRAFTY IAGO SEEKS TO RUIN HIS ENEMY CASSIO

The great soldier at once sets out for Cyprus, Desdemona being left in the care of " honest Iago," as Othello still thinks him faithful, and Iago's wife, Emilia, is asked to attend on Desdemona. Cassio follows in another vessel; Iago, with Desdemona, setting sail in a third. Cassio is the first to arrive, his vessel having lost Othello's in a storm, and Iago, who " has had most favourable and happy speed," reaches the island before the Moor. Iago's hatred of Cassio for having been preferred by Othello is speedily seen, and his crafty mind is at work to ruin the lieutenant, whom Desdemona treats with greater friendliness than she does Iago.

SCENES FROM SHAKESPEARE'S TRAGEDIES

ROMEO AT THE TOMB OF JULIET—FROM ROMEO AND JULIET

OTHELLO WATCHES THE SLEEPING DESDEMONA—FROM OTHELLO, THE MOOR OF VENICE

When Othello arrived, soon after Desdemona, he was not displeased to hear that the Turkish ships had all been shattered in the storm which had so nearly wrecked his own vessel, for now he was able to devote more time to his bride, " my fair warrior," as he lovingly called her. On the night of his arrival he bade Cassio keep order in the castle, and see there should be no disturbance among the soldiers. The crafty Iago, however, now began to work his plot, plying the luckless Cassio with wine until he became intoxicated, and in a drunken brawl wounded Montano, the governor of the island, whom Othello was to replace.

Coming on the scene of the disgraceful brawl, Othello heard an account of it from Iago, who was the cause of all the trouble; and, thinking Iago was trying to shield Cassio by making light of the matter, he said, with sorrow, " Cassio, I love thee, but never more be officer of mine," appointing Iago to the charge of the guard. Thus, the first part of the villain's scheme of treachery had succeeded. But worse, far worse, was yet to come.

Poor Cassio now appealed to Desdemona that she might intercede with her husband on his behalf. This the gentle Desdemona did; but Iago's new villainy was to make Othello believe she pleaded for Cassio because she had fallen in love with him. So well did he instil the poison of doubt into Othello's mind that at length the Moor began to lose faith in his wife, and, believing she had ceased to love him, became almost mad with jealousy.

Chance favoured the evil designs of Iago, as it so happened that, before they were married, Othello had given Desdemona a beautifully-worked handkerchief supposed to be of magic power, to make its owner loved and amiable; but to make her become hateful to her lover if ever she should lose it. Iago longed to possess this, and urged his wife to steal it.

One day, when Othello was in an ill mood of doubting, and complained of a pain in his head, Desdemona offered him the handkerchief; but he put it from him, saying, " Your napkin is too little," and it fell to the floor, where Emilia quickly picked it up and passed it to Iago. This fateful little handkerchief now became a tool of great mischief, as it was conveyed to Cassio's house by Iago; and poor Cassio, finding it, presented it to a woman as a pretty thing, not knowing to whom it had belonged, and still less guessing that Othello had been brought by Iago to watch him with the handkerchief, as a proof that Cassio had received from Desdemona a gift she should have esteemed so precious.

Othello, now believing that his wife had ceased to love him, determined to kill her; but as she lay asleep in bed he bent over her and kissed her, she looked so beautiful. His kiss awakened her, and in answer to her frightened questions he bade her say her prayers, telling her he knew of her love for Cassio. In vain did poor Desdemona plead her innocence; her jealous husband covered her with the bedclothes and smothered her.

She was not yet dead when Emilia got into the room and told of her husband Iago's evil doings, exclaiming that the misguided Moor had murdered a saint, whose last words were of love for Othello.

Iago, who has come in, stabs his wife for denouncing him, and then runs out; but others arrive, and Iago is brought back, Othello in his anger wounding him.

Realising in an awful agony how beguiled he had been to trust so vile a man and mistrust so good a wife, Othello stabbed himself, and, falling upon the body of his innocent bride, exclaimed with his dying breath :

I kissed thee ere I killed thee; no way but this,
Killing myself, to die upon a kiss.

MACBETH

DUNCAN, King of Scotland, was harassed by rebellion and invasion, but both rebels and invaders were routed by his brave generals, Macbeth and Banquo. When the news of Macbeth's victories came to Duncan, he gave the title of the defeated rebel lord to Macbeth.

Returning from the battlefield and not knowing of his new honours, Macbeth, while crossing a weird heath, came upon three witches, who greeted him as Thane of Glamis, a title to which he knew he had succeeded, but also as Thane of Cawdor, of which he had not heard. Then they added that he should be King hereafter. Almost as soon as the witches

THE TROUBLED CONSCIENCE OF LADY MACBETH

LADY MACBETH WALKING IN HER SLEEP, CONSCIENCE-STRICKEN BY WICKED DEEDS

disappeared, messengers arrived from King Duncan to announce Macbeth's new honour as Thane of Cawdor. This set him wondering whether the final prophecy of the kingship could be true, and he at once wrote to his wife to tell her the strange news.

When the King had met Macbeth, and confirmed his honours, the route of the King's journey led by Macbeth's castle, and the general hastened forward to prepare to receive the King as his guest. As he arrived at the castle Lady Macbeth was reading the letter in which the prophecy of the witches was told. She was much more prompt in action and bold in execution than her husband, and the moment she heard of the prophecy and of King Duncan's approach, she decided that he should never leave the castle alive. When her husband approached she greeted him as

> Great Glamis! worthy Cawdor!
> Greater than both, by the all-hail hereafter!

and instantly revealed her dreadful intention of quick murder.

THE TERRIBLE DEED BY WHICH MACBETH BECAME KING OF SCOTLAND

That night, after the aged Duncan had behaved most graciously to his host and hostess, he was murdered by Macbeth, acting under the imperious will of his wife, who declared that she would have done it if Duncan had not resembled her father as he slept. The guards outside the King's chamber had been made drunk, and by them the blood-stained daggers were laid.

When other visitors arrived and roused the inmates of the castle during the night, Macbeth and his wife appeared, and Macbeth, pretending to have been moved by instant fury, concealed his part in the murder by killing the sleeping guards outside the room. The play shows the working of remorse in the minds of the guilty pair, who had been faithless to the King in order to fulfil the prophecy of the witches and make way for Macbeth to take the kingship. Macbeth now succeeds Duncan as King; but he still has a trouble on his mind besides the memory of his guilt. The witches had followed their prophecy that he would be King, by adding that Banquo's descendants would be kings, and Banquo would be happier than Macbeth.

To defeat this prophecy Macbeth arranges that Banquo and his son shall be murdered. Macbeth now becomes more and more uneasy as he contemplates his crimes. He even envies his victims:

> Duncan is in his grave;
> After life's fitful fever he sleeps well;
> Treason has done his worst; nor steel, nor poison,
> Malice domestic, foreign levy, nothing
> Can touch him further.

But neither Macbeth nor his wife can sleep well. Still she urges him on, and especially conjures him to be genial at the great banquet they are giving that night, with Banquo as one of the guests.

THE MYSTERIOUS PROPHECIES OF THE THREE WITCHES

Meantime, lurking murderers have sprung upon Banquo and killed him as he approached the palace. But his son Fleance escapes, and still leaves room for the fulfilment of the witches' prophecy. At the banquet the ghost of Banquo takes his seat at the table, seen by the horrified Macbeth, but unseen by the rest of the guests. Under his terror at this apparition Macbeth behaves so strangely that only the self-possession of his wife prevents suspicion from being aroused. In his nervous distress under the remorse he feels, Macbeth again seeks the witches, who urge him on by mysterious prophecies which he does not understand. They tell him, for instance, that he shall never be vanquished till Birnam Wood shall come to his castle of Dunsinane. Meantime, Macbeth's enemies are gathering strength around him.

At last even the resolution of Lady Macbeth gives way. She walks in her sleep, and tries to wash bloodstains from her hands as she walks. Conscience is at work, and when Malcolm, son of Duncan, who has come, with English help, to depose the usurper, approaches Dunsinane, Macbeth has no longer her support; indeed, the news of her death reaches him as he is preparing for his final defence.

THE CRY OF DESPAIR FROM A MAN OVERTHROWN BY HIS AMBITION

He hears the news as a thoroughly disillusioned man who by his misuse of life has found it meaningless. This is all he has to say of it—the outcry of a man wrecked by a false ambition:

> Tomorrow, and tomorrow, and tomorrow,
> Creeps in this petty pace from day to day,
> To the last syllable of recorded time;
> And all our yesterdays have lighted fools
> The way to dusty death. Out, out, brief candle!

Life's but a walking shadow, a poor player
That struts and frets his hour upon the stage,
And then is heard no more; it is a tale
Told by an idiot, full of sound and fury,
Signifying nothing.

But, though he is hopeless at the last, he loses not his soldierly courage, and is braver than he was when murder of the helpless was his aim. Even when he heard that Birnam Wood was coming to Dunsinane, for the enemy were carrying great boughs from it to conceal their numbers, he did not quail, but exclaimed:

Ring the alarum-bell! Blow, wind! Come, wrack;
At least we'll die with harness on our back.

And rushing forth, he died in single combat with his deadly foe Macduff, whose family he had slain. And so the retribution for a life of lawless ambition redeemed only by bravery was completed.

THE TRAGEDY OF KING LEAR

Long ago there was a King of Britain whose name was Lear. He was over eighty years old at the time of the story. Old and worn with the cares of his kingdom he decided that the time had come to give up his crown and his possessions, and spend his few remaining years in peace.

But King Lear had no son to succeed him; he had only three daughters. The eldest of these was Goneril, wife of the Duke of Albany; the second was named Regan, who was married to the Duke of Cornwall; and the youngest and most beautiful, Cordelia, was still unmarried. Between his three daughters the aged King determined to divide his kingdom, so he called them together to tell them of his purpose, saying that he would give the largest share to the one that loved him most.

Goneril, a selfish, cold-hearted woman, pretended that she loved him more than her eyesight, grace, health, beauty, honour, even more than life itself. Regan, who was like her elder sister in character, protested that even the extravagant declaration of Goneril's love for her father was not strong enough for her. All her joy, she said, was in finding favour with her father.

Carried away by the loving words of these two false, selfish women, the old King gave each a third of his kingdom; but when the kind-hearted Cordelia, who did truly love her father, would not exaggerate the terms of her love beyond those which a dutiful daughter should employ, Lear was enraged at her, and gave her nothing, dividing her share of his kingdom between her two sisters.

Cordelia, however, was not without consolation, as the King of France, who loved her for her sweet and gentle nature, made her his Queen. So insensible to reason had the old King grown that the faithful Earl of Kent was banished because he had ventured to plead with Lear on behalf of Cordelia. The kingdom of Britain was now divided between Goneril and Regan, whose husbands, the Duke of Albany and the Duke of Cornwall, thus shared the power of the old ruler. Lear fondly hoped to spend his days between the homes of his two children, attended by a retinue of one hundred followers. But he had not been long in Goneril's palace before he discovered that her love for him was all a sham. His daughter did everything she could to make his life unhappy, so that he was forced to leave with all his followers.

He went to the castle of the Earl of Gloucester, an old friend of his, who had acted in regard to his own two sons almost as foolishly as Lear had done to his own daughters. Gloucester's son Edmund, an evil-minded, selfish, and unscrupulous man, was his favourite, while, Edgar, his proper heir, a brave and honest son, had unjustly been forced by Edmund's scheming to leave the home of his father.

At Gloucester's castle more sorrow was in store for Lear, as there he met his daughter Regan, who had come to plan with Edmund how she might escape the nuisance of her father and his followers. Goneril also came to the castle, and the two daughters did all they could to make the poor old King unhappy.

Utterly broken-hearted, Lear now wandered away, accompanied only by his jester but followed soon after by the faithful Earl of Kent, who had disguised himself in order to be of service to his old King. On a wild and lonely heath, and in the midst of a great storm, they came upon a hovel inhabited by one who seemed to be a madman, but was really Edgar, the banished son of Gloucester, who was feigning madness.

Now, the Earl of Gloucester would gladly have stood by Lear in his trouble, though he had been warned against rendering him assistance. Gloucester, however, told his false son Edmund that he meant to help King Lear in secret, and also showed him a letter, just received, which brought the news that a French army was coming to attack the British. Here was Edmund's chance. He bore the letter to the Duke of Cornwall, and also told him of his father's intentions to succour the unhappy King. For this service his father's earldom was given to Edmund.

THE RETRIBUTION THAT CAME TO THE BRUTAL DUKE OF CORNWALL

In the meantime Gloucester had housed in a farm near his castle, not only Lear and the jester, but Kent and his own son Edgar, both of whom were, of course, disguised. He then had the King sent on to Dover, where the warriors of the country were gathering to meet the French, with whom was Cordelia.

The Duke of Cornwall was quickly on the track of Gloucester, whom he had arrested, and in his anger at the earl's efforts to save the King he blinded him, but was mortally wounded himself by one of his own followers, enraged at his cowardly brutality.

The tragedy was reaching its height, for the sightless earl was now led to Dover by none other than his own son Edgar; and, nearing the town, he came upon King Lear, gone out of his mind, fantastically decked with flowers. A follower of Goneril, meeting them, sought to kill the Earl of Gloucester, but Edgar fought and slew the man, and discovered that he was the bearer of a love-letter from the faithless Goneril to his own step-brother Edmund.

THE HAPPY REUNION OF LEAR AND HIS DAUGHTER CORDELIA

Lear was now brought to the French camp at Dover, where his daughter Cordelia, who had never ceased to love her father, received him tenderly and tried to console him, when they were made prisoners by the victorious British.

Lear now wants only Cordelia, and when she proposes they shall see her sisters, he refuses her request.

No, no, no, no! Come, let's away to prison;
We two alone will sing like birds in the cage:
When thou dost ask me blessing, I'll kneel down,
And ask of thee forgiveness; so we'll live,

And pray, and sing, and tell old tales, and laugh
At gilded butterflies, and hear poor rogues
Talk of court news; and we'll talk with them too,
Who loses and who wins; who's in, who's out;
And take upon us the mystery of things,
As if we were God's spies; and we'll wear out,
In a walled prison, packs and sets of great ones
That ebb and flow by the moon.

But the war between France and Britain was not so fierce as that which now raged between Goneril and Regan. These two faithless sisters had both fallen in love with the villain Edmund. When Edgar gave Goneril's letter to the Duke of Albany, the duke challenged Edmund to a duel, just after the battle had been fought in which King Lear and Cordelia had been taken prisoners.

THE SAD NOTE ON WHICH THE GREAT TRAGEDY ENDS

Edmund was fatally wounded by the duke; but meanwhile the two unhappy women who had been the cause of all this sad tragedy had settled matters in a drastic way. Goneril had contrived to poison her sister Regan, out of jealousy at her love for Edmund, and she, when her own guilty secret was laid bare by the discovery of her love-letter, stabbed herself and died.

All too late, Edmund, now dying of his wounds, and repenting of his evil conduct, asked that the life of Cordelia might be spared; but, at the very moment when he was breathing his last, the weird figure of the old King carrying the dead body of Cordelia appeared. She had been strangled in prison. The last blow in the great tragedy had been struck.

The Duke of Albany, who had always been friendly to King Lear, despite the evil influence of his wife, would now have had the aged King resume his power, but that was hopeless; his heart was broken and death was on him.

Vex not his ghost: O! let him pass; he hates him
That would upon the rack of this tough world
Stretch him out longer.

In these immortal lines Kent takes farewell of the master he had served so loyally through good and evil fortune. Lear had made shipwreck of his hopes, but at the last pity for his sufferings silenced criticism.

The duke, however, showed his feeling for Lear by rewarding both Edgar and Kent for the services they had rendered to the poor old King in his hour of need.

The Story of the Most Beautiful Book in the World

The Apostles go out into the world to preach

THE VISION OF PETER

HAVE we ever thought how strange a thing it is that after the ignominious death of Jesus, the son of a carpenter in a despised village, his religion, which he had left in the hands of eleven uneducated men, who had all forsaken Him and fled in the hour of his downfall, should have spread, in the lifetime of those very men, to nations and countries far away from Jerusalem ?

This is the most wonderful fact of human history. We cannot exaggerate its wonder. Nothing in the least resembling it had ever occurred before or has occurred since. It stands out in the history of humanity as an event that it is impossible to deny, and equally impossible to explain on purely human grounds.

Imagine that a carpenter's son from a village in Essex appeared in London with twelve labourers and fishermen, preaching a new religion and prophesying the downfall of Christianity. Imagine that the twelve labourers and fishermen were not very loyal to their leader, that they rather doubted the truth of what he said, and that as soon as the police stepped in and arrested him they all deserted him.

Imagine that the archbishops and bishops proved by law that this innocent preacher should be put to death, and that he was hanged like a murderer. What should we say if we found that after his death the labourers and fishermen who had followed him, and who had deserted him, spread the knowledge of his life and work throughout Europe, converting peoples from their religion, and filling the whole world with his name ? What should we say to such an extraordinary event as that ?

That would be wonderful enough, but it would not equal the wonder of Christianity. For the Gospel of Christianity, which is nothing more or less than the Character of Christ, spread among the nations before there was printing, before there was a railway or a telegraph, and before civilisation had reached a gentleness and kindness which, owing to Christ Himself, is now the characteristic of social life. It was a triumph of sweetness, beauty, and humility, at a time when blood was on the hands of rulers and princes, and when mankind was degraded by sin.

We can see how this revolution took place by following the narrative of Paul's life; but we must leave him for the present at his home in Tarsus while we read about a striking incident in the life of Peter, the consequences of which have impressed themselves upon the ages.

GREAT FIGURES OF THE OLD TESTAMENT · THE LIFE OF JESUS

The persecutions inflicted by Paul had driven many devout Nazarenes from Jerusalem. Rather than give up their faith in Jesus, they fled to distant towns and there began life afresh. In the seaside town of Joppa there was a community of these Nazarenes, and Peter went on a visit to them. He stayed in the house of one Simon, who was a tanner, and we can see how very humble must have been the beginning of Christianity for the head of the brotherhood to stay in the house of a man following a trade which was detested by the Jews. There were special Jewish laws against tanners. One Rabbi says: " The world cannot exist without tanners, but woe unto him who is a tanner." The fact that they handled animal hides rendered them vile in the eyes of strict Jews.

THE FEEBLE BIRTH OF THE MIGHTIEST MOVEMENT IN THE WORLD

If Peter had no better house open to him in the fine city of Joppa than this miserable dwelling of Simon the tanner, the religion of the Nazarenes must indeed have been in a feeble condition.

And so, indeed, it was. The followers of Jesus still believed that His revelation was particularly, if not wholly, for the Jews; they felt the same contempt for foreigners as the rest of their race; they hoped to see the ideas of Jesus adopted in the ordinary Jewish worship.

One or two converts had realised a greater truth. There were Stephen, the first martyr, and the cultured Philip, who had brought foreigners into the brotherhood of Jesus. But the apostles held back. In any case every converted foreigner had to become a Jew, a disciple of the Mosaic law. Peter now and then seems to have had some idea of a wider field for Christ's Gospel; but he was certainly not a missionary to the foreigners. Therefore we see that the religion of Jesus at the outset was nothing but a very small and insignificant Jewish sect ; a sect which had to be secret because of its powerful enemies.

THE STRANGE VISION THAT CAME TO PETER

One day, in the house of Simon the tanner, Peter rose and mounted to the roof, like a pious Jew, to say his mid-day prayer. From the flat roof of this Eastern house he saw the blue sea creeping over the bleached sands, and felt the heat of the noonday sun beating down upon

him. As he prayed he became hungry, and, probably exhausted by his hard life, his scant fare, and the pitiless glare beating up from the hot, white roof into his eyes, he fell into a swoon.

In this trance he saw an immense movement in the sky, as if it were a gigantic linen sheet being lowered by ropes at the four corners, and saw within it all manner of birds, fowls, and reptiles. " Rise, Peter," said a Voice within him; " kill, and eat." Hungered and exhausted as he was, the Jew in him cried out: " Not so, Lord! " for among these creatures there were those which the law of Moses forbade all Jews to eat.

It was because the Jews were so strict about their diet, and because they would not eat certain animals, such as swine— which they never even mentioned by name—that they looked with loathing and contempt on other nations. " Not so, Lord; for I have never eaten any thing that is common or unclean."

The Voice answered, " What God hath cleansed, that call not thou common."

THE RICH CENTURION WHO SENT FOR THE HUMBLE FISHERMAN

Clear as the brilliant sun to which he woke was the meaning of this vision; but, as his eyes were dazzled by the light, so was his soul too dazed to realise in all its wonderful fullness the meaning of his vision. He was pondering it in his heart when he heard the voices of three foreigners in the street below, inquiring for him at the door of Simon's house. One of these men was a soldier.

He went down and asked what they wanted. They told him that Cornelius, the centurion of Caesarea, desired that he should come to him on a visit.

At once the full meaning of the vision flashed upon his mind. Cornelius was a foreigner, a man of power, a good man, respected, even by the Jews. Peter realised that God had moved the heart of this great man towards Jesus of Nazareth. He saw how important a thing had happened, and on his journey to Caesarea he took with him six of the Nazarenes at Joppa to witness what should follow.

The scene was a striking one. Cornelius, whose imagination had been kindled by stories of Jesus, was waiting in his house with several friends and kinsmen for the humble apostle. As soon as he saw him he went forward and bowed his knee to the fisherman.

"Stand up," said Peter; "I myself also am a man." That was finely said. They went in together and talked, and Peter said : "Ye know how that it is an unlawful thing for a man that is a Jew to come unto one of another nation; but God hath shewed me that I should not call any man common or unclean." Cornelius related that a vision had bid him send for Peter, and he concluded by asking the apostle to speak what God commanded him. Then Peter uttered these remarkable words :

"Of truth I perceive that God is no respecter of person; but in every nation he that feareth Him, and w o r k e t h righteousness, is accepted w i t h Him." Having spoken t h e s e words, he told the story of Jesus, and showed that it was to this Jesus of Nazareth that all the prophets had pointed through the ages.

His words made a great effect. T.h e Nazarenes who were with him felt the power of the Holy Spirit afresh, and saw in those about them the same transfiguring effect. Peter, witnessing the descent of the Spirit upon these foreigners, cried out: "Can any man forbid water, that these should not be baptised?" And he baptised them all into the religion of Jesus.

How was this great event received by the Nazarenes in Jerusalem? When Peter returned he was met with a complaint. The brethren gathered there blamed Peter bitterly for having associated with the Gentiles, for eating with them, and for admitting them to the brotherhood.

But Peter related the exact details of his vision and what happened afterwards; and they "held their peace, and glorified God, saying, Then hath God also to the Gentiles granted repentance unto life."

Dean Farrar brings vividly home to us the horror that a true Jew would feel at such acts as Peter's. "To associate with them" he says, "to enter their houses, was not that pollution enough? To touch in familiar intercourse men who had never received the seal of the covenant—was not that sufficiently horrible? But to *eat with them*—to eat food prepared by Gentiles; to taste meat which had been illegally killed by Gentile hands; to take food from dishes which any sort of unclean insect or animal might have d e f i l e d —was it to be thought of without a shudder?"

Truly, to the Jew it was a fearful thing that Peter had done. He had defied the law of Moses.

Now do we see how poor and insignificant was the state of the brotherhood immediately after the resurrection of Jesus? What was it but a little frightened, secret faction of the Jews, paying far more attention to the Jewish religion than to the grand and illuminating words of Jesus?

But Peter had taken a step destined to change the history of the world. By crossing the threshold of the Roman's house in Caesarea he really carried Christianity from Asia to Europe; by sitting down to meat with this foreigner he transplanted Christianity from Judaism to the hearts of all people. The great miracle had begun. Christianity was rescued from its peril of becoming a narrow sectarian creed and founded firmly as a religion for all mankind.

And yet only grudgingly did the Nazarenes in Jerusalem accept the new conditions.

PETER

(Next chapter in this group, page 6297)

WHAT IS WRONG IN THIS STREET SCENE?

At first glance this picture seems to show the kind of familiar street scene we notice everyday when we are out shopping with Mother, or as we go to school. But if we take a closer look we shall see that there are a great number of things wrong about it, for in his drawing the artist has made at least twenty-two mistakes. A list of them appears on page 6300.

The Interests and Pleasures of Life for All Indoors and Out

LITTLE GIFTS IN FELT

IF you have never tried making things in felt, you have something to look forward to, because felt is so easy to handle. It is very firm, and as it never frays, the cut edges can, if preferred, be left as they are, so saving much work.

An endless variety of things can be made in felt, from the kind of little gifts shown on this page to a rug for your own room.

MONEY-BAG EGG COSY

FOR this novel egg cosy, cut two straight strips of felt in contrasting shades, one for the outside and the other for the lining. The outside strip should be nine inches wide by five inches deep, and the lining eight and three-quarter inches wide by three-and-a-half inches deep.

Double the lining and fasten the two side edges together and, with matching embroidery thread, use the "stab" stitch. Gather the top edge closely. In "stab" stitch, the needle is pushed straight through the material and the thread pulled taut, the needle being pushed back the same side as it comes out each time. This is a most useful method of joining two pieces of felt which are usually too thick to be put together successfully with running stitch.

Join the outside strip of felt in the same way, and stitch it along the folded edge so that both sides match. Take a narrow strip of the same felt as the lining, an eighth of an inch wide and six inches long, taper the ends, and fashion it into the £ sign. This should be stuck or stitched in place. (In

sticking felt, use a firm paste and apply sparingly. A good way to do this is to put a little paste on a saucer and smear it on the back of the felt with an ordinary small cork used as a brush.)

Next slip the lining inside the cover which is then turned under at the bottom and the two stitched together. Gather the top three-quarters of an inch in from the edge and finish with a narrow bow at one side. Four of these egg cosies make a set. A tea cosy to match can be made in the same way, using a piece of felt about 22–24 inches long and 12 inches wide, adjusting the size if necessary, to suit the teapot.

KETTLE HOLDER

YOU need two four-inch squares of rather thick felt for the kettle holder. Cut off all the corners to match, stitch a loop of cherry-coloured felt to one corner, and at the same corner sew the two squares together. Cut out three red cherries (using a farthing), one or two pointed green leaves, a small

bent brown branch, and three slender green stalks for the fruit. Shape a small dent at the top of each cherry where the stalk should join. Arrange the design naturally and stick it down.

If it needs pressing, do this with a *dry* cloth and an iron which is not too hot. To damp felt in any way may shrink it.

CRAFTS · GAMES · NEEDLEWORK · PUZZLES · SCIENCE EXPERIMENTS

A MATCHBOX CONTAINER

FELT can be used up to the very last scrap, and this matchbox container could hold all your felt fragments which otherwise might get lost, though it could have many other uses, too. Cover the outside of the  box in felt, button-holing it in place. Cut two small pieces of felt to fit the ends, and in the centre of one of these stitch a small curtain ring. Button-hole-stitch this strip to the cover to close up one end of the box. Stick on the decorations, and if you are copying the example, mark lines on the fins and tail of the fish with indelible pencil or with one or two embroidery stitches. Look among the scraps for a wee round for the fish's eye and for ragged bits to represent seaweed. Stick the other piece of felt on the end of the matchbox tray and sew a curtain ring in the centre of this, taking the stitches right through both felt and tray, so that it can be pulled out easily.

COMPACT CASE

THIS is a small case to take a powder compact, a mirror, or a powder-puff for the handbag. It can be made larger, however, for a handkerchief sachet, a night-dress case, or a cushion cover, simply by varying the size of the circles. The felt for the two circles here was marked on the wrong side with a chalk line drawn round a tumbler and then cut out.

The design on this case shows how leaves and flowers can be separated with good effect. A leaf is made from a small oval held in place by a single long stitch, which makes the centre vein, while the flowers are small circles cut out to the size of a thimble, and then shaped a little to show five petals. Each flower has a small contrasting centre. The edge of the decorated circle is then turned back for a short distance, and the flowers are sewn along this turn-back, as if holding it down. To finish, the two circles are stitched together for two-thirds of the way round.

TAPE-MEASURE TIDY

TAPE-MEASURES have a habit of getting mislaid, and Mother would appreciate one in this neat little holder. Cut a straight strip five inches long by one-and-a-half inches wide, and two small pieces one-and-a-half inches square each. Decorate each square in any way you fancy.

To decorate it as shown, cut two circles of felt, in any colour suitable for a flower. Shape each into six petals. Cut a tiny circle in yellow for the flower centre, and with a single stitch fasten centre and flower circles to one of the felt squares. Trace a butterfly from a picture and cut it out in felt. Holding the wings together, oversew the body on the under side—this has the effect of making the wings stand up—and stitch the body of the butterfly to the other square of felt. Stick felt shapes on to the wings, and a scrap of yellow to the tip of each antenna. Then buttonhole one square to either end of the long strip. Fold a tape-measure in four and slip it in.

KEEPING A MEMORY BOOK

WHEN you have finished reading a newspaper, a magazine, or a book, how much do you remember of what you have read ? A lot depends on what you *want* to remember. What you are most interested in will always stay longest in your mind. But the mind is very much like a lumber-room. The more you try to cram into it the more untidy it becomes and the more difficult it is to find anything you want.

A good idea is to keep a Memory Book. The ideal book for the purpose is one of those fair-sized Index Books that can be obtained from any good stationers or printer's shop for a few shillings. It is worth saving up your money to buy one, for it will save you a great deal of time and trouble when you have it working properly.

Inside the front cover of your Index Book you will find all the letters of the alphabet, from A to Z, usually printed in red. Under each letter print the general heading of the subjects in which you are most interested and on which you wish to collect information. Under " B," for instance, you could make the heading " Birds " or " Battleships " ; under " S," " Sporting Records " or " Strange Customs." Remember to use a separate page of each letter for each subject. This will allow you plenty of room to add further details to your notes from other sources.

In this way you will build up for yourself quite a handy personal encyclopedia, and constant reference to your Memory Book will make you a real expert at " quiz " programmes, or if you are asked to take part in a " Brains Trust " at your local Youth Club.

Also you will soon find that one Index Book is not sufficient to contain all you know. In fact, you may end up with a library.

HOW TO FIND OUR WAY IN A WOOD

MOST of us at some time or other during our holiday rambles have been lost in a wood. Perhaps trying to save time we left the pathway, or we may have wanted to explore, and have wandered farther than we realised. Then, unless we happen to have a compass, we may walk about aimlessly for hours. But we need not be lost, for Nature has supplied us with an unfailing series of signs, which, if known and studied, show us the north, south, east, and west as clearly and truly as any compass.

We must find a full-grown tree that stands slightly apart from its fellows, and look carefully at the bark. It will be harder, lighter, and drier on the south side; while on the north side it will be considerably darker in tone, and often at the roots on the north side we shall find a clump of moss. Nearly all the hardwood trees, such as the oak, the ash, and the elm, have moss growing on the north side; while on that side the leaves are longer, of darker green, and have lighter veins than those found on the south side. Again, spiders build on the south side.

One of the surest ways of discovering the compass points is to find a sawn or cut stump. The rings of wood seen in the section will be found to be thicker on the south side than on the north, so that the heart of the stump is nearer the north side. All these signs are given to us by the effects of the Sun. Stones that have rested in the same spot for some time usually have moss on the side facing north, while at best on the south side we shall find only a thin covering of harsh, half-dried moss. On the north side of a hill, ferns, mosses, and late flowers grow, and this side is at all times greener with vegetation. In winter nests of insects will be found in the crevices on the south side of trees with rough bark.

If we are on a marsh, small bushes will act as compasses, their leaves and limbs showing the same differences as we have seen on the trees in the wood. But if we want to find our way back again the same way as we came, we can make a tracking stick.

An old walking stick, broom handle, or a stout branch will do for this. If the tip is not very broad we shall have to put a block of wood on the end, fixing this with a nail in the same way as a broom head is attached to its handle. Into the underside of this block we drive large nails, arranging them in a definite pattern, like a triangle or the outline of a footprint. Then if we use this as an ordinary walking stick in the soft ground as we go, we should have a perfect track to follow coming home.

THE WHIRLING KALEIDOSCOPE

HERE is an interesting scientific toy that can be made by any boy or girl.

Take a pair of compasses, and on a piece of stiff, white cardboard draw the figure shown here, making it about three or four inches in diameter. Then cut out the disc with a sharp penknife, and cut a round hole in the centre, following the circumference of the inner circle. If the toy is to work properly there must be no jagged edges, hence the importance of using a very sharp penknife.

The next thing is to paint the disc. Leave the outer circle white, but colour the three inside divisions, making one bright red, the next one royal blue, and the third yellow. Be sure to get the colours vivid and not too dark.

As soon as the disc is dry it is ready for use. To get a succession of colour changes pass a piece of flexible string through the central hole, and, holding one end firmly in each hand, turn the string once or twice rapidly and then pull taut.

DIAGRAM OF THE DISC

The disc will have been set revolving by the twisting of the string, and when that is pulled tight the disc will continue to turn rapidly on it. As it does so the colours will blend, and as different parts of the centre hole touch the string in turn, the combinations of colour will vary wonderfully.

While the disc gives pleasure as a toy, it is also of considerable scientific value, and we should know the reason for the curious changes.

Owing to the rapid spinning of the disc, our eyes are unable to follow the individual colours as they go round, and so they become merged. Blue, yellow, and red mix in various ways, giving all the colours of the rainbow. The reason why the positions of the colours keep changing as we spin the disc on the string is that the colour which touches the string is always in the centre, and revolves less rapidly than the other colours, being nearer the axis on which the card turns.

ANSWERS TO THE PUZZLE GAME ON PAGE 6058

ON page 6058 appears a natural history puzzle game in which seven well-known things are described. These are the various articles referred to: 1. The common sweet chestnut; 2. Herrings; 3. Tea; 4. Silk; 5. Oats; 6. Honey; 7. Apples.

SIMPLE FIRST-AID IN THE HOME

Accidents will happen, and it is just as well that we should know what to do, for by acting promptly we can often prevent much suffering.

CUTS, WOUNDS, AND BRUISES

A DIRTY flesh-wound should be either washed, or, if no water is obtainable, wiped with a clean handkerchief, and bandaged with another. It is better to cover the wound with a piece of blank white paper, such as notepaper, rather than let a soiled handkerchief touch it. Whenever possible the wound should be washed in lukewarm water, cleansed properly with an antiseptic, then covered with lint, and finally bandaged. The edges of a clean cut should be pressed together, and covered with an antiseptic plaster or dressing.

A bruise can be relieved by putting on a cold compress—a pad of soft cloth wrung out in cold water. Ice, if available, is even more soothing.

BURNS AND SCALDS

A BURN is caused by dry heat, a scald by moist heat, usually boiling water. When the injured part is covered with clothing this must be carefully removed, and if it adheres to the skin it should be cut away from around the injured part with clean scissors. Air must be immediately excluded. This can easily be done, if warm water is at hand, by putting the injured part in water at the normal temperature of the body, 98.4 degrees, until a dressing can be prepared, otherwise it should be covered with soft material kept in place by a bandage.

Burns should be treated at once with a solution of bicarbonate of soda, a dessertspoonful to a pint of warm water, or for speed to prevent blistering, the bicarbonate can be put on dry and afterwards damped. The part should then be kept covered, and in the case of a bad burn or scald, as in that of all but the slightest of injuries, the patient should be treated for shock—kept warm and quiet and given some weak sweet tea.

For burns on the face, make a mask of cottonwool or any soft material, leaving a hole for nose and mouth, and soak this in the bicarbonate solution. Keep the mask damp with the solution.

INSECT BITES AND STINGS

INSECT bites can be extremely painful, some people being more prone to them than others. A great deal of discomfort can be avoided if exposed parts are smeared lightly with oil of lavender before going into the garden or out into the country, especially on a damp summer day or in the evening.

Calamine lotion and methylated spirit, mixed in equal quantities, dabbed on a bite will relieve pain and swelling.

When a sting is left in the flesh, it should be taken out, if possible with a sterilised needle. Rub the spot with a piece of washing soda damped, or with the wet blue bag; or damp it with methylated spirit or bicarbonate solution. Cover with a dry dressing.

SOMETHING IN THE EYE

IF a piece of grit or a tiny fly should get into the eye, resist the temptation to rub it. Try to find out where the object is. Pull down the lower lid, and if it can then be seen, gently lever it out with the corner of a clean handkerchief twisted to a point and damped.

When the particle is on the upper eyelid, try this simple method first. Lift the top lid away from the eye, push the lower one up underneath the top and let both go. The lashes of the bottom lid act as a brush and should sweep the object out. Another way is to roll back the top lid on a match stick, and use the handkerchief tip, or a small camel hair brush, to take out the object.

If neither of these methods is successful after one or two attempts, pull down the bottom eyelid and put on a drop of castor oil or liquid medicinal paraffin. This should be done also if the grit is fixed on the eyeball, and in that case the eye should afterwards be bandaged, with a small pad of cottonwool, or something equally soft, between the bandage and the closed lid. Then a doctor should be consulted as soon as possible.

COLD BLISTERS

COLD blisters, or herpes, to give them their proper name, which often come on the lips when a cold is developing, are unsightly and painful. A dab of eau de Cologne in the very early stages should prevent the blisters forming.

HOT FOMENTATIONS

FOMENTATIONS are used on wounds which have become septic or inflamed or to relieve pain. For an open sore, a fresh piece of boracic lint is necessary for each application, but where the skin is unbroken, a piece of plain lint or flannel can do duty several times.

The piece of lint should be large enough, when doubled, to cover the injury. It is also necessary to have a piece of oiled silk a little larger all round than the fomentation, a pad of cotton wool, a bandage, a clean cloth or a small towel, and a basin.

Roll the lint up in the centre of the cloth, which should be laid in the basin with its two ends overhanging the edge. Cover with boiling water, then lift the fomentation clear by the two dry ends of the cloth, and twist to wring out the water.

Quickly unrolling the cloth, take out the lint and put it over the affected part. Cover with the oiled silk, then with the cotton wool, and bandage to keep it in place.

The Story of the Boundless Universe and All Its Wondrous Worlds

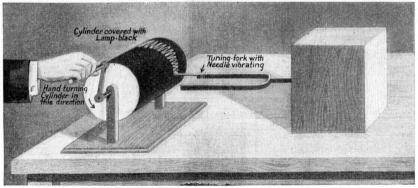

If a needle is attached to a tuning-fork, and the fork is fixed in a block of wood and then struck, the vibrating needle will draw a wavy line on a slowly revolving cylinder.

MUSIC AND NOISE

WE know that sound waves agree in many ways with other kinds of waves, like the waves of the sea, or the waves of light. We must now go on to study the nature of these sound waves; and the first thing we discover is that they differ from other waves in one highly important respect.

In the sea the wave runs along the surface, but the movements of the water, which make the wave, are not at all along the surface of the sea; they are up-and-down movements. Of course, it looks to our eyes as if the water were really running along, but it is not; the wave is running along; the water itself is only rising and falling.

The proper way of saying this is that the vibration is at right angles to (or away from) the line of the wave. The wave is moving along in one direction, and the particles of water which make the wave are moving at right angles to that direction. They are moving, not along, but up and down. The movement might just as well be from side to side, but in any case it is a *transverse* vibration—that is to say, a vibration across. Now, what we have learned about the waves of the sea is true of the waves of light; but it is not true of sound waves. The great point about

sound waves is that the movement of the air, or whatever the medium happens to be, is not at right angles to the path of the wave, but is a movement to and fro in the line of the wave. Let us think of a stretched string that is vibrating and imagine it is giving a little series of blows to the air that is next to it; or let us think of a fist moving backwards and forwards in the air, making a number of quick taps.

That is the way a sound wave is started. When the air is tapped it is squeezed, but it is elastic, and in between the taps it springs back, and so it is alternately condensed and expanded, and the wave is made up of these to-and-fro movements of the particles of air in the line of the wave.

It is really not difficult to form in our minds an accurate picture of the way in which the wave travels. All we need do is to place on a table a row of billiard balls, all touching one another. Suppose we now roll another billiard ball against the ball at one end of the row. Each ball in turn is squeezed, and passes the pressure on to the next one, with the result that the ball at the other end of the row is shot out by itself. Each ball in turn is pressed and relaxed. That is what happens to the air when a sound wave travels through it, and we may imagine what the wave is

ASTRONOMY · GEOLOGY · GEOGRAPHY · CHEMISTRY · PHYSICS · LIFE

made to travel by particles of air bump-ing against each other in their to-and-fro movement, as the billiard balls bump each against the next.

That is all we need to know about the nature of sound waves, but the next ques-tion we may naturally ask is: What makes the difference between the sounds we call noises and those we call musical notes? Or, in the case of music full of discords, what marks the line between pleasing sound on the one hand, and, for many, displeasing sound on the other?

Well, the case of music teaches us that there is no shape and absolute line to be drawn between noise and music, as there are many sounds and combinations of sounds which are pleasant and musical to one ear and unpleasant to another. Nevertheless, though there is room for difference of opinion at the margin be-tween the two kinds of sounds, we can answer without hesitation that the differ-ence between what everyone would call a noise and what everyone would call music, depends on whether the waves making the sound are regular or irregular.

THE SHAPE OF THE MUSICAL SOUNDS OF AN ORCHESTRA

When we take a rich and complicated musical sound made by a large orchestra, the resulting wave is regular and yet irreg-ular. The ear of a child, or any untrained ear, may not perceive the regularity, and to such an ear the sound may be a noise; but the ear of a musician may perceive that the sound really is regular, and has a definite shape, and to him it may be a splendid musical experience. Also, there may be room in music sometimes for sounds which are partly regular, and therefore musical, and partly irregular, and therefore noise. Certain of the metal and drum-like instruments which are struck in the modern orchestra owe their value to this mixture of noise and music.

We do not really know why waves which strike the ear in a regular way should be called pleasant and why those which are irregular should be called un-pleasant; but it seems natural that a regu-lar, even, steady flow of impulses into the hearing part of the brain should be pleasant, and we can imagine why it should be unpleasant for the nerve cells to be disturbed by waves without order or rhythm, all mixed up together, and per-haps liable to throw out of order the living machinery of the cells. Perhaps we may fairly compare the difference between the effects of music and noise to the difference between rocking a baby and shaking it.

The most simple, but by no means the most interesting, difference between musical notes is in their loudness; and what has to be said about this is true equally of noises.

THE POWER OF THE EAR TO DISTINGUISH BETWEEN VARIOUS SOUNDS

Loudness of sound depends on the size of the waves that cause it. The proper word in this connection is not size, but *amplitude*. The greater the amplitude of the waves, the louder the sound. If sound waves were like water waves, then a very faint sound would correspond to a little ripple, and a very loud sound to waves " mountains high." There is some-thing to be added to this, however, be-cause, when we use such a word as loud-ness, it is evident that we have to reckon not only with what is outside the ear, but also with the ear itself. Now, it is the fact that if we take notes of various pitch, high and low, all having the same amplitude of waves, they do not sound equally loud. Thus, though it is true that the loudness of a given note depends on its amplitude, when we compare different notes we find that if the amplitude be all the same, the higher in pitch they are the louder they sound. In other words, our ears are more sensitive to high notes than to low notes.

From the point of view of music this is extremely important. It means that when we are listening to voices singing together or to something played on the piano, our ears always give more value to the higher notes than to the lower ones.

WHY HIGH NOTES ARE ALWAYS HEARD BETTER THAN LOW NOTES

The basses, the tenors, and the con-traltos, for instance, may be making as much sound as the sopranos, but, our ears being more sensitive to high tones, we hear the sopranos best. That is why the sopranos are usually given what we call the tune to sing, while the basses, tenors, and contraltos are only given something which accompanies the tune.

So when we are playing the piano, if the tune is in the top notes of the right hand we can use both hands and all our fingers with equal force, and the tune will stand out clearly to the ear, because the ear is more sensitive to high tones. But sometimes a piece is written with the tune for the left hand, and the accompaniment for the right hand. In such a case, if both hands play with equal force we shall not hear the tune properly, but shall mainly hear a meaningless accompaniment. The player, therefore, must in such a case play lightly with his right hand, and pick the notes out strongly with his left hand, so as to compensate for the fact that the ear is more sensitive to high than to low notes.

On the other hand, it is very interesting to observe that, so far as the startling, or fear-producing, effect is concerned, low notes are vastly more powerful than high ones. The sudden sound of a flute, even loudly sounded, and of course, being high-pitched, sharply heard by the ear, has no startling quality at all compared with a roll of distant thunder or any kind of sound that resembles a growl. It is very noticeable in babies and small children that a low-pitched voice may frighten them, even though it is heard far less intensely by the ear than a high-pitched voice would be.

HOW TO DRAW A PICTURE OF A SOUND ON A SHEET OF PAPER

So much for the loudness of sounds. Our next concern is with the pitch of musical tones; and it is easy to show that the difference between a high note and a low note lies in the difference between the number of waves that strike the ear in a given time. It is not difficult to prove this, because we can take a tuning-fork and set it vibrating, and make one of the prongs, or something attached to one of them, scratch a record of what happens on a piece of smoked paper, which we can move at a known rate close to the fork.

In this way we get an up-and-down line marked on the paper, and may actually count the number of vibrations made in each second by the particular fork. We then find that the greater the number of vibrations, the higher the pitch of the sound. Gradually the tuning-fork ceases to sound, and the note becomes fainter; but its pitch does not alter, however faint it is. If we look at the record made by the fork on the paper we can see the reason of this. The size of the waves steadily lessens as the fork loses its energy, and so the sound becomes fainter; but the number of waves in each second remains the same, however small they are, and that is why the pitch of the note is unaltered.

The best instrument for studying the pitch of musical sounds is called the siren. Siren was the name given to an imaginary kind of being, half woman and half bird, who sang so beautifully that no one could resist her; and it is by way of a joke that the name has been given to the modern siren, which produces notes that belong to the musical order but certainly could never charm anyone. The siren is simply an arrangement by which air is blown along a tube; but across the nozzle of the tube there is turning a flat piece of metal with a lot of holes in it, so that the air can only pass through when the holes come opposite the tube.

HOW THE SIREN IS MADE TO PRODUCE ITS SHRILL SOUND

If we know how many holes there are, and how often the disc spins in a second, we can tell the number of waves which are being produced to make the sound that we hear. If we begin very slowly there may be perhaps only ten holes coming opposite the tube in a second; that simply means ten puffs in a second.

It is true that we may hear each of these as a little puff; and we do so because each little puff starts something or other vibrating at a rate which we can hear. But the ten puffs in a second, taken together, do not make a sound for us. However, if the number reaches twelve or thirteen a few people will hear an extremely deep, low-pitched note, and people with ordinary, healthy ears should hear a low note when the puffs reach about sixteen a second. As we increase the number, the pitch of the note we hear rises until it becomes an intensely high whistle. There may be now thirty thousand puffs in each second, or more.

THE HIGH-PITCHED NOTES THAT LIONS AND CATS CAN HEAR

If a number of people are listening, especially people of different ages, it will be found that one after another ceases to hear anything at all, while others still hear an intensely high whistling note.

Sir Francis Galton once made some interesting experiments with animals in this connection. He found that lions and cats were peculiarly sensitive to the notes of an extremely high-pitched whistle, though other animals did not seem to be aware of them at all.

(Next chapter in this group, page 6303)

ITALY'S GREAT CRAFTSMAN

MICHAEL ANGELO AS HE STANDS OUTSIDE
THE UFFIZI PALACE IN FLORENCE

MICHAEL ANGELO WORKING ON HIS PICTURE
OF THE LAST JUDGMENT IN THE SISTINE CHAPEL

MICHAEL ANGELO CONTEMPLATES ONE OF HIS GREAT STATUES

The Story of Immortal Folk Whose Work Will Never Die

Michael Angelo　　　　　Raphael　　　　　Leonardo da Vinci

THE MASTER MEN OF ITALY
MICHAEL ANGELO · LEONARDO · RAPHAEL

IN that great gallery of immortal men that Italy has given to mankind, a gallery, unmatched in art by any other land, three stand out like giants: Michael Angelo, Leonardo da Vinci, and Raphael. In their lives we can see all the working out of ideals, the personal endeavour criss-crossed with fate, that makes such an ever-changing picture of Italy in the Great Years.

The century which held the lives of these three is the golden century of European art. What a wealth of genius lay in Italy then! How little men knew their good fortune when they could see Michael Angelo, Leonardo, and Raphael all together in Rome and in Florence, hear them speak, see them walk, and behold the mingled richness that their hands had wrought! Certainly these three great artists had plaudits enough from the people. But Italy was so used to genius that she simply took them as better than other artists, and she took artists as a matter of course. Now, in a world barren of such greatness, the lives of three supreme geniuses falling so near together seems a miracle.

Michael Angelo, the greatest of the three, was set by character and circum-stance most apart. His real name was Michelangelo Buonarroti, and he was born in 1475 in the castle of Caprese, in the Arezzo Mountains, near Florence—near enough for the great Republic to claim him as her own. Florence was then at the height of her prosperity, and Michael Angelo marked the summit of her achievements in art. He lived to see her dragged down, hum-bled, her high estate and her pride sacri-ficed to the quarrels of her nobles and the political disturbances of Italy at that time.

His father, Ludovico, was a descendant of a noble Florentine family, and at the time of Michael Angelo's birth was Mayor of Caprese. When the boy was still young the father returned to Florence and left him with his nurse in the home of a stone-cutter of Settignano, near by. Michael Angelo never forgot the joy of those childhood years. " If there is anything good in me," he once said, " it comes from the pure air of your Arezzo hills."

The boy presently came to live with his parents in Florence, and was sent to school. His father seemed to grow poorer and poorer, and looked about for posts in commerce and in law for his sons. He wanted Michael Angelo, the eldest, to become a notary.

EXPLORERS · INVENTORS · WRITERS · ARTISTS · SCIENTISTS

But the boy's heart, as we may imagine, was not in his books. He was punished many times for his truancy and bad scholarship, to no effect. He still spent all the hours he could steal wandering about Florence, where the picturesqueness, colour, and grandeur of her Tuscan nobility and her rich traders combined to make a pageant of daily life.

THE ARTIST WHO RECOGNISED THE GENIUS OF MICHAEL ANGELO

One of the young Michael Angelo's best friends was an apprentice of Ghirlandajo, the painter. In the master's absence the boy spent many happy hours, and " played about " with pencil and paper to his heart's content. He also made many studies in secret, imitating the style of the painters he liked the best. One of these came under the eye of Ghirlandajo, and, recognising an unusual gift, he went himself to the boy's father and persuaded him to allow Michael Angelo to take up art instead of law.

Ludovico consented, and on the first day of April, 1488, his son, aged thirteen, became apprenticed to Ghirlandajo. It seemed almost from the first that no lessons were necessary. All that was needed to develop Michael Angelo's genius his new life gave to him—an unlimited chance of drawing. He soon outstripped the other apprentices; they could but stand and stare at his sketches wherein an almost uncanny knowledge of form revealed itself. One day he made a sketch of Ghirlandajo and some of the apprentices and the master, seeing it by chance, exclaimed, " the boy knows more than I do."

LORENZO MEDICI AND WHAT HE DID FOR ART AND LEARNING

We can rarely think of a life like Michael Angelo's without remembering that fortune never comes with both hands full. This man of superb genius knew nothing of the art of living. He was bitter, moody, unfriendly, save to one or two, had few pleasant places in his life; it seemed that if he wandered into a green patch it was at once ploughed and salted with disappointment. He was always intolerant of all save what seemed to him the best, and his best was, even to himself, an inaccessible height.

It is probable that Michael Angelo's happiest years fell in his boyhood. Before he had been in Ghirlandajo's studio a year he was noticed by Lorenzo Medici.

This Lorenzo the Magnificent, as he was called, deserves a special place in our regard. There is scarcely an artist of any merit of his time whom he did not freely help. His name is continually peeping out of records. Without him the world would have been incredibly poorer—though it must be said that a good deal of his "magnificence " was paid for out of public money.

Lorenzo took Michael Angelo into his own house, and there for two years the boy lived, one among the company of painters, scholars, and poets whom the Medici prince delighted to honour. There he gained his true education—absorbing the conversation of educated men. There he learned something of the art of making verse—for he wrote quite a number of sonnets of a certain merit during his life.

Unfortunately for Michael Angelo and many others, in 1492 Lorenzo died, and his son Piero became head of the house of Medici. Piero showed himself to be a very unworthy successor of Lorenzo. The pleasant company of intelligent and artistic people was scattered, and Michael Angelo returned to his father's house.

THE ONE THING THAT MATTERED IN THE LIFE OF MICHAEL ANGELO

A little later the artist was called to Rome by one of the Cardinals who had seen some of his work. For five years he stayed there, fulfilling orders first for one patron and then another. His life was austere, of a hardness we can scarcely comprehend. His hours of work were necessarily long, because, although he had by now pupils, and assistants of his own, he never deputed to them the finishing of a piece of work, as so many artists of the day were content to do. He was merciless to himself, ate little, slept little. All that mattered was his work.

Presently we hear of him in Florence again, and this time to some purpose. The authorities showed him a huge block of marble which some other artist had discarded. From this Michael Angelo fashioned his colossal David. Half Florence gathered to see this man flinging his mallet about, making the chips of marble fly, working in a fierce, apparently careless manner that held them speechless. The David made him famous; he found it difficult to cope with the commissions that came to him.

In 1505 a new power rose in his life. He was summoned to Rome by Pope Julius II.

This extraordinary man, who only "reigned" ten years, had an extraordinary effect on all Italy, and on her artists. He was at heart a soldier, but in addition to making Italy ring with the sound of his sword he made Rome ring with the sound of artists' and builders' chisels. He called in Michael Angelo; two years later he summoned Raphael; he had Bramante rebuilding St. Peter's, and a number of other artists. He was not so much a kindly patron, like Lorenzo, as a master, and a most difficult master, as we shall presently see.

It seemed that for the rest of his life Michael Angelo was at the mercy of first one pope and then another, making plans at their orders, which were changed before they could be fulfilled. The sheer waste of these years of his prime makes one of the saddest chapters in art's story.

First, Julius must have a gigantic monument made for his own tomb, embodying a great array of figures which should show his exploits. Nothing was too good for the sculptor who was to make the pope immortal. But the work was no sooner begun than his holiness lost interest. He even forgot to give the sculptor ordinary wages for daily needs. Poor Michael Angelo strode up to the pope's palace one day in desperation, and was rudely dismissed by a servant.

THE SHAMEFUL TREATMENT OF A GREAT GENIUS IN ROME

The sculptor flung himself out of Rome in a rage and returned the same day to Florence. Whereupon the pope suddenly changed his mind again, and must have his monument. But he did not know the man he was dealing with. Papal briefs which would have made others tremble in their shoes did not make Michael Angelo move an eyelash. He had finished with His Holiness.

Three times the pope sent to the chief men of Florence ordering Michael Angelo to be sent at once back to Rome. In the end, for the sake of Florence, the sculptor, sick at heart, obeyed. At that time Julius was at Bologna, brewing trouble. Michael Angelo went to him there and made a bronze statue of Julius, at his orders, with a sword in his hand.

In 1508 he was back at Rome, secretly joyed at the thought of continuing the work on the monument. But that Tragedy of the Tomb, as a writer has called it, was only just begun. It was destined to cast a shadow over the sculptor's life for some forty years. Pope Julius thought he did not want a tomb just now; he wanted the ceiling of the Sistine Chapel painted. Four years went by, while the sculptor, having begged in vain that Raphael the painter might do it, got through that enormous labour.

A TERRIBLE DISAPPOINTMENT AFTER FIVE YEARS OF GOOD WORK

As soon as the frescoes were finished Michael Angelo turned eagerly to his sculpture, and he succeeded in devoting a year's work to the tomb of Julius II. But very soon there was a new pope. As Leo X, Cardinal Giovanni Medici, son of Lorenzo, took the place of Julius.

Leo X had known Michael Angelo when he was a boy at home, and soon after his accession he gave him orders for work—this time architecture. Poor Michael Angelo! He was obliged once more to lay down his tools and proceed to Florence, where the new pope wanted him to build a façade for the church of St. Lorenzo. But this man of superhuman gifts could not resist the joy of any true, creative work. We hear of him next at Carrara, where a large number of men quarried marble at his orders. In his mind he saw the work done—the finest thing Italy had ever seen, please God, said Michael Angelo. Five years passed.

Great columns of marble had been dragged to Florence, workshops were busy there; the most noble façade in Christendom was in the making under the guidance of this indomitable man. Then, quite suddenly, the pope changed his mind. He did not want the façade after all.

The artist's indignation, poured out white hot, rather frightened the pope. His Holiness confided to Sebastian del Piombo, the painter, that Michael Angelo was too much for him.

FATE INTERRUPTS THE WORK OF MICHAEL ANGELO

Presently still another pope, Clement VII, again a Medici, cast his shadow over the artist's path. This time he was ordered to build the Laurentian Library, and set up the new sacristy of St. Lorenzo, wherein the tombs of the Medici should be enshrined. There was scope enough in the scheme of the work, with its bas reliefs and six great sarcophagi, and portrait statues, to rouse the fervour of an ordinary man, let alone Michael Angelo. Forgetting all that lay behind, he plunged once more into a vast labour. Clement was kinder and more thoughtful than the sculptor's previous masters had been, and for a time all went well. Then fate stopped the work. Once more the Medici were expelled from Florence. The terrible internal strife that made Italian history about this time a long battle scene, shook first the capital and then the chief towns. In 1529 Florence was besieged; and her leading men, looking round for someone to direct the defences, applied to Michael Angelo.

THE LOVELY FIGURES MADE IN SECRET WHILE FLORENCE WAS AT WAR

The work he did would make anyone think he had been born to be a military engineer. Traces of his fortifications are still in existence. He took on all this extra labour, and worked at the Medici tombs as well. While Florence was being battered at, shaken, he worked in secret at figures for the tombs of the men who had helped to make Florence immortal.

A sharp division came in the sculptor's life in 1534 when his father, at the age of ninety, passed away. Michael Angelo left Florence then for Rome, and never returned to the lovely city on the Arno. He had no sooner arrived in Rome than Clement died. The new pope, Paul III, at once called in the man whose name was now famous throughout Italy, and instituted him artist in chief to the Vatican. At this period the famous Last Judgment was painted on the eastern wall of the Sistine Chapel. A little later he started on the frescoes in a chapel of the Vatican; by the time they were finished he was 74.

In 1547 Michael Angelo was made architect to St. Peter's, and there he spent the last ten years of his working life. The dome of this great church remains as a testimony for all time to the labour of a man who, judged by ordinary standards, was approaching an extreme old age.

TWO FRIENDS WHO BRIGHTENED THE LAST YEARS OF A GREAT LIFE

Two people had made a fleeting brightness in the artist's later years—his faithful servant Urbino, and good Vittoria Colonna, the Marchesa of Pescara. This lady and Michael Angelo were great Bible readers, poetry readers, thinkers, students of religion, and their intimacy was very

beautiful. In a life so barren of human joys as Michael Angelo's, where the mere thought of marriage had been shut out, this friendship must have counted for a great deal. With her death Michael Angelo felt that his last earthly happiness had gone. He died peacefully in February 1564, and a whole nation mourned him.

To pass from the life of Michael Angelo to that of Leonardo da Vinci is like passing from magnificent and gloomy mountains and valleys to a pleasant, sunlit plain.

Perhaps this great difference between them was the reason why, when their paths crossed, these two great geniuses did not look with friendliness at each other. Michael Angelo was haughty and cold, and Leonardo was polite and urbane and very sensitive. Like most artists, he resented the sculptor's superiority, and it did not make the position any easier when Leonardo said, " I was a great painter while you were but a youth." But if time has justified Michael Angelo's superiority, time has also made Leonardo an intensely interesting and lovable personality.

THE SINGING BOY WHO LOVED THE FLOWERS AND BIRDS

Leonardo was born in 1452 at Vinci, near Florence. He always insisted on calling himself Leonardo the Florentine; but history has not been kind to him in this one detail. His father, Piero, was a lawyer, an important man in Florence, and had a fine house there, where Leonard lived until he was twenty-four.

The glimpses that we have of Leonardo's early life are intensely interesting; we feel that he was a man to be loved at sight. He went through his boyhood days happy and singing, so that people smiled when they looked at him. Flowers, birds, and animals were his friends. He went out for long rambling days in the country, and always came back with more treasures for his menagerie.

Anything that was alive was beloved by Leonardo—toads, serpents, bats and " creepy-crawlies " innumerable. Where Leonardo was, no animal was ill treated. Many and many a time he bought the little singing birds in the street and the market-place, and afterwards gave himself the intense pleasure of taking the cage far from the town and freeing the prisoner.

Much as he loved " all creatures great and small," he had a special overwhelming

THREE MEN WHOSE NAMES WILL NEVER DIE

RAPHAEL AT WORK IN THE VATICAN, SKETCHING A MOTHER AND CHILD FOR ONE OF HIS GLORIOUS FRESCOES

MICHAEL ANGELO AND HIS GREAT FRIEND VITTORIA COLONNA

RAPHAEL AND A LADY FRIEND

LEONARDO DA VINCI SHOWS HIS IDEA FOR A FLYING MACHINE TO HIS PATRON LUDOVICO SFORZA —FROM THE PAINTING BY ELEANOR FORTESCUE-BRICKDALE

love for horses. There was never a steed too wild for Leonardo to tame and ride. He became a superb horseman; made drawings and studies of horses in every imaginable position, and wrote an interesting book on horses and their anatomy.

THE TRUE ARTIST WHOSE SOUL WAS TUNED LIKE A PERFECT INSTRUMENT

Wherever he went he carried a note-book and sketch-book. Sometimes he would wander up and down the streets of Florence just looking for beautiful things, so that his eyes and soul became sensitive to beauty, tuned like a perfect instrument. He grew up into a handsome, athletic man, with much personal charm and great conversational gifts.

There was nothing in Leonardo of that blindness to all things save art which marked the youth of so many painters. He was naturally of a brilliant intellect, and loved equally music and mathematics, astronomy and poetry. The greatest marvel in the mentality of this man, who is one of Nature's wonders, was the mixture of scientific and artistic genius. He was a gifted musician, and shares with Raphael the first place in Italian painting. He filled a great number of books with notes on all kinds of subjects and scientific inventions that dealt with subjects as varied as canals, flying machines, and the use of steam. It is nothing today to find a young man thus occupied; but we live in a scientific age. Leonardo lived in an age when scientific knowledge was slight.

Before his boyhood years were over Leonardo decided that much as he loved the pursuit of knowledge he loved art more. And at the age of eighteen he was apprenticed to Andrea Verrocchio the painter, but it appears that he busied himself as much with the chisel as the brush. Presently his name appeared on the roll of the Painters' Guild, and Lorenzo Medici became his patron.

AMUSING GLIMPSES OF THE DAILY LIFE OF LEONARDO DA VINCI

Leonardo left a great mass of papers and manuscript books dealing with the daily events of his life. Here and there a brief note is very interesting: " Today I began two Virgin Maries." " Today I begin this new book and a new model of the horse." We get amusing glimpses from his own notes and public records of the conditions of an artist's life—as when he was working for some monks in Florence and they very kindly paid him in advance. There is a record, about this time, of the payment to Leonardo, by these monks, of one lira and six soldi for painting their clock. A soldo is a half-penny and a lira is nominally about tenpence. But in those days, of course, the value of money was much greater than it is now.

But in spite of these many personal records, there are great gaps in the life of Leonardo which have never been successfully filled by the men who have written about him. Between 1481, when he was living in Florence, and 1487, when he appears at the court of Milan in the service of Ludovico Sforza, nothing is known of him. The Sforza family played a great part in the career of Leonardo. One of Ludovico's projects was to raise a huge equestrian statue in honour of his father, one of the finest commanders Italy has known, who rose from the peasantry to be fighting leader and Duke of Milan.

THE HIGH OPINION LEONARDO HAD OF HIS OWN POWERS

Ludovico was a great friend of Lorenzo Medici, and he wrote him asking if he could suggest a man capable of making such a statue. Lorenzo knew the kind of person Ludovico was, and it pleased him to send Leonardo with another musician to Ludovico's castle in Milan. The artist bore a present of a silver lute, a present from the Medici prince to the Sforza duke. Whether Lorenzo really wrote, saying " This is the man," the writers do not say. But Leonardo heard of the great project and thought it would be a task exactly suited to his gifts, and he wrote to Ludovico asking for the commission.

He explained that he was a born engineer and could design cannon and engines of war; and in times of peace he was the equal of anyone in the matter of architecture of private and public buildings, and in the matter of conducting water from one place to another. He went on: " I can execute sculpture, whether in marble, bronze, or terracotta, and in painting I can do as much as any other man, be he who he may. I could engage to execute the bronze horse in eternal memory of your father and the illustrious house of Sforza. And if any of the above-mentioned things should appear to you impossible or impracticable

THE MASTER PAINTER OF ITALY

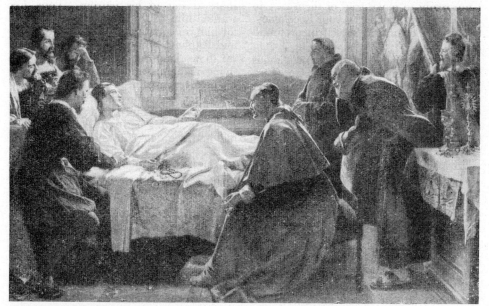

THE LAST MOMENTS OF RAPHAEL—FROM THE PAINTING BY HENRY O'NEIL

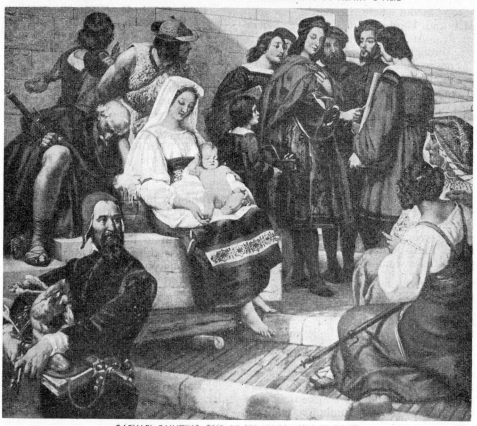

RAPHAEL PAINTING ONE OF HIS MADONNAS IN ROME

The pictures on these pages are reproduced by courtesy of Messrs. Alinari, Manelli, Photochrom, and others.

I am ready to make trial of them . . . in any place that may please your Excellency, to whom I commend myself in profound humility."

This letter is one of the most famous written by any artist. Its apparent lack of humility is excused by the fact that all the statements are true. Ludovico was quick to draw into his service this man of gifts who had already charmed him by his conversation and gift for playing the lute. Leonardo was engaged as artist-in-chief to the Count of Milan at a salary of two thousand ducats—about four thousand pounds.

PERHAPS THE FINEST PORTRAIT OF A WOMAN THE WORLD HAS KNOWN

Ludovico found his artist-in-chief a little trying, because of his trick of leaving one project for another, his passion for beginning again, and his utter inability to be really satisfied with anything he had done. It was always the next model of a horse that was going to be the perfect one. On the whole, Leonardo was very well and kindly treated by the Sforza family. And, although war ploughed its way through the pleasant fields of his life, he never suffered in soul through its destructions as Michael Angelo did.

We have already noticed, in our chapters on art, Leonardo's extraordinary method of painting a picture. To an outsider it seemed that most of his time was spent in front of the easel in rapt contemplation, the brush idle. A vision seemed to enfold him; he forgot about the passage of time, forgot to eat and drink. The fruit of this long sojourn in the mysterious land of the spirit would be a few brush strokes. But those, piled one on another during the patient years, created a picture like the Mona Lisa, perhaps the most wonderful portrait of a woman yet known.

THE TRAIL OF HAPPINESS THAT LEONARDO LEFT BEHIND HIM

Leonardo travelled a great deal up and down Italy, working for this person and that. Wherever he went he left a radiant memory of his delightful personality and conversation. He must have been the most brilliant man in a brilliant generation. He never lost his passion for mathematics and invention, and more than once was employed as a military engineer during the small wars troubling Italy at this time. As he got older he became still

more trying to his patrons. Pope Leo wanted him badly to paint some pictures for him, in company with Michael Angelo and Raphael. But Leonardo gave himself up to working out his lovely dream of a flying machine, and the Pope waited for his pictures in vain.

In 1515 Leonardo passed into the service of the King of France, and presently went to live near his patron. He was getting old and soon laid down his brush. He died in 1519 at Amboise, in France.

Italy could not know then, with Raphael only a year longer to live, that her two supreme painters were passing. One had made the name of Florence glorious, another the name of Urbino.

It must have been a matter of regret to the proud Florentines that Raphael could not in any case be claimed by them. Urbino lay on the other side of the Apennines, outside the Tuscan border. Raphael was born there in 1483. His father was a painter—not very distinguished, but of sufficient merit to form an excellent master for his son. The boy was of a sweet-tempered, serious nature, and passed his childhood very happily. He must have learned to draw at a very early age, for when he was only eleven his father realised that the boy was outstripping him and needed to be trained under a better artist than he could hope to be.

THE AMAZING SKILL OF YOUNG RAPHAEL WITH HIS BRUSH

Perugino the painter was living in Perugia at that time, and Raphael's father made arrangements for him to take the boy into his studio. A little later Giovanni died, leaving Raphael an orphan.

It seemed that all his energy and thought ran in the one single course of painting. In this way he was very different from Leonardo and Michael Angelo, his two compeers. Before his youth was passed he had attained such skill that all who saw his work marvelled.

When he was twenty-one he paid his first visit to Florence. Just then the Medici were in exile, and the sister of the Duke of Urbino sent a letter of introduction for the young painter to Piero Soderini, who was ruling in the Medici's place. The letter throws a faint light on the Raphael of that time. " He is a discreet and amiable youth," wrote the lady, and she begged that for the sake of his father to whom the Duke had been attached, Soderini would be good to him.

Raphael's chief interest in Florence was the Council Chamber decorations and the cartoons prepared for them by Michael Angelo and Leonardo. All Florence, and indeed towns outside Florence, were talking of the rivalry of these two men, and Raphael lost no time in seeking the Council Chamber. The work he saw there had a tremendous effect on him.

We hear of him presently at Perugia again painting pictures for churches. Then he returned to Florence, and stayed there until he was twenty-five. By this time, although many years younger, he was equal in fame with Leonardo and Michael Angelo. All Italy was whispering about him. But success had not spoiled him; he was still a most indefatigable student and worker. He had none of the tempestuousness of Michael Angelo, none of the exceeding charm and brilliance of Leonardo; he remained the discreet and amiable person recommended to Piero Soderini. And his portrait, painted by himself a little later, fulfils the description of the lady at Urbino.

THE WORK THAT BROUGHT WEALTH AND FAME TO RAPHAEL

Raphael's life was divided into two halves, as Michael Angelo's had been, by the entry into it of Pope Julius II. This powerful old man had got the sculptor in Rome and was furious because Leonardo was busy on some public works in Florence and could not free himself. Julius looked round for another genius. " Where is this young man everyone is talking of ? " he asked. " This Raphael of Urbino ? Send for him at once."

Raphael was in Florence at the time, with two or three pictures not quite finished. When the Pope's summons came he dared not delay an hour. He begged Bartolommeo and Ghirlandajo to finish the work for him, and went to Rome with all speed. There he was set to work on the famous wall paintings in the Vatican.

Raphael made a number of friends in Rome, rich men and men of letters. He found himself famous above all others, and wealthy. He was called The Master, and pupils paid him a court unequalled in the realm of art since. None of the bitter trials that marred Michael Angelo's life and work came his way.

Leonardo, then an old man, came to Rome, and lived in Raphael's house with him. His other friends, like Bartolommeo, also came, and each had the same friendliness given them—a friendliness touched with a charming deference in the case of Leonardo. Raphael seemed not to know what it was to be jealous or bitter. His fellow artists, with the exception perhaps of poor, difficult Michael Angelo, never knew what it was to feel any rivalry in Raphael. But Rome seemed to divide itself in half, one part extolling Raphael, the other Michael Angelo, as the greatest artist on earth.

HOW THE FAME OF THE MASTER SPREAD TO OTHER LANDS

As the work at the Vatican, the wall paintings, the cartoons for the Sistine tapestries, drew to a close, Raphael had become famous not only in Italy but in Europe. Henry the Eighth of England and Francis the First of France both invited him to Court, with no result. He stayed in Rome; succeeded Bramante as architect to the Pope, now Leo X, in 1514; and a little later on he became Inspector of Antiquities in Rome, with full power to buy any art treasures he wished. A great number of men, architects, sculptors, painters, wood-carvers, mosaic workers, were employed by him, and his workshops were as friendly as his house. Such was the man's gift for genial and courteous living.

A large body of pupils, about fifty, went with him daily to and from his studio. Michael Angelo met him, and scowled, and said something about Raphael walking as if at the head of an army. The painter laughed and said that he, Michael Angelo, looked like an executioner on his way to the scaffold.

THE FINE TRIBUTE TO RAPHAEL IN THE LETTER OF A FRIEND

But Raphael did not walk at the head of his army a great while longer. He laid down his brush in the prime of life. In 1520 one of his friends wrote to another at Venice: " On the night of Good Friday, the most gentle and excellent of painters, Raphael of Urbino, died, to the infinite grief of all men, but especially of the learned for whom . . . he was preparing a plan of the antique monuments of Rome . . . Now this glorious work has been interrupted by the envious hand of Death, who has robbed us of this youthful master at the age of 37, and on his own birthday."

IN THE BATTLE OF JUTLAND LITTLE JACK CORNWELL STOOD AT HIS GUN TO THE LAST
The story is told on page 6196. This picture, issued by the Fine Arts Publishing Company, is by Mr. Frank Salisbury.

The Great Stories of the World That Will Be Told for Ever

THE RACE FOR THE LIFEBOAT

A LITTLE girl named Margaret, who was born and bred in a fishing village on the Scottish coast, was sleeping alone with her mother one summer night.

While the dark hours wore away the wind rose, and the waves grew big and threatening as they came dashing on to the rocky shore. The mothers and sisters in the fisher cottages awoke and started at the sound. They knew that it meant danger to their dear ones away in the fishing-boats.

As morning dawned they stood on the shore straining their eyes in search of sails. While they waited there in trouble and fear they saw, to their dismay, a ship heaving up and down on the waves, drifting nearer and nearer to the sharp rocks, and helpless to save herself.

The little crowd of women, children, and feeble old men on the beach stretched out their hands helplessly toward the men in the rigging. There was not a fishing-boat left on the shore; all the strong men and boys were away fishing, and who among that group of people could have launched a boat in such a sea? Yet it was heart-breaking to watch men perish before their eyes. " If only the lifeboat men could know! " cried a woman.

Margaret heard what she said, and a bright thought came to her. She asked if the ship could hold together while she ran for the lifeboat four miles away along the coast. Someone shouted that she would not be able to cross the stream, but Margaret was off. Four miles, and the flooded burn lay before her! It raged like an animal; its banks were flooded; and, worst of all, the small plank bridge had been carried away in the rushing flood.

Into the water Margaret plunged. It nearly carried her off her feet, and she gasped and shuddered as it chilled her through and through. Then, rallying all her strength, she forced her body against the current, and inch by inch pressed on. And so the worst was over, and she was out of the stream.

At last the tottering feet of this brave little maid reached the village street, and she had just strength to cry out that there was a ship on the rocks before she lost consciousness. But she had done her work. Kind womanly hands clasped her, and the crew of the lifeboat were quickly in their places. The boat was launched.

Margaret's deed was not in vain, for the lifeboat was in time, and saved the crew of the ship on the rocks.

IMAGINATION · CHIVALRY · LEGENDS · GOLDEN DEEDS · FAIRY TALES

STEFAN OF RUMANIA

STEFAN CEL MARE is one of the national heroes of Rumania. He reigned in Moldavia for nearly the whole of the second half of the fifteenth century.

During his reign King Stefan fought fifty battles, of which he lost only two. They were nearly all against the Turks. His country was the gateway between the Christian and Mohammedan worlds. He fought not only for the country but for its faith, so much so that, although he was Orthodox, the Pope sent him a crown and gave him the title of Defender of the Faith.

Once, having lost a battle and been badly wounded, Stefan fled to the castle where his fair wife and his loving mother were safely hidden. He arrived in the dead of night. A cold wind was howling in the darkness and the rain was falling fast. He banged at the castle gate, and his mother appeared at an opening and said, " Who is that knocking? "

" Your son Stefan," came the reply.

" Thou liest," was the answer. " My son would only come back if he were victorious, or else die for his country."

" Oh, give me entrance, my wounds are sore," Stefan cried, but the answer came:

" Go, if thou really be my son. Shame not my white hairs, but go and die on the battlefield for thy country. Let the old and young crown thy grave with flowers, and not thy old age with the name of traitor. Get thee hence! "

Not a word said Stefan, but he turned the head of his weary horse and climbed the mountain-side to a lonely place where a hermit lived.

He asked the hermit's advice as to what course he should follow. The wise old man, pointing to the valley below, where the scattered army lay, said:

" Thou hast the right to make thy country into a graveyard, but not to give it as a prey to thy foes."

Straightway Stefan sounded his bugle. The followers who were left alive came to his side, and he sent them to gather the people for the defence of their land.

Then, in some miraculous way, Stefan found himself at the other side of the country, where he came to a little house with an old woman sitting at the door.

" Good-morrow, good man, what is thy name and thy errand? " she asked. " I have but little to give, but if thou wilt take of what I have I will share it with pleasure," she said.

" I am Stefan, and I want men to fight for the country," said the weary prince.

" I have seven grown sons; take them," the old woman said. " It breaks my heart to part with them, but they are yours."

Stefan won the battle and gave the old woman her sons again, and to the seven sons he gave the seven mountains near their home, which still bear the name of the Seven Brothers.

Stefan went on fighting for the rest of his life, and died of a wound. His old age was crowned with the famous name of Stefan cel Mare—Stephen the Great.

THE MAN WHO WENT THROUGH FIRE

THE scene of this story is the great oil wells on the side of Persia that slopes down into Iraq.

Glowing oil furnaces drive the pumps of a great petroleum well in a village where Robert Leiper Lindsay is in charge, with James Still as his assistant.

Now imagine this. Suddenly a valve bursts, and a hissing gust of oil spurts into the air under a pressure of 700 pounds to the square inch. The open, blazing furnaces are only thirty yards away, and the air around is filled with the liquid fuel they burn. If the oil in the air is set on fire the whole compound will be destroyed.

The quick mind of Lindsay sees at once that the pumps must be stopped and the supply of oil feeding the furnaces must be cut off; so he calls to his assistant to shut off the pumps, and sets out to cut off the furnace supply.

But to get to the furnaces he must pass through the fountain of streaming oil, and arrive at the furnaces with his clothes saturated with petroleum. He knows what the end will be, but he does not shrink. He passes through the oil shower, turns off the oil-tap of the furnaces, and then turns away, and falls, a blazing torch.

His assistant is successful in shutting off the pumps, but is cut off by heat and smoke, and is almost stifled. He manages, however, to escape through a window and limit the damage, so that the work of the well can go on.

He lived, too, to bear witness to the undaunted heroism of his mate, whom duty had carried to almost instant death.

VIEILLARD-CHRYSANTHEME

This is a French translation of the story told in English on page 3496

Il y avait une fois un grand seigneur et un brave jardinier qui avaient une chose en commun, leur amour profond pour les fleurs.

Souvent Tsugaru quittait son palais pour se rendre au jardin, et ses courtisans pour le vieux Kikuo; ensemble ils discouraient des soins à donner aux plantes. Ils aimaient surtout les chrysanthèmes; en effet, Kikuo était un sobriquet qui voulait dire Vieillard-Chrysanthème: on l'avait surnommé ainsi à cause de son habileté à cultiver ces fleurs.

Un jour un ennemi fit la guerre à Tsugaru, tua ses soldats, incendia son palais, et foula aux pieds son jardin. Tout le monde s'enfuit devant les troupes victorieuses de l'ennemi; seul Kikuo resta avec son maître jusqu'à ce que tout espoir fût perdu; alors il s'enfuit avec lui dans les montagnes.

Tsugaru était navré; d'ailleurs son existence luxueuse ne l'avait guère préparé à la vie rude qu'il lui fallait mener; il tomba malade et mourut, la main dans celle de son fidèle jardinier.

Kikuo était si triste qu'il ne lui restait aucun désir de vivre, pas même pour revoir une fleur. Mais, au bout d'un jour, il sortit de son abattement, et fit les préparatifs nécessaires à l'enterrement de son maître. Il voulait autant que possible faire honneur à son seigneur. Il n'y avait pas d'argent pour payer un cortège superbe, avec des prêtres, des bannières, et un tombeau magnifique. Tout ce que Kikuo put faire fut de planter autour de la tombe de son maître une bordure de ses fleurs favorites, large de trente mètres.

Kikuo vécut des années dans les montagnes, cultivant ce nouveau jardin. Enfin, à l'âge de quatre-vingt-deux ans, il tomba malade à son tour.

Un soir, il entendit des chuchotemens devant sa cabane, et, levant la tête, il vit à l'entrée une foule de beaux petits enfants vêtus d'or, de blanc, et de rose. Ces petits lui tendaient les bras, et l'appelaient d'une voix caressante ressemblant au souffle du vent dans les herbes:

" Kikuo ! Nous sommes tes Enfants-Chrysanthèmes. Nous t'aimons, Kikuo. Nous voudrions te venir en aide, mais c'est impossible. Tu mourras dans trente jours. Mais où tu iras nous te suivrons, cher père ! "

Soudain la vision s'évanouit. Le lendemain, le vieillard raconta l'histoire à un bûcheron de ses amis, qui venait le soigner pendant sa maladie. Et, en effet, trente jours plus tard le vieux jardinier s'endormit pour la dernière fois, et lorsque le bûcheron se rendit à la tombe de Tsugaru, il n'y restait pas un seul chrysanthème. Tsugaru et Kikuo, entourés des Enfants-Chrysanthèmes, s'étaient retrouvés dans quelque jardin bienheureux.

HEROES OF THE LIGHTHOUSE

A TALE that stirs our blood and makes us proud of mankind comes from France, from the lighthouse at Kerdonis, Belle-Isle. In the lighthouse were the keeper and his wife and their two children, the elder of whom was only ten.

While repairing his lantern the lighthouseman was taken ill. Though she alone could help him, and though his life was in danger, his wife left his side to light the lamp, and then returned to find him dying. Suddenly the little boy cried, " Mother, the lamp is not turning ! "

The lighthouse lamp was one of those which go round and round. Should it remain fixed it would deceive sailors at sea, and probably wreck their ships. Again the poor woman left her dying husband to examine the machinery, only to find that it had completely broken down.

The grief-stricken mother then took her boy and girl, who sat weeping by their father's bed, and set them to turn the lamp by hand all through the night.

They sat in the tower, this little brother and sister, aged seven and ten, faithfully turning the lantern; nor did they rest from nine oclock at night till seven the next morning, for the night was black and a tempest raged at sea.

By their united strength the lantern was made to revolve throughout the stormy night, and while they turned the lantern to give light and save life the light passed out of their father's eyes and the life passed out of his body. Below their mother was weeping over their dead father.

Help came from outside too late to save him, or to spare the tiny heroes from the vigil of this dreadful night.

JACK CORNWELL

JOHN TRAVERS CORNWELL was first-class boy on the Chester, one of the British ships at the battle of Jutland, in May 1916.

In the official despatches describing that terrible contest, many names were mentioned of gallant officers who performed lustrous deeds; many instances were cited of the fine handling of ships which make a Briton's blood leap with pride; but in all this stirring record was nothing to excel the story of the boy Cornwell.

His admiral, Sir David Beatty, singled him out for mention above all others, this unassuming, gallant-hearted lad. Let this famous sailor tell us the story in his own official language.

Boy (1st class) John Travers Cornwell, of the Chester, was mortally wounded early in the action.

He nevertheless remained standing alone at a most exposed post till the end of the action, with the gun's crew dead and wounded all around him. He was under sixteen and a half years.

I regret that he has since died, but I recommend his case for special recognition in justice to his memory, and as an acknowledgment of the high example set by him.

Jack was sight-setter for the gun. This necessitated his being stationed during the fighting in a quite unprotected position. Within less than five minutes of the opening of the battle his gun was put out of action by an enemy shell, and at the same moment he was wounded to death.

But, says his captain, " he remained steady at his most exposed post at the gun, waiting for orders. His gun would not bear on the enemy; all but two of the ten of the gun-crew were killed or wounded, and he was the only one who was in such an exposed position. *But he felt he might be needed*, and, indeed, he might have been; so he stayed there, standing and waiting under heavy fire, with just his own brave heart and God's help to support him."

First-class Boy Cornwell felt himself one of those whom England expected to do their duty.

They bore him back to Grimsby, and there, in the hospital, the nurses asked him how the battle had gone. " Oh, we carried on all right," he said simply.

He knew of our victory and was content, and he said nothing of his own immortal deed. He lived only twenty-four hours after being carried into the hospital, and his mother arrived from London too late. " I know Mother is coming; give her my love," were his last words.

The little hero's body was buried at Manor Park Cemetery, but when the news of his heroism was published he became a national hero. Dead though he be, his memory has become immortal.

THE BOY WHO SAVED HIS FAMILY

ABOUT two hundred years ago the Huguenots, who were the Protestants of France, were being bitterly persecuted for their religious beliefs. In the village of Thorigne lived a weaver named Daniel Bonnet. He had a wife and three children, the youngest being a little boy of five.

As they were Huguenots, suffering great hardships, they decided to leave France and go to America, where they would be free to worship God in whatever way they liked.

When all was ready they started off; but in order to get away safely they put their three children on the back of a donkey and covered them over with vegetables. Then they set off as though they were going to market, for if it had been known that they were going they would have been stopped.

Not long after they had left the village one of the soldiers saw them, and, suspecting that they had hidden their children under the vegetables, he rode up and said with a sneer: " Going to market are you? Then I will try if your carrots are tender."

With that he drove his sword into the load on the donkey's back with all his might, but, hearing no sound, he thought he must have been mistaken in his suspicions, and galloped off.

We can imagine the agony which the poor parents felt. They dared not stop to see what had happened, but had to go on until they were far away from everyone and out of sight.

When at last they took off the vegetables they found their little boy had been stabbed through the thigh. The little fellow looked up at them, and said, feebly but with pride : " But I did not speak, Mother," and then fainted away.

Thanks to his courage, the family were able to escape across the sea, and to found a new home in a happier land.

Nature's Wonderful Living Family in Earth and Air and Sea

This picture of Summer, by E. A. Hornel, is the property of the Walker Art Gallery

BUTTERFLIES AND MOTHS

HUMAN genius has never invented anything lovelier than a butterfly, or anything as wonderful. In the lore and legend of the ancients, in the fairy tales beloved by us all, nothing excels the surprise, the startling succession from repulsiveness to dainty charm, of this creature's strange career.

It is a delightful fact that any child may observe for itself the entire amazing life-cycle of these little wonder people of the gardens and the wilds, beginning with the tiny egg, feeding the caterpillar which results, guarding the chrysalis into which the grub passes, and finally witnessing the rending of that tomb-like husk, and the bursting forth of a winged thing of the air, lovely as a floating flower, scented like one, the perfect butterfly.

Men deeply versed in the subject have sought to classify the eggs in the hope of recognising species by them, but the attempt fails. Take the eggs from their natural surroundings and mix them with others, and they are hopeless as a guide. And the difficulties go deeper than that. There are times when, in the presence of the perfect insect, we are puzzled to say why one is a butterfly and another a moth. It is simple enough to distinguish between a clothes moth and a cabbage-haunting butterfly; but there are features in which moths so closely approach the butterflies as to make it a delicate matter to define the border line.

In effect the border line is much less sharply drawn by Nature than by entomologists. We who have followed this course of study have seen in almost every aspect of higher life how one form emerges in another, how, though many links are snapped, sufficient remain to reveal to us the unity, the one-ness of Creation, the branching out of a multitude of species from a common stem.

And so it is here again. There are definite formulas to guide us, but exceptions abound to keep alive our sense of the extremely fluid character of the boundaries between the two kinds of our present group.

First, then, a butterfly flies by day, a moth by night. That holds good to this extent, that butterflies never fly by night; but, as against that, there are many moths which fly by day. Indeed, in warm latitudes, where bats and other night-flying enemies of insects abound, moths which pursue their calling in the hours of darkness are rarities.

PREHISTORIC LIFE · MAMMALS · BIRDS · REPTILES · FISHES · INSECTS

Another comprehensive rule is that butterflies have their antennae thickened at the extremities, after the manner of little clubs, while moths have their antennae fringed or feathered. But we look at a Burnet moth to find thickened antennae-ends here, and are reminded again that our law is not without exceptions.

A LITTLE STRANGER THAT WAS WORTH ITS WEIGHT IN DIAMONDS

Rule number three is that the butterfly, when at rest, raises its wings over its back, so that they are at an angle of 90 degrees to the body, whereas the moth reposes, with its wings down, in penthouse fashion, the rear wings hooked to the front pair. Yet some kinds of Skipper butterflies when resting flatten out their wings moth-wise, though they are free of the hook-and-eye attachments.

Not that we know all there is to be learned. There is always the possibility of fresh discoveries even in lands so thoroughly worked over as Great Britain. During 1924 Frederick Weiss, a professor at Manchester University, reported the presence, in numbers, of unique moths which had a fine family in the hollow of a tree on Kersal Moor, near Manchester.

In no respect more wonderful than any other moth, this little stranger was deemed worth more than its weight in diamonds from the fact that it had never before been seen alive in England. If we but knew how that family of moths came to so unlikely a place we should have a new chapter to add to the fascinating story of the migration of these frail insects.

These migrations are mystifying. We receive from the Continent, sometimes as single spies, sometimes in whole battalions, the Clouded Yellow, the Pale Clouded Yellow butterflies, the lovely Painted Lady, the Red Admiral; sometimes, too, though more rarely, the precious Black-veined White, the Bath White, the Camberwell Beauty, and the Long and the Short Tailed Blues.

THE MYSTERY OF THE PAINTED LADY'S YEARLY FLIGHT OVERSEA

Darwin saw clouds of butterflies streaming out to sea from South America; more recently they have been seen bravely flying 1200 miles from the nearest possible land, Africa. Midsummer madness or the might of an overwhelming air current must be responsible for such great flights as these, but the regular occurrence of flocks of butterflies from the Continent within our island gates makes us wonder whether they come by accident or design.

Does our lovely voyaging Painted Lady yearly set her wings at a venture and flap careless with the singing sea winds, or is she fired with the impulse which animates the birds, to go forth and conquer new worlds for her children?

We are as puzzled to see the little beauties mounted on jewelled wings in our midst, as people in an arid land are to see dry watercourses suddenly become torrents in the midst of unbroken drought. The torrents have come because heavy rains have fallen far away; the butterflies have come to us, because some wordless order from Nature has bidden them rise and fly to us and elsewhere, their Promised Land. We see the effect but dimly surmise the cause.

The unexpected coming to us of these fair visitors from afar does not exhaust the perplexities of distribution. We find just as much food for wonder in the goings and comings of species which are our own. Which is the more thrilling, the finding by Professor Weiss of rare moths in a tree hollow on a Manchester moor or the amazing story of the moths of an Argyllshire coalmine?

EXQUISITE GEMS OF BEAUTY FROM NATURE'S MATCHLESS STORE

Here we have no rare moth, but common examples of the Noctulids, as strangely housed as those frogs, toads, and birds which have been found in the workings of gold mines in South Africa. Presumably Noctulid eggs or caterpillars must have been carried down this coalpit on fodder bought for the mine ponies. For there are the moths and their young, breeding in rapidly succeeding generations, the caterpillars feeding on the horse's fodder, the moths maturing, flying in the darkness and laying more eggs where the caterpillars may profitably pass their youth.

The way in which moths and butterflies hide their eggs must often effect remarkable changes of habitat in this way, but there is a twin mystery of a different order attaching to the question.

It should be advantageous for the eggs to lie snug and unobserved of creatures to which an insect egg is a dainty. Yet eggs of the moth and butterfly are among the most exquisite gems of beauty;

lustrous as pearls, daintier than hand-wrought jewels, fluted, ribbed, patterned in a score of different ways, perfect as works of art, yet contrived with marvellous skill for the admission of the substance which renders them fertile, and compounded of such material as to afford the larvae their first meal from the shells when hatching has taken place.

Such beauty as this, we might think, would but render the eggs conspicuous and so expose them to danger; there is safety in obscurity. But the plan succeeds, and the charm of form, texture, and colouration by which the eggs are characterised must be accepted as another item of evidence that Nature has, throughout her scheme, the same desire for beauty which she reveals in the features of a lovely woman, in the colours of the rainbow, in the eye of a deer, in the grace of a tiger, and the symmetry of a noble tree.

The second element of mystery as to the eggs is how the parents know where to lay them.

Any boy or girl collector knows where to look for the eggs or larvae of the species. They know what to expect from the dead nettle, from the privet, from the lime, from the cabbage, from the oak and the apple.

A SUPREMELY WONDERFUL THING IN THE LIFE OF A CATERPILLAR

The perfect insect goes back to the foliage or tree-trunk on which it was nurtured in an earlier form of existence. This is supremely wonderful. No moth or butterfly eats. At most they drink the nectar of sugary flowers, or, as in the case of the dashing Red Admiral, sip the juices of decaying flesh or the fluid of a puddle. But solid food has no meaning for them. They have no mouth parts for such food; some have not even the apparatus for the taking of moisture.

Yet all lay their eggs in a place which is to be cradle and larder to the caterpillars into which those eggs will turn. Each moth or butterfly goes back to its appointed plant or other growth to deposit its eggs, never straying to the wrong sort. Their progeny will inherit the riches in which they themselves can have no share.

It is always the right food on which they lay their eggs. Some caterpillars are such lusty fellows that they thrive on a generalised diet, and can go from one plant type to another without ill effect. Generally, however, there is one food, and one only, for a species, and if that fails, the caterpillar will die in the midst of abundance, starved where a myriad other caterpillars of different species flourish. The parents, to whom solid food has no meaning, infallibly find it for the offspring which they may never live to see, which will never be able to return them thanks.

THE UNERRING INSTINCT THAT ANSWERS NATURE'S SOUNDLESS CALL

In a sense, but only partially, this return to the cradle stock resembles the return of the adult cuckoo for egg-laying to nests similar to that in which it was reared. But the cuckoo passes through no transformation, no stage of forgetting. It is fed by its foster parents and remembers them, their nests, and their habits.

Between the caterpillar stage and that of the perfect insect there is a gulf as of living death, when all recollection of food eaten must be obliterated. Yet Nature, by some secret, soundless call, hails the parent to the appointed tree or bush or weed, and there, on the very substance essential to the creature yet unborn, the egg is fixed. There is no more perfect example in the world of unerring instinct.

Like the flies, the moths and butterflies when they leave the chrysalis are fully developed; there is no after-growth for them, whether they be tiny moths of the leaf-mining group, a mere eighth of an inch across the wings, or the giant Atlas moth of Africa, the Titan of all the Lepidoptera, which, of bat-like proportions, has a wing span of nearly a foot !

For the three stages of life, the larva, the chrysalis, and the perfect insect, or imago, condition, the caterpillar must eat such quantities of food that all actual growth may be then accomplished. The succeeding steps are those of change, not extension of size.

MAGIC OF THE BUTTERFLY'S GLORIES REVEALED IN ONE BIG WORD

The ugly word Lepidoptera is the scientific description of the whole order of moths and butterflies. It tells in a single group of letters the magic of the butterfly's glories. All these insects have their wings covered with scales, and their name means scale-winged.

Not the faintest suggestion occurs in the make-up of a caterpillar that such a process is to be wrought in its adult condition. The skin may be smooth, it may be spiny, hairy, armed with sharp prickles tipped with natural gum, but never a vestige of scales. Except that it has a very complicated head, with tough, horny jaws, eyes, and feelers, it might be a worm with legs.

Yet how different is its career from that of the worm. Having eaten the shells of the eggs from which they emerge, the caterpillars begin a campaign of gorging and splitting. There is no other word for it. They live to eat. Behind the head are three pairs of jointed, horny legs and claws which serve in the main to grip the food on which the larva feeds.

These occupy that part of the body which will be the chest or thorax of the butterfly, and from which three pairs of legs and two pairs of wings will arise. From the rear part of the caterpillar's body spring four pairs of fleshy false legs, pro-legs as they are called, which will vanish in the chrysalis stage. Behind these again are two claspers at the end of the body.

THE ENORMOUS APPETITE OF DIFFERENT FORMS OF LARVAL LIFE

These claspers play an important part in the activities of geometer caterpillars, commonly known as span worms. Here the larvae have only two pairs of pro-legs instead of the customary three, and, instead of marching forward with the flowing motion of the ordinary caterpillar, it arches its body, then, gripping by the claspers and pro-legs, throws itself forward, retaining its grip in the manner described until the fore part of the body has reached a new position.

Like most other insects, caterpillars breathe by means of air tubes which open to the surface of the body. These we may see for ourselves along the sides of the body. The grub dies if these are sealed, and so it is a matter for wonder that the poor thing does not meet with disaster when the time comes for it to moult. For the caterpillar does moult; its entire skin has to be cast, again and again.

It eats and eats till it can eat no more, till the body has grown so great that its skin must burst unless the larva gets out of it As the time of crisis approaches the grub grows lethargic and its appetite fails. It might be sickening for death instead of for a new jacket, so ill it seems.

But at the appointed moment the skin splits down the back, and out crawls the caterpillar with a new and lustrous skin already in position beneath that which it discards as outgrown.

Appetite again returns, and once more the story of gorging is continued. The amount of food eaten is truly enormous, when we consider the size of the diner. The privet hawk-moth caterpillar devours 11,000 times its own weight in food during its larval life. The larva of Polyphemus consumes three-quarters of a pound of leaves and half an ounce of water during its lusty two months' career, a quantity equal to 86,000 times the weight of itself at birth.

THE PLUNDERERS OF MAN'S CULTIVATED FOOD PLANTS

It is not surprising, then, that caterpillars can do enormous damage to the cultivated food plants and trees of mankind; and that the last part of their name should apparently come from " piller "—a plunderer.

A caterpillar that is a menace to apple-growers is that of the winter moth. Female winter moths are wingless. They lay their eggs on the branches of fruit trees and die. The caterpillars devour the foliage, then, when about to undergo their change, descend to the ground and bury themselves in the earth or in crannies of the bark of the tree.

The new generation of males, when they leave the pupa stage, fly like other moths; but the females, in order to meet their mates and lay their eggs, must climb the tree trunks, like caterpillars. To prevent them from getting up and sowing the seeds of ruin amid the branches, fruit-growers placed bands of grease-proof paper heavily smeared with a thick treacly substance round the boles of the trees. Thus thousands of crawling females were caught.

THE FRUIT-GROWER'S WAY WITH HIS CATERPILLAR FOES

At times their numbers were so great that, like the rabbits which at last over-top the wire defences of Australian farms, using the heaps of their own dead as a footpath, the females of the winter moth were able to crawl over *their* dead to the boughs beyond.

Grease-banding of trees is still prac-tised, but most fruit-growers nowadays deal with the winter-moth caterpillars by means of spraying their trees with an arsenical wash. This poisons the caterpillars' food without damaging the tree.

Another of the apple-grower's enemies is the caterpillar of the codlin moth. This caterpillar eats its way into an apple, and the fruit farmer protects his apples by spraying the young fruit with the lead arsenate as soon as the petals of the blossom have fallen. This poisons the young caterpillar when it begins its journey into the apple. Sometimes the lead arsenate has to be applied several times during June and July; and in the U.S.A., codlin moths produce so many broods that apples have to be sprayed right up to the time they are picked, after which they have to be washed before they are sold.

In our own gardens we have sometimes seen the melancholy skeletons of cabbages bearing witness to the vast appetite of the caterpillars of the Large and Small White butterflies often called Cabbage butterflies—and to the gardener's neglect; and many of us have made extra pocket money by collecting caterpillars from cabbage leaves.

It is indeed fortunate for man that the caterpillar hosts are reduced by the weather, and by birds, mice, moles, and certain insects which feed on them.

THE GOAT-MOTH CATERPILLAR'S AMAZING POWER OF DESTRUCTION

One of the heartiest eaters among caterpillars is that of the goat-moth, which finally reaches a weight 72,000 times as great as the weight it represented when newly hatched from the egg. But the goat-moth caterpillar is one of the marvels of the tribe. Its egg is laid in a chink in the bark, whence, when hatched, the larva creeps into the tree, gnawing a way before it as it goes.

At first its tunnellings are small, like itself, but as time goes on these become considerable, so that at the end of three, four, or five years of the larval stage the caterpillar has done serious damage to the tree which is its home and its meals.

But there are other places than the interior of oak trees for caterpillars. We find them in the woods of many trees, in reeds, down in the soil among roots, but, of course, mainly on the foliage of vegetation. For defence, most of them depend upon protective resemblance to their surroundings. The beautiful markings of the hawk-moth caterpillars harmonise extraordinarily with their leafy background flecked with light, and so do the colour schemes of hundreds of others.

THE CATERPILLAR'S WONDERFUL LIFE-LINE OF SELF-SPUN SILK

Those that are less highly specialised in colour scheme retire to the soil when day dawns, or tunnel the leaves and live there, or spin tents of web and live in numbers together. Others are defended from enemies by poisonous hairs.

Then there are the leaf-rollers, which cement together two sides of a leaf or two different leaves, and in that make their home, rendered snug by a couch of web spun from their silk gland. They leave open one end of the retreat, and from that, at the first sign of danger, they back out, spin a strand of web, and so descend out of harm's way. Many others have the same reliance on this self-furnished lifeline, and we may see hosts of caterpillars lowering themselves from lime and poplar and oak, swaying from the ladder of silk which is being fabricated before our eyes from the gland beneath the head.

It is in this situation that the poisonous species distil their venom. Some merely cause a flow of virus at a touch, but others, like the puss-moth larva, spit out their poison a considerable distance, like little snakes, which at the moment they seem to resemble. These caterpillars are to be avoided by unshaded eyes, for the fluid causes great pain, temporary blindness, and blistering of a sensitive skin.

WHEN THE GREAT HOUR COMES FOR THE MOTH AND THE CATERPILLAR

Well, whatever the kind, the great hour comes for change. The last meal has been eaten; the caterpillar must prepare for the paramount marvel of its life. It is to become a chrysalis. With the butterflies the outer skin goes, a wisp of silk is woven round the golden husk, and all is over. But the moths invest themselves in elaborate domains of silk.

The woolly bears weave their now useless hairs into their silken cocoons; the larvae of the Dicranura masticate such difficult material as wood and even sandstone, and mix that with their silk.

Most wonderful of all, a recently discovered African moth, of the Nyctemera group, wraps itself in a cloak of bubbles of its own creating, like the citadel of the cuckoo-spit, and in that passes its time of trance.

Some moths and butterflies have two batches of eggs a year; some only one. Adult insects will in most cases result in the same season from the earlier batch of eggs. Those laid later in the year may carry the cycle as far as the chrysalis stage, which will suffice to withstand the rigours of winter.

THE MARVELLOUS TRANSFORMATION WITHIN THE CHRYSALIS

There are cases, of course, like the goat-moth and the hawk-moths and others, in which the caterpillars themselves sleep through the winter. The writer had an experience of this with 250 tiger-caterpillars, which were accidentally starved for a fortnight at a critical time of their career, yet survived, thin and miserable, to resume feeding at Christmas and to complete their change in the following year.

Within the chrysalis a marvellous transformation takes place. Not always, for we do not permit it to happen with the majority of silk-moth cocoons. This moth, however, has become an entirely domesticated species, bred in captivity. The females do not seek to fly away, nor the caterpillars to wander, but rest in the place where they are hatched and fed.

Silk of unmatched quality is produced by these caterpillars, woven, scores and scores of yards of thread to a single cocoon, to form a rest and refuge while the change from grub to moth is achieved. Only a sufficient number to keep up stocks is permitted to undergo the complete change. The remainder, when the cocoons are spun and the caterpillar deeply entranced within, are steeped in hot water, which destroys life and leaves the human owner to unwind the silk and weave it.

Probably bees have been the most beneficial insects we have ever had, but from the dawn of trade and manufacture no other little creature has so romantically enriched the world as the silkworm moth.

THE ROMANTIC ORIGIN OF THE SILK INDUSTRY IN EUROPE

For thousands of years silk has been an abundant industry in China. From China silk-moth eggs were stolen by two Persian monks nearly 1500 years ago, and brought hidden in hollow bamboos to Europe. From that small stock descended all the silkworms which, century after century, spun the silk that made France and Italy

famous all over the earth for their products from this delightful material.

During the second part of the nineteenth century disease attacked the European stocks of silk-moths. One of the most important of the industries of two great nations was threatened, and a despairing call was made to that great genius, Louis Pasteur, to check the malady. He had never seen a cocoon, knew nothing of the life-story of the insect. But, nothing doubting, he went to Henri Fabre and asked to see the cocoon which he understood the caterpillars formed.

Fabre handed him one. Pasteur shook it near his ear and said with surprise, " Why, it makes a noise; there's something inside."

Fabre explained that it was the chrysalis, and Pasteur asked him what he meant. " I mean the sort of mummy into which the caterpillar changes before becoming a moth," answered the famous old naturalist.

" And has every cocoon a chrysalis inside it ? " asked the astonished scientist.

" Obviously," replied Fabre; "it is to protect the chrysalis that the caterpillar spins its cocoons."

" Really! " said the great man, humbly. From that time the modest Pasteur studied and toiled, mastered his subject, and stamped out the disease which had baffled Fabre and all the other naturalists.

FROM THE UGLY DUCKLING TO THE BEAUTIFUL SWAN OF THE LEGEND

Yes, the cocoon is to protect the chrysalis during one of the master changes of creation. A loathly grub enters the cocoon, divests itself of its skin for the last time, and lies like a hibernating or paralysed animal. It is quite inert, helpless, so cold that you think it dead unless you hold it in your warm hand and see it faintly wriggle. But as it lies there, motionless, what a miracle of transformation is in progress.

Nothing remains unchanged, save perhaps the system of breathing. Jaws, claws, claspers, pro-legs, digestive system, even the very outline, all go, yet if we patiently watch the horny case day after day, we may see a new wonder coming into existence before our eyes. The shape of the head, legs and thorax gradually appear upon the chrysalis case, the spiracles show themselves along the sides; the first rough draft of the Master Artist's

BRITISH BUTTERFLIES

We give on these pages a series of pictures of British Butterflies in their natural colours, together with the egg, caterpillar, and chrysalis of each. Pictures in colour of Foreign Butterflies and Moths appear on pages 1417 to 1420; pictures of British Moths and their Caterpillars are given facing page 5935; and the Caterpillars of a number of Foreign Moths appear on pages 6209 and 6210.

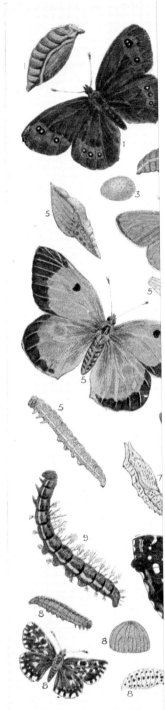

1. Large Skipper (Augiades sylvanus) 2. Pale Clouded Yellow (Colias hyale) 3. Silver spotted Skipper (Augiades comma) 4. Painted Lady (Pyrameis cardui) 5. Silver-washed Fritillary (Argynnis paphia) 6. Large White (Pieris brassicae) 7. Chalk Hill Blue (Lycaena Corydon) 8. Camberwell Beauty (Vanessa antiopa) 9. Large Blue (Nomiades arion)

1. Northern Brown or Scotch A...
or Holly Blue (Cyaniris argiolus)
edusa) 6. White Admiral (Lim...
(Hesperia malvae) 9. Red Ad...

1. C...
3. H...
gonia...

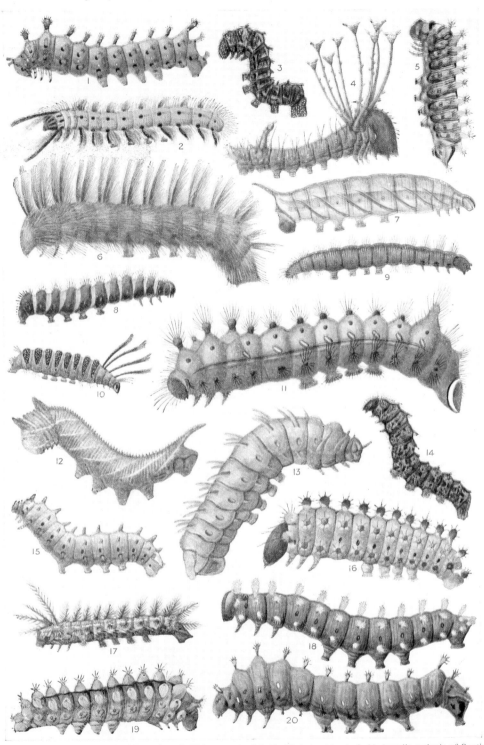

1. Pearl bordered Fritillary
Tip (Euchloe cardamines)
phasia sinapis) 6. Green-
Blue (Lycaena aegon) 9. I

1. Samia gloveri of the Rocky Mountains 2. Vishnu moth of India (Trabala vishnu) 3. Nudaurelia cytheria of South Africa 4. Syssphinx molina of Central America 5. Orizaba silk-moth of Mexico (Rothschildia orizaba) 6. Gonometer robusta of Rhodesia 7. Chaerocampa celeris of India 8. Eusemia bisma of India 9. Anticyra combusta of India 10. Phalanna polymena of India 11. Moon silk-moth of India (Actias selene) 12. Four-horned sphinx of U.S.A. (Ceratonia amyntor) 13. Atlas silk-moth of India (Attacus atlas) 14. Thyella tyrrhaea of South Africa 15. Phylosamia cynthia of China 16. Telea polyphemus of U.S.A. 17. Automeris pamina of U.S.A. 18. Coloradia venata of Argentina 19. Jorulla silk-moth of Mexico (Rothschildia jorulla) 20. Columbian silk-moth of U.S.A. (Samia columbia)

work is seen in low relief on the case of chitin. The given hour arrives and the resurrection has come. A hideous grub has vanished; a winged creature, fair as flowers, is here in its place. The case is slowly forced apart from within and the Sleeping Princess is astir and emerging. Or, if you will, the Ugly Duckling has been transformed, and the Swan of legend is before us.

THE MARVELLOUS COLOURS OF THE SCALES ON A BUTTERFLY'S WING

However, without such aids to appreciation we may for ourselves behold and value the marvel revealed for our delight. Out of the sheltering husk comes a trembling feeble promise of perfection. Its wings are strangely doubled and bent, its scales are all upright, like the coat of a suffering horse. Courage and strength come with the occasion. A rush or blood is swept from the central supply along the veins of the wings, which straighten out and become pinions of power. The scales, packed as we first see them for economy of space in the prison, settle into their correct positions, and the effect is as if new colour and radiance had suddenly descended on the little stranger.

The colour we see on those magic wings is due both to pigments within and also on the walls of the bag-like scales, and to the breaking up of light by the ridges of the scales as they lie on the wing like slates on a roof.

Therefore, something of this majesty of colour is due to that refraction of light which is so familiar in the rainbow, but here is produced by scales our eyes cannot see apart from each other.

Nor is this the end of the tale of beauty and wonder. Butterflies have often been called aerial flowers. Little did those who first bestowed the name dream that butterflies possess not only the colour of flowers, but a kindred scent.

THE SECRET WIRELESS CODE THAT PUZZLES THE NATURALIST

This is not, apparently, the gift of all, but of many, and some common to the knowledge of us all are heirs of the great bequest. In some cases scent glands are local; in others they are widely diffused. The scales of the wings include certain scent plumules, from which a grateful perfume is broadcast, apparently at the will of the owner. We suppose that to be so from the fact that the scent glands

communicate with air tubes, by means of which pneumatic pressure can be exerted to scatter the gracious odour as the butterfly desires.

In our common Clouded Yellow butterfly these scent patches are restricted to well defined areas along the wing, a particular in which this species has its parallel in a tropical representative of our common Brimstone butterfly.

Our Fritillaries have the scent organs along the middle nervures of the fore wings; the Meadow browns and their closest kindred have them on the discs of the fore wings; the Skippers also have scent patches, but in varying positions for different species.

In human society it is women who delight to have scent about their apparel, but in Nature we find only the male butterflies endowed with the gift of creating a sweet atmosphere with which to attract the opposite sex. The fact that she is a lady suffices as recommendation for the female in the moth and butterfly world.

THE MYSTERY OF HOW THE MALE SUITOR TRACES HIS LADY

She can easily trace her scented suitor, but how can he trace her ? There we have another mystery of the Lepidoptera. There seems no doubt that they have means of communication unknown to us. A naturalist places a female moth a prisoner in a tiny open-fronted cage, out in his garden at night, when none of her species appears to be within range. Males flock at once to her dungeon from all quarters of the compass.

" They flew for miles " we often hear it said, but there is no proof as to the distance from which the anxious lovers come. That the presence of a little female of their kind does attract the males in astounding numbers is all we know. Even if they fly to her only from hundreds of yards instead of miles, the fact is sufficiently notable. How do they know, out of sight, out of hearing, that she is there ?

Sight it cannot be, for though moths' eyes are large, and the insects fly well in the dark, the things they see are such as reflect the little light available. All the white flowers which open and scent the air at night are moth lighthouses, stored with nectar for them alone. Even human beings, with their different type of vision, can see white in comparative darkness. But a tiny distant moth ? No, it cannot be vision which draws distant wooers and gallants to the little caged princess.

The more we advance into the mysterious domain of wireless, the more men incline to believe that insects in general, and moths and butterflies in particular, have their own natural equivalent of our artificial system. They may be sending out cries which our ears are too dull to catch, and their antennae may be the aerials to arrest the sound waves so created. We may never know the truth, but it is certain that entomologists will never rest content so long as the mystery remains unsolved.

The great Death's Head moth enters beehives and steals the honey of the workers. The bees could instantly sting it to death if they chose, but because it has a cry similar to the murmuring of their queen they leave it unharmed to pillage them at will. That is a Death's Head habit today, inherited and passed on from generation to generation, but it had a beginning, a conscious inception, as this new habit of the winter moths has had in our own time. There is art, there is craft, there is intelligence of a sort in every phase of animal life, if we have but the patience to explore and the good fortune to discover its operations.

THE ROMANCE AND LOVELINESS OF THE BUTTERFLIES THAT GLADDEN THE EYE

Repellent and destructive in the caterpillar stage, moths and butterflies are things to gladden the eyes and senses in their complete condition. That is, if we can forget the damage for which their progeny is responsible.

Who is there so dead to romance and loveliness as to ban from the scheme of open-air beauties the Admirals, the Peacocks, the Swallow-tails, the noble Swifts, the dashing Hawks and Emperors, the score of species which have Beauty as part of their man-given titles—the Belted Beauty, the Bordered, the Brindled, the Camberwell, the Lilac, the Marbled, the Willow Beauty, and the rest. It is hopeless to begin a catalogue, for it requires entire books to deal with colours, shapes, habits, localities.

Nearly every moth and every butterfly performs useful service, in fertilising the vegetable growths from which it draws its food supplies, or in some compensatory act. Every destructive group of caterpillars has its cousins at work for the good of our land.

Take the clothes-moth, for example. This moth, as a moth, is harmless. It lays its eggs on our woollen clothes, carpets, tapestries, and what not. The caterpillars are the villains of the story; they eat the material and ruin it, spoiling the one good suit which a poor man saves for Sundays and weddings, the one good carpet in his house, the one lovely example of tapestry in church or mansion.

THE PENALTIES OF MAN'S INTERFERENCE WITH THE COURSE OF NATURE

In the very same group of moths are those whose caterpillars are a curse to granaries, where they eat much grain and ruin more. Yet the same tribe affords us excellent allies in the fungus-moth and the four-spotted black, which devours rotting wood and the other sad debris of the wayside.

The natural enemies of caterpillars are birds, innocent reptiles, and insect-eating insects. We have killed the birds and banished the reptiles, and the other parasites cannot keep pace with the enormous increase for which our system of cultivation has made way. Every year we have caterpillar plagues of some sort.

The Pea moth sullies our peas, in which we find its hateful larvae; there is a moth that haunts the foliage of our currants, another that tunnels them; a moth that bores into the stems of corn.

Indeed, we have scarcely a single growth in forest, garden, or moor for which Nature has not provided a hungry parasite in the shape of caterpillar from moth or butterfly. Of the little wretches whose larvae mine the leaves of our flowers and vegetables, already over 200 species are known in England alone; and where they flourish not a plant remains unmarred.

THE CATERPILLAR AS ONE OF THE GRAVEST PROBLEMS OF OUR OPEN-AIR LIFE

Caterpillars are indeed one of the gravest problems of our open-air life. They are the occasion of huge loss to the agriculturist and fruit farmer; they cause unending disappointment and dismay to those whose joy is a garden, large or small.

That is the serious side of the question. The other is concerned with the aesthetic. We like to have butterflies as well as Brussels sprouts and roses, but how to combine them is a puzzle too profound for most of us.

The Story of the Things We See About Us Every Day

THE MAKING OF A TUNNEL

WHEN a new railway is wanted and land cannot be bought, the human moles dig through the clay or gravel deep beneath the city streets; or they blast their way through a rocky mountain or dig beneath a river.

The site of a tunnel having been fixed, a working shaft is first sunk to the required depth. The engineer prefers, if possible, to sink his shaft in clay. If the tunnel is to be continued through good clay, or through dry sand or gravel, a heading will be driven and the sides and roof will be temporarily supported by timber as the work progresses. Later the tunnel is lined with bricks or concrete, the timber supports being removed; or it may be found necessary, as digging progresses, to place iron segments in position ring by ring, especially if the tunnel is near the surface, with heavy weights such as buildings bearing on it.

Sometimes the ground is loose and apt to cave in; sometimes it is water-bearing. Then the tunnellers use the wonderful Greathead shield, which is like a huge section of smooth iron tube with a projecting hood and cutting edge in front.

When tunnelling is to begin the shield is assembled piece by piece at the base of the shaft, and the tunnel is dug out for a short distance. The shield is then pushed forward into the tunnel by several hydraulic rams. Toward the front of the shield is a diaphragm, in which is an opening large enough to allow a man to pass into the fore part, beneath the hood. Here the men who do the actual digging are able to work at the face, passing out through the hole the material, which is hoisted to the surface.

Should water trickle into the workings it is overcome by putting in an airlock at a convenient point so that the pressure of the air in the tunnel can be controlled to keep the water from running in. The air pressure is regulated to balance the water pressure at about the middle of the shield, but even so water seeps in at the bottom. It is prevented from coming into the tunnel by caulking between the segments with which the tunnel is lined. As the workmen in front of the shield dig away to the required distance of one foot eight inches they pug the face of the earth with clay to keep the air from escaping.

Let us now see how the tunnellers made the famous Mersey Tunnel, which was cut largely through Red Triassic sandstone.

INDUSTRIES · HOW THINGS ARE MADE · WHERE THEY COME FROM

The Mersey Tunnel, which joins Liverpool and Birkenhead, is the biggest underwater tunnel in the world. The diameter is 44 feet, or, if the thickness of its walls is included, 46 feet.

NEARLY THREE MILES OF TUNNELS BENEATH THE RIVER MERSEY

The main tunnel is over two miles long, and on both sides of the river are branch tunnels leading to the docks. These have an external diameter of 28 feet. The total length of tunnels is nearly three miles. The construction went forward on several sections simultaneously.

In the first place a shaft was sunk on each side of the river. Both shafts were of 21-feet diameter and 190 feet deep. Until the Red Triassic sandstone was reached it was necessary to line the two shafts with cast iron.

About halfway down the shafts two small tunnels were driven out toward the river from each side. These tunnels were 15 feet wide and 12 feet high, except in two places where circumstances compelled them to be made only of 11 feet 8 inches in diameter. These pilot tunnels were driven on levels that were to be the top and bottom of the main tunnel.

Excavation started with pneumatic hammers, but later explosives were used. To prevent too much cracking of the sandstone, half-pound charges of gelignite were fired, each by a separate fuse.

In all 147,000 pounds of explosive were used in making these tunnels, and when the ends met midway between Birkenhead and Liverpool there was a difference of only about half an inch in the line and level of the halves of the top tunnel and a fraction of an inch more in the case of the lower headings.

HOW THE TOP HALF WAS COMPLETED BEFORE THE LOWER WAS BEGUN

A full-sized section of tunnel was constructed as an experiment, and when the two pilot tunnels were completed early in April 1928 work began on a mile-long section of the tunnel proper.

First of all the top half of the tunnel was made. At intervals along the top pilot tunnel large chambers, nearly 20 feet long, were made. Then excavation was continued from both ends of each chamber until a junction was made with the next. Thus the construction continued, the semi-circular tunnel being lined throughout with cast-iron segments.

A small space was left between the iron lining and the rock face. As the sections were placed in position this space was packed with small pieces of rock and was grouted with sand and cement through holes left in the segments for the purpose. The joints between the segments were closed with lead caulking. Then the tunnel was lined with concrete.

While the top half of the tunnel was being made the debris excavated was passed down chutes into the lower pilot tunnel. Here it fell into skips which were hauled by electric locomotives to the shafts, where electric lifts raised the material to the surface.

The lower half of the main tunnel was then made in a similar way, from the lower pilot tunnel, the two halves being joined and made watertight.

THE GREAT SEMI-CIRCULAR SHIELD AND ITS 24 HYDRAULIC RAMS

There still remained the approach tunnels, two on the Birkenhead side and two in Liverpool, and a junction chamber on each side where the approach tunnels joined the main under-river road. In making the tunnel which runs beneath Dale Street a semi-circular shield was used with a diameter of 46 feet nine and a half inches and a length of 12 feet six inches. As the excavation proceeded the shield, weighing 200 tons, was pushed forward by 24 hydraulic rams exercising a pressure of 2400 tons.

The great junction chambers have concrete side walls five feet thick and the arched roofs are of steel joists and concrete. Excavations were made for the walls and roof, which were built in bit by bit, and not until their completion was the great central mass of rock removed.

During the colossal undertaking of making these underground highways about 800,000 cubic yards of rock and other material, weighing 1,200,000 tons, were removed. More than 82,000 tons of cast-iron lining and a million bolts were used, with 140 miles of lead caulking to make watertight joins between the plates. Steel reinforcement weighed more than 3000 tons, and concrete, 150,000 cubic yards, weighed 270,000 tons. Blasting operations accounted for 560,000 pounds of explosive, and during excavation 7482 million gallons of water were pumped from the workings.

PICTURE-STORY OF TUNNELLING

The first step in making a tunnel is to sink a shaft from which the burrowing out of the earth can be started. In this picture we are looking up a shaft sunk for the making of a tunnel of London's water-supply system.

THE MECHANICAL MOLE AT WORK

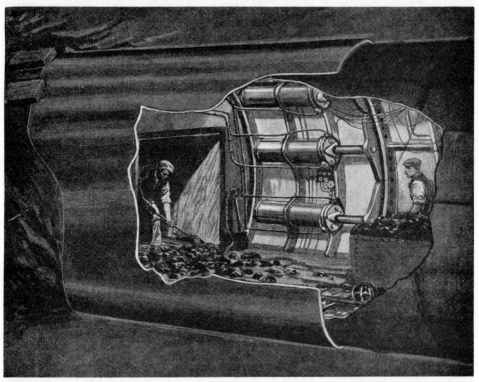

When a tunnel is to be driven through loose or water-bearing ground the wonderful Greathead Shield is used. This is a modern improvement of the shield invented by Brunel for building the Thames Tunnel. The shield, which has a smooth exterior or skin, as it is called, is driven forward by the powerful hydraulic rams seen in the picture. A short tunnel is cut into the earth in front of the shield with the aid of Ingersoll-Rand pneumatic shovels, and the roof is supported with wood if necessary. The shield is then pushed forward by the rams, which exert a pressure of about 3000 pounds for each square inch. The feet of these rams push against the last completed ring of the tunnel, as seen above, and a cutting edge in front of the shield bites into the earth. This example is twelve feet in diameter, and in twenty-four hours fifteen feet of tunnel can be driven.

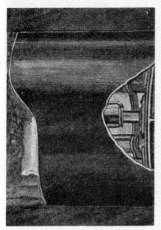 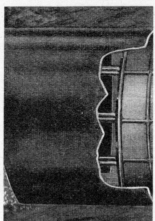 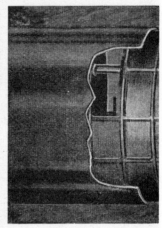

In the picture on the left we see the progress of the digging in front of the shield, the men being protected from falling material by the hood. In the centre picture the shield is moving forward; and on the right we see the shield as far forward as it will go, one foot eight inches, which allows just enough room to place the iron segments in position after the loose clay has been shovelled away. The rams are then drawn in again.

THE FIRST HIGHWAY UNDER THE THAMES

Many tunnels now run under London's river, but the first of these was the Thames Tunnel, built by Sir Marc Isambard Brunel, and opened in 1843. It is shown here in sections, and the first idea of how to bore it was given to Brunel by a little sea-creature, the teredo, which had honeycombed a piece of timber which the engineer picked up at Chatham.

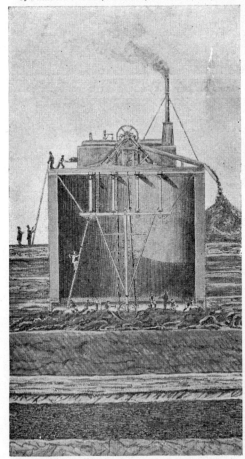

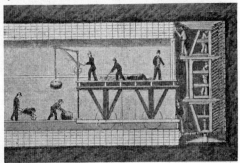

A shield was lowered into the shaft, and moved forward as men dug out the tunnel.

A huge caisson or tower was built, weighing hundreds of tons, and men worked inside this, digging out the gravel while the caisson sank by its own weight.

The difficulties were enormous, and several times the tunnel partially collapsed, as shown here, and the waters rushed in. But after seventeen years, success crowned the great effort.

REMOVING CLAY AND LINING THE WALLS

Whatever method of excavating is used, the material dug out has to be removed from where the shield is working, conveyed to the shaft, and raised to the surface. In this picture the clay is being dug out by pneumatic spades.

When the material dug out has been carried away and the shield moves forward the roof and sides of the tunnel need support. For this purpose segments of iron (or of concrete, as here) are placed in position.

PLACING IRON SEGMENTS IN POSITION

When a tunnel is lined with iron the heavy iron segments are placed in position with the aid of this apparatus known as an erector, which has a large counter-balance at one end. In this picture a segment which is being placed is suspended by a hook and chain from the other end as the workman on the left steadies it.

Just as the lock in a river enables the passage of boats from one level to another without unduly wasting the water of the higher level, so an air-lock enables trolleys, workmen, and so on, to pass into the tunnel without a great loss of compressed air. Here we see two air-locks side by side, one of them being open and the other closed.

THE BEGINNING OF A RAILWAY TUNNEL

Before work began on the three-mile Woodhead railway tunnel under the Pennines, a great deal of preliminary drilling took place in the various pilot headings to test the nature of the ground which lay ahead, and particularly that which lay above. Here are men at work during the early stages of the tunnelling.

In this picture we see work in progress on one of the small pilot tunnels of the Woodhead Tunnel. Earth and rock which have been blasted out are removed by a mechanical shovel loader.

THE TWO HALVES BECOME ONE TUNNEL

In making the Mersey Tunnel the top half was excavated and lined with iron segments before work began on the lower half, which is here seen being excavated. 82,000 tons of segments were used in lining the tunnel.

This picture shows the great tunnel completely lined with segments. The structure at the top of the tunnel is a great roadway suspended from the roof, along which the excavated material from the lower half of the tunnel was removed.

BUILDING THE ROAD AND LINING THE TUNNEL

The roadway in the Mersey Tunnel is built of concrete, reinforced with steel rods which are anchored to the sides of the tunnel. It is supported on two twelve-inch walls of similar material, which are placed 21 feet apart.

The iron lining of the tunnel was itself lined with concrete by filling in each boxlike segment. Then a reinforcing mesh was attached to the face of the upper part of the tunnel, which was lined with a waterproof cement rendering an inch thick. These men are preparing the reinforcement.

THE GREAT SHIELD AND THE TUNNEL IT MAKES

Owing to the nature of the ground through which one of the approach tunnels was made it was necessary to use a great shield for the excavations. Unlike the shield shown on page 6216, this was of semi-circular section, and as the digging progressed. the shield was moved forward by 24 hydraulic rams, seen clearly in this picture.

A junction in the wonderful Mersey tunnel between Liverpool and Birkenhead.

THROUGH MOUNTAINS AND UNDER A CITY

Here is a scene during the construction of the 15-mile tunnel which carries the water of Loch Treig through Ben Nevis. The rough rock sides are here seen receiving a lining of concrete.

A truck full of excavated material from a tunnel for an extension to London's Underground Railways is here seen about to be hoisted up the shaft.

The latest British tunnel to be completed is the Woodhead railway tunnel under the Pennines. Here we see work in progress.

Sometimes when it is necessary to enlarge an existing tunnel the new is made round the old. In this case, Underground trains continued to run through the tunnel on the left without interruption while a larger tunnel for a station was built.

Plain Answers to the Questions of the Children of the World

HOW DID MEN LEARN TO TALK?

What is baby trying to say?

Anything that expresses to someone else what is going on in our minds is, in a way, a sort of talking. We can tell by a baby's face, long before it can talk, something of what it wants and feels. We can also tell by a baby's cry a great deal of what it wants and feels. Now, that cry is made with its voice, just as talking is made, and is really a sort of untaught talking. It is made in the same way, and it serves the same purpose. Different kinds of cries have different meanings. Then, also, we not only move our faces and make sounds with our voices, but we move our hands and arms. In some parts of the world these movements or gestures have definite meanings, and people can talk to each other in this way without saying a word. This is called " gesture language."

In the same way different kinds of sounds—and that is all words are in themselves—come to have special meanings of their own ; and that is what happens when we talk. The simplest words are those which a baby will make all the world over when it first tries to talk. You only have to breathe out through your mouth and separate your lips twice to say mamma. This, or something very like it, is the baby's name for its mother in all languages, and if men forgot how to talk, the new babies would soon make a beginning with *mamma*. Is it not beautiful to think that language began in this way?

One of the interesting questions often asked about talking is why there are so many languages. It is worth thinking over. Very many words really begin in imitation of sounds. You know, words like buzz, whirr, pop, and so on. People who study language know that far more words begin in this way than most people think. Apart from that, however, we often have to make words simply by inventing them. The word does not matter as long as everyone is agreed as to what it means. A word is only a name. You would still be you if you had been called Tom instead of Harry, or Monica instead of Marjorie. Shakespeare says in one of the best-known passages in his plays :

What's in a name?
A rose by any other name would smell as sweet.

So in different parts of the world different names have been invented ; but really different languages are a thousand times more alike than we think. Latin, Greek, Italian, Spanish, Portuguese, and French are really close relatives, because the

FIRE · WIND · WATER · LIFE · MIND · SLEEP · HOW · WHY · WHERE

different peoples who speak them are in large measure descended from the same people. So, nowadays, we can often learn the history of a nation by its language. English is probably the finest language in the world for all purposes, but it is a very funny mixture. This word mixture, for instance, is Latin, and so are tens of thousands of English words. Many others are a sort of French, and many others Anglo-Saxon, which is very like German. We say *father*, the Germans *vater*, the Romans said *pater*, the French say *pere*, and so on. All these words are really the same.

What is Maundy Money?

At Westminster Abbey, on the Thursday before Easter every year, specially minted silver coins called Maundy money are given to a number of old men and women. This is done in accordance with a very ancient custom founded on the words spoken by Christ at the Last Supper: " A new commandment I give unto you." The word Maundy comes from the Latin mandatum, commandment.

In former centuries it was the custom for the reigning sovereign, on Maundy Thursday, to wash the feet of as many poor people as there were years in his age, and to give them meat, money, and clothes. King James II was the last English monarch to carry out this chastening task. The gifts, however, continued to be distributed, and already, in the reign of Charles II, the first special Maundy coins had been minted.

Nowadays the Maundy money takes the place of gifts of clothes. The coins, minted for the occasion, are silver penny, twopenny, threepenny, and fourpenny (groat) pieces, without milled edges. They are legal tender; that is they could be used to buy things.

At the yearly Maundy ceremony at Westminster Abbey these unique coins are distributed by the Lord High Almoner, who represents the Queen.

Why Have We Different Tastes in Eating?

We know that no two people look quite the same. Everyone's face is differently made from every other face. We know that when we take prints of the markings on people's fingers they always differ from one another. And, as people differ in their faces and in their skins, so they differ in deeper things. No two brains are quite the same, and so no two people have quite the same tastes. But, also, people's bodies have different needs. One body may require a good deal of fat, and may be very capable of digesting fat, and so that person will like fat and oily things—which may be less good for another, who will like it less. Then, again, at different ages we have different food requirements. Children are very active, and since they are small, lose their heat quickly. They therefore require a large proportion of food to supply them with energy and heat. Perhaps the best of such foods is sugar, and that is the good reason why children and young people like sweets and sweet things more than most grown-up people do. This is not greed, but the demand of the body for what it specially needs. Thus tastes differ, too, in different parts of the world.

Why does Grass Turn Yellow After Being Made into Hay?

If there were no microbes in the world this would not happen; but nearly all the changes that happen in the bodies of living things after they die are due to microbes. This is as true of fish that turns bad as of grass that turns yellow when it is made into hay. Perhaps we are apt to forget that grass is part of the body of a living thing, but so it certainly is. It consists of those parts of certain plants which are called their leaves.

These leaves, like all other leaves, have the special duty of feeding on the carbon dioxide of the air by the aid of sunlight, and for this purpose they contain a very wonderful chemical substance called *chlorophyll*, the colour of which is green. Like all other chemical compounds which are very complicated, chlorophyll is very easily broken up and changed into something else. On the other hand, most simple compounds, like water, are very difficult to break up.

When the leaves of grass die by being cut, the very first compound that suffers from the change is this delicate and unstable chlorophyll. It is broken up into compounds, some of which have a yellow colour. We see the same thing in the leaves of a tree in autumn, which the tree has killed by corking up the channels through which they got their food.

Where Does the Swastika Come From ?

This symbol, a hooked cross which was used by the Nazis in Germany, has been traced to the pottery of Elam in the early days of civilisation in Mesopotamia. It was used for the ornamentation of spindle whorls in ancient Troy about 3000 B.C. It has been found on seals in Knossos. It was familiar in ancient Greece, and to the Incas in South America before the Spaniards came; and it is found as decoration in China, Tibet, Japan, Persia, India, North Africa, and Scandinavia.

Its form varies, one type being the triskilion in the arms of both Sicily and the Isle of Man. A right-handed swastika is regarded in India as the symbol of Ganesa, god of wisdom and prudence, and also as the sun of the upper world; the left-handed swastika being both the symbol of the goddess Kali and the symbol of the sun in the underworld.

Can We Measure the Speed of a Thought ?

We sometimes say " as quick as thought," as if thought were the quickest thing in the world; but that is far from true. When we think, waves of something travel along the nerves inside our brains, and if we want to measure the speed of thought, the best way to do so is to measure the rate at which a nerve-current travels from point to point.

This cannot be done directly in anyone's brain; but we can do it in other ways. We can take a long nerve, such as we find in the arm or the leg, and by the use of delicate electrical clocks we can find how fast it carries its messages. About the speed of an express train is what we find. That is very slow compared with the speed of the Earth, and slowness itself compared with the speed of light. So " as quick as lightning " means far more, *millions* of times more actually, than " as quick as thought."

Now we can do another thing. We can find out how long a person takes to distinguish between, say, a red colour and a blue colour. When he sees red he is to do a certain thing, and when he sees blue he is to do something else—as quickly as he can. We can measure exactly how many hundredths of a second this takes

to do; then we can subtract the time taken in running to and from the brain, and we find that most of the time was spent in the brain—in the thinking.

Why Does Water Boil when put on Lime ?

The answer to this depends on a very interesting chemical process. Water does not exactly boil when put on lime, but it is certainly true that the water is made very hot; and our question really should be: Where does this heat come from? Lime is a compound of the metal calcium and oxygen. It is therefore called the oxide of calcium, and each molecule that makes up this compound contains one atom of each of these elements; so chemists write it by this *formula* or sign—CaO—Ca for calcium and O for oxygen. If water gets to this oxide, the water and the oxide combine very powerfully. It is as if the quicklime (as it is often called) drank up the water and slaked its thirst, and so we now call it slaked lime. This slaked lime is oxide of calcium plus water, and its formula is simply the two formulas added together, CaO, H_2O. The best way of writing this is $Ca(OH)_2$. The small 2 means that there are two parts each of oxygen and hydrogen. As in most other cases of chemical action (just as when a fire burns) heat is produced by this slaking of lime, and that makes the lime and the extra water very hot.

Why Can we See the Whole Circle of the Moon When it is Not Shining ?

The reason is that the Earth shines brightly by the Sun's light, just as the Moon does; and the Earth's light is sometimes enough to light up the Moon so that we can sometimes see even the part of its face that is not lit by the Sun.

There is a curious and celebrated mistake in a famous English poem which shows that the poet did not at all understand the Moon, and apparently had never seen what we have seen. It is The Ancient Mariner, by Coleridge, who speaks of

> The horned moon, with one bright star
> Within the nether tip.

Of course, no one ever saw a star within either tip of the crescent Moon, because the rest of the Moon is there, and would hide the star. The nearest star is many millions of miles farther away than the Moon.

How Big is the Gulf Stream and How Fast Does it Flow?

The Gulf Stream, the most rapidly moving of all the ocean currents, is that portion of the equatorial drift which has passed through the Caribbean Sea and the Gulf of Mexico. Having flowed into the Gulf of Mexico quite easily, it finds itself considerably enclosed, and has to obtain some way of escape. The easiest path is the narrow passage between Florida and Cuba, and in that confined outlet the Gulf Stream becomes concentrated like water in the nozzle of a hose.

When it is passing through the channel at the end of the Yucatan peninsula its speed is only about a quarter of a mile an hour, and its width is ninety miles, while its depth is almost a thousand fathoms, or considerably over a mile. When it emerges from Florida its width has narrowed down to fifty miles, and its depth is only 350 fathoms, or less than half a mile.

THE WAY THE GULF STREAM GOES

At the same time its speed has increased to four miles an hour, the swiftest movement in its whole course.

Soon after escaping from this narrow passage-way the Gulf Stream becomes wider and deeper once more, and its rate of progress is slower—only about ten or fifteen miles a day. Then, as the current loses speed, its boundaries become less well defined, and in the open ocean it is detected more by its temperature, colour, and life than by its motion. It is estimated that every day the Gulf Stream carries past Florida 436 million million tons of water.

The Gulf Stream is warm because it is composed of water that comes from the Tropics, where the hot rays from the overhead Sun pour directly down and heat the upper layers of the sea.

How Many Seeds Come from One Plant?

A German botanist who devoted many years of study to this subject, gives this list of plants with the average number of seeds produced by each in a single season:

Henbane	- 10,000	Fleabane	- 120,000
Radish	- 12,000	Tobacco	- 360,000
Shepherd's Purse	- 64,000	Flixweed	- 730,000

But these are as nothing compared with the number of seeds produced by some of the orchids. One of these, the acropera, was estimated by Darwin to produce 74 million seeds in a season. Even that is small compared with the production of ferns, most of which produce spores far in excess of any seed-bearing plants. The golden polypody produces about a hundred million spores, not on the whole plant, but on a single leaf; and on each leaf the marattia produces 2800 millions, while the angiopteris has 4000 millions on a leaf. The fungus is even more prolific, as we can understand when we realise that the cloud of dust from a bursting puffball is made up of millions of tiny spores.

But the bacteria are the most wonderful of all plant forms from the production point of view. A well-known scientist states that under suitable conditions, and in a suitable temperature, a cell of the *bacillus subtilis* will take about twenty minutes to divide into two. If this process were repeated continuously, and every cell thus formed did the same, the product of one germ in a single night would amount to over 130 millions.

Even with seed-bearing plants the results of production would be amazing should every seed become a plant and every plant yield seed. If a henbane plant developed 10,000 seeds in one year and 10,000 plants grew from these, producing 10,000 seeds each, at the end of five years there would be ten thousand million million plants, which would produce a hundred million million million seeds, and the whole of the dry land on the Earth would be occupied with growing henbane plants. Another plant, the flixweed, would, if unchecked for three years, produce enough plants to cover the land surface of the globe two thousand times over. So amazingly prolific is Nature in maintaining the plant world, but, of course, the enemies against which the plants have to contend are many, and the majority of seeds and young plants are destroyed.

HOW LONG DOES AN ANIMAL LIVE?

How long do animals live ? It is one of the questions most often asked, but rarely answered with satisfaction. There is not enough experience to make satisfactory answers possible, but we have done our best in making up this table. We do not give these ages as definite, but the figures are based on cases known or are the opinion of accepted authorities. It is not known whether artificial conditions of captivity or domestication may be favourable or unfavourable to long life. There is also to be considered the great difference between average and potential length of life, as shown in human life. The figures in this table, representing years, may be accepted as about the best available.

Albatross	46	Gnu	15	Peacock	40
Alligator	about 60	Goat	13	Pelican	52
Amazon Parrot	40	Goat Moth (larva) about 4		Pheasant	20
Anteater	14	Golden Eagle	104	Pigeon (Common)	35
Antelope usually about 14		Goose	over 65	Pike	15
Armadillo	13	Greenfinch	23	Porcupine	20
		Greenfly .. a few weeks		Python	21
Badger	probably 14	Grosbeak	21		
Bat (Fruit)	17	Gull (Herring)	44	Quagga	16
Bee (Bumble) a summer		Hare .. probably 10		Rabbit .. old at 10	
Bee (Hive)	a summer	Hartebeest	13	Raccoon .. probably 19	
Bee (Queen) up to 5		Hedgehog	3	Rat .. usually 3	
Bee (Workers)	1	Heron	22	Ratel	23
Blackbird	over 20	Herring Gull	44	Raven	69
Boa Constrictor	23	Hippopotamus : one		Rhinoceros	40
Boar	about 20	lived at a Zoo for 30			
Bullfinch	19	Horse old at 35		Salmon	13
Bunting	13	Hyena	24	Sea Anemone	50
Bustard	30			Sheep .. old at 14	
Butterfly a few weeks		Ibis	26	Skink	20
				Skylark probably 12	
Camel	about 24	Jackal .. .. old at 14		Sloth	11
Canary	20			Slow Worm	31
Carp	40	Kangaroo	13	Snail (Garden)	5
Cassowary	about 26	Katydid 2-3 months		Snail (Edible) about 7	
Cattle	about 30	Kites about 25		Snail (Viviparous) about 10	
Chimpanzee	about 26	Lemur	25	Snail (Sea) about 30	
Civet	15	Leopard probably 20		Snakes about 22	
Cockatoo(Sulphur-Crested)81		Lion .. over 30		Sparrow	14
Condor	52	Lizards sometimes 31		Spider (Garden) 6 months	
Cormorant	23	Llama about 20		Squirrel (Grey)	15
Crane	30	Long-nosed Viper	22	Stags probably 19	
Crocodile probably 30		Lynx	14	Stork	30
		Magpie	21	Swallow	9
Dog .. usually 25		Marmot	13	Swan	25
Dormouse	5	Marten	10		
Dove (Barbary Turtle) 35		Mayfly (as fly) a few days		Tapir	30
Duck about 25		Mongoose	10	Thrush	15
		Monkeys about 30		Tiger .. probably 19	
Eagle (Golden)	104	Mouflon (wild sheep) 19		Toad	36
Eel	55	Mouse usually 2		Tortoise at least 100	
Eland	15	Mussel (Freshwater) over 15		Tortoise (Giant)	200
Elephant over 70				Turtle Dove (Barbary) 35	
Emu	28	Nightingale	25		
		Nylghaie	12	Viper (Long-nosed)	22
Flamingo	27			Viper (Water)	21
Flying Fox	17	Orang Utan about 26		Vulture (Egyptian)	118
Fowls about 25		Ostrich about 35			
Frog	15	Owl (Tawny)	26	Wapiti	22
Fruit Bat	17	Owl (Eagle)	68	Wasp (Queen)	1
				Wasp .. a summer	
Gazelle	11	Palm Civet	15	Wolf .. old at 16	
Giraffe probably 28		Parrot (Amazon)	40	Wombat	26
Glass Snake	17	Parrot (Grey)	93		

Will the World's Food Supply Ever Run Short ?

It is quite certain that, as people cannot live without enough food, there never will be more people than there is food for. The struggle for life is, in the first place, a struggle for food, and for a large number of people all over the world the struggle is so severe that many babies and children are killed by it every year, directly or indirectly.

But the number of people in the world steadily increases, and doubtless always has increased since mankind came to be; and steadily the amount of food has been increased by human effort. Men learned how to tame and care for sheep and oxen and goats, and so obtained flesh and milk; and this pastoral stage—pastoral comes from the word pastor, which means a shepherd—yielded to the agricultural stage of growing crops, which supports far more human life than the pastoral stage alone can.

It is probable that some day there must be a limit, though we are nowhere near it yet. When freed from the insects which carry disease, Africa alone will be capable of holding and feeding five hundred million people more than it does now.

Has a Fish a Voice ?

It has, and in one sense strictly so, because its sound proceeds from the vibrations of the swim-bladder, situated below the backbone and containing air or gas and enabling the fish to accommodate itself to varying levels. It is the equivalent of the lung in land animals, but in some fish it has become an organ for the production of sounds. The bark of the conger is one of them, the grunts of the gurnards and of the John Dory are others.

In recent years the sounds have been examined, and some recorded under water by the United States Naval Ordnance Laboratory in conjunction with the Bermuda Biological Station. At depths of 200 fathoms the North American toad fish produces a sound like that of an aeroplane engine. Drum-like fish sounds do not actually proceed from the swimming bladder, but are made by a muscle at the side of it, which contracts 24 times a second. In the cat-fish this produces something like the beating of a tom-tom, and in other fishes sounds like that of kettle drums. Honks, hisses, the mooing of an afflicted cow, the grating of teeth, or the drilling of a roadway all mingle in a concert which, conducted 50 feet or more below the surface, can sometimes be heard six feet above it.

Why is the End of an Anvil Tapered ?

The tapered end of the anvil, which is called the beak because it resembles a bird's beak, is to enable the blacksmith to shape curved articles of iron, such as a horse-shoe. These are beaten out round the gradually narrowing beak. In earlier days the anvil had a beak at each end, and as this gave the appearance of a pair of horns on the head of an ox, the anvil was called a bickern, a word which means two-horned. An anvil with one beak is sometimes mistakenly called a bickern.

Why has Water no Taste ?

It is true that pure water has no taste, but probably not one in ten thousand of those who read this question has ever known water that had no taste. None of us has ever tasted pure water unless we have been to the chemist's and tasted water that has been distilled. The ordinary water we drink has quantities of air dissolved in it, and these give it a taste. It also has a certain amount of salts dissolved in it. If we boil water we drive off the gases in it, and then it does become tasteless and flat. That is why tea is spoiled if we allow the water to *go on* boiling before we make the tea. Why pure water should have no taste is very plain. Our bodies mainly consist of water. The nerves of taste, and their endings in the tongue, mostly consist of water themselves, and they live in water. Therefore water does not excite them. If it did we should be tasting it all the time.

What are Parliamentary Whips ?

There are two meanings to the word Whip. A Whip is an official who ensures that sufficient members of his party are in the House at any given moment. Whips also act as liaison officers between the leaders and the members of their party.

The term whip also refers to the printed circular which gives details of forthcoming business and is issued weekly by each party to its members. This printed whip underlines—with two or three lines—the more important business on which divisions are expected.

How is a Carillon Worked?

The carillon, as a peal of bells is called, from an old French word, is now becoming much better known in England, for several have been brought into use in recent years. One is at Loughborough, and another at Bournville, the famous industrial village founded by George Cadbury. A carillon has been described as a series of bells so hung and arranged as to be capable of being played as a musical instrument, either by means of machinery or by a keyboard. If the carillon is played by machinery the method is automatic,

PLAYING THE BOURNVILLE CARILLON

the same as that used for chimes on church bells; the tunes are set on a revolving barrel, which is driven by heavy weights, as in a grandfather's clock. But the carillon which is free to play any tune has stationary bells struck by hammers connected by wires to a keyboard, at which the player sits. The keyboard is also fitted with pedals for the lower notes, to be worked by the feet. The keys, which project, are struck with the closed hand, the little finger being protected with a leather covering. As the key has to move the weight of the clapper, the blow, especially for the lower notes, must be strong—hence the value of the pedals. Carillons may consist of from 35 to 49 bells. The Bournville carillon has 42, and

the Loughborough carillon, which is to be rung "every day for ever" in memory of men who fell in war, has 47.

Some modern carillons are rung by apparatus which calls for little physical exertion by the ringer. One device has a short keyboard similar to that of a piano, and a light touch on the key rings the bells by electro-pneumatic mechanism.

Why Has the Sonnet Always Fourteen Lines?

The answer, given in a single sentence, seems to be that it is because fourteen lines were thought to be the best for this form of elegiac verse by its 13th-century Italian inventor, and that successive poets have followed the example. The 19th-century English writer, Theodore Watts-Dunton, who studied the history and development of the sonnet with much care, tells us that "the poet's quest from the very first has been to write a poem in fourteen lines so arranged that they should, better than any other number and arrangement of verses, produce a certain melodic effect upon the ear." The Italian model was perfected by Dante and Petrarch and was followed by Milton. In it the first eight lines or octave rhyme abba, abba; the other six or sextet rhyme more freely. In the Shakespearean form three quatrains with six alternate rhyme sounds are followed by a rhymed couplet.

Why Does Everything Seem to Spin Round When We are Dizzy?

When anyone feels dizzy and perhaps almost about to faint, his brain cannot properly control the working of his eyes. They may move round from side to side, perhaps independently instead of together, and so it may look as if things were spinning round. Another reason for dizziness has to do with a wonderful part of the body near the ear without which none of us could sit upright, much less stand, though few people have ever heard of it. This organ, which used to be thought to have something to do with hearing, really controls our balance. In some people it suffers from a disease, and these people constantly suffer from dizziness and an unpleasant feeling that everything is spinning round.

As every child knows, we can make ourselves dizzy by spinning round several times in one direction. This disturbs the organ of balance, about which we have been speaking, and this disturbance it is that gives us the feeling. If you turn round the other way you put things right by restoring the original state of affairs within the balancing organ. The name for the feeling that things are spinning round is *vertigo*; *vert* simply means *turn*.

Why Do Birds Cast Their Feathers?

Feathers become worn and torn and broken, and must be replaced. We do not know how birds manage to moult their feathers; it is one of the wonderful provisions of Nature, whose effects we see without being able to say exactly how they are caused. But the moulting of birds is similar to what takes place in other forms of animal life. Horses grow long coats of hair in winter which they shed in summer. Dogs cast their coats. Snakes cast their skins; crabs and other shell-fish cast their shells. If a crab lived always in one shell his body could never grow any bigger. At a certain time in the year his flesh becomes very watery, so that he can draw those great claws of his through the narrow opening at the top of the shells in which they are enclosed, and he comes out of his shell almost as soft and pulpy as an egg in its skin with its shell removed. Birds are never left bare like this. They moult gradually. Yet some are so completely robbed of their strong feathers that, being defenceless, they go into hiding until the new ones grow.

What is a Billycock Hat?

It was first called a Billy Coke, after the famous Billy Coke of Norfolk, who was the first Lord Leicester. He wore a hat of this kind about the beginning of the Victorian era, and it became associated with him, like Wellington boots with the Iron Duke, or as the brougham became associated with Lord Brougham.

What Makes the Sound in the Organ?

When the organist puts his finger on a key, he allows air to enter the pipe that corresponds to the key he touches. The air is thrown into vibration in the pipe, and this spreads in all directions through the air and makes the sound we hear. It is really a vibrating column of air that produces the sound, while in the piano it is a vibrating string transferring its vibrations to the air around it. So the organ is really a huge wind instrument, as the other is a stringed instrument. The rate at which the column of air vibrates decides the note we hear, and depends on the length of the column, which, of course, depends on the length of the pipe. Thus, a pipe 32 feet long will hold a column of air that vibrates just half as fast as the column in a pipe 16 feet long, and the note of the longer pipe will be exactly an octave below the other. It would not do if there were nothing but a plain pipe, because, of course, the air would simply rush through it with a hiss. At one end of the pipe there must be something to throw it into vibrations, a "tongue," which may be made of various materials and shapes according to the *quality* of the note we want. But the *pitch* of the note is decided by the length of the pipe.

What is a Pyrrhic Victory?

Pyrrhus, king of Epirus, when helping the Greeks against the Romans in Italy in 280 B.C., won two battles with such severe losses in killed and wounded that he was compelled to retreat into Sicily. Thus a victory won at a cost so great as to make it worthless is called a Pyrrhic victory.

Who is Chanticleer?

The poetical name for a cock, derived from his clear crowing. The cock takes a prominent place in the medieval fables about animals, such as those in the ancient book Reynard the Fox. In these stories, Chanticleer shows himself daring enough to dupe Reynard, though the fox is famous for tricks. One day, Reynard, starving as usual, had slyly smuggled himself into a poultry yard and devoured the poor cock. Having eaten his full, he was slouching along when peasants came across his way and reproached the animal for his cruel mischief and cunning. Chanticleer heard the talk from where he languished, suffocating, in the stomach of the fox. "Why don't you answer these unjust accusations?" he whispered, and, as the unwary Reynard opened his mouth, the other jumped out and escaped.

The French poet Edmond Rostand (1868–1918) made Chanticleer the chief character of a drama where all the actors play the parts of animals, a work whose popularity owes as much to the originality of the subject as to the lyrics of the poet.

Why is a Food Tin Generally Round ?

Round tins are easier to make than square tins, but the main reason for making them this shape is because it embodies the principle of the arch, which helps greatly in giving them strength. A round tin can stand a great deal of knocking about, and also a great deal of pressure, without losing its shape.

Do All Things Move in Space ?

Of course, the Sun and the Moon, and even, as we now know, what used to be called the " fixed stars," have motions of their own—their *proper* motions, as they are called, proper really meaning " belonging to "; but the motion which proves that the Earth is moving is called their *apparent* motion, for it only seems or appears. The Earth is moving, and not they. The marks of this motion are that it is *common to all* the heavenly bodies, though their own or proper motions may all be quite different from each other; and that it is daily, or *diurnal*, which is Latin for daily. The best proof of the Earth's motion, then, is the *common, apparent, diurnal* motion of the heavenly bodies, which can only mean that the Earth spins right round on itself once a day; just as the best proof of a train's motion is the *common, apparent* motion of everything on both sides of it—common, or shared in by all objects, even including animals running in opposite directions to each other. That, of course, is their own or *proper* motion. Everything moves.

Why does Red Irritate a Bull ?

It is very difficult to be quite sure of the truth of this question, and we ought to be sure of the fact before we try to explain it. No one has made experiments to prove that red really irritates the bull more than any other bright colour. Still, it is probable that red, perhaps just because it is usually the brightest of colours, does irritate a bull; though if the red colour were on something that did not move, perhaps it would have much less effect. People have thought that bulls are irritated by red because it is the colour of blood; but we do not think that is so. A certain amount of study of human beings seems to suggest that different colours differ in their effect on the nervous system, and that while such colours as green and violet are soothing, yellow and red are exciting. Of course, it takes very little to irritate a bull; only the saying is so popular, perhaps, because it applies so well to ourselves. We are all apt to fire up at some particular subject, as the bull is supposed to do at a red rag.

Does a Bridge Expand in the Sun ?

A bridge expands in the sun or in the daytime or in the summer, and shrinks in the shade or at night or in winter. The rule is that heat makes everything expand. So we may say that everything occupies more or less space according to the amount of heat in it—that is, of course, if other circumstances, such as the pressure round the thing, are kept the same. Metals have a striking way of changing their volume, or size, under the influence of heat, and so this change is very noticeable in the case of iron or steel bridges. If the engineer does not know that bridges expand, he will build a bridge that is certain soon to get strained, and even to crack. He has to reckon on the amount of expansion that will occur under the influence of such heat as the bridge is likely to be exposed to, and he must allow for it. In a big bridge like the Forth Bridge, many inches have to be allowed for its change of size when hot or cold.

Does a Spider Ever Run Out of Web ?

In a general way a spider does not run out of the material of which it spins its web while it can find enough to eat. There used to be a legend that after the common garden spider had spun the web of wondrous circular pattern three times it would spin no more. But there is no proof of this old story. If accident or mischief should destroy the garden spider's web overnight another web will be found in its place next morning, for the spider applies to its web-spinning the maxim of try, try, try again while the summer lasts.

The common garden spider lives only for a summer, and the silk, being a secretion of its body, is dependent on the spider's daily nourishment. When the winter comes the garden spider dies, though in a very mild winter it may survive till another year. But there are other spiders which hibernate through the winter, hidden away in crevices, and when spring comes they begin again their spinning.

Does Smoke Always Come From a Fire?

There is no real reason why smoke should always come from a fire, and there are many ways of making fires which produce no smoke. There are, in fact, some cities in which no one is allowed to make fires that produce smoke. The reason why smoke comes from our ordinary fires is the same as the reason for a great many other facts that we can notice. It is, indeed, the reason which explains the making of the coal in the first place. Carbon will not burn unless it is hot enough, and it is less easily burned than most of the other things that can burn. So a certain quantity of carbon is apt to go unburned, though this will happen far less if we keep the fire hot enough, which is to be done by giving it a good supply of air. If we make a forced draught, and keep up a steady, quick flow of fresh air—that is to say, of fresh oxygen—to the fire, then we shall find that all the carbon is burned up, and no smoke will be produced.

Why Cannot we See the Spokes of a Wheel When it Goes Very Fast?

The reason is that the marks made, so to speak, by anything on the retina at the back of the eye do not instantly fade away, but last for a small fraction of a second. The real marvel here is that these images on the retina last for such a short time, and that it is so quickly ready to receive new ones. Still, the images do last for a little while, and if a wheel goes round at all quickly, the marks made by the spokes at the different parts of their journey run into each other, and we see no distinct spokes at all, but only a faint blur inside the circle of the wheel. The first answer to this question that would naturally suggest itself to our minds is, that the spokes of the wheel cannot be seen when it turns quickly because they are moving too fast for the eye to catch. That, however, is not the case at all, and a simple experiment will show that the first explanation is the true one, and not this, likely though it sounds. If we set a wheel spinning in darkness, and then have a single flash of electric light just for an instant, we catch a glimpse of the spokes of the wheel as if the wheel were not moving at all.

Why Does Glass Not Break if Put in Cold Water and Boiled?

Almost everything gets bigger, or *expands*, when it is made hot; and it gets smaller, or *contracts*, when made cool. If, then, we take a thing all in one piece, and do not heat every part of it to the same extent at the same time—something will have to go. That is what happens when a tumbler is cracked in the way we all know; but if the tumbler is put into water, and then the water is boiled, the *whole glass* expands equally, there is no strain between the inside and the outside, and so there is no reason why it should break.

Why is the Sky Blue?

This was found out by the 19th-century British physicist, John Tyndall. The sky gets its light from the Sun. When the Sun is away the sky is dark. Therefore, the blue of the sky must be somehow thrown to our eyes from something in the sky which keeps all the other colours in the white light of the Sun, and throws back the blue, and that is what happens.

The sky is filled with countless tiny specks of what we may call dust, specks of solid stuff hanging in the air. These are of just such a size that they catch the bigger waves of light, which make the other colours, but throw to our eyes the shorter waves of light, which make blue. If you could do away with all the solid stuff in the air, the sky would be dark, and all the light of the daytime would come directly from the Sun. Skylight is reflected sunlight, but only the blue part of it.

How Can a Duckling Swim Without Being Taught?

The answer is partly instinct. It is only fair to remember that in any case it is much easier for animals to swim than it is for us; and it is also fair to us to remember that some people do swim almost without being taught. Sometimes an insect, which has never seen anyone do the thing it has to do, does it perfectly; but in the case of the higher animals, like the cat and the duckling, the question of being taught comes in. The kitten may partly learn to purr through hearing its mother purr, and the duckling, though perhaps its mother does not actually teach it anything, gets confidence from its mother. It sees that she can swim, and that helps it.